The Definitive Guide to Django

Web Development Done Right, Second Edition

Adrian Holovaty and Jacob Kaplan-Moss

The Definitive Guide to Django: Web Development Done Right, Second Edition

Copyright © 2009 by Adrian Holovaty and Jacob Kaplan-Moss

ISBN 13: 978-1-4302-1936-1

ISBN (electronic): 978-1-4302-1937-8

Printed and bound in the United States of America 9 8 7 6 5 4 3 2 1

Trademarked names may appear in this book. Rather than use a trademark symbol with every occurrence of a trademarked name, we use the names only in an editorial fashion and to the benefit of the trademark owner, with no intention of infringement of the trademark.

Java™ and all Java-based marks are trademarks or registered trademarks of Sun Microsystems, Inc., in the US and other countries. Apress, Inc., is not affiliated with Sun Microsystems, Inc., and this book was written without endorsement from Sun Microsystems, Inc.

Lead Editor: Duncan Parkes
Technical Reviewer: Sean Legassick
Editorial Board: Clay Andres, Steve Anglin, Mark Beckner, Ewan Buckingham, Tony Campbell,
    Gary Cornell, Jonathan Gennick, Michelle Lowman, Matthew Moodie, Jeffrey Pepper, Frank Pohlmann,
    Ben Renow-Clarke, Dominic Shakeshaft, Matt Wade, Tom Welsh
Project Managers: Grace Wong and James Markham
Copy Editors: Nancy Sixsmith and Candace English
Associate Production Director: Kari Brooks-Copony
Production Editor: Katie Stence
Compositor: Patrick Cunningham
Proofreader: April Eddy
Indexer: BIM Indexing & Proofreading Services
Artist: April Milne
Cover Designer: Kurt Krames
Manufacturing Director: Tom Debolski

Distributed to the book trade worldwide by Springer-Verlag New York, Inc., 233 Spring Street, 6th Floor, New York, NY 10013. Phone 1-800-SPRINGER, fax 201-348-4505, e-mail orders-ny@springer-sbm.com, or visit http://www.springeronline.com.

For information on translations, please contact Apress directly at 2855 Telegraph Avenue, Suite 600, Berkeley, CA 94705. Phone 510-549-5930, fax 510-549-5939, e-mail info@apress.com, or visit http://www.apress.com.

Apress and friends of ED books may be purchased in bulk for academic, corporate, or promotional use. eBook versions and licenses are also available for most titles. For more information, reference our Special Bulk Sales–eBook Licensing web page at http://www.apress.com/info/bulksales.

The source code for this book is available to readers at http://www.apress.com.

This book is dedicated to the Django community.

Contents at a Glance

PART 1 ▪▪▪ Getting Started

PART 2 ▪▪▪ Advanced Usage

PART 3 ■■■ Other Django Features

PART 4 ■■■ Appendixes

Contents

PART 1 ■■■ Getting Started

PART 2 ■■■ **Advanced Usage**

PART 3 ■■■ Other Django Features

PART 4 ■■■ Appendixes

About the Authors

ADRIAN HOLOVATY is a cocreator and co–Benevolent Dictator for Life of Django. He runs a Web start-up called EveryBlock. He lives with his wife in Chicago and spends his free time attempting to play guitar in the style of Django Reinhardt.

JACOB KAPLAN-MOSS is a lead developer and co–Benevolent Dictator for Life of Django. Jacob is a partner at Revolution Systems, a consultancy that helps companies make the most of open source software. Jacob previously worked for the *Lawrence Journal-World*, the locally owned newspaper in Lawrence, Kansas where Django was developed. At *Journal-World* Jacob was the lead developer of Ellington, a commercial Web-publishing platform for media companies.

About the Technical Reviewer

 **SEAN LEGASSICK** has been creating software for over 15 years. His work designing the architecture of South African open source framework Chisimba has contributed significantly to software-engineering capacity-building in Africa and other areas of the developing world. He is a cofounder of MobGeo, a start-up developing innovative location-aware mobile marketing solutions. Away from the world of software, he writes on politics and culture.

Acknowledgments

Thanks to the many people who contributed to our online first drafts, and thanks to the folks at Apress for their great editing.

Preface

Welcome to the second edition of *The Definitive Guide to Django*, informally known as The Django Book! This book aims to teach you how to use the Django Web framework to develop Web sites efficiently.

When Jacob Kaplan-Moss and I wrote the first edition of this book, Django was still in a pre-1.0 stage. Once Django version 1.0 was released, with its several backward-incompatible changes, the first edition inevitably became outdated and people began demanding an update. I'm happy to report this edition covers Django 1.1 and should serve you well for some time.

My thanks go to the many contributors who posted comments, corrections, and rants to `http://djangobook.com/`, the accompanying Web site for this book, where I posted chapter drafts as I wrote them. You guys are great.

Adrian Holovaty
Cocreator and co–Benevolent Dictator for Life, Django

Introduction

In the early days, Web developers wrote every page by hand. Updating a Web site meant editing HTML; a "redesign" involved redoing every single page, one at a time.

As Web sites grew and became more ambitious, it quickly became obvious that that situation was tedious, time-consuming, and ultimately untenable. A group of enterprising hackers at NCSA (the National Center for Supercomputing Applications, where Mosaic, the first graphical Web browser, was developed) solved this problem by letting the Web server spawn external programs that could generate HTML dynamically. They called this protocol the Common Gateway Interface, or CGI, and it changed the Web forever.

It's hard now to imagine what a revelation CGI must have been: instead of treating HTML pages as simple files on disk, CGI allows you to think of your pages as resources generated dynamically on demand. The development of CGI ushered in the first generation of dynamic Web sites.

However, CGI has its problems: CGI scripts need to contain a lot of repetitive "boilerplate" code, they make code reuse difficult, and they can be difficult for first-time developers to write and understand.

PHP fixed many of these problems, and it took the world by storm—it's now by far the most popular tool used to create dynamic Web sites, and dozens of similar languages and environments (ASP, JSP, etc.) have followed PHP's design closely. PHP's major innovation is its ease of use: PHP code is simply embedded into plain HTML. The learning curve for someone who already knows HTML is extremely shallow.

But PHP has its own problems; its very ease of use encourages sloppy, repetitive, ill-conceived code. Worse, PHP does little to protect programmers from security vulnerabilities, and thus many PHP developers found themselves learning about security only once it was too late.

These and similar frustrations led directly to the development of the current crop of "third- generation" Web-development frameworks. These frameworks—Django and Ruby on Rails appear to be the most popular these days—recognize that the Web's importance has escalated of late.

With this new explosion of Web development comes yet another increase in ambition; Web developers are expected to do more and more every day.

Django was invented to meet these new ambitions. Django lets you build deep, dynamic, interesting sites in an extremely short time. Django is designed to let you focus on the fun, interesting parts of your job while easing the pain of the repetitive bits. In doing so, it provides high-level abstractions of common Web-development patterns, shortcuts for frequent programming tasks, and clear conventions on how to solve problems. At the same time, Django tries to stay out of your way, letting you work outside the scope of the framework as needed.

We wrote this book because we firmly believe that Django makes Web development better. It's designed to quickly get you moving on your own Django projects, and then ultimately teach you everything you need to know to successfully design, develop, and deploy a site that you'll be proud of.

We're extremely interested in your feedback. The online version of this book—available at http://djangobook.com/—will let you comment on any part of the book and discuss it with other readers. We'll do our best to read all the comments posted there, and to respond to as many as possible. If you prefer e-mail, please drop us a line at feedback@djangobook.com. Either way, we'd love to hear from you!

We're glad you're here, and we hope you find Django as exciting, fun, and useful as we do.

PART 1

■ ■ ■

Getting Started

CHAPTER 1

■■■

Introduction to Django

This book is about Django, a Web-development framework that saves you time and makes Web development a joy. Using Django, you can build and maintain high-quality Web applications with minimal fuss.

At its best, Web development is an exciting, creative act; at its worst, it can be a repetitive, frustrating nuisance. Django lets you focus on the fun stuff—the crux of your Web application—while easing the pain of the repetitive bits. In doing so, it provides high-level abstractions of common Web development patterns, shortcuts for frequent programming tasks, and clear conventions for how to solve problems. At the same time, Django tries to stay out of your way, letting you work outside the scope of the framework as needed.

The goal of this book is to make you a Django expert. The focus is twofold. First, we explain, in depth, what Django does and how to build Web applications with it. Second, we discuss higher-level concepts where appropriate, answering the question "How can I apply these tools effectively in my own projects?" By reading this book, you'll learn the skills needed to develop powerful Web sites quickly, with code that is clean and easy to maintain.

What Is a Web Framework?

Django is a prominent member of a new generation of *Web frameworks*—but what does that term mean, precisely?

To answer that question, let's consider the design of a Web application written in Python *without* a framework. Throughout this book, we'll take this approach of showing you basic ways to get work done *without* shortcuts, in the hope that you'll recognize why shortcuts are so helpful. (It's also valuable to know how to get things done without shortcuts because shortcuts aren't always available. And most importantly, knowing *why* things work the way they do makes you a better Web developer.)

One of the simplest, most direct ways to build a Python Web app from scratch is to use the Common Gateway Interface (CGI) standard, which was a popular technique circa 1998. Here's a high-level explanation of how it works: create a Python script that outputs HTML, then save the script to a Web server with a `.cgi` extension and visit the page in your Web browser. That's it.

Here's a sample Python CGI script that displays the ten most recently published books from a database. Don't worry about syntax details; just get a feel for the basic things it's doing.

```python
#!/usr/bin/env python

import MySQLdb

print "Content-Type: text/html\n"
print "<html><head><title>Books</title></head>"
print "<body>"
print "<h1>Books</h1>"
print "<ul>"

connection = MySQLdb.connect(user='me', passwd='letmein', db='my_db')
cursor = connection.cursor()
cursor.execute("SELECT name FROM books ORDER BY pub_date DESC LIMIT 10")

for row in cursor.fetchall():
    print "<li>%s</li>" % row[0]

print "</ul>"
print "</body></html>"

connection.close()
```

First, to fulfill the requirements of CGI, this code prints a "Content-Type" line, followed by a blank line. It prints some introductory HTML, connects to a database, and runs a query to retrieve the names of the latest ten books. Looping over those books, it generates an HTML list of the titles. Finally, it prints the closing HTML and closes the database connection.

With a one-off page like this one, the write-it-from-scratch approach isn't necessarily bad. For one thing, this code is simple to comprehend—even a novice developer can read these 16 lines of Python and understand everything it does, from start to finish. There's nothing else to learn, no other code to read. It's also simple to deploy: just save this code in a file that ends with .cgi, upload that file to a Web server, and visit that page with a browser.

Despite its simplicity, this approach has a number of problems and annoyances. Ask yourself these questions:

- What happens when multiple parts of your application need to connect to the database? Surely that database-connecting code shouldn't need to be duplicated in each individual CGI script. The pragmatic thing to do would be to refactor it into a shared function.

- Should a developer *really* have to worry about printing the "Content-Type" line and remembering to close the database connection? This sort of boilerplate reduces programmer productivity and introduces opportunities for mistakes. These setup- and teardown-related tasks would best be handled by some common infrastructure.

- What happens when this code is reused in multiple environments, each with a separate database and password? At this point, some environment-specific configuration becomes essential.

- What happens when a Web designer who has no experience coding Python wishes to redesign the page? One wrong character could crash the entire application. Ideally, the logic of the page—the retrieval of book titles from the database—would be separate from the HTML display of the page so that a designer could edit the latter without affecting the former.

These problems are precisely what a Web framework intends to solve. A Web framework provides a programming infrastructure for your applications so that you can focus on writing clean, maintainable code without having to reinvent the wheel. In a nutshell, that's what Django does.

The MVC Design Pattern

Let's dive in with a quick example that demonstrates the difference between the previous approach and a Web framework's approach. Here's how you might write the previous CGI code using Django. The first thing to note is that we split it over three Python files (models.py, views.py, urls.py) and an HTML template (latest_books.html):

```python
# models.py (the database tables)

from django.db import models

class Book(models.Model):
    name = models.CharField(max_length=50)
    pub_date = models.DateField()



# views.py (the business logic)

from django.shortcuts import render_to_response
from models import Book

def latest_books(request):
    book_list = Book.objects.order_by('-pub_date')[:10]
    return render_to_response('latest_books.html', {'book_list': book_list})



# urls.py (the URL configuration)

from django.conf.urls.defaults import *
import views

urlpatterns = patterns('',
    (r'^latest/$', views.latest_books),
)
```

```
# latest_books.html (the template)

<html><head><title>Books</title></head>
<body>
<h1>Books</h1>
<ul>
{% for book in book_list %}
<li>{{ book.name }}</li>
{% endfor %}
</ul>
</body></html>
```

Again, don't worry about the particulars of syntax; just get a feel for the overall design. The main thing to note here is the *separation of concerns*:

- The models.py file contains a description of the database table, represented by a Python class. This class is called a *model*. Using it, you can create, retrieve, update, and delete records in your database using simple Python code rather than writing repetitive SQL statements.

- The views.py file contains the business logic for the page. The latest_books() function is called a *view*.

- The urls.py file specifies which view is called for a given URL pattern. In this case, the URL /latest/ will be handled by the latest_books() function. In other words, if your domain is example.com, any visit to the URL http://example.com/latest/ will call the latest_books() function.

- The latest_books.html file is an HTML template that describes the design of the page. It uses a template language with basic logic statements—for example, {% for book in book_list %}.

Taken together, these pieces loosely follow a pattern called Model-View-Controller (MVC). Simply put, MVC is way of developing software so that the code for defining and accessing data (the model) is separate from request-routing logic (the controller), which in turn is separate from the user interface (the view). (We'll discuss MVC in more depth in Chapter 5.)

A key advantage of such an approach is that components are *loosely coupled*. Each distinct piece of a Django-powered Web application has a single key purpose and can be changed independently without affecting the other pieces. For example, a developer can change the URL for a given part of the application without affecting the underlying implementation. A designer can change a page's HTML without having to touch the Python code that renders it. A database administrator can rename a database table and specify the change in a single place rather than having to search and replace through a dozen files.

In this book, each component of MVC gets its own chapter. Chapter 3 covers views, Chapter 4 covers templates, and Chapter 5 covers models.

Django's History

Before we dive into more code, we should take a moment to explain Django's history. We noted earlier that we'll be showing you how to do things *without* shortcuts so that you more fully understand the shortcuts. Similarly, it's useful to understand *why* Django was created, because knowledge of the history will put into context why Django works the way it does.

If you've been building Web applications for a while, you're probably familiar with the problems in the CGI example we presented earlier. The classic Web developer's path goes something like this:

1. Write a Web application from scratch.

2. Write another Web application from scratch.

3. Realize the application from step 1 shares much in common with the application from step 2.

4. Refactor the code so that application 1 shares code with application 2.

5. Repeat steps 2–4 several times.

6. Realize you've invented a framework.

This is precisely how Django itself was created!

Django grew organically from real-world applications written by a Web-development team in Lawrence, Kansas, USA. It was born in the fall of 2003, when the Web programmers at the *Lawrence Journal-World* newspaper, Adrian Holovaty and Simon Willison, began using Python to build applications.

The World Online team, responsible for the production and maintenance of several local news sites, thrived in a development environment dictated by journalism deadlines. For the sites—including LJWorld.com, Lawrence.com, and KUsports.com—journalists (and management) demanded that features be added and entire applications be built on an intensely fast schedule, often with only days' or hours' notice. Thus, Simon and Adrian developed a time-saving Web-development framework out of necessity—it was the only way they could build maintainable applications under the extreme deadlines.

In summer 2005, after having developed this framework to a point where it was efficiently powering most of World Online's sites, the team, which now included Jacob Kaplan-Moss, decided to release the framework as open source software. They released it in July 2005 and named it Django, after the jazz guitarist Django Reinhardt.

Now, several years later, Django is a well-established open source project with tens of thousands of users and contributors spread across the planet. Two of the original World Online developers (the "Benevolent Dictators for Life," Adrian and Jacob) still provide central guidance for the framework's growth, but it's much more of a collaborative team effort.

This history is relevant because it helps explain two key things. The first is Django's "sweet spot." Because Django was born in a news environment, it offers several features (such as its admin site, covered in Chapter 6) that are particularly well suited for "content" sites—sites like Amazon.com, Craigslist, and The Washington Post that offer dynamic, database-driven information. Don't let that turn you off, though—although Django is particularly good for developing those sorts of sites, that doesn't preclude it from being an effective tool for building any sort of dynamic Web site. (There's a difference between being *particularly effective* at something and being *ineffective* at other things.)

The second matter to note is how Django's origins have shaped the culture of its open source community. Because Django was extracted from real-world code rather than being an academic exercise or a commercial product, it is acutely focused on solving Web-development problems that Django's developers themselves have faced—and continue to face. As a result, Django itself is actively improved on an almost daily basis. The framework's maintainers have a vested interest in making sure Django saves developers time, produces applications that are easy to maintain, and performs well under load. If nothing else, the developers are motivated by their own selfish desires to save themselves time and enjoy their jobs. (To put it bluntly, they eat their own dog food.)

How to Read This Book

In writing this book, we tried to strike a balance between readability and reference, with a bias toward readability. Our goal with this book, as stated earlier, is to make you a Django expert, and we believe the best way to teach is through prose and plenty of examples, rather than providing an exhaustive but bland catalog of Django features. (As the saying goes, you can't expect to teach somebody how to speak a language merely by teaching them the alphabet.)

With that in mind, we recommend that you read Chapters 1 through 12 in order. They form the foundation of how to use Django; once you've read them, you'll be able to build and deploy Django-powered Web sites. Specifically, Chapters 1 through 7 are the "core curriculum," Chapters 8 through 11 cover more-advanced Django usage, and Chapter 12 covers deployment. The remaining chapters, 13 through 20, focus on specific Django features and can be read in any order.

The appendixes are for reference. They, along with the free documentation at http://www.djangoproject.com/, are probably what you'll flip back to occasionally to recall syntax or find quick synopses of what certain parts of Django do.

Required Programming Knowledge

Readers of this book should understand the basics of procedural and object-oriented programming: control structures (e.g., if, while, for), data structures (lists, hashes/dictionaries), variables, classes, and objects.

Experience in Web development is, as you may expect, very helpful, but it's not required to understand this book. Throughout the book, we try to promote best practices in Web development for readers who lack this experience.

Required Python Knowledge

At its core, Django is simply a collection of libraries written in the Python programming language. To develop a site using Django, you write Python code that uses these libraries. Learning Django, then, is a matter of learning how to program in Python and understanding how the Django libraries work.

If you have experience programming in Python, you should have no trouble diving in. By and large, the Django code doesn't perform a lot of "magic" (i.e., programming trickery whose implementation is difficult to explain or understand). For you, learning Django will be a matter of learning Django's conventions and APIs.

If you don't have experience programming in Python, you're in for a treat. It's easy to learn and a joy to use! Although this book doesn't include a full Python tutorial, it highlights Python features and functionality where appropriate, particularly when code doesn't immediately make sense. Still, we recommend you read the official Python tutorial, available online at `http://docs.python.org/tut/`. We also recommend Mark Pilgrim's free book *Dive Into Python* (Apress, 2004), available at `http://www.diveintopython.org/` and published in print by Apress.

Required Django Version

This book covers Django 1.1.

Django's developers maintain backward compatibility within "major version" numbers. This commitment means that, if you write an application for Django 1.1, it will still work for 1.2, 1.3, 1.9, and any other version number that starts with "1." Once Django hits 2.0, though, your applications might need to be rewritten—but version 2.0 is a long way away. As a point of reference, it took more than three years to release version 1.0. (This is very similar to the compatibility policy that applies to the Python language itself: code that was written for Python 2.0 works with Python 2.6, but not necessarily with Python 3.0.) Given that this book covers Django 1.1, it should serve you well for some time.

Getting Help

One of the greatest benefits of Django is its kind and helpful user community. For help with any aspect of Django—from installation to application design to database design to deployment—feel free to ask questions online.

- The Django users mailing list is where thousands of Django users hang out to ask and answer questions. Sign up for free at `http://www.djangoproject.com/r/django-users`.

- The Django IRC channel is where Django users hang out to chat and help each other in real time. Join the fun by logging on to #django on the Freenode IRC network.

What's Next?

In the next chapter, we'll get started with Django, covering installation and initial setup.

CHAPTER 2

■ ■ ■

Getting Started

Installing Django is a multistep process because of the multiple moving parts in modern Web development environments. In this chapter, we'll walk you through how to install the framework and its few dependencies.

Because Django is "just" Python code, it runs anywhere Python does—including on some cell phones! But this chapter just covers the common scenarios for Django installations. We'll assume that you're installing it either on a desktop/laptop machine or on a server.

Later on (in Chapter 12), we'll cover how to deploy Django to a production site.

Installing Python

Django is written purely in Python, so the first step in installing the framework is to make sure that you have Python installed.

Python Versions

The core Django framework works with any Python version from 2.3 to 2.6, inclusive. Django's optional Geographic Information Systems (GIS) support requires Python 2.4 to 2.6.

If you're not sure which version of Python to install and you have complete freedom over the decision, pick the latest one in the 2.*x* series: version 2.6. Although Django works equally well with any version from 2.3 to 2.6, the later versions of Python have performance improvements and additional language features you might like to use in your applications. Plus, certain third-party Django add-ons that you might want to use might require a version newer than Python 2.3, so using a later version of Python keeps your options open.

DJANGO AND PYTHON 3.0

At the time of writing, Python 3.0 was released, but Django didn't yet support it. Python 3.0 introduced a substantial number of backward-incompatible changes to the language, so we expect that most major Python libraries and frameworks, including Django, will take a few years to catch up.

If you're new to Python and are wondering whether to learn Python 2.*x* or Python 3.*x*, our advice is to stick with Python 2.*x*.

Installation

If you're on Linux or Mac OS X, you probably have Python already installed. Type `python` at a command prompt (or in Applications/Utilities/Terminal in OS X). If you see something like this, Python is installed:

```
Python 2.4.1 (#2, Mar 31 2005, 00:05:10)
[GCC 3.3 20030304 (Apple Computer, Inc. build 1666)] on darwin
Type "help", "copyright", "credits" or "license" for more information.
>>>
```

Otherwise, you'll need to download and install Python. It's fast and easy, and detailed instructions are available at `http://www.python.org/download/`.

Installing Django

At any given time, two distinct versions of Django are available to you: the latest official release and the bleeding-edge *trunk* version. The version you decide to install depends on your priorities. Do you want a stable and tested version of Django, or do you want a version containing the latest features, perhaps so you can contribute to Django itself, at the expense of stability?

We recommend sticking with an official release, but it's important to know that the trunk development version exists because you'll find it mentioned in the documentation and by members of the community.

Installing an Official Release

Official releases have a version number, such as 1.0.3 or 1.1, and the latest one is always available at `http://www.djangoproject.com/download/`.

If you're on a Linux distribution that includes a package of Django, it's a good idea to use the distributor's version. That way, you'll get security updates along with the rest of your system packages.

If you don't have access to a prepackaged version, you can download and install the framework manually. To do so, first download the tarball, which will be named something similar to `Django-1.0.2-final.tar.gz`. (It doesn't matter which local directory you download this file into; the installation process will put Django's files in the right place.) Then unzip it and run `setup.py install`, as you do with most Python libraries.

Here's how that process looks on Unix systems:

1. `tar xzvf Django-1.0.2-final.tar.gz`

2. `cd Django-*`

3. `sudo python setup.py install`

On Windows, we recommend using 7-Zip (`http://www.djangoproject.com/r/7zip/`) to unzip `.tar.gz` files. Once you've unzipped the file, start up a DOS shell (the command prompt) with administrator privileges and run the following command from within the directory whose name starts with `Django-`:

```
python setup.py install
```

In case you're curious, Django's files will be installed into your Python installation's `site-packages` directory—a directory where Python looks for third-party libraries. Usually it's in a place similar to `/usr/lib/python2.4/site-packages`.

Installing the Trunk Version

The latest and greatest Django development version is referred to as the *trunk* version, and it's available from Django's Subversion repository. You should consider installing this version if you want to work on the bleeding edge or if you want to contribute code to Django itself.

Subversion is a free, open source revision-control system, and the Django team uses it to manage changes to the Django codebase. You can use a Subversion client to grab the very latest Django source code and you can update your local version of the Django code, known as your *local checkout*, at any given time to get the latest changes and improvements made by Django developers.

When using trunk, keep in mind there's no guarantee things won't be broken at any given moment. With that said, though, some members of the Django team run production sites on trunk, so they have an incentive to keep it stable.

To grab the latest Django trunk, follow these steps:

1. Make sure that you have a Subversion client installed. You can get the software free from `http://subversion.tigris.org/` and you can find excellent documentation at `http://svnbook.red-bean.com/`.

   If you're on a Mac with OS X 10.5 or later, you're in luck; Subversion should already be installed. You can verify this by typing `svn --version` in the Terminal.

2. Check out the trunk using the command `svn co http://code.djangoproject.com/svn/django/trunk djtrunk`.

3. Locate your Python installation's `site-packages` directory, which is usually in a place similar to `/usr/lib/python2.4/site-packages`. If you have no idea, type this command from a command prompt:

   ```
   python -c 'import sys, pprint; pprint.pprint(sys.path)'
   ```

   The resulting output should include your `site-packages` directory.

   Within the `site-packages` directory, create a file called `django.pth` and edit it to contain the full path to your `djtrunk` directory to it. For example, the file could contain just this line:

   ```
   /home/me/code/djtrunk
   ```

4. Place `djtrunk/django/bin` on the system path. This directory includes management utilities such as `django-admin.py`.

■Tip If `.pth` files are new to you, you can learn more about them at `http://www.djangoproject.com/r/python/site-module/`.

After downloading from Subversion and following the preceding steps, there's no need to run `python setup.py install`—you just did the work by hand!

Because the Django trunk changes often with bug fixes and feature additions, you'll probably want to update it every once in a while. To update the code, just run the command `svn update` from within the `djtrunk` directory. When you run that command, Subversion will contact `http://code.djangoproject.com`, determine whether any of Django's code has changed, and update your local version of the code with any changes that have been made since you last updated. It's quite slick.

Finally, if you use trunk, you should know how to figure out which version of trunk you're running. Knowing your version number is important if you ever need to reach out to the community for help or if you submit improvements to the framework. In these cases, you should tell people which trunk version (also known as a *revision number* or *changeset*) that you're using. To find out your revision number, type `svn info` from within the `djtrunk` directory, and look for the number after Revision. This number is incremented each time Django is changed, whether through a bug fix, feature addition, documentation improvement, or anything else. Among some members of the Django community, it's a badge of honor to be able to say, "I've been using Django since [insert very low revision number here]."

Testing the Django Installation

For some post-installation positive feedback, take a moment to test whether the installation worked. In a command shell, change into another directory (*not* the directory that contains the `django` directory) and start the Python interactive interpreter by typing `python`. If the installation was successful, you should be able to import the module `django`:

```
>>> import django
>>> django.VERSION
(1, 1, 0, 'final', 1)
```

INTERACTIVE INTERPRETER EXAMPLES

The *Python interactive interpreter* is a command-line program that lets you write a Python program interactively. To start it, run the command `python` at the command line.

Throughout this book, we feature example Python interactive interpreter sessions. You can recognize these examples by the triple greater-than signs (>>>) that designate the interpreter's prompt. If you're copying examples from this book, don't copy those greater-than signs.

Multiline statements in the interactive interpreter are padded with three dots (...). For example:

```
>>> print """This is a
... string that spans
... three lines."""
This is a
string that spans
three lines.
>>> def my_function(value):
...     print value
>>> my_function('hello')
hello
```

Those three dots at the start of the additional lines are inserted by the Python shell—they're not part of our input. We include them to be faithful to the actual output of the interpreter. If you copy our examples to follow along, don't copy those dots.

Setting Up a Database

At this point, you could very well begin writing a Web application with Django because Django's only hard-and-fast prerequisite is a working Python installation. However, odds are you'll be developing a *database-driven* Web site, in which case you'll need to configure a database server.

If you just want to start playing with Django, skip ahead to the "Starting a Project" section—but keep in mind that all the examples in this book assume that you have a working database set up.

Django supports four database engines:

- PostgreSQL (http://www.postgresql.org/)
- SQLite 3 (http://www.sqlite.org/)
- MySQL (http://www.mysql.com/)
- Oracle (http://www.oracle.com/)

For the most part, all the engines work equally well with the core Django framework. (A notable exception is Django's optional GIS support, which is much more powerful with PostgreSQL than with other databases.) If you're not tied to any legacy system and have the freedom to choose a database back-end, we recommend PostgreSQL, which achieves a fine balance between cost, features, speed, and stability.

Setting up the database is a two-step process:

1. First, you'll need to install and configure the database server. This process is beyond the scope of this book, but each of the four database back-ends has rich documentation on its Web site. (If you're on a shared hosting provider, the server is probably set up already.)

2. Second, you'll need to install the Python library for your particular database back-end. This is a third-party bit of code that allows Python to interface with the database. We outline the specific, per-database requirements in the following sections.

If you're just playing around with Django and don't want to install a database server, consider using SQLite. SQLite is unique in the list of supported databases in that it doesn't require either of the preceding steps if you're using Python 2.5 or higher. It merely reads and writes its data to a single file on your filesystem, and Python versions 2.5 and higher include built-in support for it.

On Windows, obtaining database driver binaries can be frustrating. If you're eager to jump in, we recommend using Python 2.5 and its built-in support for SQLite.

Using Django with PostgreSQL

If you use PostgreSQL, you'll need to install either the `psycopg` or `psycopg2` package from `http://www.djangoproject.com/r/python-pgsql/`. We recommend `psycopg2` because it is newer, more actively developed, and can be easier to install. Either way, remember whether you're using version 1 or 2; you'll need this information later.

If you're using PostgreSQL on Windows, you can find precompiled binaries of `psycopg` at `http://www.djangoproject.com/r/python-pgsql/windows/`.

If you're on Linux, check whether your distribution's package-management system offers a package called `python-psycopg2`, `psycopg2-python`, `python-postgresql`, or something similar.

Using Django with SQLite 3

If you're using Python version 2.5 or higher, you're in luck: no database-specific installation is required because Python ships with SQLite support. Skip ahead to the next section.

If you're working with Python 2.4 or older, you'll need SQLite 3—*not* version 2—from `http://www.djangoproject.com/r/sqlite/` and the `pysqlite` package from `http://www.djangoproject.com/r/python-sqlite/`. Make sure that you have `pysqlite` version 2.0.3 or higher.

On Windows, you can skip installing the former (the separate SQLite binaries) because they're statically linked into the `pysqlite` binaries.

If you're on Linux, check whether your distribution's package-management system offers a package called `python-sqlite3`, `sqlite-python`, `pysqlite`, or something similar.

Using Django with MySQL

Django requires MySQL 4.0 or above. The 3.*x* versions don't support nested subqueries and some other fairly standard SQL statements.

You'll also need to install the MySQLdb package from http://www.djangoproject.com/r/python-mysql/.

If you're on Linux, check whether your distribution's package-management system offers a package called python-mysql, python-mysqldb, mysql-python, or something similar.

Using Django with Oracle

Django works with Oracle Database Server versions 9i and higher.

If you're using Oracle, you'll need to install the cx_Oracle library, available at http://cx-oracle.sourceforge.net/. Use version 4.3.1 or higher, but avoid version 5.0 because of a bug in that version of the driver.

Using Django Without a Database

As mentioned earlier, Django doesn't actually require a database. If you just want to use it to serve dynamic pages that don't hit a database, that's perfectly fine.

With that said, bear in mind that some of the extra tools bundled with Django *do* require a database, so if you choose not to use a database, you'll miss out on those features. (We highlight these features throughout this book.)

Starting a Project

Once you've installed Python, Django, and (optionally) your database server/library, you can take the first step of developing a Django application by creating a *project*.

A project is a collection of settings for an instance of Django, including database configuration, Django-specific options, and application-specific settings.

If this is your first time using Django, you'll have to take care of some initial setup. Create a new directory to start working in, perhaps something like /home/username/djcode/.

WHERE SHOULD THIS DIRECTORY LIVE?

If your background is in PHP, you're probably used to putting code under the Web server's document root (in a location such as /var/www). With Django, you don't do that. It's not a good idea to put any of this Python code within your Web server's document root because in doing so you risk the possibility that people will be able to view your raw source code over the Web. That's not good.

Put your code in a directory **outside** of the document root.

Change into the directory you created and run the command `django-admin.py startproject mysite`. This will create a `mysite` directory in your current directory.

■Note `django-admin.py` should be on your system path if you installed Django via its `setup.py` utility. If you're using trunk, you'll find `django-admin.py` in `djtrunk/django/bin`. Because you'll be using `django-admin.py` often, consider adding it to the system path. On Unix, you can do so by symlinking from `/usr/local/bin` by using a command such as `sudo ln -s /path/to/django/bin/django-admin.py /usr/local/bin/django-admin.py`. On Windows, you'll need to update your `PATH` environment variable. If you installed Django from a packaged version for your Linux distribution, `django-admin.py` might be called `django-admin` instead.

If you see a "permission denied" message when running `django-admin.py startproject`, you'll need to change the file's permissions. To do this, navigate to the directory where `django-admin.py` is installed (for example, `cd /usr/local/bin`) and run the command `chmod +x django-admin.py`.

The `startproject` command creates a directory containing four files:

```
mysite/
    __init__.py
    manage.py
    settings.py
    urls.py
```

These files are as follows:

- `__init__.py`: A file required for Python to treat the `mysite` directory as a package (a group of Python modules). It's an empty file, and you normally won't add anything to it.

- `manage.py`: A command-line utility that lets you interact with this Django project in various ways. Type `python manage.py help` to get a feel for what it can do. You should never have to edit this file; it's created in the directory purely for convenience.

- `settings.py`: Settings/configuration for this Django project. Take a look at it to get an idea of the types of settings available, along with their default values.

- `urls.py`: The URLs for this Django project. Think of it as the "table of contents" of your Django-powered site. At the moment, it's empty.

Despite their small size, these files already constitute a working Django application.

Running the Development Server

For more post-installation positive feedback, let's run the Django development server to see the bare-bones application in action.

The Django development server (also called the *runserver* after the command that launches it) is a built-in, lightweight Web server you can use while developing your site. It's included with Django so you can develop your site rapidly, without having to deal with configuring your production server (Apache, for example) until you're ready for production. The development server watches your code and automatically reloads it, making it easy for you to change your code without needing to restart anything.

To start the server, change into the project directory (cd mysite) if you haven't already, and run this command:

```
python manage.py runserver
```

You'll see something like this:

```
Validating models...
0 errors found.

Django version 1.0, using settings 'mysite.settings'
Development server is running at http://127.0.0.1:8000/
Quit the server with CONTROL-C.
```

This launches the server locally on port 8000, accessible only to connections from your own computer. Now that it's running, visit http://127.0.0.1:8000/ with your Web browser. You'll see a "Welcome to Django" page shaded in a pleasant pastel blue. It worked!

One final important note about the development server is worth mentioning before proceeding. Although this server is convenient for development, resist the temptation to use it in anything resembling a production environment. The development server can handle only a single request at a time reliably, and it has not gone through a security audit of any sort. When the time comes to launch your site, see Chapter 12 for information on how to deploy Django.

CHANGING THE DEVELOPMENT SERVER'S HOST OR PORT

By default, the runserver command starts the development server on port 8000, listening only for local connections. If you want to change the server's port, pass it as a command-line argument:

```
python manage.py runserver 8080
```

When you specify an IP address, you tell the server to allow nonlocal connections, which is especially helpful if you want to share a development site with other members of your team. The IP address 0.0.0.0 tells the server to listen on any network interface:

```
python manage.py runserver 0.0.0.0:8000
```

After this is done, other computers on your local network will be able to view your Django site by visiting your IP address in their Web browsers (for example, http://192.168.1.103:8000/)

Note that you'll have to consult your network settings to determine your IP address on the local network. Unix users can run ifconfig in a command prompt to get this information; Windows users can run ipconfig.

What's Next?

Now that you have everything installed and the development server running, you're ready to learn the basics of serving Web pages with Django in Chapter 2.

CHAPTER 3

■■■

Views and URLconfs

In the previous chapter, we explained how to set up a Django project and run the Django development server. In this chapter, you'll learn the basics of creating dynamic Web pages with Django.

Your First Django-Powered Page: Hello World

As a first goal, let's create a Web page that outputs that famous example message: "Hello world."

If you were publishing a simple "Hello world" Web page without a Web framework, you'd simply type "Hello world" into a text file, call it hello.html, and upload it to a directory on a Web server somewhere. Notice that you specified two key pieces of information about that Web page: its contents (the string "Hello world") and its URL (http://www.example.com/hello.html, or maybe http://www.example.com/files/hello.html if you put it in a subdirectory).

With Django, you specify those same two things, but in a different way. The contents of the page are produced by a *view function*, and the URL is specified in a *URLconf*. First, let's write the "Hello world" view function.

Your First View

Within the mysite directory that django-admin.py startproject made in the last chapter, create an empty file called views.py. This Python module will contain the views for this chapter. Note that there's nothing special about the name views.py—Django doesn't care what the file is called, as you'll see in a bit—but it's a good idea to call it views.py as a convention for the benefit of other developers reading your code.

A "Hello world" view is simple. Here's the entire function, plus import statements, which you should type into the views.py file:

```
from django.http import HttpResponse

def hello(request):
    return HttpResponse("Hello world")
```

Let's step through this code one line at a time:

- First, you import the class HttpResponse, which lives in the django.http module. You need to import this class because it's used later in the code.

- Next, you define a function called hello—the view function.

- Each view function takes at least one parameter, called request by convention. This is an object that contains information about the current Web request that has triggered this view, and it's an instance of the class django.http.HttpRequest. In this example, you don't do anything with request, but it must be the first parameter of the view nonetheless.

- Note that the name of the view function doesn't matter; it doesn't have to be named in a certain way for Django to recognize it. We called it hello because that name clearly indicates the gist of the view, but it could just as well be named hello_wonderful_ beautiful_world, or something equally revolting. The next section, "Your First URLconf," will shed light on how Django finds this function.

- The function is a simple one-liner: it merely returns an HttpResponse object that has been instantiated with the text "Hello world".

The main lesson is this: a view is just a Python function that takes an HttpRequest as its first parameter and returns an instance of HttpResponse. In order for a Python function to be a Django view, it must do these two things. (There are exceptions, but we'll get to them later.)

Your First URLconf

If at this point you run python manage.py runserver again, you'll still see the "Welcome to Django" message, with no trace of the "Hello world" view anywhere. That's because the mysite project doesn't yet know about the hello view; you need to tell Django explicitly that you're activating this view at a particular URL. (Continuing the previous analogy of publishing static HTML files, at this point you've created the HTML file but haven't uploaded it to a directory on the server yet.) To hook a view function to a particular URL with Django, use a URLconf.

A *URLconf* is like a table of contents for a Django-powered Web site. Basically, it's a mapping between URLs and the view functions that should be called for those URLs. It's how you tell Django, "For this URL, call this code, and for that URL, call that code." For example, "When somebody visits the URL /foo/, call the view function foo_view(), which lives in the Python module views.py."

When you executed django-admin.py startproject in the previous chapter, the script created a URLconf for you automatically: the file urls.py. By default, it looks something like this:

```
from django.conf.urls.defaults import *

# Uncomment the next two lines to enable the admin:
# from django.contrib import admin
# admin.autodiscover()
```

```
urlpatterns = patterns('',
    # Example:
    # (r'^mysite/', include('mysite.foo.urls')),

    # Uncomment the admin/doc line below and add 'django.contrib.admindocs'
    # to INSTALLED_APPS to enable admin documentation:
    # (r'^admin/doc/', include('django.contrib.admindocs.urls')),

    # Uncomment the next line to enable the admin:
    # (r'^admin/', include(admin.site.urls)),
)
```

This default URLconf includes some commonly used Django features commented out, so activating those features is as easy as uncommenting the appropriate lines. If you ignore the commented-out code, here's the essence of a URLconf:

```
from django.conf.urls.defaults import *

urlpatterns = patterns('',
)
```

Let's step through this code one line at a time:

- The first line imports all objects from the django.conf.urls.defaults module, which is Django's URLconf infrastructure. This includes a function called patterns.

- The second line calls the function patterns and saves the result into a variable called urlpatterns. The patterns function gets passed only a single argument: the empty string. (The string can be used to supply a common prefix for view functions, which we'll cover in Chapter 8.)

The main thing to note is the variable urlpatterns, which Django expects to find in the URLconf module. This variable defines the mapping between URLs and the code that handles those URLs. By default, the URLconf is empty—the Django application is a blank slate.

■Note That's how Django knew to show you the "Welcome to Django" page in the last chapter. If your URLconf is empty, Django assumes that you just started a new project, so it displays that message.

To add a URL and view to the URLconf, just add a Python tuple mapping a URL pattern to the view function. Here's how to hook in the hello view:

```
from django.conf.urls.defaults import *
from mysite.views import hello

urlpatterns = patterns('',
    ('^hello/$', hello),
)
```

■Note We removed the commented-out code for brevity. You can choose to leave those lines in if you want.

Two changes were made:

- First, the `hello` view was imported from its module: `mysite/views.py`, which translates into `mysite.views` in Python import syntax. (This assumes that `mysite/views.py` is on the Python path; see the sidebar for details.)
- Next, the line (`'^hello/$', hello`) was added to `urlpatterns`. This line is referred to as a *URLpattern*. It's a Python tuple in which the first element is a pattern-matching string (a regular expression; more on this in a bit) and the second element is the view function to use for that pattern.

In a nutshell, Django was told that any request to the URL `/hello/` should be handled by the `hello` view function.

PYTHON PATH

The *Python path* is the list of directories on your system where Python looks when you use the Python `import` statement.

For example, let's say your Python path is set to `['', '/usr/lib/python2.4/site-packages', '/home/username/djcode']`. If you execute the Python statement `from foo import bar`, Python will look for a module called `foo.py` in the current directory. (The first entry in the Python path, an empty string, means "the current directory.") If that file doesn't exist, Python will look for the file `/usr/lib/python2.4/site-packages/foo.py`. If that file doesn't exist, it will try `/home/username/djcode/foo.py`. Finally, if *that* file doesn't exist, it will raise `ImportError`.

If you're interested in seeing the value of your Python path, start the Python interactive interpreter and type this:

```
>>> import sys
>>> print sys.path
```

You usually don't have to worry about setting your Python path—Python and Django take care of things for you automatically behind the scenes. (Setting the Python path is one of the things that the `manage.py` script does.)

It's worth discussing the syntax of this URLpattern because it might not be immediately obvious. Although you want to match the URL `/hello/`, the pattern looks a bit different from that. Here's why:

- Django removes the slash from the front of every incoming URL before it checks the URLpatterns. This means that the URLpattern doesn't include the leading slash in /hello/. (At first, this requirement might seem counterintuitive, but it simplifies things—such as the inclusion of URLconfs within other URLconfs, which we'll cover in Chapter 8.)

- The pattern includes a caret (^) and a dollar sign ($). These regular expression characters have a special meaning: the caret means "require that the pattern matches the start of the string," and the dollar sign means "require that the pattern matches the end of the string."

- This concept is best explained by an example. If you had used the pattern '^hello/' (without a dollar sign at the end), *any* URL starting with /hello/ would match (for example, /hello/foo and /hello/bar, not just /hello/). Similarly, if you leave off the initial caret character (for example, 'hello/$'), Django would match *any* URL that ends with hello/, such as /foo/bar/hello/. If you simply use hello/ without a caret *or* a dollar sign, any URL containing hello/ would match (for example, /foo/hello/bar). Thus, you use both the caret and dollar sign to ensure that only the URL /hello/ matches—nothing more, nothing less.

- Most URLpatterns start with carets and end with dollar signs, but it's nice to have the flexibility to perform more sophisticated matches.

- You might be wondering what happens if someone requests the URL /hello (that is, *without* a trailing slash). Because the URLpattern requires a trailing slash, that URL would *not* match. However, by default, any request to a URL that *doesn't* match a URLpattern and *doesn't* end with a slash will be redirected to the same URL with a trailing slash. (This is regulated by the APPEND_SLASH Django setting, which is covered in Appendix D.)

- If you're the type of person who likes all URLs to end with slashes (which is the preference of Django's developers), all you need to do is add a trailing slash to each URLpattern and leave APPEND_SLASH set to True. If you prefer your URLs *not* to have trailing slashes, or if you want to decide it on a per-URL basis, set APPEND_SLASH to False and put trailing slashes in your URLpatterns as you see fit.

The other thing to note about this URLconf is that the hello view function was passed as an object without calling the function. This is a key feature of Python (and other dynamic languages): functions are first-class objects, which means that you can pass them around just like any other variables. Cool stuff, eh?

To test the changes to the URLconf, start the Django development server, as you did in Chapter 2, by running the command python manage.py runserver. (If you left it running, that's fine, too. The development server automatically detects changes to your Python code and reloads as necessary, so you don't have to restart the server between changes.) The server is running at the address http://127.0.0.1:8000/, so open up a Web browser and go to http://127.0.0.1:8000/hello/. You should see the text "Hello world"—the output of your Django view.

Hooray! You made your first Django-powered Web page.

A Quick Note About 404 Errors

At this point, the URLconf defines only a single URLpattern: the one that handles requests to the URL /hello/. What happens when you request a different URL?

To find out, try running the Django development server and visiting a page such as http://127.0.0.1:8000/goodbye/, http://127.0.0.1:8000/hello/subdirectory/, or even http://127.0.0.1:8000/ (the site "root"). You should see a "Page not found" message (see Figure 3-1). Django displays this message because you requested a URL that's not defined in your URLconf.

The utility of this page goes beyond the basic 404 error message. It also tells you precisely which URLconf Django used and every pattern in that URLconf. From that information, you should be able to tell why the requested URL threw a 404.

Naturally, this is sensitive information intended only for you, the Web developer. If this were a production site deployed live on the Internet, you wouldn't want to expose that information to the public. For that reason, this "Page not found" page is displayed only if your Django project is in *debug mode*. We'll explain how to deactivate debug mode later. For now, just know that every Django project is in debug mode when you first create it, and if the project is not in debug mode, Django outputs a different 404 response.

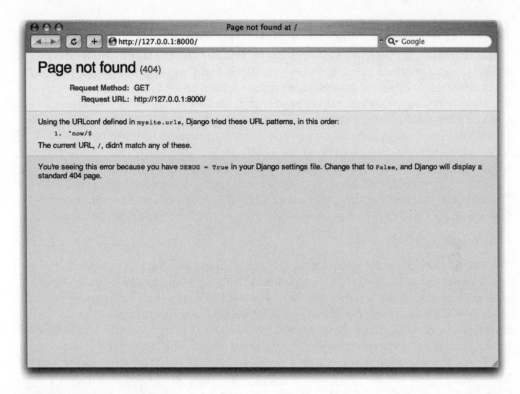

Figure 3-1. *Django's 404 page*

A Quick Note About the Site Root

As explained in the last section, you'll see a 404 error message if you view the site root: http://127.0.0.1:8000/. Django doesn't magically add anything to the site root; that URL is not special-cased in any way. It's up to you to assign it to a URLpattern, just like every other entry in your URLconf.

The URLpattern to match the site root is a bit counterintuitive, though, so it's worth mentioning. When you're ready to implement a view for the site root, use the URLpattern '^$', which matches an empty string. Here's an example:

```
from mysite.views import hello, my_homepage_view

urlpatterns = patterns('',
    ('^$', my_homepage_view),
    # ...
)
```

How Django Processes a Request

Before continuing to the second view function, let's pause to learn a little more about how Django works. Specifically, when you view your "Hello world" message by visiting http://127.0.0.1:8000/hello/ in your Web browser, what does Django do behind the scenes?

It all starts with the *settings file*. When you run python manage.py runserver, the script looks for a file called settings.py in the same directory as manage.py. This file contains all sorts of configuration for this particular Django project, all in uppercase: TEMPLATE_DIRS, DATABASE_NAME, and so on. The most important setting is called ROOT_URLCONF. ROOT_URLCONF tells Django which Python module should be used as the URLconf for this Web site.

Remember when django-admin.py startproject created the files settings.py and urls.py? The autogenerated settings.py contains a ROOT_URLCONF setting that points to the autogenerated urls.py. Open the settings.py file and see for yourself; it should look like this:

```
ROOT_URLCONF = 'mysite.urls'
```

This corresponds to the file mysite/urls.py. When a request comes in for a particular URL—say, a request for /hello/—Django loads the URLconf pointed to by the ROOT_URLCONF setting. Then it checks each of the URLpatterns in that URLconf, in order, comparing the requested URL with the patterns one at a time, until it finds one that matches. When it finds one that matches, it calls the view function associated with that pattern, passing it an HttpRequest object as the first parameter. (We'll cover the specifics of HttpRequest later.)

As you saw in the first view example, a view function must return an HttpResponse. Once it does this, Django does the rest, converting the Python object to a proper Web response with the appropriate HTTP headers and body (the content of the Web page).

In summary, here are the steps:

1. A request comes in to /hello/.

2. Django determines the root URLconf by looking at the ROOT_URLCONF setting.

3. Django looks at all the URLpatterns in the URLconf for the first one that matches /hello/.

4. If it finds a match, it calls the associated view function.

5. The view function returns an HttpResponse.

6. Django converts the HttpResponse to the proper HTTP response, which results in a Web page.

You now know the basics of how to make Django-powered pages. It's quite simple, really: just write view functions and map them to URLs via URLconfs.

Your Second View: Dynamic Content

The "Hello world" view was instructive for demonstrating the basics of how Django works, but it wasn't an example of a *dynamic* Web page because the contents of the page are always the same. Every time you view /hello/, you'll see the same thing; it might as well be a static HTML file.

For the second view, let's create something more dynamic: a Web page that displays the current date and time. This is a nice and simple next step because it doesn't involve a database or any user input; just the output of the server's internal clock. It's only marginally more exciting than "Hello world," but it will demonstrate a few new concepts.

This view needs to do two things: calculate the current date and time, and return an `HttpResponse` containing that value. If you have experience with Python, you know that Python includes a `datetime` module for calculating dates. Here's how to use it:

```
>>> import datetime
>>> now = datetime.datetime.now()
>>> now
datetime.datetime(2008, 12, 13, 14, 9, 39, 2731)
>>> print now
2008-12-13 14:09:39.002731
```

That's simple enough, and it has nothing to do with Django. It's just Python code. (We want to emphasize that you should be aware of what code is "just Python" vs. code that is Django-specific. As you learn Django, we want you to be able to apply your knowledge to other Python projects that don't necessarily use Django.)

To make a Django view that displays the current date and time, you just need to hook this `datetime.datetime.now()` statement into a view and return an `HttpResponse`. Here's how it looks:

```
from django.http import HttpResponse
import datetime

def current_datetime(request):
    now = datetime.datetime.now()
    html = "<html><body>It is now %s.</body></html>" % now
    return HttpResponse(html)
```

As with the `hello` view function, this should live in `views.py`. Note that we hid the `hello` function from this example for brevity, but for the sake of completeness, here's what the entire `views.py` looks like:

```
from django.http import HttpResponse
import datetime

def hello(request):
    return HttpResponse("Hello world")

def current_datetime(request):
    now = datetime.datetime.now()
    html = "<html><body>It is now %s.</body></html>" % now
    return HttpResponse(html)
```

■**Note** From now on, we won't display previous code in code examples except when necessary. You should be able to tell from context which parts of an example are new and which are old.

Let's step through the changes made to `views.py` to accommodate the `current_datetime` view:

- An `import datetime` was added to the top of the module, so you can calculate dates.

- The new `current_datetime` function calculates the current date and time as a `datetime.datetime` object and then stores it as the local variable `now`.

- The second line of code within the view constructs an HTML response using Python's "format-string" capability. The `%s` within the string is a placeholder, and the percent sign after the string means "Replace the `%s` in the preceding string with the value of the variable `now`." The `now` variable is technically a `datetime.datetime` object, not a string, but the `%s` format character converts it to its string representation, which is something like this: `"2008-12-13 14:09:39.002731"`. It will result in an HTML string such as `"<html><body>It is now 2008-12-13 14:09:39.002731.</body></html>"`.

- Yes, the HTML is invalid, but we're trying to keep the example simple and short.

- Finally, the view returns an `HttpResponse` object that contains the generated response—just as we did in `hello`.

After adding that to `views.py`, add the URLpattern to `urls.py` to tell Django which URL should handle this view. Something like `/time/` would make sense:

```
from django.conf.urls.defaults import *
from mysite.views import hello, current_datetime

urlpatterns = patterns('',
    ('^hello/$', hello),
    ('^time/$', current_datetime),
)
```

Two changes were made. First, we imported the `current_datetime` function at the top. Second, and more importantly, we added a URLpattern mapping the URL `/time/` to that new view. Getting the hang of this?

With the view written and URLconf updated, fire up the `runserver` and visit `http://127.0.0.1:8000/time/` in your browser. You should see the current date and time.

DJANGO'S TIME ZONE

Depending on your computer, the date and time might be a few hours off. That's because Django is time zone–aware and defaults to the `America/Chicago` time zone. (It has to default to *something*, and that's the time zone where the original developers live.) If you live elsewhere, you'll want to change it in `settings.py`. See the comment in that file for a link to an up-to-date list of worldwide time zone options.

URLconfs and Loose Coupling

Now is a good time to highlight a key philosophy behind URLconfs and behind Django in general: the principle of *loose coupling*. Simply put, loose coupling is a software-development approach that values the importance of making pieces interchangeable. If two pieces of code are loosely coupled, changes made to one of the pieces will have little or no effect on the other.

Django's URLconfs are a good example of this principle in practice. In a Django Web application, the URL definitions and the view functions they call are loosely coupled; that is, the decision of what the URL should be for a given function and the implementation of the function itself resides in two separate places. This lets you switch out one piece without affecting the other.

For example, consider the current_datetime view. If you wanted to change the URL for the application—say, to move it from /time/ to /current-time/—you could make a quick change to the URLconf without having to worry about the view itself. Similarly, if you wanted to change the view function—altering its logic somehow—you could do that without affecting the URL to which the function is bound.

Furthermore, if you wanted to expose the current-date functionality at *several* URLs, you could easily take care of that by editing the URLconf, without having to touch the view code. In this example, the current_datetime is available at two URLs. It's a contrived example, but this technique can come in handy:

```
urlpatterns = patterns('',
    ('^hello/$', hello),
    ('^time/$', current_datetime),
    ('^another-time-page/$', current_datetime),
)
```

URLconfs and views are loose coupling in action. We'll continue to point out examples of this important philosophy throughout this book.

Your Third View: Dynamic URLs

In the current_datetime view, the contents of the page—the current date/time—were dynamic, but the URL (/time/) was static. In most dynamic Web applications, though, a URL contains parameters that influence the output of the page. For example, an online bookstore might give each book its own URL (for example, /books/243/ and /books/81196/).

Let's create a third view that displays the current date and time offset by a certain number of hours. The goal is to craft a site so that the page /time/plus/1/ displays the date/time one hour into the future, the page /time/plus/2/ displays the date/time two hours into the future, the page /time/plus/3/ displays the date/time three hours into the future, and so on.

A novice might think to code a separate view function for each hour offset, which might result in a URLconf like this:

```
urlpatterns = patterns('',
    ('^time/$', current_datetime),
    ('^time/plus/1/$', one_hour_ahead),
    ('^time/plus/2/$', two_hours_ahead),
    ('^time/plus/3/$', three_hours_ahead),
    ('^time/plus/4/$', four_hours_ahead),
)
```

Clearly, this line of thought is flawed. Not only would this result in redundant view functions but also the application is fundamentally limited to supporting only the predefined hour ranges: one, two, three, or four hours. If you decided to create a page that displayed the time *five* hours into the future, you'd have to create a separate view and URLconf line for that, furthering the duplication. You need to do some abstraction here.

A WORD ABOUT PRETTY URLS

If you're experienced in another Web development platform, such as PHP or Java, you might want to use a query string parameter—something like /time/plus?hours=3, in which the hours would be designated by the hours parameter in the URL's query string (the part after the ?).

You *can* do that with Django (and we'll tell you how in Chapter 8 but one of Django's core philosophies is that URLs should be beautiful. The URL /time/plus/3/ is far cleaner, simpler, more readable, easier to recite to somebody aloud, and just plain prettier than its query string counterpart. Pretty URLs are a characteristic of a quality Web application.

Django's URLconf system encourages pretty URLs by making it easier to use pretty URLs than *not* to.

How then do you design the application to handle arbitrary hour offsets? The key is to use *wildcard URLpatterns*. As mentioned previously, a URLpattern is a regular expression; hence, you can use the regular expression pattern \d+ to match one or more digits:

```
urlpatterns = patterns('',
    # ...
    (r'^time/plus/\d+/$', hours_ahead),
    # ...
)
```

(We're using the # ... to imply there might be other URLpatterns that we trimmed from this example.)

This new URLpattern will match any URL such as /time/plus/2/, /time/plus/25/, or even /time/plus/100000000000/. Come to think of it, let's limit it so that the maximum allowed offset is 99 hours. That means we want to allow either one- or two-digit numbers—and in regular expression syntax, that translates into \d{1,2}:

```
(r'^time/plus/\d{1,2}/$', hours_ahead),
```

■**Note** When building Web applications, it's always important to consider the most outlandish data input possible and decide whether the application should support that input. We've curtailed the outlandishness here by limiting the offset to 99 hours.

One important detail introduced here is that r character in front of the regular expression string. This character tells Python that the string is a "raw string"—its contents should not interpret backslashes. In normal Python strings, backslashes are used for escaping special characters—such as in the string '\n', which is a one-character string containing a newline. When you add the r to make it a raw string, Python does not apply its backslash escaping, so r'\n' is a two-character string containing a literal backslash and a lowercase *n*. There's a natural collision between Python's use of backslashes and the backslashes that are found in regular expressions, so it's strongly suggested that you use raw strings any time you're defining a regular expression in Python. From now on, all the URLpatterns in this book will be raw strings.

Now that a wildcard is designated for the URL, you need a way of passing that wildcard data to the view function, so that you can use a single view function for any arbitrary hour offset. You can do this by placing parentheses around the data in the URLpattern that you want to save. In the case of the example, you want to save whatever number was entered in the URL, so put parentheses around \d{1,2}, like this:

```
(r'^time/plus/(\d{1,2})/$', hours_ahead),
```

If you're familiar with regular expressions, you'll be right at home here; you're using parentheses to *capture* data from the matched text.

The final URLconf, including the previous two views, looks like this:

```
from django.conf.urls.defaults import *
from mysite.views import hello, current_datetime, hours_ahead

urlpatterns = patterns('',
    (r'^hello/$', hello),
    (r'^time/$', current_datetime),
    (r'^time/plus/(\d{1,2})/$', hours_ahead),
)
```

With that taken care of, let's write the hours_ahead view.

CODING ORDER

In this example, the URLpattern was written first and the view was written second, but in the previous examples, the view was written first and then the URLpattern was written. Which technique is better? Well, every developer is different.

If you're a big-picture type of person, it might make the most sense to you to write all the URLpatterns for your application at the same time, at the start of your project, and then code up the views. This has the advantage of giving you a clear to-do list, and it essentially defines the parameter requirements for the view functions you'll need to write.

If you're more of a bottom-up developer, you might prefer to write the views first and then anchor them to URLs afterward. That's OK, too.

In the end, it comes down to which technique fits your brain the best. Both approaches are valid.

hours_ahead is very similar to the current_datetime view written earlier with one key difference: it takes an extra argument the number of hours of offset. Here's the view code:

```
from django.http import Http404, HttpResponse
import datetime

def hours_ahead(request, offset):
    try:
        offset = int(offset)
    except ValueError:
        raise Http404()
    dt = datetime.datetime.now() + datetime.timedelta(hours=offset)
    html = "<html><body>In %s hour(s), it will be %s.</body></html>" % (offset, dt)
    return HttpResponse(html)
```

Let's step through this code one line at a time:

- The view function, hours_ahead, takes *two* parameters: request and offset.

- request is an HttpRequest object, just as in hello and current_datetime. We'll say it again: each view *always* takes an HttpRequest object as its first parameter.

- offset is the string captured by the parentheses in the URLpattern. For example, if the requested URL were /time/plus/3/, offset would be the string '3'. If the requested URL were /time/plus/21/, offset would be the string '21'. Note that captured values will always be *strings*, not integers, even if the string is composed of only digits such as '21'.

■**Note** Technically, captured values will always be *Unicode objects*, not plain Python byte strings, but don't worry about this distinction at the moment.

- We decided to call the variable offset, but you can call it whatever you want as long as it's a valid Python identifier. The variable name doesn't matter; all that matters is that it's the second argument to the function, after request. (It's also possible to use keyword, instead of positional, arguments in a URLconf. We cover that in Chapter 8.)

- The first thing you do within the function is call int() on offset. This converts the string value to an integer.

- Note that Python will raise a ValueError exception if you call int() on a value that cannot be converted to an integer, such as the string 'foo'. In this example, if you encounter the ValueError, you raise the exception django.http.Http404, which, as you can imagine, results in a 404 "Page not found" error.

- Astute readers will wonder how we could ever reach the ValueError case, given that the regular expression in the URLpattern—(\d{1,2})—captures only digits, and therefore offset will only ever be a string composed of digits. The answer is that we won't because the URLpattern provides a modest but useful level of input validation, *but* we still check for the ValueError in case this view function ever gets called in some other way. It's good practice to implement view functions such that they don't make any assumptions about their parameters. Loose coupling, remember?

- In the next line of the function, we calculate the current date/time and add the appropriate number of hours. You've already seen datetime.datetime.now() from the current_datetime view; the new concept here is that you can perform date/time arithmetic by creating a datetime.timedelta object and adding to a datetime.datetime object. The result is stored in the variable dt.

- This line also shows why we called int() on offset—the datetime.timedelta function requires the hours parameter to be an integer.

- Next, the HTML output of this view function is constructed, just as with current_datetime. A small difference in this line from the previous line is that it uses Python's format-string capability with *two* values, not just one. Hence, there are two %s symbols in the string and a tuple of values to insert: (offset, dt).

- Finally, an HttpResponse of the HTML is returned. By now, this is old hat.

With that view function and URLconf written, start the Django development server (if it's not already running), and visit http://127.0.0.1:8000/time/plus/3/ to verify it works. Then try http://127.0.0.1:8000/time/plus/5/. Then http://127.0.0.1:8000/time/plus/24/. Finally, visit http://127.0.0.1:8000/time/plus/100/ to verify that the pattern in the URLconf accepts only one- or two-digit numbers; Django should display a "Page not found" error in this case, just as you saw in the section "A Quick Note About 404 Errors" earlier. The URL http://127.0.0.1:8000/time/plus/ (with *no* hour designation) should also throw a 404.

Django's Pretty Error Pages

Take a moment to admire the fine Web application you've made so far and now you'll break it! Let's deliberately introduce a Python error into the views.py file by commenting out the offset = int(offset) lines in the hours_ahead view:

```
def hours_ahead(request, offset):
    # try:
    #     offset = int(offset)
    # except ValueError:
    #     raise Http404()
    dt = datetime.datetime.now() + datetime.timedelta(hours=offset)
    html = "<html><body>In %s hour(s), it will be %s.</body></html>" % (offset, dt)
    return HttpResponse(html)
```

Load up the development server and navigate to /time/plus/3/. You'll see an error page with a significant amount of information, including a TypeError message displayed at the very top: "unsupported type for timedelta hours component: unicode".

What happened? Well, the `datetime.timedelta` function expects the `hours` parameter to be an integer, and the bit of code that converted `offset` to an integer was commented out. That caused `datetime.timedelta` to raise the `TypeError`. It's the typical kind of small bug that every programmer runs into at some point.

The point of this example was to demonstrate Django error pages. Take some time to explore the error page and get to know the various bits of information it gives you.

Here are some things to notice:

- At the top of the page, you get the key information about the exception: the type of exception, any parameters to the exception (the `"unsupported type"` message in this case), the file in which the exception was raised, and the offending line number.

- Under the key exception information, the page displays the full Python traceback for this exception. This is similar to the standard traceback you get in Python's command-line interpreter, except it's more interactive. For each level ("frame") in the stack, Django displays the name of the file, the function/method name, the line number, and the source code of that line.

- Click the line of source code (in dark gray), and you'll see several lines from before and after the erroneous line, to give you context.

- Click "Local vars" under any frame in the stack to view a table of all local variables and their values, in that frame, at the exact point in the code at which the exception was raised. This debugging information can be a great help.

- Note the "Switch to copy-and-paste view" text under the "Traceback" header. Click those words, and the traceback will switch to an alternate version that can be easily copied and pasted. Use this when you want to share your exception traceback with others to get technical support—such as the kind folks in the Django IRC chat room or on the Django users' mailing list.

- Underneath, the "Share this traceback on a public Web site" button will do this work for you in just one click. Click it to post the traceback to `http://www.dpaste.com/`, where you'll get a distinct URL that you can share with other people.

- Next, the "Request information" section includes a wealth of information about the incoming Web request that spawned the error: GET and POST information, cookie values, and metainformation, such as Common Gateway Interface (CGI) headers. Appendix G has a complete reference of all the information that a request object contains.

- Below the "Request information" section, the "Settings" section lists all the settings for this particular Django installation. (We already mentioned `ROOT_URLCONF` and we'll show you various Django settings throughout the book. All the available settings are covered in detail in Appendix D.)

The Django error page is capable of displaying more information in certain special cases, such as the case of template syntax errors. We'll get to those later, when we discuss the Django template system. For now, uncomment the `offset = int(offset)` lines to get the view function working properly again.

Are you the type of programmer who likes to debug with the help of carefully placed `print` statements? You can use the Django error page to do so—just without the `print` statements. At any point in your view, temporarily insert an `assert False` to trigger the error page. Then you can view the local variables and state of the program. Here's an example using the `hours_ahead` view:

```python
def hours_ahead(request, offset):
    try:
        offset = int(offset)
    except ValueError:
        raise Http404()
    dt = datetime.datetime.now() + datetime.timedelta(hours=offset)
    assert False
    html = "<html><body>In %s hour(s), it will be %s.</body></html>" % (offset, dt)
    return HttpResponse(html)
```

Finally, it's obvious that much of this information is sensitive—it exposes the innards of your Python code and Django configuration—and it would be foolish to show this information on the public Internet. A malicious person could use it to attempt to reverse-engineer your Web application and do nasty things. For that reason, the Django error page is displayed only when your Django project is in debug mode. We'll explain how to deactivate debug mode in Chapter 12. For now, just know that every Django project is in debug mode automatically when you start it. (Sound familiar? The "Page not found" errors, described earlier in this chapter, work the same way.)

What's Next?

So far, we've been writing the view functions with HTML hard-coded directly in the Python code. We've done that to keep things simple while we demonstrated core concepts, but in the real world, this is nearly always a bad idea.

Django ships with a simple yet powerful template engine that allows you to separate the design of the page from the underlying code. You'll dive into Django's template engine in the next chapter.

CHAPTER 4

■ ■ ■

Templates

In the previous chapter, you may have noticed something peculiar in how we returned the text in our example views. Namely, the HTML was hard-coded directly in our Python code, like this:

```python
def current_datetime(request):
    now = datetime.datetime.now()
    html = "<html><body>It is now %s.</body></html>" % now
    return HttpResponse(html)
```

Although this technique was convenient for the purpose of explaining how views work, it's not a good idea to hard-code HTML directly in your views. Here's why:

- Any change to the design of the page requires a change to the Python code. The design of a site tends to change far more frequently than the underlying Python code, so it would be convenient if the design could change without needing to modify the Python code.

- Writing Python code and designing HTML are two different disciplines, and most professional Web-development environments split these responsibilities between separate people (or even separate departments). Designers and HTML/CSS coders shouldn't be required to edit Python code to get their job done.

- It's most efficient if programmers can work on Python code and designers can work on templates at the same time, rather than one person waiting for the other to finish editing a single file that contains both Python and HTML.

For these reasons, it's much cleaner and more maintainable to separate the design of the page from the Python code itself. We can do this with Django's *template system*, which we discuss in this chapter.

Template-System Basics

A Django template is a string of text that is intended to separate the presentation of a document from its data. A template defines placeholders and various bits of basic logic (template tags) that regulate how the document should be displayed. Usually templates are used for producing HTML, but Django templates are equally capable of generating any text-based format.

Let's start with a simple example template. This Django template describes an HTML page that thanks a person for placing an order with a company. Think of it as a form letter:

```html
<html>
<head><title>Ordering notice</title></head>

<body>

<h1>Ordering notice</h1>

<p>Dear {{ person_name }},</p>

<p>Thanks for placing an order from {{ company }}. It's scheduled to
ship on {{ ship_date|date:"F j, Y" }}.</p>

<p>Here are the items you've ordered:</p>

<ul>
{% for item in item_list %}
    <li>{{ item }}</li>
{% endfor %}
</ul>

{% if ordered_warranty %}
    <p>Your warranty information will be included in the packaging.</p>
{% else %}
    <p>You didn't order a warranty, so you're on your own when
    the products inevitably stop working.</p>
{% endif %}

<p>Sincerely,<br />{{ company }}</p>

</body>
</html>
```

This template is basic HTML with some variables and template tags thrown in. Let's step through it:

- Any text surrounded by a pair of braces (e.g., {{ person_name }}) is a *variable*. This means "insert the value of the variable with the given name." How do we specify the values of the variables? We'll get to that in a moment.

- Any text that's surrounded by curly braces and percent signs (e.g., {% if ordered_ warranty %}) is a *template tag*. The definition of a tag is quite broad: a tag just tells the template system to "do something."

  This example template contains a for tag ({% for item in item_list %}) and an if tag ({% if ordered_warranty %}).

  A for tag works very much like a for statement in Python, letting you loop over each item in a sequence. An if tag, as you may expect, acts as a logical "if" statement. In this particular case, the tag checks whether the value of the ordered_warranty variable evaluates to True. If it does, the template system will display everything between the {% if ordered_warranty %} and {% else %}. If not, the template system will display everything between {% else %} and {% endif %}. Note that the {% else %} is optional.

- Finally, the second paragraph of this template contains an example of a *filter*, which is the most convenient way to alter the formatting of a variable. In this example, {{ ship_ date|date:"F j, Y" }}, we're passing the ship_date variable to the date filter, giving the date filter the argument "F j, Y". The date filter formats dates in a given format, as specified by that argument. Filters are attached using a pipe character (|), as a reference to Unix pipes.

Each Django template has access to several built-in tags and filters, many of which are discussed in the sections that follow. Appendix F contains the full list of tags and filters, and it's a good idea to familiarize yourself with that list so you know what's possible. It's also possible to create your own filters and tags; we'll cover that in Chapter 9.

Using the Template System

Let's dive into Django's template system so you can see how it works—but we're *not* yet going to integrate it with the views that we created in the previous chapter. Our goal here is to show you how the system works independent of the rest of Django. (Usually you'll use the template system within a Django view, but we want to make it clear that the template system is just a Python library that you can use *anywhere*, not just in Django views.)

Here is the most basic way you can use Django's template system in Python code:

1. Create a Template object by providing the raw template code as a string.

2. Call the render() method of the Template object with a given set of variables (the *context*). This returns a fully rendered template as a string, with all of the variables and template tags evaluated according to the context.

In code, it looks like this:

```
>>> from django import template
>>> t = template.Template('My name is {{ name }}.')
>>> c = template.Context({'name': 'Adrian'})
>>> print t.render(c)
My name is Adrian.
>>> c = template.Context({'name': 'Fred'})
>>> print t.render(c)
My name is Fred.
```

The following sections describe these steps in much more detail.

Creating Template Objects

The easiest way to create a Template object is to instantiate it directly. The Template class lives in the django.template module, and the constructor takes one argument, the raw template code. Let's dip into the Python interactive interpreter to see how this works in code.

From the mysite project directory created by django-admin.py startproject (as covered in Chapter 2), type python manage.py shell to start the interactive interpreter.

A SPECIAL PYTHON PROMPT

If you've used Python before, you may be wondering why we're running python manage.py shell instead of just python. Both commands will start the interactive interpreter, but the manage.py shell command has one key difference from python: before starting the interpreter, it tells Django which settings file to use. Many parts of Django—including the template system—rely on your settings, and you won't be able to use them unless the framework knows which settings to use.

If you're curious, here's how it works behind the scenes. Django looks for an environment variable called DJANGO_SETTINGS_MODULE, which should be set to the import path of your settings.py. For example, DJANGO_SETTINGS_MODULE might be set to 'mysite.settings', assuming mysite is on your Python path.

When you run python manage.py shell, the command takes care of setting DJANGO_SETTINGS_MODULE for you. We're encouraging you to use python manage.py shell in these examples to minimize the amount of tweaking and configuring you have to do.

As you become more familiar with Django, you'll likely stop using manage.py shell and will set DJANGO_SETTINGS_MODULE manually in your .bash_profile or other shell-environment configuration file.

Let's go through some template-system basics:

```
>>> from django.template import Template
>>> t = Template('My name is {{ name }}.')
>>> print t
```

If you're following along interactively, you'll see something like this:

```
<django.template.Template object at 0xb7d5f24c>
```

That `0xb7d5f24c` will be different every time, but it isn't relevant; it's a Python thing (the Python "identity" of the `Template` object, if you must know).

When you create a `Template` object, the template system compiles the raw template code into an internal, optimized form, ready for rendering. But if your template code includes any syntax errors, the call to `Template()` will cause a `TemplateSyntaxError` exception:

```
>>> from django.template import Template
>>> t = Template('{% notatag %}')
Traceback (most recent call last):
  File "<stdin>", line 1, in ?
  ...
django.template.TemplateSyntaxError: Invalid block tag: 'notatag'
```

The term *block tag* here refers to {% notatag %}. *Block tag* and *template tag* are synonymous.

The system raises a `TemplateSyntaxError` exception for any of the following cases:

- Invalid tags
- Invalid arguments to valid tags
- Invalid filters
- Invalid arguments to valid filters
- Invalid template syntax
- Unclosed tags (for tags that require closing tags)

Rendering a Template

Once you have a `Template` object, you can pass it data by giving it a *context*. A context is simply a set of template variable names and their associated values. A template uses a context to populate its variables and evaluate its tags.

A context is represented in Django by the `Context` class, which lives in the `django.template` module. Its constructor takes one optional argument: a dictionary mapping variable names to variable values. Call the `Template` object's `render()` method with the context to "fill" the template:

```
>>> from django.template import Context, Template
>>> t = Template('My name is {{ name }}.')
>>> c = Context({'name': 'Stephane'})
>>> t.render(c)
u'My name is Stephane.'
```

We should point out here that the return value of `t.render(c)` is a Unicode object—not a normal Python string. You can tell this by the `u` in front of the string. Django uses Unicode objects instead of normal strings throughout the framework. If you understand the repercussions of that, be thankful for the sophisticated things Django does behind the scenes to make it work. If you don't understand the repercussions of that, don't worry for now; just know that Django's Unicode support makes it relatively painless for your applications to support a wide variety of character sets beyond the basic "A–Z" of the English language.

Variable names must begin with a letter (A–Z or a–z) and may contain additional letters, digits, underscores, and dots. (Dots are a special case we'll discuss in the section "Context Variable Lookup.") Variable names are case-sensitive.

Here's an example of template compilation and rendering, using a template similar to the example at the beginning of this chapter:

```
>>> from django.template import Template, Context
>>> raw_template = """<p>Dear {{ person_name }},</p>
...
... <p>Thanks for placing an order from {{ company }}. It's scheduled to
... ship on {{ ship_date|date:"F j, Y" }}.</p>
...
... {% if ordered_warranty %}
... <p>Your warranty information will be included in the packaging.</p>
... {% else %}
... <p>You didn't order a warranty, so you're on your own when
... the products inevitably stop working.</p>
... {% endif %}
...
... <p>Sincerely,<br />{{ company }}</p>"""
>>> t = Template(raw_template)
>>> import datetime
>>> c = Context({'person_name': 'John Smith',
...     'company': 'Outdoor Equipment',
...     'ship_date': datetime.date(2009, 4, 2),
...     'ordered_warranty': False})
>>> t.render(c)
u"<p>Dear John Smith,</p>\n\n<p>Thanks for placing an order from Outdoor
Equipment. It's scheduled to\nship on April 2, 2009.</p>\n\n\n<p>You
didn't order a warranty, so you're on your own when\nthe products
inevitably stop working.</p>\n\n\n<p>Sincerely,<br />Outdoor Equipment
</p>"
```

Let's step through this code one statement at a time:

1. First we import the classes Template and Context, which both live in the module django.template.

2. We save the raw text of our template into the variable raw_template. Note that we use triple quotation marks to designate the string, because it wraps over multiple lines; in contrast, strings within single quotation marks cannot be wrapped over multiple lines.

3. Next we create a template object, t, by passing raw_template to the Template class constructor.

4. We import the datetime module from Python's standard library because we'll need it in the following statement.

5. We create a Context object, c. The Context constructor takes a Python dictionary, which maps variable names to values. Here, for example, we specify that the person_name is 'John Smith', company is 'Outdoor Equipment', and so forth.

6. Finally, we call the render() method on our template object, passing it the context. This returns the rendered template—that is, it replaces template variables with the actual values of the variables, and it executes any template tags.

Note that the "You didn't order a warranty" paragraph was displayed because the ordered_warranty variable evaluated to False. Also note the date, April 2, 2009, which is displayed according to the format string 'F j, Y'. (We'll explain format strings for the date filter in Appendix E.)

If you're new to Python, you may wonder why this output includes newline characters ('\n') rather than displaying the line breaks. That's happening because of a subtlety in the Python interactive interpreter: the call to t.render(c) returns a string, and by default the interactive interpreter displays the *representation* of the string rather than the printed value of the string. If you want to see the string with line breaks displayed as true line breaks rather than '\n' characters, use the print statement: print t.render(c).

Those are the fundamentals of using the Django template system: just write a template string, create a Template object, create a Context, and call the render() method.

Multiple Contexts, Same Template

Once you have a Template object, you can render multiple contexts through it. Consider this example:

```
>>> from django.template import Template, Context
>>> t = Template('Hello, {{ name }}')
>>> print t.render(Context({'name': 'John'}))
Hello, John
>>> print t.render(Context({'name': 'Julie'}))
Hello, Julie
>>> print t.render(Context({'name': 'Pat'}))
Hello, Pat
```

Whenever you're using the same template source to render multiple contexts like this, it's more efficient to create the Template object *once*, and then call render() on it multiple times:

```
# Bad
for name in ('John', 'Julie', 'Pat'):
    t = Template('Hello, {{ name }}')
    print t.render(Context({'name': name}))
```

```
# Good
t = Template('Hello, {{ name }}')
for name in ('John', 'Julie', 'Pat'):
    print t.render(Context({'name': name}))
```

Django's template parsing is quite fast. Behind the scenes, most of the parsing happens via a call to a single regular expression. This is in stark contrast to XML-based template engines, which incur the overhead of an XML parser and tend to be orders of magnitude slower than Django's template-rendering engine.

Context Variable Lookup

In the examples so far, we've passed simple values in the contexts—mostly strings, plus a datetime.date example. However, the template system elegantly handles more-complex data structures, such as lists, dictionaries, and custom objects.

The key to traversing complex data structures in Django templates is the dot character (.). Use a dot to access dictionary keys, attributes, methods, or indices of an object.

This is best illustrated with a few examples. For instance, suppose you're passing a Python dictionary to a template. To access the values of that dictionary by dictionary key, use a dot:

```
>>> from django.template import Template, Context
>>> person = {'name': 'Sally', 'age': '43'}
>>> t = Template('{{ person.name }} is {{ person.age }} years old.')
>>> c = Context({'person': person})
>>> t.render(c)
u'Sally is 43 years old.'
```

Similarly, dots also allow access of object attributes. For example, a Python datetime.date object has year, month, and day attributes, and you can use a dot to access those attributes in a Django template:

```
>>> from django.template import Template, Context
>>> import datetime
>>> d = datetime.date(1993, 5, 2)
>>> d.year
1993
>>> d.month
5
>>> d.day
2
>>> t = Template('The month is {{ date.month }} and the year is {{ date.year }}.')
>>> c = Context({'date': d})
>>> t.render(c)
u'The month is 5 and the year is 1993.'
```

This example uses a custom class, demonstrating that variable dots also allow attribute access on arbitrary objects:

```
>>> from django.template import Template, Context
>>> class Person(object):
...     def __init__(self, first_name, last_name):
...         self.first_name, self.last_name = first_name, last_name
>>> t = Template('Hello, {{ person.first_name }} {{ person.last_name }}.')
>>> c = Context({'person': Person('John', 'Smith')})
>>> t.render(c)
u'Hello, John Smith.'
```

Dots can also refer to *methods* on objects. For example, each Python string has the methods upper() and isdigit(), and you can call those in Django templates using the same dot syntax:

```
>>> from django.template import Template, Context
>>> t = Template('{{ var }}–{{ var.upper }}–{{ var.isdigit }}')
>>> t.render(Context({'var': 'hello'}))
u'hello–HELLO–False'
>>> t.render(Context({'var': '123'}))
u'123–123–True'
```

Note that you do *not* include parentheses in the method calls. Also, it's not possible to pass arguments to the methods; you can only call methods that have no required arguments. (We explain this philosophy later in this chapter.)

Finally, dots are also used to access list indices, as in this example:

```
>>> from django.template import Template, Context
>>> t = Template('Item 2 is {{ items.2 }}.')
>>> c = Context({'items': ['apples', 'bananas', 'carrots']})
>>> t.render(c)
u'Item 2 is carrots.'
```

Negative list indices are not allowed. For example, the template variable {{ items.-1 }} would cause a TemplateSyntaxError.

PYTHON LISTS

A reminder: Python lists have 0-based indices. The first item is at index 0, the second is at index 1, and so on.

Dot lookups can be summarized like this: when the template system encounters a dot in a variable name, it tries the following lookups, in this order:

- Dictionary lookup (e.g., foo["bar"])

- Attribute lookup (e.g., foo.bar)

- Method call (e.g., foo.bar())

- List-index lookup (e.g., foo[2])

The system uses the first lookup type that works. It's short-circuit logic.

Dot lookups can be nested multiple levels deep. For instance, the following example uses {{ person.name.upper }}, which translates into a dictionary lookup (person['name']) and then a method call (upper()):

```
>>> from django.template import Template, Context
>>> person = {'name': 'Sally', 'age': '43'}
>>> t = Template('{{ person.name.upper }} is {{ person.age }} years old.')
>>> c = Context({'person': person})
>>> t.render(c)
u'SALLY is 43 years old.'
```

Method-Call Behavior

Method calls are slightly more complex than the other lookup types. Here are some things to keep in mind.

If, during the method lookup, a method raises an exception, the exception will be propagated unless the exception has an attribute silent_variable_failure whose value is True. If the exception *does* have a silent_variable_failure attribute, the variable will render as an empty string, as in this example:

```
>>> t = Template("My name is {{ person.first_name }}.")
>>> class PersonClass3:
...     def first_name(self):
...         raise AssertionError, "foo"
>>> p = PersonClass3()
>>> t.render(Context({"person": p}))
Traceback (most recent call last):
...
AssertionError: foo

>>> class SilentAssertionError(AssertionError):
...     silent_variable_failure = True
>>> class PersonClass4:
...     def first_name(self):
...         raise SilentAssertionError
>>> p = PersonClass4()
>>> t.render(Context({"person": p}))
u'My name is .'
```

- A method call will work only if the method has no required arguments. Otherwise, the system will move to the next lookup type (list-index lookup).

- Obviously, some methods have side effects and it would be foolish at best, and possibly even a security hole, to allow the template system to access them.

  Say, for instance, you have a BankAccount object that has a delete() method. If a template includes something like {{ account.delete }}, where account is a BankAccount object, the object would be deleted when the template is rendered!

  To prevent this, set the function attribute alters_data on the method:

  ```
  def delete(self):
      # Delete the account
  delete.alters_data = True
  ```

- The template system won't execute any method marked in this way. Continuing the current example, if a template includes {{ account.delete }} and the delete() method has alters_data=True, then the delete() method will not be executed when the template is rendered. Instead it will fail silently.

How Invalid Variables Are Handled

By default, if a variable doesn't exist the template system renders it as an empty string, failing silently. Consider this example:

```
>>> from django.template import Template, Context
>>> t = Template('Your name is {{ name }}.')
>>> t.render(Context())
u'Your name is .'
>>> t.render(Context({'var': 'hello'}))
u'Your name is .'
>>> t.render(Context({'NAME': 'hello'}))
u'Your name is .'
>>> t.render(Context({'Name': 'hello'}))
u'Your name is .'
```

The system fails silently rather than raising an exception because it's intended to be resilient to human error. In this case, all of the lookups failed because variable names have the wrong case or name. In the real world, it's unacceptable for a Web site to become inaccessible due to a small template syntax error.

Playing with Context Objects

Most of the time, you'll instantiate Context objects by passing in a fully populated dictionary to Context(). But you can add and delete items from a Context object once it's been instantiated, too, using standard Python dictionary syntax:

```
>>> from django.template import Context
>>> c = Context({"foo": "bar"})
>>> c['foo']
'bar'
>>> del c['foo']
>>> c['foo']
Traceback (most recent call last):
  ...
KeyError: 'foo'
>>> c['newvariable'] = 'hello'
>>> c['newvariable']
'hello'
```

Basic Template Tags and Filters

As we've mentioned already, the template system ships with built-in tags and filters. The sections that follow provide a rundown of the most common tags and filters.

Tags

The following sections outline the common Django tags.

if/else

The {% if %} tag evaluates a variable, and if that variable is True (i.e., it exists, is not empty, and is not a False Boolean value), the system will display everything between {% if %} and {% endif %}, as in this example:

```
{% if today_is_weekend %}
    <p>Welcome to the weekend!</p>
{% endif %}
```

An {% else %} tag is optional:

```
{% if today_is_weekend %}
    <p>Welcome to the weekend!</p>
{% else %}
    <p>Get back to work.</p>
{% endif %}
```

PYTHON "TRUTHINESS"

In Python and in the Django template system, these objects evaluate to False in a Boolean context:

- An empty list ([ ]).
- An empty tuple (( )).
- An empty dictionary ({ }).
- An empty string (' ').
- Zero (0).
- The special object None.
- The object False (obviously).
- Custom objects that define their own Boolean context behavior. (This is advanced Python usage.)

Everything else evaluates to True.

The {% if %} tag accepts and, or, or not for testing multiple variables, or to negate a given variable. Consider this example:

```
{% if athlete_list and coach_list %}
    Both athletes and coaches are available.
{% endif %}

{% if not athlete_list %}
    There are no athletes.
{% endif %}

{% if athlete_list or coach_list %}
    There are some athletes or some coaches.
{% endif %}

{% if not athlete_list or coach_list %}
    There are no athletes or there are some coaches.
{% endif %}

{% if athlete_list and not coach_list %}
    There are some athletes and absolutely no coaches.
{% endif %}
```

{% if %} tags don't allow and and or clauses within the same tag, because the order of logic would be ambiguous. For example, this is invalid:

```
{% if athlete_list and coach_list or cheerleader_list %}
```

The use of parentheses for controlling order of operations is not supported. If you find yourself needing parentheses, consider performing logic outside the template and passing the result of that as a dedicated template variable. Or just use nested {% if %} tags, like this:

```
{% if athlete_list %}
    {% if coach_list or cheerleader_list %}
        We have athletes, and either coaches or cheerleaders!
    {% endif %}
{% endif %}
```

Multiple uses of the same logical operator are fine, but you can't combine different operators. For example, this is valid:

```
{% if athlete_list or coach_list or parent_list or teacher_list %}
```

There is no {% elif %} tag. Use nested {% if %} tags to accomplish the same thing:

```
{% if athlete_list %}
    <p>Here are the athletes: {{ athlete_list }}.</p>
{% else %}
    <p>No athletes are available.</p>
    {% if coach_list %}
        <p>Here are the coaches: {{ coach_list }}.</p>
    {% endif %}
{% endif %}
```

Make sure to close each {% if %} with an {% endif %}. Otherwise, Django will throw a TemplateSyntaxError.

for

The {% for %} tag allows you to loop over each item in a sequence. As in Python's for statement, the syntax is for X in Y, where Y is the sequence to loop over and X is the name of the variable to use for a particular cycle of the loop. Each time through the loop, the template system will render everything between {% for %} and {% endfor %}.

For example, you could use the following to display a list of athletes given a variable athlete_list:

```
<ul>
{% for athlete in athlete_list %}
    <li>{{ athlete.name }}</li>
{% endfor %}
</ul>
```

Add reversed to the tag to loop over the list in reverse:

```
{% for athlete in athlete_list reversed %}
...
{% endfor %}
```

It's possible to nest {% for %} tags:

```
{% for athlete in athlete_list %}
    <h1>{{ athlete.name }}</h1>
    <ul>
    {% for sport in athlete.sports_played %}
        <li>{{ sport }}</li>
    {% endfor %}
    </ul>
{% endfor %}
```

A common pattern is to check the size of the list before looping over it, and outputting some special text if the list is empty:

```
{% if athlete_list %}
    {% for athlete in athlete_list %}
        <p>{{ athlete.name }}</p>
    {% endfor %}
{% else %}
    <p>There are no athletes. Only computer programmers.</p>
{% endif %}
```

Because this pattern is so common, the for tag supports an optional {% empty %} clause that lets you define what to output if the list is empty. This example is equivalent to the previous one:

```
{% for athlete in athlete_list %}
    <p>{{ athlete.name }}</p>
{% empty %}
    <p>There are no athletes. Only computer programmers.</p>
{% endfor %}
```

There is no support for "breaking out" of a loop before the loop is finished. If you want to accomplish this, change the variable you're looping over so that it includes only the values you want to loop over. Similarly, there is no support for a "continue" statement that would instruct the loop processor to return immediately to the front of the loop. (See the section "Philosophies and Limitations" later in this chapter for the reasoning behind this design decision.)

Within each {% for %} loop, you get access to a template variable called forloop. This variable has a few attributes that give you information about the progress of the loop:

- forloop.counter is always set to an integer representing the number of times the loop has been entered. This is one-indexed, so the first time through the loop, forloop. counter will be set to 1. Here's an example:

  ```
  {% for item in todo_list %}
      <p>{{ forloop.counter }}: {{ item }}</p>
  {% endfor %}
  ```

- forloop.counter0 is like forloop.counter, except it's zero-indexed. Its value will be set to 0 the first time through the loop.

- `forloop.revcounter` is always set to an integer representing the number of remaining items in the loop. The first time through the loop, `forloop.revcounter` will be set to the total number of items in the sequence you're traversing. The last time through the loop, `forloop.revcounter` will be set to 1.

- `forloop.revcounter0` is like `forloop.revcounter`, except it's zero-indexed. The first time through the loop, `forloop.revcounter0` will be set to the number of elements in the sequence, minus 1. The last time through the loop, it will be set to 0.

- `forloop.first` is a Boolean value set to `True` if this is the first time through the loop. This is convenient for special-casing:

```
{% for object in objects %}
    {% if forloop.first %}<li class="first">{% else %}<li>{% endif %}
    {{ object }}
    </li>
{% endfor %}
```

- `forloop.last` is a Boolean value set to `True` if this is the last time through the loop. A common use for this is to put pipe characters between a list of links:

```
{% for link in links %}{{ link }}{% if not forloop.last %} | {% endif %}{%
endfor %}
```

The preceding template code might output something like this:

```
Link1 | Link2 | Link3 | Link4
```

Another common use for this is to put a comma between words in a list:

```
Favorite places:
{% for p in places %}{{ p }}{% if not forloop.last %}, {% endif %}{% endfor %}
```

- `forloop.parentloop` is a reference to the `forloop` object for the *parent* loop, in case of nested loops. Here's an example:

```
{% for country in countries %}
    <table>
    {% for city in country.city_list %}
        <tr>
        <td>Country #{{ forloop.parentloop.counter }}</td>
        <td>City #{{ forloop.counter }}</td>
        <td>{{ city }}</td>
        </tr>
    {% endfor %}
    </table>
{% endfor %}
```

The magic `forloop` variable is available only within loops. After the template parser has reached `{% endfor %}`, `forloop` disappears.

CONTEXT AND THE FORLOOP VARIABLE

Inside the {% for %} block, the existing variables are moved out of the way to avoid overwriting the magic forloop variable. Django exposes this moved context in forloop.parentloop. You generally don't need to worry about this, but if you supply a template variable named forloop (though we advise against it, because it could confuse fellow template authors), it will be named forloop.parentloop while inside the {% for %} block.

ifequal/ifnotequal

The Django template system deliberately is not a full-fledged programming language and thus does not allow you to execute arbitrary Python statements. (More on this idea in the section "Philosophies and Limitations.") However, it's quite a common template requirement to compare two values and display something if they're equal—and Django provides an {% ifequal %} tag for that purpose.

The {% ifequal %} tag compares two values and displays everything between {% ifequal %} and {% endifequal %} if the values are equal.

This example compares the template variables user and currentuser:

```
{% ifequal user currentuser %}
    <h1>Welcome!</h1>
{% endifequal %}
```

The arguments can be hard-coded strings, with either single or double quotes, so the following is valid:

```
{% ifequal section 'sitenews' %}
    <h1>Site News</h1>
{% endifequal %}

{% ifequal section "community" %}
    <h1>Community</h1>
{% endifequal %}
```

Just like {% if %}, the {% ifequal %} tag supports an optional {% else %}:

```
{% ifequal section 'sitenews' %}
    <h1>Site News</h1>
{% else %}
    <h1>No News Here</h1>
{% endifequal %}
```

Only template variables, strings, integers, and decimal numbers are allowed as arguments to {% ifequal %}. These are valid examples:

```
{% ifequal variable 1 %}
{% ifequal variable 1.23 %}
{% ifequal variable 'foo' %}
{% ifequal variable "foo" %}
```

Any other types of variables, such as Python dictionaries, lists, or Booleans, can't be hard-coded in {% ifequal %}. These are invalid examples:

```
{% ifequal variable True %}
{% ifequal variable [1, 2, 3] %}
{% ifequal variable {'key': 'value'} %}
```

If you need to test whether something is true or false, use the {% if %} tags instead of {% ifequal %}.

Comments

Just as in HTML or Python, the Django template language allows for comments. To designate a comment, use {# #}:

```
{# This is a comment #}
```

The comment will not be output when the template is rendered.

Comments using this syntax cannot span multiple lines. This limitation improves template parsing performance. In the following template, the rendered output will look exactly the same as the template (i.e., the comment tag will not be parsed as a comment):

```
This is a {# this is not
a comment #}
test.
```

If you want to use multiline comments, use the {% comment %} template tag, like this:

```
{% comment %}
This is a
multiline comment.
{% endcomment %}
```

Filters

As explained earlier in this chapter, template filters are simple ways of altering the value of variables before they're displayed. Filters use a pipe character, like this:

```
{{ name|lower }}
```

This displays the value of the {{ name }} variable after being filtered through the lower filter, which converts text to lowercase.

Filters can be *chained*—that is, they can be used in tandem such that the output of one filter is applied to the next. Here's an example that converts the first element in a list to uppercase:

```
{{ my_list|first|upper }}
```

Some filters take arguments. A filter argument comes after a colon and is always in double quotes. Here's an example:

```
{{ bio|truncatewords:"30" }}
```

This displays the first 30 words of the `bio` variable.

The following are a few of the most important filters. Appendix F covers the rest.

- `addslashes`: Adds a backslash before any backslash, single quote, or double quote. This is useful if the produced text is included in a JavaScript string.

- `date`: Formats a `date` or `datetime` object according to a format string given in the parameter, as in this example:

  ```
  {{ pub_date|date:"F j, Y" }}
  ```

  Format strings are defined in Appendix F.

- `length`: Returns the length of the value. For a list, this returns the number of elements. For a string, this returns the number of characters. (Python experts, note that this works on any Python object that knows how to determine its own length—that is, any object that has a `__len__()` method.)

Philosophies and Limitations

Now that you've gotten a feel for the Django template language, we should point out some of its intentional limitations, along with some philosophies behind why it works the way it works.

More than any other component of Web applications, template syntax is highly subjective, and programmers' opinions vary wildly. The fact that Python alone has dozens, if not hundreds, of open source template-language implementations supports this point. Each was likely created because its developer deemed all existing template languages inadequate. (In fact, it is said to be a rite of passage for a Python developer to write his or her own template language! If you haven't done this yet, consider it. It's a fun exercise.)

With that in mind, you might be interested to know that Django doesn't require you to use its template language. Because Django is intended to be a full-stack Web framework that provides all the pieces necessary for Web developers to be productive, many times it's more convenient to use Django's template system than other Python template libraries, but it's not a strict requirement in any sense. As you'll see in the upcoming section "Using Templates in Views," it's very easy to use another template language with Django.

Still, it's clear we have a strong preference for the way Django's template language works. The template system has roots in how Web development is done at World Online and the combined experience of Django's creators. Here are a few of our philosophies:

- *Business logic should be separated from presentation logic.* Django's developers see a template system as a tool that controls presentation and presentation-related logic—and that's it. The template system shouldn't support functionality that goes beyond this basic goal.

  For that reason, it's impossible to call Python code directly within Django templates. All "programming" is fundamentally limited to the scope of what template tags can do. It *is* possible to write custom template tags that do arbitrary things, but the out-of-the-box Django template tags intentionally do not allow for arbitrary Python-code execution.

- *Syntax should be decoupled from HTML/XML.* Although Django's template system is used primarily to produce HTML, it's intended to be just as usable for non-HTML formats, such as plain text. Some other template languages are XML based, placing all template logic within XML tags or attributes, but Django deliberately avoids this limitation. Requiring valid XML for writing templates introduces a world of human mistakes and hard-to-understand error messages, and using an XML engine to parse templates incurs an unacceptable level of overhead in template processing.

- *Designers are assumed to be comfortable with HTML code.* The template system isn't designed so that templates necessarily are displayed nicely in WYSIWYG editors such as Dreamweaver. That is too severe a limitation and wouldn't allow the syntax to be as friendly as it is. Django expects template authors to be comfortable editing HTML directly.

- *Designers are assumed not to be Python programmers.* The template-system authors recognize that Web-page templates are most often written by *designers*, not *programmers*, and therefore should not assume Python knowledge.

  However, the system also intends to accommodate small teams in which the templates *are* created by Python programmers. It offers a way to extend the system's syntax by writing raw Python code. (More on this in Chapter 9.)

- *The goal is not to invent a programming language.* The goal is to offer just as much programming-esque functionality, such as branching and looping, that is essential for making presentation-related decisions.

Using Templates in Views

You've learned the basics of using the template system; now let's use this knowledge to create a view. Recall the current_datetime view in mysite.views, which we started in the previous chapter. Here's what it looks like:

```python
from django.http import HttpResponse
import datetime

def current_datetime(request):
    now = datetime.datetime.now()
    html = "<html><body>It is now %s.</body></html>" % now
    return HttpResponse(html)
```

Let's change this view to use Django's template system. At first you might think to do something like this:

```
from django.template import Template, Context
from django.http import HttpResponse
import datetime

def current_datetime(request):
    now = datetime.datetime.now()
    t = Template("<html><body>It is now {{ current_date }}.</body></html>")
    html = t.render(Context({'current_date': now}))
    return HttpResponse(html)
```

Sure, that uses the template system, but it doesn't solve the problems we pointed out in the introduction of this chapter. Namely, the template is still embedded in the Python code, so true separation of data and presentation isn't achieved. Let's fix that by putting the template in a *separate file*, which this view will load.

You might first consider saving your template somewhere on your filesystem and using Python's built-in file-opening functionality to read the contents of the template. Here's what that might look like, assuming the template was saved as the file /home/djangouser/templates/mytemplate.html:

```
from django.template import Template, Context
from django.http import HttpResponse
import datetime

def current_datetime(request):
    now = datetime.datetime.now()
    # Simple way of using templates from the filesystem.
    # This is BAD because it doesn't account for missing files!
    fp = open('/home/djangouser/templates/mytemplate.html')
    t = Template(fp.read())
    fp.close()
    html = t.render(Context({'current_date': now}))
    return HttpResponse(html)
```

This approach, however, is inelegant for these reasons:

- It doesn't handle the case of a missing file, as noted in the code. If the file mytemplate.html doesn't exist or isn't readable, the open() call will raise an IOError exception.

- It hard-codes your template location. If you were to use this technique for every view function, you'd be duplicating the template locations—not to mention that it involves a lot of typing!

- It includes a lot of boring boilerplate code. You've got better things to do than to write calls to open(), fp.read(), and fp.close() each time you load a template.

To solve these issues, we'll use *template loading* and *template inheritance*.

Template Loading

Django provides a convenient and powerful API for loading templates from the filesystem, with the goal of removing redundancy both in your template-loading calls and in your templates themselves.

To use this template-loading API, first you'll need to tell the framework where you store your templates. The place to do this is in your *settings file*—the settings.py file that we mentioned in the last chapter, when we introduced the ROOT_URLCONF setting.

If you're following along, open settings.py and find the TEMPLATE_DIRS setting. By default, it's an empty tuple, likely containing some autogenerated comments:

```
TEMPLATE_DIRS = (
    # Put strings here, like "/home/html/django_templates"
    # or "C:/www/django/templates".
    # Always use forward slashes, even on Windows.
    # Don't forget to use absolute paths, not relative paths.
)
```

This setting tells Django's template-loading mechanism where to look for templates. Pick a directory where you'd like to store your templates and add it to TEMPLATE_DIRS, like so:

```
TEMPLATE_DIRS = (
    '/home/django/mysite/templates',
)
```

There are a few things to note:

- You can specify any directory you want, as long as the directory and templates within that directory are readable by the user account under which your Web server runs. If you can't think of an appropriate place to put your templates, we recommend creating a templates directory within your project (i.e., within the mysite directory you created in Chapter 2).

- If your TEMPLATE_DIRS contains only one directory, don't forget the comma at the end of the directory string!

  Bad:

  ```
  # Missing comma!
  TEMPLATE_DIRS = (
      '/home/django/mysite/templates'
  )
  ```

  Good:

  ```
  # Comma correctly in place.
  TEMPLATE_DIRS = (
      '/home/django/mysite/templates',
  )
  ```

Python requires commas within single-element tuples to disambiguate the tuple from a parenthetical expression. This is a common newbie gotcha.

- If you're on Windows, include your drive letter and use Unix-style forward slashes rather than backslashes, as follows:

```
TEMPLATE_DIRS = (
    'C:/www/django/templates',
)
```

- It's simplest to use absolute paths (i.e., directory paths that start at the root of the filesystem). If you want to be a bit more flexible and decoupled, though, you can take advantage of the fact that Django settings files are just Python code by constructing the contents of TEMPLATE_DIRS dynamically, as in this example:

```
import os.path

TEMPLATE_DIRS = (
    os.path.join(os.path.dirname(__file__), 'templates').replace('\\','/'),
)
```

This example uses the "magic" Python variable __file__, which is automatically set to the file name of the Python module in which the code lives. It gets the name of the directory that contains settings.py (os.path.dirname), joins that with templates in a cross-platform way (os.path.join), then ensures that everything uses forward slashes instead of backslashes (in the case of Windows).

While we're on the topic of dynamic Python code in settings files, we should point out that it's very important to avoid Python errors in your settings file. If you introduce a syntax error or a runtime error, your Django-powered site will likely crash.

With TEMPLATE_DIRS set, the next step is to change the view code to use Django's template-loading functionality rather than hard-coding the template paths. Returning to our current_datetime view, let's change it like so:

```
from django.template.loader import get_template
from django.template import Context
from django.http import HttpResponse
import datetime

def current_datetime(request):
    now = datetime.datetime.now()
    t = get_template('current_datetime.html')
    html = t.render(Context({'current_date': now}))
    return HttpResponse(html)
```

In this example, we're using the function django.template.loader.get_template()rather than loading the template from the filesystem manually. The get_template() function takes a template name as its argument, figures out where the template lives on the filesystem, opens that file, and returns a compiled Template object.

Our template in this example is current_datetime.html, but there's nothing special about that .html extension. You can give your templates whatever extension makes sense for your application, or you can leave off extensions entirely.

To determine the location of the template on your filesystem, get_template() combines your template directories from TEMPLATE_DIRS with the template name that you pass to get_template(). For example, if your TEMPLATE_DIRS is set to '/home/django/mysite/templates', the get_template() call would look for the template /home/django/mysite/templates/current_datetime.html.

If get_template() cannot find the template with the given name, it raises a TemplateDoesNotExist exception. To see what that looks like, fire up the Django development server by running python manage.py runserver within your Django project's directory. Then point your browser at the page that activates the current_datetime view (e.g., http://127.0.0.1:8000/time/). Assuming DEBUG is set to True and you haven't yet created a current_datetime.html template, you should see a Django error page highlighting the TemplateDoesNotExist error, as shown in Figure 4-1.

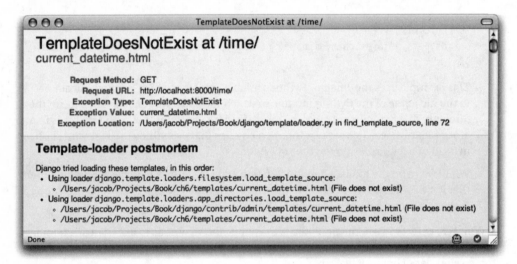

Figure 4-1. *The error page shown when a template cannot be found*

This error page is similar to the one we explained in Chapter 3, with one additional piece of debugging information: a "Template-loader postmortem" section. This section tells you which templates Django tried to load, along with the reason each attempt failed (e.g., "File does not exist"). This information is invaluable when you're trying to debug template-loading errors.

Moving along, create the current_datetime.html file within your template directory using the following template code:

```
<html><body>It is now {{ current_date }}.</body></html>
```

Refresh the page in your Web browser, and you should see the fully rendered page.

render_to_response()

We've shown you how to load a template, fill a Context, and return an HttpResponse object with the result of the rendered template. We've optimized it to use get_template() instead of hard-coding templates and template paths. But it still requires a fair amount of typing to do those things. Because these steps are such a common idiom, Django provides a shortcut that lets you load a template, render it, and return an HttpResponse—all in one line of code.

This shortcut is a function called render_to_response(), which lives in the module django. shortcuts. Most of the time you'll be using render_to_response() rather than loading templates and creating Context and HttpResponse objects manually—unless your employer judges your work by total lines of code written.

Here's the ongoing current_datetime example rewritten to use render_to_response():

```
from django.shortcuts import render_to_response
import datetime

def current_datetime(request):
    now = datetime.datetime.now()
    return render_to_response('current_datetime.html', {'current_date': now})
```

What a difference! Let's step through the code changes:

- We no longer have to import get_template, Template, Context, or HttpResponse. Instead, we import django.shortcuts.render_to_response. The import datetime remains.

- Within the current_datetime function, we still calculate now, but the template loading, context creation, template rendering, and HttpResponse creation are all taken care of by the render_to_response() call. Because render_to_response() returns an HttpResponse object, we can simply return that value in the view.

The first argument to render_to_response() is the name of the template to use. The second argument, if given, should be a dictionary to use in creating a Context for that template. If you don't provide a second argument, render_to_response() will use an empty dictionary.

The locals() Trick

Consider our latest incarnation of current_datetime:

```
def current_datetime(request):
    now = datetime.datetime.now()
    return render_to_response('current_datetime.html', {'current_date': now})
```

Many times, as in this example, you'll find yourself calculating some values, storing them in variables (e.g., now in the preceding code), and sending those variables to the template. Particularly lazy programmers should note that it's slightly redundant to have to give names for temporary variables *and* give names for the template variables. It also means extra typing.

So if you're one of those lazy programmers and you like keeping code particularly concise, you can take advantage of a built-in Python function called `locals()`. It returns a dictionary mapping all local variable names to their values, where *local* means all variables that have been defined within the current scope. Thus, the preceding view could be rewritten like so:

```
def current_datetime(request):
    current_date = datetime.datetime.now()
    return render_to_response('current_datetime.html', locals())
```

Here, instead of manually specifying the context dictionary as before, we pass the value of `locals()`, which will include all variables defined at that point in the function's execution. As a consequence, we've renamed the `now` variable to `current_date`, because that's the variable name that the template expects. In this example, `locals()` doesn't offer a *huge* improvement, but this technique can save you some typing if you have several template variables to define— or if you're lazy.

One thing to watch out for when using `locals()` is that it includes *every* local variable, which may comprise more variables than you actually want your template to have access to. In the previous example, `locals()` will also include `request`. Whether this matters to you depends on your application and your level of perfectionism.

Subdirectories in get_template()

It can get unwieldy to store all of your templates in a single directory. You might like to store templates in subdirectories of your template directory, and that's fine. In fact, we recommend doing so; some more-advanced Django features (such as the generic views system, which we cover in Chapter 11) expect this template layout as a default convention.

Storing templates in subdirectories of your template directory is easy. In your calls to get_template(), just include the subdirectory name and a slash before the template name, like so:

```
t = get_template('dateapp/current_datetime.html')
```

Because `render_to_response()` is a small wrapper around `get_template()`, you can do the same thing with the first argument to `render_to_response()`, like this:

```
return render_to_response('dateapp/current_datetime.html', {'current_date': now})
```

There's no limit to the depth of your subdirectory tree. Feel free to use as many subdirectories as you like.

■**Note** Windows users, be sure to use forward slashes rather than backslashes. `get_template()` assumes a Unix-style file-name designation.

The include Template Tag

Now that we've covered the template-loading mechanism, we can introduce a built-in template tag that takes advantage of it: {% include %}. This tag allows you to include the contents of another template. The argument to the tag should be the name of the template to include, and the template name can be either a variable or a hard-coded (quoted) string, in either single or double quotes. Anytime you have the same code in multiple templates, consider using {% include %} to remove the duplication.

These two examples include the contents of the template nav.html. The examples are equivalent and illustrate that either single or double quotes are allowed:

```
{% include 'nav.html' %}
{% include "nav.html" %}
```

This example includes the contents of the template includes/nav.html:

```
{% include 'includes/nav.html' %}
```

The following example includes the contents of the template whose name is contained in the variable template_name:

```
{% include template_name %}
```

As in get_template(), the template's file name is determined by adding the template directory from TEMPLATE_DIRS to the requested template name.

Included templates are evaluated with the context of the template that's including them. For example, consider these two templates:

```
# mypage.html

<html>
<body>
{% include "includes/nav.html" %}
<h1>{{ title }}</h1>
</body>
</html>


# includes/nav.html

<div id="nav">
    You are in: {{ current_section }}
</div>
```

If you render mypage.html with a context containing current_section, then the variable will be available in the included template, as you would expect.

If, in an {% include %} tag, a template with the given name isn't found, Django will do one of two things:

- If DEBUG is set to True, you'll see the TemplateDoesNotExist exception on a Django error page.
- If DEBUG is set to False, the tag will fail silently, displaying nothing in the place of the tag.

Template Inheritance

Our template examples so far have been tiny HTML snippets, but in the real world you'll be using Django's template system to create entire HTML pages. This leads to a common Web-development problem: across a Web site, how does one reduce the duplication and redundancy of common page areas, such as sitewide navigation?

A classic way of solving this problem is to use *server-side includes*, directives you can embed within your HTML pages to include one Web page inside another. Indeed, Django supports that approach, with the {% include %} template tag just described. But the preferred way of solving this problem with Django is to use a more elegant strategy called *template inheritance*.

In essence, template inheritance lets you build a base "skeleton" template that contains all the common parts of your site and defines "blocks" that child templates can override.

Let's see an example of this by creating a more complete template for our current_ datetime view, by editing the current_datetime.html file:

```
<!DOCTYPE HTML PUBLIC "-//W3C//DTD HTML 4.01//EN">
<html lang="en">
<head>
    <title>The current time</title>
</head>
<body>
    <h1>My helpful timestamp site</h1>
    <p>It is now {{ current_date }}.</p>

    <hr>
    <p>Thanks for visiting my site.</p>
</body>
</html>
```

That looks just fine, but what happens when we want to create a template for another view—say, the hours_ahead view from Chapter 3? If we want again to make a nice, valid, full HTML template, we'd create something like this:

```
<!DOCTYPE HTML PUBLIC "-//W3C//DTD HTML 4.01//EN">
<html lang="en">
<head>
    <title>Future time</title>
</head>
```

```
<body>
    <h1>My helpful timestamp site</h1>
    <p>In {{ hour_offset }} hour(s), it will be {{ next_time }}.</p>

    <hr>
    <p>Thanks for visiting my site.</p>
</body>
</html>
```

Clearly, we've just duplicated a lot of HTML. Imagine if we had a more typical site, including a navigation bar, a few style sheets, perhaps some JavaScript—we'd end up putting all sorts of redundant HTML into each template.

The server-side include solution to this problem is to factor out the common bits in both templates and save them in separate template snippets, which are then included in each template. Perhaps you'd store the top bit of the template in a file called header.html:

```
<!DOCTYPE HTML PUBLIC "-//W3C//DTD HTML 4.01//EN">
<html lang="en">
<head>
```

And perhaps you'd store the bottom bit in a file called footer.html:

```
    <hr>
    <p>Thanks for visiting my site.</p>
</body>
</html>
```

With an include-based strategy, headers and footers are easy. It's the middle ground that's messy. In this example, both pages feature a title—<h1>My helpful timestamp site</h1>—but that title can't fit into header.html because the <title> on both pages is different. If we included the <h1> in the header, we'd have to include the <title>, which wouldn't allow us to customize it per page. See where this is going?

Django's template-inheritance system solves these problems. You can think of it as an inside-out version of server-side includes. Instead of defining the snippets that are *common*, you define the snippets that are *different*.

The first step is to define a *base template*—a skeleton of your page that *child templates* will later fill in. Here's a base template for our ongoing example:

```
<!DOCTYPE HTML PUBLIC "-//W3C//DTD HTML 4.01//EN">
<html lang="en">
<head>
    <title>{% block title %}{% endblock %}</title>
</head>
<body>
    <h1>My helpful timestamp site</h1>
    {% block content %}{% endblock %}
    {% block footer %}
    <hr>
    <p>Thanks for visiting my site.</p>
    {% endblock %}
</body>
</html>
```

This template, which we'll call `base.html`, defines a simple HTML skeleton document that we'll use for all the pages on the site. It's the job of child templates to override, add to, or leave alone the contents of the blocks. (If you're following along, save this file to your template directory as `base.html`.)

We're using a template tag here that you haven't seen before: the `{% block %}` tag. All the `{% block %}` tags do is tell the template engine that a child template may override those portions of the template.

Now that we have this base template, we can modify our existing `current_datetime.html` template to use it:

```
{% extends "base.html" %}

{% block title %}The current time{% endblock %}

{% block content %}
<p>It is now {{ current_date }}.</p>
{% endblock %}
```

While we're at it, let's create a template for the `hours_ahead` view from Chapter 3. (If you're following along with code, we'll leave it up to you to change `hours_ahead` to use the template system instead of hard-coded HTML.) Here's what that could look like:

```
{% extends "base.html" %}

{% block title %}Future time{% endblock %}

{% block content %}
<p>In {{ hour_offset }} hour(s), it will be {{ next_time }}.</p>
{% endblock %}
```

Isn't this beautiful? Each template contains only the code that's *unique* to that template. No redundancy needed. If you need to make a sitewide design change, just make the change to `base.html`, and all of the other templates will immediately reflect the change.

Here's how it works. When you load the template `current_datetime.html`, the template engine sees the `{% extends %}` tag, noting that this template is a child template. The engine immediately loads the parent template—in this case, `base.html`.

At that point, the template engine notices the three `{% block %}` tags in `base.html` and replaces those blocks with the contents of the child template. So, the title we've defined in `{% block title %}` will be used, as will the `{% block content %}`.

Note that since the child template doesn't define the `footer` block, the template system uses the value from the parent template instead. Content within a `{% block %}` tag in a parent template is always used as a fallback.

Inheritance doesn't affect the template context. In other words, any template in the inheritance tree will have access to every one of your template variables from the context.

You can use as many levels of inheritance as needed. One common way of using inheritance is the following three-level approach:

1. Create a `base.html` template that holds the main look and feel of your site. This is the stuff that rarely, if ever, changes.

2. Create a `base_SECTION.html` template for each "section" of your site (e.g., `base_photos.html` and `base_forum.html`). These templates extend `base.html` and include section-specific styles/design.

3. Create individual templates for each type of page, such as a forum page or a photo gallery. These templates extend the appropriate section template.

This approach maximizes code reuse and makes it easy to add items to shared areas, such as sectionwide navigation.

Here are some guidelines for working with template inheritance:

- If you use `{% extends %}` in a template, it must be the first template tag in that template. Otherwise, template inheritance won't work.

- Generally, the more `{% block %}` tags in your base templates, the better. Remember, child templates don't have to define all parent blocks, so you can fill in reasonable defaults in a number of blocks and then define only the ones you need in the child templates. It's better to have more hooks than fewer hooks.

- If you find yourself duplicating code in a number of templates, it probably means you should move that code to a `{% block %}` in a parent template.

- If you need to get the content of the block from the parent template, use `{{ block.super }}`, which is a "magic" variable providing the rendered text of the parent template. This is useful if you want to add to the contents of a parent block instead of completely overriding it.

- You may not define multiple `{% block %}` tags with the same name in the same template. This limitation exists because a block tag works in both directions. That is, a block tag doesn't just provide a hole to fill; it also defines the content that fills the hole in the *parent*. If there were two similarly named `{% block %}` tags in a template, that template's parent wouldn't know which one of the blocks' content to use.

- The template name you pass to `{% extends %}` is loaded using the same method that `get_template()` uses. That is, the template name is appended to your `TEMPLATE_DIRS` setting.

- In most cases, the argument to `{% extends %}` will be a string, but it can be a variable if you don't know the name of the parent template until runtime. This lets you do some cool, dynamic stuff.

What's Next?

You now have the basics of Django's template system under your belt. What's next?

Many modern Web sites are *database-driven*: the content of the Web site is stored in a relational database. This allows a clean separation of data and logic (in the same way views and templates allow the separation of logic and display).

The next chapter covers the tools Django gives you to interact with a database.

CHAPTER 5

■ ■ ■

Models

In Chapter 3, we covered the fundamentals of building dynamic Web sites with Django: setting up views and URLconfs. As we explained, a view is responsible for doing *some arbitrary logic*, and then returning a response. In one of the examples, our arbitrary logic was to calculate the current date and time.

In modern Web applications, the arbitrary logic often involves interacting with a database. Behind the scenes, a *database-driven Web site* connects to a database server, retrieves some data out of it, and displays that data on a Web page. The site might also provide ways for site visitors to populate the database on their own.

Many complex Web sites provide some combination of the two. Amazon.com, for instance, is a great example of a database-driven site. Each product page is essentially a query into Amazon's product database formatted as HTML, and when you post a customer review, it gets inserted into the database of reviews.

Django is well suited for making database-driven Web sites because it comes with easy yet powerful tools for performing database queries using Python. This chapter explains that functionality: Django's database layer.

■**Note** While it's not strictly necessary to know basic relational database theory and SQL in order to use Django's database layer, it's highly recommended. An introduction to those concepts is beyond the scope of this book, but keep reading even if you're a database newbie. You'll probably be able to follow along and grasp concepts based on the context.)

The "Dumb" Way to Do Database Queries in Views

Just as Chapter 3 detailed a "dumb" way to produce output within a view (by hard-coding the text directly within the view), there's a "dumb" way to retrieve data from a database in a view. It's simple: just use any existing Python library to execute an SQL query and do something with the results.

In this example view, we use the MySQLdb library (available via http://www.djangoproject.com/r/python-mysql/) to connect to a MySQL database, retrieve some records, and feed them to a template for display as a Web page:

```
from django.shortcuts import render_to_response
import MySQLdb

def book_list(request):
    db = MySQLdb.connect(user='me', db='mydb', passwd='secret', host='localhost')
    cursor = db.cursor()
    cursor.execute('SELECT name FROM books ORDER BY name')
    names = [row[0] for row in cursor.fetchall()]
    db.close()
    return render_to_response('book_list.html', {'names': names})
```

This approach works, but some problems should jump out at you immediately:

- We're hard-coding the database connection parameters. Ideally, these parameters would be stored in the Django configuration.

- We're having to write a fair bit of boilerplate code: creating a connection, creating a cursor, executing a statement, and closing the connection. Ideally, all we'd have to do is specify which results we want.

- It ties us to MySQL. If, down the road, we switch from MySQL to PostgreSQL, we'll have to use a different database adapter (e.g., psycopg rather than MySQLdb), alter the connection parameters, and—depending on the nature of the SQL statement—possibly rewrite the SQL. Ideally, the database server we're using would be abstracted, so that a database server change could be made in a single place. (This feature is particularly useful if you're building an open source Django application that you want to be used by as many people as possible.)

As you might expect, Django's database layer aims to solve these problems. Here's a sneak preview of how the previous view can be rewritten using Django's database API:

```
from django.shortcuts import render_to_response
from mysite.books.models import Book

def book_list(request):
    books = Book.objects.order_by('name')
    return render_to_response('book_list.html', {'books': books})
```

We'll explain this code a little later in the chapter. For now, just get a feel for how it looks.

The MTV (or MVC) Development Pattern

Before we delve into any more code, let's take a moment to consider the overall design of a database-driven Django Web application.

As we mentioned in previous chapters, Django is designed to encourage loose coupling and strict separation between pieces of an application. If you follow this philosophy, it's easy to make changes to one particular piece of the application without affecting the other pieces.

In view functions, for instance, we discussed the importance of separating the business logic from the presentation logic by using a template system. With the database layer, we're applying that same philosophy to data access logic.

Those three pieces together—data access logic, business logic, and presentation logic—comprise a concept that's sometimes called the *Model-View-Controller* (MVC) pattern of software architecture. In this pattern, "Model" refers to the data access layer, "View" refers to the part of the system that selects what to display and how to display it, and "Controller" refers to the part of the system that decides which view to use, depending on user input, accessing the model as needed.

WHY THE ACRONYM?

The goal of explicitly defining patterns such as MVC is mostly to streamline communication among developers. Instead of having to tell your coworkers, "Let's make an abstraction of the data access, then let's have a separate layer that handles data display, and let's put a layer in the middle that regulates this," you can take advantage of a shared vocabulary and say, "Let's use the MVC pattern here."

Django follows this MVC pattern closely enough that it can be called an MVC framework. Here's roughly how the M, V, and C break down in Django:

- *M*, the data-access portion, is handled by Django's database layer, which is described in this chapter.

- *V*, the portion that selects which data to display and how to display it, is handled by views and templates.

- *C*, the portion that delegates to a view depending on user input, is handled by the framework itself by following your URLconf and calling the appropriate Python function for the given URL.

Because the "C" is handled by the framework itself and most of the excitement in Django happens in models, templates, and views, Django has been referred to as an *MTV framework*. In the MTV development pattern,

- *M* stands for "Model," the data access layer. This layer contains anything and everything about the data: how to access it, how to validate it, which behaviors it has, and the relationships between the data.

- *T* stands for "Template," the presentation layer. This layer contains presentation-related decisions: how something should be displayed on a Web page or other type of document.

- *V* stands for "View," the business logic layer. This layer contains the logic that accesses the model and defers to the appropriate template(s). You can think of it as the bridge between models and templates.

If you're familiar with other MVC Web-development frameworks, such as Ruby on Rails, you may consider Django views to be the "controllers" and Django templates to be the "views." This is an unfortunate confusion brought about by differing interpretations of MVC.

In Django's interpretation of MVC, the "view" describes the data that gets presented to the user; it's not necessarily just *how* the data looks, but *which* data is presented. In contrast, Ruby on Rails and similar frameworks suggest that the controller's job includes deciding which data gets presented to the user, whereas the view is strictly *how* the data looks, not *which* data is presented.

Neither interpretation is more "correct" than the other. The important thing is to understand the underlying concepts.

Configuring the Database

With all of that philosophy in mind, let's start exploring Django's database layer. First, we need to take care of some initial configuration; we need to tell Django which database server to use and how to connect to it.

We'll assume you've set up a database server, activated it, and created a database within it (e.g., using a CREATE DATABASE statement). If you're using SQLite, no such setup is required because SQLite uses standalone files on the filesystem to store its data.

As with TEMPLATE_DIRS in the previous chapter, database configuration lives in the Django settings file, called settings.py by default. Edit that file and look for the database settings:

```
DATABASE_ENGINE = ''
DATABASE_NAME = ''
DATABASE_USER = ''
DATABASE_PASSWORD = ''
DATABASE_HOST = ''
DATABASE_PORT = ''
```

Here's a rundown of each setting.

- DATABASE_ENGINE tells Django which database engine to use. If you're using a database with Django, DATABASE_ENGINE must be set to one of the strings shown in Table 5-1.

Table 5-1. *Database Engine Settings*

Setting	Database	Required Adapter
postgresql	PostgreSQL	psycopg version 1.x, http://www.djangoproject.com/r/python-pgsql/1/.
postgresql_psycopg2	PostgreSQL	psycopg version 2.x, http://www.djangoproject.com/r/python-pgsql/.
mysql	MySQL	MySQLdb, http://www.djangoproject.com/r/python-mysql/.
sqlite3	SQLite	No adapter needed if using Python 2.5+. Otherwise, pysqlite, http://www.djangoproject.com/r/python-sqlite/.
oracle	Oracle	cx_Oracle, http://www.djangoproject.com/r/python-oracle/.

- Note that for whichever database back-end you use, you'll need to download and install the appropriate database adapter. Each one is available for free on the Web; just follow the links in the "Required Adapter" column in Table 5-1. If you're on Linux, your distribution's package-management system might offer convenient packages. (Look for packages called python-postgresql or python-psycopg.) For example:

```
DATABASE_ENGINE = 'postgresql_psycopg2'
```

- DATABASE_NAME tells Django the name of your database. For example:

```
DATABASE_NAME = 'mydb'
```

If you're using SQLite, specify the full filesystem path to the database file on your filesystem. For example:

```
DATABASE_NAME = '/home/django/mydata.db'
```

As for where to put that SQLite database, we're using the /home/django directory in this example, but you should pick a directory that works best for you.

- DATABASE_USER tells Django which username to use when connecting to your database. If you're using SQLite, leave this blank.

- DATABASE_PASSWORD tells Django which password to use when connecting to your database. If you're using SQLite or have an empty password, leave this blank.

- DATABASE_HOST tells Django which host to use when connecting to your database. If your database is on the same computer as your Django installation (i.e., localhost), leave this blank. If you're using SQLite, leave this blank.

  MySQL is a special case here. If this value starts with a forward slash ('/') and you're using MySQL, MySQL will connect via a Unix socket to the specified socket, for example:

```
DATABASE_HOST = '/var/run/mysql'
```

Once you've entered those settings and saved settings.py, it's a good idea to test your configuration. To do this, run python manage.py shell, as in the last chapter, from within the mysite project directory. (As discussed in the previous chapter, manage.py shell is a way to run the Python interpreter with the correct Django settings activated. This is necessary in our case because Django needs to know which settings file to use in order to get your database connection information.)

In the shell, type these commands to test your database configuration:

```
>>> from django.db import connection
>>> cursor = connection.cursor()
```

If nothing happens, then your database is configured properly. Otherwise, check the error message for clues about what's wrong. Table 5-2 shows some common errors.

Table 5-2. *Database Configuration Error Messages*

Error Message	Solution
You haven't set the DATABASE_ENGINE setting yet.	Set the DATABASE_ENGINE setting to something other than an empty string. Valid values are shown in Table 5-1.
Environment variable DJANGO_SETTINGS_MODULE is undefined.	Run the command python manage.py shell rather than python.
Error loading _____ module: No module named _____.	You haven't installed the appropriate database-specific adapter (e.g., psycopg or MySQLdb). Adapters are *not* bundled with Django, so it's your responsibility to download and install them on your own.
_____ isn't an available database back-end.	Set your DATABASE_ENGINE setting to one of the valid engine settings described previously. Perhaps you made a typo?
Database _____ does not exist	Change the DATABASE_NAME setting to point to a database that exists, or execute the appropriate CREATE DATABASE statement in order to create it.
Role _____ does not exist	Change the DATABASE_USER setting to point to a user that exists, or create the user in your database.
Could not connect to server	Make sure DATABASE_HOST and DATABASE_PORT are set correctly, and make sure the database server is running.

Your First App

Now that you've verified the connection is working, it's time to create a *Django app*—a bundle of Django code, including models and views, that lives together in a single Python package and represents a full Django application.

It's worth explaining the terminology here, because this tends to trip up beginners. We already created a *project* in Chapter 2, so what's the difference between a *project* and an *app*? The difference is that of configuration vs. code:

- A project is an instance of a certain set of Django apps, plus the configuration for those apps.

- Technically, the only requirement of a project is that it supplies a settings file, which defines the database connection information, the list of installed apps, the TEMPLATE_DIRS, and so forth.

- An app is a portable set of Django functionality, usually including models and views, that lives together in a single Python package.

- For example, Django comes with a number of apps, such as a commenting system and an automatic admin interface. A key thing to note about these apps is that they're portable and reusable across multiple projects.

There are very few hard-and-fast rules about how you fit your Django code into this scheme. If you're building a simple Web site, you may use only a single app. If you're building a complex Web site with several unrelated pieces such as an e-commerce system and a message board, you'll probably want to split those into separate apps so that you'll be able to reuse them individually in the future.

Indeed, you don't necessarily need to create apps at all, as evidenced by the example view functions we've created so far in this book. In those cases, we simply created a file called `views.py`, filled it with view functions, and pointed our URLconf at those functions. No "apps" were needed.

However, there's one requirement regarding the app convention: if you're using Django's database layer (models), you must create a Django app. Models must live within apps. Thus, in order to start writing our models, we'll need to create a new app.

Within the `mysite` project directory, type this command to create a `books` app:

```
python manage.py startapp books
```

This command does not produce any output, but it does create a `books` directory within the `mysite` directory. Let's look at the contents of that directory:

```
books/
    __init__.py
    models.py
    tests.py
    views.py
```

These files will contain the models and views for this app.

Have a look at `models.py` and `views.py` in your favorite text editor. Both files are empty, except for comments and an import in `models.py`. This is the blank slate for your Django app.

Defining Models in Python

As we discussed earlier in this chapter, the "M" in "MTV" stands for "Model." A Django model is a description of the data in your database, represented as Python code. It's your data layout—the equivalent of your SQL CREATE TABLE statements—except it's in Python instead of SQL, and it includes more than just database column definitions. Django uses a model to execute SQL code behind the scenes and return convenient Python data structures representing the rows in your database tables. Django also uses models to represent higher-level concepts that SQL can't necessarily handle.

If you're familiar with databases, your immediate thought might be, "Isn't it redundant to define data models in Python instead of in SQL?" Django works the way it does for several reasons:

- Introspection requires overhead and is imperfect. In order to provide convenient data-access APIs, Django needs to know the database layout *somehow*, and there are two ways of accomplishing this. The first way is to explicitly describe the data in Python, and the second way is to introspect the database at runtime to determine the data models.

- This second way seems cleaner, because the metadata about your tables lives in only one place, but it introduces a few problems. First, introspecting a database at runtime obviously requires overhead. If the framework had to introspect the database each time it processed a request, or even only when the Web server was initialized, this would incur an unacceptable level of overhead. (While some believe that level of overhead is acceptable, Django's developers aim to trim as much framework overhead as possible.) Second, some databases, notably older versions of MySQL, do not store sufficient metadata for accurate and complete introspection.

- Writing Python is fun, and keeping everything in Python limits the number of times your brain has to do a "context switch." It helps productivity if you keep yourself in a single programming environment/mentality for as long as possible. Having to write SQL, then Python, and then SQL again is disruptive.

- Having data models stored as code rather than in your database makes it easier to keep your models under version control. This way, you can easily keep track of changes to your data layouts.

- SQL allows for only a certain level of metadata about a data layout. Most database systems, for example, do not provide a specialized data type for representing e-mail addresses or URLs. Django models do. The advantage of higher-level data types is higher productivity and more reusable code.

- SQL is inconsistent across database platforms. If you're distributing a Web application, for example, it's much more pragmatic to distribute a Python module that describes your data layout than separate sets of CREATE TABLE statements for MySQL, PostgreSQL, and SQLite.

A drawback of this approach, however, is that it's possible for the Python code to get out of sync with what's actually in the database. If you make changes to a Django model, you'll need to make the same changes inside your database to keep your database consistent with the model. We'll discuss some strategies for handling this problem later in this chapter.

Finally, we should note that Django includes a utility that can generate models by intro-specting an existing database. This is useful for quickly getting up and running with legacy data. We'll cover this in Chapter 18.

Your First Model

As an ongoing example in this chapter and the next chapter, we'll focus on a basic book/author/publisher data layout. We use this as our example because the conceptual relation-ships between books, authors, and publishers are well known, and this is a common data layout used in introductory SQL textbooks. You're also reading a book that was written by authors and produced by a publisher!

We'll suppose the following concepts, fields, and relationships:

- An author has a first name, a last name, and an e-mail address.

- A publisher has a name, a street address, a city, a state/province, a country, and a Web site.

- A book has a title and a publication date. It also has one or more authors (a many-to-many relationship with authors) and a single publisher (a one-to-many relationship—aka foreign key—to publishers).

The first step in using this database layout with Django is to express it as Python code. In the models.py file that was created by the startapp command, enter the following:

```
from django.db import models

class Publisher(models.Model):
    name = models.CharField(max_length=30)
    address = models.CharField(max_length=50)
    city = models.CharField(max_length=60)
    state_province = models.CharField(max_length=30)
    country = models.CharField(max_length=50)
    website = models.URLField()

class Author(models.Model):
    first_name = models.CharField(max_length=30)
    last_name = models.CharField(max_length=40)
    email = models.EmailField()

class Book(models.Model):
    title = models.CharField(max_length=100)
    authors = models.ManyToManyField(Author)
    publisher = models.ForeignKey(Publisher)
    publication_date = models.DateField()
```

Let's quickly examine this code to cover the basics. The first thing to notice is that each model is represented by a Python class that is a subclass of django.db.models.Model. The parent class, Model, contains all the machinery necessary to make these objects capable of interacting with a database—and that leaves our models responsible solely for defining their fields, in a nice and compact syntax. Believe it or not, this is all the code we need to write to have basic data access with Django.

Each model generally corresponds to a single database table, and each attribute on a model generally corresponds to a column in that database table. The attribute name corresponds to the column's name, and the type of field (e.g., CharField) corresponds to the database column type (e.g., varchar). For example, the Publisher model is equivalent to the following table (assuming PostgreSQL CREATE TABLE syntax):

```
CREATE TABLE "books_publisher" (
    "id" serial NOT NULL PRIMARY KEY,
    "name" varchar(30) NOT NULL,
    "address" varchar(50) NOT NULL,
    "city" varchar(60) NOT NULL,
    "state_province" varchar(30) NOT NULL,
    "country" varchar(50) NOT NULL,
    "website" varchar(200) NOT NULL
);
```

Indeed, Django can generate that CREATE TABLE statement automatically, as we'll show you in a moment.

The exception to the one-class-per-database-table rule is the case of many-to-many relationships. In our example models, Book has a ManyToManyField called authors. This designates that a book has one or many authors, but the Book database table doesn't get an authors column. Rather, Django creates an additional table—a many-to-many "join table"—that handles the mapping of books to authors.

For a full list of field types and model syntax options, see Appendix B.

Finally, note we haven't explicitly defined a primary key in any of these models. Unless you instruct it otherwise, Django automatically gives every model an autoincrementing integer primary key field called id. Each Django model is required to have a single-column primary key.

Installing the Model

We've written the code; now let's create the tables in our database. In order to do that, the first step is to *activate* these models in our Django project. We do that by adding the books app to the list of "installed apps" in the settings file.

Edit the settings.py file again, and look for the INSTALLED_APPS setting. INSTALLED_APPS tells Django which apps are activated for a given project. By default, it looks something like this:

```
INSTALLED_APPS = (
    'django.contrib.auth',
    'django.contrib.contenttypes',
    'django.contrib.sessions',
    'django.contrib.sites',
)
```

Temporarily comment out all four of those strings by putting a hash character (#) in front of them. (They're included by default as a common-case convenience, but we'll activate and discuss them in subsequent chapters.) While you're at it, comment out the default MIDDLEWARE_CLASSES setting, too; the default values in MIDDLEWARE_CLASSES depend on some of the apps we just commented out. Then, add 'mysite.books' to the INSTALLED_APPS list, so the setting ends up looking like this:

```
MIDDLEWARE_CLASSES = (
    # 'django.middleware.common.CommonMiddleware',
    # 'django.contrib.sessions.middleware.SessionMiddleware',
    # 'django.contrib.auth.middleware.AuthenticationMiddleware',
)
```

```
INSTALLED_APPS = (
    # 'django.contrib.auth',
    # 'django.contrib.contenttypes',
    # 'django.contrib.sessions',
    # 'django.contrib.sites',
    'mysite.books',
)
```

As discussed in the last chapter, when you set `TEMPLATE_DIRS`, be sure to include the trailing comma in `INSTALLED_APPS` because it's a single-element tuple. By the way, this book's authors prefer to put a comma after *every* element of a tuple, regardless of whether the tuple has only a single element. This avoids the issue of forgetting commas, and there's no penalty for using that extra comma.

`'mysite.books'` refers to the `books` app we're working on. Each app in `INSTALLED_APPS` is represented by its full Python path—that is, the path of packages, separated by dots, leading to the app package.

Now that the Django app has been activated in the settings file, we can create the database tables in our database. First, let's validate the models by running this command:

```
python manage.py validate
```

The `validate` command checks whether your models' syntax and logic are correct. If all is well, you'll see the message `0 errors found`. If you don't, make sure you typed in the model code correctly. The error output should give you helpful information about what was wrong with the code.

Any time you think you have problems with your models, run `python manage.py validate`. It tends to catch all the common model problems.

If your models are valid, run the following command for Django to generate `CREATE TABLE` statements for your models in the `books` app (with colorful syntax highlighting available, if you're using Unix):

```
python manage.py sqlall books
```

In this command, `books` is the name of the app. It's what you specified when you ran the command `manage.py startapp`. When you run the command, you should see something like this:

```
BEGIN;
CREATE TABLE "books_publisher" (
    "id" serial NOT NULL PRIMARY KEY,
    "name" varchar(30) NOT NULL,
    "address" varchar(50) NOT NULL,
    "city" varchar(60) NOT NULL,
    "state_province" varchar(30) NOT NULL,
    "country" varchar(50) NOT NULL,
    "website" varchar(200) NOT NULL
)
;
```

```
CREATE TABLE "books_author" (
    "id" serial NOT NULL PRIMARY KEY,
    "first_name" varchar(30) NOT NULL,
    "last_name" varchar(40) NOT NULL,
    "email" varchar(75) NOT NULL
)
;
CREATE TABLE "books_book" (
    "id" serial NOT NULL PRIMARY KEY,
    "title" varchar(100) NOT NULL,
    "publisher_id" integer NOT NULL REFERENCES "books_publisher" ("id")
        DEFERRABLE INITIALLY DEFERRED,
    "publication_date" date NOT NULL
)
;
CREATE TABLE "books_book_authors" (
    "id" serial NOT NULL PRIMARY KEY,
    "book_id" integer NOT NULL REFERENCES "books_book" ("id")
        DEFERRABLE INITIALLY DEFERRED,
    "author_id" integer NOT NULL REFERENCES "books_author" ("id")
        DEFERRABLE INITIALLY DEFERRED,
    UNIQUE ("book_id", "author_id")
)
;
CREATE INDEX "books_book_publisher_id" ON "books_book" ("publisher_id");
COMMIT;
```

Note the following:

- Table names are automatically generated by combining the name of the app (books) and the lowercase name of the model (Publisher, Book, and Author). You can override this behavior, as detailed in Appendix B.

- As we mentioned earlier, Django adds a primary key for each table automatically—the id fields. You can override this, too.

- By convention, Django appends "_id" to the foreign key field name. As you might have guessed, you can override this behavior, too.

- The foreign key relationship is made explicit by a REFERENCES statement.

- These CREATE TABLE statements are tailored to the database you're using, so database-specific field types such as auto_increment (MySQL), serial (PostgreSQL), or integer primary key (SQLite) are handled for you automatically. The same goes for quoting of column names (e.g., using double quotes or single quotes). This example output is in PostgreSQL syntax.

The `sqlall` command doesn't actually create the tables or otherwise touch your data-base—it just prints output to the screen so you can see what SQL Django would execute if you asked it. If you wanted to, you could copy and paste this SQL into your database client, or use Unix pipes to pass it directly (e.g., `python manage.py sqlall books | psql mydb`). However, Django provides an easier way of committing the SQL to the database: the `syncdb` command:

```
python manage.py syncdb
```

Run that command and you'll see something like this:

```
Creating table books_publisher
Creating table books_author
Creating table books_book
Installing index for books.Book model
```

The `syncdb` command is a simple "sync" of your models to your database. It looks at all of the models in each app in your `INSTALLED_APPS` setting, checks the database to see whether the appropriate tables exist yet, and creates the tables if they don't yet exist. Note that `syncdb` does *not* sync changes in models or deletions of models; if you make a change to a model or delete a model, and you want to update the database, `syncdb` will not handle that. (More on this in the "Making Changes to a Database Schema" section toward the end of this chapter.)

If you run `python manage.py syncdb` again, nothing happens, because you haven't added any models to the `books` app or added any apps to `INSTALLED_APPS`. Ergo, it's always safe to run `python manage.py syncdb`—it won't clobber things.

If you're interested, take a moment to dive into your database server's command-line client and see the database tables Django created. You can manually run the command-line client (e.g., `psql` for PostgreSQL) or you can run the command `python manage.py dbshell`, which will figure out which command-line client to run, depending on your `DATABASE_SERVER` setting. The latter is almost always more convenient.

Basic Data Access

Once you've created a model, Django automatically provides a high-level Python API for work-ing with those models. Try it out by running `python manage.py shell` and typing the following:

```
>>> from books.models import Publisher
>>> p1 = Publisher(name='Apress', address='2855 Telegraph Avenue',
...     city='Berkeley', state_province='CA', country='U.S.A.',
...     website='http://www.apress.com/')
>>> p1.save()
>>> p2 = Publisher(name="O'Reilly", address='10 Fawcett St.',
...     city='Cambridge', state_province='MA', country='U.S.A.',
...     website='http://www.oreilly.com/')
>>> p2.save()
>>> publisher_list = Publisher.objects.all()
>>> publisher_list
[<Publisher: Publisher object>, <Publisher: Publisher object>]
```

These few lines of code accomplish quite a bit. Here are the highlights:

- First, import the Publisher model class. This lets you interact with the database table that contains publishers.

- Create a Publisher object by instantiating it with values for each field: name, address, and so on.

- To save the object to the database, call its save() method. Behind the scenes, Django executes an SQL INSERT statement here.

- To retrieve publishers from the database, use the attribute Publisher.objects, which you can think of as a set of all publishers. Fetch a list of *all* Publisher objects in the database with the statement Publisher.objects.all(). Behind the scenes, Django executes an SQL SELECT statement here.

One thing is worth mentioning, in case it wasn't clear from this example. When you create objects using the Django model API, Django doesn't save the objects to the database until you call the save() method:

```
p1 = Publisher(...)
# At this point, p1 is not saved to the database yet!
p1.save()
# Now it is.
```

If you want to create an object and save it to the database in a single step, use the objects. create() method. This example is equivalent to the preceding example:

```
>>> p1 = Publisher.objects.create(name='Apress',
...     address='2855 Telegraph Avenue',
...     city='Berkeley', state_province='CA', country='U.S.A.',
...     website='http://www.apress.com/')
>>> p2 = Publisher.objects.create(name="O'Reilly",
...     address='10 Fawcett St.', city='Cambridge',
...     state_province='MA', country='U.S.A.',
...     website='http://www.oreilly.com/')
>>> publisher_list = Publisher.objects.all()
>>> publisher_list
```

Naturally, you can do quite a lot with the Django database API—but first, let's take care of a small annoyance.

Adding Model String Representations

When we printed out the list of publishers, all we got was this unhelpful display that makes it difficult to tell the Publisher objects apart:

```
[<Publisher: Publisher object>, <Publisher: Publisher object>]
```

We can fix this easily by adding a method called __unicode__() to our Publisher class. A __unicode__() method tells Python how to display the "unicode" representation of an object. You can see this in action by adding a __unicode__() method to the three models:

```python
from django.db import models

class Publisher(models.Model):
    name = models.CharField(max_length=30)
    address = models.CharField(max_length=50)
    city = models.CharField(max_length=60)
    state_province = models.CharField(max_length=30)
    country = models.CharField(max_length=50)
    website = models.URLField()

    def __unicode__(self):
        return self.name

class Author(models.Model):
    first_name = models.CharField(max_length=30)
    last_name = models.CharField(max_length=40)
    email = models.EmailField()

    def __unicode__(self):
        return u'%s %s' % (self.first_name, self.last_name)

class Book(models.Model):
    title = models.CharField(max_length=100)
    authors = models.ManyToManyField(Author)
    publisher = models.ForeignKey(Publisher)
    publication_date = models.DateField()

    def __unicode__(self):
        return self.title
```

As you can see, a __unicode__() method can do whatever it needs to do in order to return a representation of an object. Here, the __unicode__() methods for Publisher and Book simply return the object's name and title, respectively, but the __unicode__() for Author is slightly more complex: it pieces together the first_name and last_name fields, separated by a space. The only requirement for __unicode__() is that it return a Unicode object. If __unicode__() doesn't return a Unicode object—if it returns, say, an integer—Python will raise a TypeError with a message such as "coercing to Unicode: need string or buffer, int found".

> ### UNICODE OBJECTS
>
> What are Unicode objects?
>
> You can think of a Unicode object as a Python string that can handle more than a million different types of characters, from accented versions of Latin characters, to non-Latin characters, to curly quotes and obscure symbols.
>
> Normal Python strings are *encoded*, which means they use an encoding such as ASCII, ISO-8859-1, or UTF-8. If you're storing fancy characters (anything beyond the standard 128 ASCII characters such as 0–9 and A–Z) in a normal Python string, you have to keep track of which encoding your string is using, or else the fancy characters might appear messed up when they're displayed or printed. Problems occur when you have data that's stored in one encoding and you try to combine it with data in a different encoding, or when you try to display it in an application that assumes a certain encoding. We've all seen Web pages and e-mail that are littered with "??? ??????" or other characters in odd places; that generally suggests there's an encoding problem.
>
> Unicode objects, however, have no encoding; they use a consistent, universal set of characters called, well, *Unicode*. When you deal with Unicode objects in Python, you can mix and match them safely without having to worry about encoding issues.
>
> Django uses Unicode objects throughout the framework. Model objects are retrieved as Unicode objects, views interact with Unicode data, and templates are rendered as Unicode. You usually won't have to worry about making sure that your encodings are right; things should just work.
>
> Note that this has been a *very* high-level, dumbed-down overview of Unicode objects, and you owe it to yourself to learn more about the topic. A good place to start is `http://www.joelonsoftware.com/articles/Unicode.html`.

For the __unicode__() changes to take effect, exit out of the Python shell and enter it again with `python manage.py shell`. (This is the simplest way to make code changes take effect.) Now the list of Publisher objects is much easier to understand:

```
>>> from books.models import Publisher
>>> publisher_list = Publisher.objects.all()
>>> publisher_list
[<Publisher: Apress>, <Publisher: O'Reilly>]
```

Make sure any model you define has a __unicode__() method—not only for your own convenience when using the interactive interpreter, but also because Django uses the output of __unicode__() in several places when it needs to display objects.

Finally, note that __unicode__() is a good example of adding *behavior* to models. A Django model describes more than the database table layout for an object; it also describes any functionality that an object knows how to do. __unicode__() is one example of such functionality—a model knows how to display itself.

Inserting and Updating Data

You've already seen this done: to insert a row into your database, first create an instance of your model using keyword arguments, like so:

```
>>> p = Publisher(name='Apress',
...          address='2855 Telegraph Ave.',
...          city='Berkeley',
...          state_province='CA',
...          country='U.S.A.',
...          website='http://www.apress.com/')
```

This act of instantiating a model class does *not* touch the database. The record isn't saved into the database until you call save(), like this:

```
>>> p.save()
```

In SQL, this can roughly be translated into the following:

```
INSERT INTO books_publisher
    (name, address, city, state_province, country, website)
VALUES
    ('Apress', '2855 Telegraph Ave.', 'Berkeley', 'CA',
     'U.S.A.', 'http://www.apress.com/');
```

Because the Publisher model uses an autoincrementing primary key id, the initial call to save() does one more thing: it calculates the primary key value for the record and sets it to the id attribute on the instance:

```
>>> p.id
52     # this will differ based on your own data
```

Subsequent calls to save() will save the record in place, without creating a new record (i.e., performing an SQL UPDATE statement instead of an INSERT):

```
>>> p.name = 'Apress Publishing'
>>> p.save()
```

The preceding save() statement will result in roughly the following SQL:

```
UPDATE books_publisher SET
    name = 'Apress Publishing',
    address = '2855 Telegraph Ave.',
    city = 'Berkeley',
    state_province = 'CA',
    country = 'U.S.A.',
    website = 'http://www.apress.com'
WHERE id = 52;
```

Note that *all* the fields will be updated, not just the ones that have been changed. Depending on your application, this may cause a race condition. See the section "Updating Multiple Objects in One Statement" to find out how to execute this (slightly different) query:

```
UPDATE books_publisher SET
    name = 'Apress Publishing'
WHERE id=52;
```

Selecting Objects

Knowing how to create and update database records is essential, but chances are that the Web applications you'll build will be doing more querying of existing objects than creating new ones. You've already seen a way to retrieve *every* record for a given model:

```
>>> Publisher.objects.all()
[<Publisher: Apress>, <Publisher: O'Reilly>]
```

This roughly translates to this SQL:

```
SELECT id, name, address, city, state_province, country, website
FROM books_publisher;
```

■**Note** Django doesn't use SELECT * when looking up data and instead lists all fields explicitly. This is by design: in certain circumstances SELECT * can be slower, and (more important) listing fields more closely follows one tenet of the Zen of Python: "Explicit is better than implicit." For more on the Zen of Python, try typing import this at a Python prompt.

Let's take a close look at each part of this Publisher.objects.all() line:

- First, we have the model we defined, Publisher. No surprise here: when you want to look up data, you use the model for that data.

- Next, we have the objects attribute, which is called a *manager*. Managers are discussed in detail in Chapter 10. For now, all you need to know is that managers take care of all "table-level" operations on data including, most important, data lookup.

- All models automatically get an objects manager; you'll use it any time you want to look up model instances.

- Finally, we have all(). This is a method on the objects manager that returns all the rows in the database. Though this object *looks* like a list, it's actually a *QuerySet*—an object that represents a specific set of rows from the database. Appendix C deals with QuerySets in detail. For the rest of this chapter, we'll just treat them like the lists they emulate.

Any database lookup is going to follow this general pattern—we'll call methods on the manager attached to the model we want to query against.

Filtering Data

Naturally, it's rare to want to select *everything* from a database at once; in most cases, you'll want to deal with a subset of your data. In the Django API, you can filter your data using the filter() method:

```
>>> Publisher.objects.filter(name='Apress')
[<Publisher: Apress>]
```

filter() takes keyword arguments that get translated into the appropriate SQL WHERE clauses. The preceding example would get translated into something like this:

```
SELECT id, name, address, city, state_province, country, website
FROM books_publisher
WHERE name = 'Apress';
```

You can pass multiple arguments into filter() to narrow down things further:

```
>>> Publisher.objects.filter(country="U.S.A.", state_province="CA")
[<Publisher: Apress>]
```

Those multiple arguments get translated into SQL AND clauses. Thus, the example in the code snippet translates into the following:

```
SELECT id, name, address, city, state_province, country, website
FROM books_publisher
WHERE country = 'U.S.A.'
AND state_province = 'CA';
```

Notice that by default the lookups use the SQL = operator to do exact match lookups. Other lookup types are available:

```
>>> Publisher.objects.filter(name__contains="press")
[<Publisher: Apress>]
```

That's a *double* underscore there between name and contains. Like Python itself, Django uses the double underscore to signal that something "magic" is happening—here, the __contains part gets translated by Django into an SQL LIKE statement:

```
SELECT id, name, address, city, state_province, country, website
FROM books_publisher
WHERE name LIKE '%press%';
```

Many other types of lookups are available, including icontains (case-insensitive LIKE), startswith and endswith, and range (SQL BETWEEN queries). Appendix C describes all of these lookup types in detail.

Retrieving Single Objects

The previous filter() examples all returned a QuerySet, which you can treat like a list. Sometimes it's more convenient to fetch only a single object instead of a list. That's what the get() method is for:

```
>>> Publisher.objects.get(name="Apress")
<Publisher: Apress>
```

Instead of a list (rather, QuerySet), only a single object is returned. Because of that, a query resulting in multiple objects will cause an exception:

```
>>> Publisher.objects.get(country="U.S.A.")
Traceback (most recent call last):
    ...
MultipleObjectsReturned: get() returned more than one Publisher --
    it returned 2! Lookup parameters were {'country': 'U.S.A.'}
```

A query that returns no objects also causes an exception:

```
>>> Publisher.objects.get(name="Penguin")
Traceback (most recent call last):
    ...
DoesNotExist: Publisher matching query does not exist.
```

The DoesNotExist exception is an attribute of the model's class: Publisher.DoesNotExist. In your applications, you'll want to trap these exceptions, like this:

```
try:
    p = Publisher.objects.get(name='Apress')
except Publisher.DoesNotExist:
    print "Apress isn't in the database yet."
else:
    print "Apress is in the database."
```

Ordering Data

As you play around with the previous examples, you might discover that the objects are being returned in a seemingly random order. You aren't imagining things; so far we haven't told the database how to order its results, so we're simply getting back data in some arbitrary order chosen by the database.

In your Django applications, you'll probably want to order your results according to a certain value—say, alphabetically. To do this, use the order_by() method:

```
>>> Publisher.objects.order_by("name")
[<Publisher: Apress>, <Publisher: O'Reilly>]
```

This doesn't look much different from the earlier all() example, but the SQL now includes a specific ordering:

```
SELECT id, name, address, city, state_province, country, website
FROM books_publisher
ORDER BY name;
```

You can order by any field you like:

```
>>> Publisher.objects.order_by("address")
[<Publisher: O'Reilly>, <Publisher: Apress>]

>>> Publisher.objects.order_by("state_province")
[<Publisher: Apress>, <Publisher: O'Reilly>]
```

To order by multiple fields (where the second field is used to disambiguate ordering in cases where the first is the same), use multiple arguments:

```
>>> Publisher.objects.order_by("state_province", "address")
[<Publisher: Apress>, <Publisher: O'Reilly>]
```

You can also specify reverse ordering by prefixing the field name with a - (that's a minus character):

```
>>> Publisher.objects.order_by("-name")
[<Publisher: O'Reilly>, <Publisher: Apress>]
```

While this flexibility is useful, using order_by() all the time can be quite repetitive. Most of the time you'll have a particular field you usually want to order by. In these cases, Django lets you specify a default ordering in the model:

```
class Publisher(models.Model):
    name = models.CharField(max_length=30)
    address = models.CharField(max_length=50)
    city = models.CharField(max_length=60)
    state_province = models.CharField(max_length=30)
    country = models.CharField(max_length=50)
    website = models.URLField()

    def __unicode__(self):
        return self.name

    class Meta:
        ordering = ['name']
```

Here, we've introduced a new concept: the class Meta, which is a class that's embedded within the Publisher class definition (it's indented to be within class Publisher). You can use this Meta class on any model to specify various model-specific options. A full reference of Meta options is available in Appendix B, but for now, we're concerned with the ordering option. If you specify this, it tells Django that unless an ordering is given explicitly with order_by(), all Publisher objects should be ordered by the name field whenever they're retrieved with the Django database API.

Chaining Lookups

You've seen how you can filter data, and you've seen how you can order it. You'll often need to do both, of course. In these cases, you simply "chain" the lookups together:

```
>>> Publisher.objects.filter(country="U.S.A.").order_by("-name")
[<Publisher: O'Reilly>, <Publisher: Apress>]
```

As you might expect, this translates to an SQL query with both a WHERE and an ORDER BY:

```
SELECT id, name, address, city, state_province, country, website
FROM books_publisher
WHERE country = 'U.S.A'
ORDER BY name DESC;
```

Slicing Data

Another common need is to look up only a fixed number of rows. Imagine that you have thousands of publishers in your database, but you want to display only the first one. You can do this using Python's standard list-slicing syntax:

```
>>> Publisher.objects.order_by('name')[0]
<Publisher: Apress>
```

This translates roughly to:

```
SELECT id, name, address, city, state_province, country, website
FROM books_publisher
ORDER BY name
LIMIT 1;
```

Similarly, you can retrieve a specific subset of data using Python's range-slicing syntax:

```
>>> Publisher.objects.order_by('name')[0:2]
```

This returns two objects, translating roughly to the following:

```
SELECT id, name, address, city, state_province, country, website
FROM books_publisher
ORDER BY name
OFFSET 0 LIMIT 2;
```

Note that negative slicing is *not* supported:

```
>>> Publisher.objects.order_by('name')[-1]
Traceback (most recent call last):
  ...
AssertionError: Negative indexing is not supported.
```

This is easy to get around, though. Just change the order_by() statement like this:

```
>>> Publisher.objects.order_by('-name')[0]
```

Updating Multiple Objects in One Statement

We pointed out in the "Inserting and Updating Data" section that the model save() method updates *all* columns in a row. Depending on your application, you might want to update only a subset of columns.

For example, suppose that you want to update the Apress Publisher to change the name from 'Apress' to 'Apress Publishing'. Using save(), it would look something like this:

```
>>> p = Publisher.objects.get(name='Apress')
>>> p.name = 'Apress Publishing'
>>> p.save()
```

This roughly translates to the following SQL:

```
SELECT id, name, address, city, state_province, country, website
FROM books_publisher
WHERE name = 'Apress';

UPDATE books_publisher SET
    name = 'Apress Publishing',
    address = '2855 Telegraph Ave.',
    city = 'Berkeley',
    state_province = 'CA',
    country = 'U.S.A.',
    website = 'http://www.apress.com'
WHERE id = 52;
```

■Note This example assumes that Apress has a publisher ID of 52.

You can see in this example that Django's save() method sets *all* the column values, not just the name column. If you're in an environment in which other columns of the database might change because of some other process, it's smarter to change *only* the column you need to change. To do this, use the update() method on QuerySet objects. Here's an example:

```
>>> Publisher.objects.filter(id=52).update(name='Apress Publishing')
```

The SQL translation here is much more efficient and has no chance of race conditions:

```
UPDATE books_publisher
SET name = 'Apress Publishing'
WHERE id = 52;
```

The update() method works on any QuerySet, which means that you can edit multiple records in bulk. Here's how you might change the country from 'U.S.A.' to USA in each Publisher record:

```
>>> Publisher.objects.all().update(country='USA')
2
```

The update() method has a return value: an integer that represents how many records changed. In the preceding example, it was 2.

Deleting Objects

To delete an object from your database, simply call the object's delete() method:

```
>>> p = Publisher.objects.get(name="O'Reilly")
>>> p.delete()
>>> Publisher.objects.all()
[<Publisher: Apress Publishing>]
```

You can also delete objects in bulk by calling `delete()` on the result of any `QuerySet`. This is similar to the `update()` method shown in the last section:

```
>>> Publisher.objects.filter(country='USA').delete()
>>> Publisher.objects.all().delete()
>>> Publisher.objects.all()
[]
```

Be careful when deleting your data! As a precaution against deleting all the data in a particular table, Django requires you to explicitly use `all()` if you want to delete *everything* in your table.

For example, this doesn't work:

```
>>> Publisher.objects.delete()
Traceback (most recent call last):
  File "<console>", line 1, in <module>
AttributeError: 'Manager' object has no attribute 'delete'
```

But it does work if you add the `all()` method:

```
>>> Publisher.objects.all().delete()
```

If you're just deleting a subset of your data, you don't need to include `all()`. To repeat a previous example:

```
>>> Publisher.objects.filter(country='USA').delete()
```

What's Next?

After reading this chapter, you now have enough knowledge of Django models to be able to write basic database applications. Chapter 10 will provide some information on more advanced usage of Django's database layer.

Once you've defined your models, the next step is to populate your database with data. You might have legacy data, in which case Chapter 18 will give you advice about integrating with legacy databases. You might rely on site users to supply your data, in which case Chapter 7 will teach you how to process user-submitted form data.

But in some cases, you or your team might need to enter data manually, in which case it would be helpful to have a Web-based interface for entering and managing data. The next chapter covers Django's admin interface, which exists precisely for that reason.

■ ■ ■

## CHAPTER 6

The Django Admin Site

For a certain class of Web sites, an *admin interface* is an essential part of the infrastructure. This is a Web-based interface, limited to trusted site administrators, that enables the adding, editing, and deletion of site content. Some common examples are: the interface you use to post to your blog, the back-end site managers use to moderate user-generated comments, the tool your clients use to update the press releases on the Web site you built for them.

There's a problem with admin interfaces, though: it's boring to build them. Web development is fun when you're developing public-facing functionality, but building admin interfaces is always the same. You have to authenticate users, display and handle forms, validate input, and so on. It's boring and it's repetitive.

So what's Django's approach to these boring, repetitive tasks? It does it all for you—in just a couple of lines of code, no less. With Django, building an admin interface is a solved problem.

This chapter is about Django's automatic admin interface. The feature works by reading metadata in your model to provide a powerful and production-ready interface that site administrators can start using immediately. We discuss how to activate, use, and customize this feature.

Note that we recommend reading this chapter even if you don't intend to use the Django admin site, because we introduce a few concepts that apply to all of Django, regardless of admin-site usage.

The django.contrib Packages

Django's automatic admin is part of a larger suite of Django functionality called `django.contrib`—the part of the Django codebase that contains various useful add-ons to the core framework. You can think of `django.contrib` as Django's equivalent of the Python standard library—optional, de facto implementations of common patterns. They're bundled with Django so that you don't have to reinvent the wheel in your own applications.

The admin site is the first part of `django.contrib` that we're covering in this book; technically, it's called `django.contrib.admin`. Other available features in `django.contrib` include a user-authentication system (`django.contrib.auth`), support for anonymous sessions (`django.contrib.sessions`), and even a system for user comments (`django.contrib.comments`). You'll get to know the various django.contrib features as you become a Django expert, and we'll spend some more time discussing them in Chapter 16. For now, just know that Django ships with many nice add-ons, and django.contrib is generally where they live.

Activating the Admin Interface

The Django admin site is entirely optional, because only certain types of sites need this functionality. That means you'll need to take a few steps to activate it in your project.

First, make a few changes to your settings file:

1. Add 'django.contrib.admin' to the INSTALLED_APPS setting. (The order of INSTALLED_APPS doesn't matter, but we like to keep things alphabetical so it's easy for a human to read.)

2. Make sure INSTALLED_APPS contains 'django.contrib.auth', 'django.contrib.contenttypes', and 'django.contrib.sessions'. The Django admin site requires these three packages. (If you're following along with our ongoing mysite project, note that we commented out these three INSTALLED_APPS entries in Chapter 5. Uncomment them now.)

3. Make sure MIDDLEWARE_CLASSES contains 'django.middleware.common.CommonMiddleware', 'django.contrib.sessions.middleware.SessionMiddleware', and 'django.contrib.auth.middleware.AuthenticationMiddleware'. (Again, if you're following along, note that we commented them out in Chapter 5, so uncomment them.)

Second, run python manage.py syncdb. This step will install the extra database tables that the admin interface uses. The first time you run syncdb with 'django.contrib.auth' in INSTALLED_APPS, you'll be asked about creating a superuser. If you don't do this, you'll need to run python manage.py createsuperuser separately to create an admin user account; otherwise you won't be able to log in to the admin site. (Potential gotcha: the python manage.py createsuperuser command is available only if 'django.contrib.auth' is in your INSTALLED_APPS.)

Third, add the admin site to your URLconf (in urls.py, remember). By default, the urls.py generated by django-admin.py startproject contains commented-out code for the Django admin, and all you have to do is uncomment it. For the record, here are the bits you need to make sure are in there:

```
# Include these import statements...
from django.contrib import admin
admin.autodiscover()

# And include this URLpattern...
urlpatterns = patterns('',
    # ...
    (r'^admin/', include(admin.site.urls)),
    # ...
)
```

With that bit of configuration out of the way, now you can see the Django admin site in action. Just run the development server (`python manage.py runserver`, as in previous chapters) and visit `http://127.0.0.1:8000/admin/` in your Web browser.

Using the Admin Site

The admin site is designed to be used by nontechnical users, and as such it should be pretty self-explanatory. Nevertheless, we'll give you a quick walkthrough of the basic features.

The first thing you'll see is a login screen, as shown in Figure 6-1.

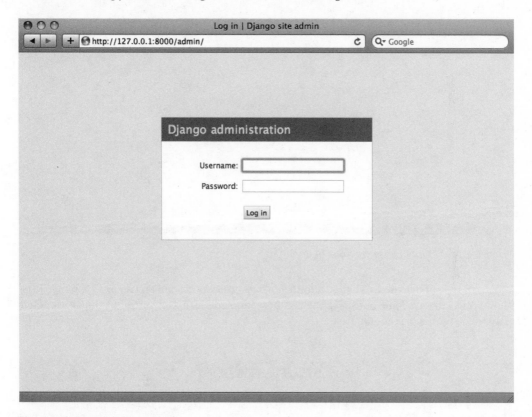

Figure 6-1. *Django's login screen*

Log in with the username and password you set up when you added your superuser. If you're unable to log in, make sure you've actually created a superuser—try running `python manage.py createsuperuser`.

Once you're logged in, the first thing you'll see will be the admin home page (Figure 6-2). This page lists all the available types of data that can be edited on the admin site. At this point, because we haven't activated any of our own models yet, the list is sparse: it includes only Groups and Users, which are the two default admin-editable models.

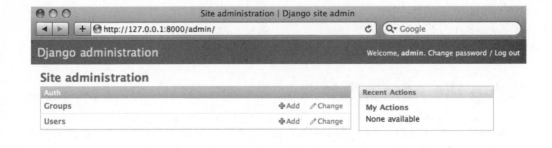

Figure 6-2. *The Django admin home page*

Each type of data in the Django admin site has a *change list* and an *edit form*. Change lists show you all the available objects in the database, and edit forms let you add, change, or delete particular records in your database.

OTHER LANGUAGES

If your primary language is not English and your Web browser is configured to prefer a language other than English, you can make a quick change to see whether the Django admin site has been translated into your language. Just add 'django.middleware.locale.LocaleMiddleware' to your MIDDLEWARE_CLASSES setting, making sure it appears *after* 'django.contrib.sessions.middleware.SessionMiddleware'.

When you've done that, reload the admin index page. If a translation for your language is available, then the various parts of the interface—from the Change Password and Log Out links at the top of the page to the Groups and Users links in the middle—will appear in your language instead of English. Django ships with translations for dozens of languages.

For much more on Django's internationalization features, see Chapter 19.

Click the Change link in the Users row to load the change-list page for users (Figure 6-3).

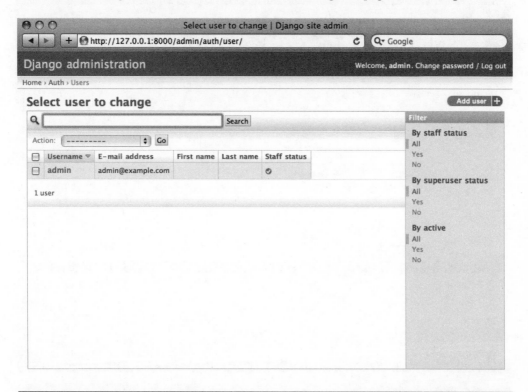

Figure 6-3. *The user change-list page*

This page displays all users in the database; you can think of it as a prettied-up Web version of a `SELECT * FROM auth_user;` SQL query. If you're following along with our ongoing example, you'll see only one user here, assuming you've added only one, but once you have more users, you'll probably find the filtering, sorting, and searching options useful. Filtering options are at the right, sorting is available by clicking a column header, and the search box at the top lets you search by username.

Click the username of the user you created, and you'll see the edit form for that user (Figure 6-4).

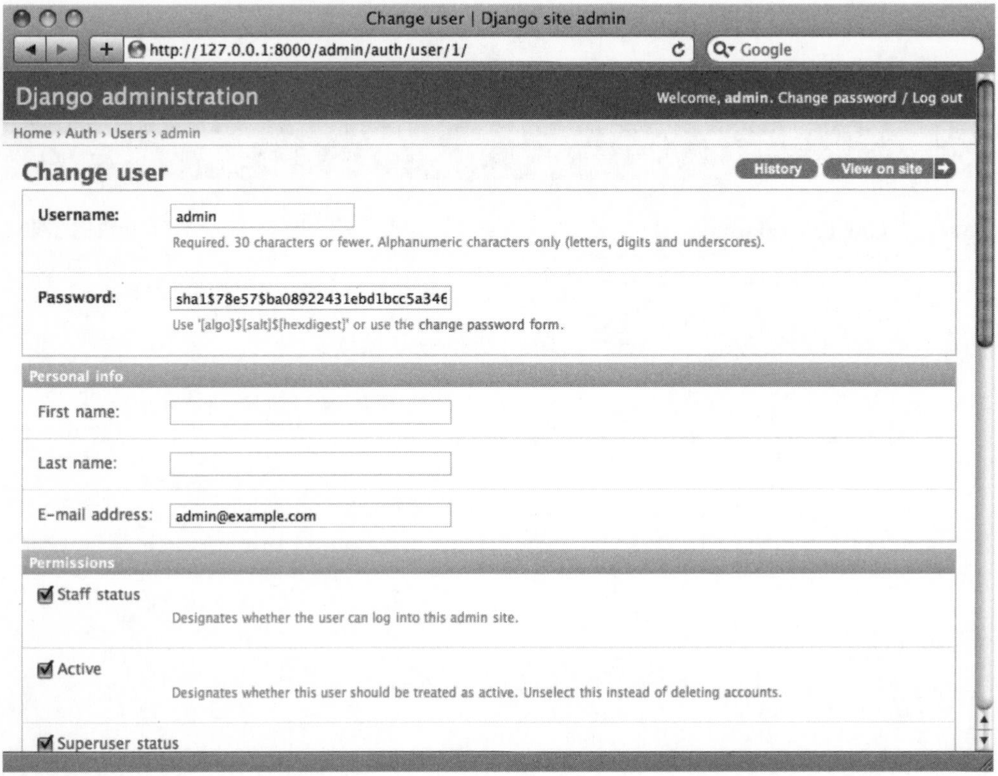

Figure 6-4. *The user edit form*

This page lets you change the attributes of the user, like the first/last names and various permissions. (Note that to change a user's password, you should click Change Password Form under the password field rather than editing the hashed code.) Another thing to note here is that fields of different types get different widgets—for example, date/time fields have calendar controls, Boolean fields have check boxes, and character fields have simple text input fields.

You can delete a record by clicking the Delete button at the bottom left of the record's edit form. That'll take you to a confirmation page, which, in some cases, will display any dependent objects that will be deleted, too. (For example, if you delete a publisher, any book with that publisher will be deleted, as well!)

You can add a record by clicking Add in the appropriate column of the admin home page. This will give you an empty version of the edit page, ready for you to fill out.

You'll notice that the admin interface handles input validation for you. Try leaving a required field blank or putting an invalid date into a date field, and you'll see those errors when you try to save, as shown in Figure 6-5.

When you edit an existing object, you'll notice a History link in the upper-right corner of the window. Every change made through the admin interface is logged, and you can examine this log by clicking the History link (see Figure 6-6).

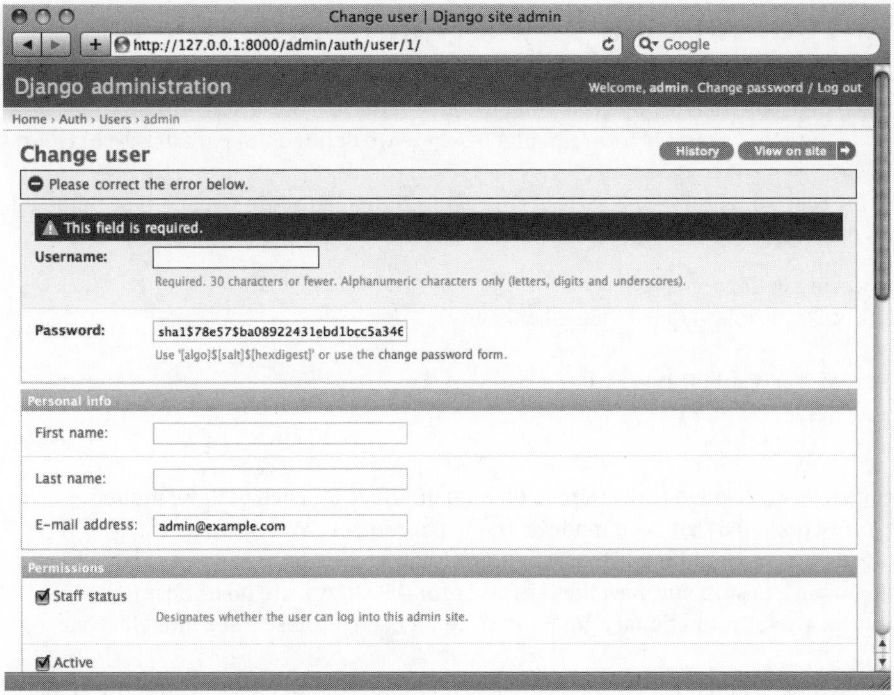

Figure 6-5. *An edit form displaying errors*

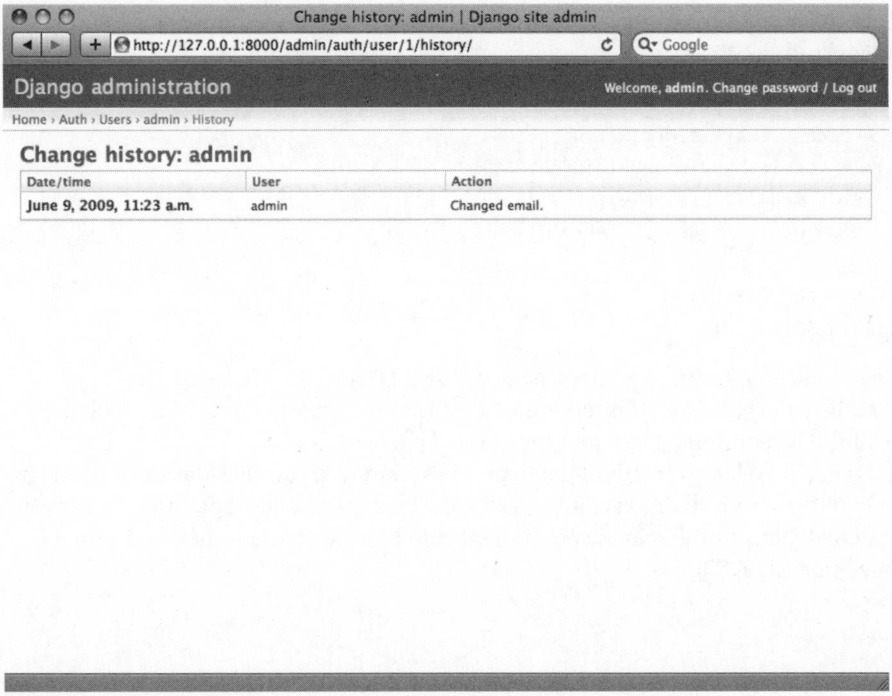

Figure 6-6. *An object history page*

Adding Your Models to the Admin Site

There's one crucial part we haven't done yet. Let's add our own models to the admin site so we can add, change, and delete objects in our custom database tables using this nice interface. We'll continue the books example from Chapter 5, where we defined three models: Publisher, Author, and Book.

Within the books directory (mysite/books), create a file called admin.py, and type in the following lines of code:

```
from django.contrib import admin
from mysite.books.models import Publisher, Author, Book

admin.site.register(Publisher)
admin.site.register(Author)
admin.site.register(Book)
```

This code tells the Django admin site to offer an interface for each of these models.

Once you've done that, go to your admin home page in your Web browser (http://127.0.0.1:8000/admin/). You should see a Books section with links for Authors, Books, and Publishers. (You might have to stop and start the runserver for the changes to take effect.)

You now have a fully functional admin interface for each of those three models. That was easy!

Take some time to add and change records, to populate your database with some data. If you followed Chapter 5's examples of creating Publisher objects (and you didn't delete them), you'll already see those records on the publisher change-list page.

One feature worth mentioning here is the admin site's handling of foreign keys and many-to-many relationships, both of which appear in the Book model. As a reminder, here's what the Book model looks like:

```
class Book(models.Model):
    title = models.CharField(max_length=100)
    authors = models.ManyToManyField(Author)
    publisher = models.ForeignKey(Publisher)
    publication_date = models.DateField()

    def __unicode__(self):
        return self.title
```

On the Django admin site's Add Book page (http://127.0.0.1:8000/admin/books/book/add/), the publisher (a ForeignKey) is represented by a select box, and the authors field (a ManyToManyField) is represented by a multiple-select box. Both fields sit next to a green plus sign that lets you add related records of that type. For example, if you click the green plus sign next to the Publisher field, you'll get a pop-up window that lets you add a publisher. After you successfully create the publisher in the pop-up, the Add Book form will be updated with the newly created publisher. Slick.

How the Admin Site Works

Behind the scenes, how does the admin site work? It's pretty straightforward.

When Django loads your URLconf from urls.py at server startup, it executes the admin. autodiscover() statement that we added as part of activating the admin. This function iterates over your INSTALLED_APPS setting and looks for a file called admin.py in each installed app. If an admin.py exists in a given app, it executes the code in that file.

In the admin.py in our books app, each call to admin.site.register() simply registers the given model with the admin. The admin site will display an edit/change interface for only models that have been explicitly registered.

The app django.contrib.auth includes its own admin.py, which is why Users and Groups showed up automatically in the admin. Other django.contrib apps, such as django.contrib. redirects, also add themselves to the admin, as do many third-party Django applications you might download from the Web.

Beyond that, the Django admin site is just a Django application, with its own models, templates, views, and URLpatterns. You add it to your application by hooking it into your URLconf, just as you hook in your own views. You can inspect its templates, views, and URL-patterns by poking around in django/contrib/admin in your copy of the Django codebase—but don't be tempted to change anything directly in there, as there are plenty of hooks for you to customize the way the admin site works. (If you do decide to poke around the Django admin application, keep in mind it does some rather complicated things in reading metadata about models, so it would probably take a good amount of time to read and understand the code.)

Making Fields Optional

After you play around with the admin site for a while, you'll probably notice a limitation— the edit forms require every field to be filled out, whereas in many cases you'd want certain fields to be optional. Let's say, for example, that we want our Author model's email field to be optional—that is, a blank string should be allowed. In the real world, you might not have an e-mail address on file for every author.

To specify that the email field is optional, edit the Book model (which, as you'll recall from Chapter 5, lives in mysite/books/models.py). Simply add blank=True to the email field, like so:

```
class Author(models.Model):
    first_name = models.CharField(max_length=30)
    last_name = models.CharField(max_length=40)
    email = models.EmailField(blank=True)
```

This tells Django that a blank value is indeed allowed for authors' e-mail addresses. By default, all fields have blank=False, which means blank values are not allowed.

There's something interesting happening here. Until now, with the exception of the __ unicode__() method, our models have served as definitions of our database tables—Pythonic expressions of SQL CREATE TABLE statements, essentially. In adding blank=True, we have begun expanding our model beyond a simple definition of what the database table looks like. Now our model class is starting to become a richer collection of knowledge about what Author objects are and what they can do. Not only is the email field represented by a VARCHAR column in the database, it's also an optional field in contexts such as the Django admin site.

Once you've added that `blank=True`, reload the author edit form (`http://127.0.0.1:8000/admin/books/author/add/`), and you'll notice the field's label—Email—is no longer bolded. This signifies it's not a required field. You can now add authors without needing to provide e-mail addresses; you won't get the loud red "This field is required" message anymore if the field is submitted empty.

Making Date and Numeric Fields Optional

A common gotcha related to `blank=True` has to do with date and numeric fields, but it requires a fair amount of background explanation.

SQL has its own way of specifying blank values—a special value called `NULL`. `NULL` could mean "unknown," or "invalid," or some other application-specific meaning. In SQL, a value of `NULL` is different from an empty string, just as the special Python object `None` is different from an empty Python string (`""`). This means it's possible for a particular character field (e.g., a `VARCHAR` column) to contain both `NULL` values and empty string values.

This can cause unwanted ambiguity and confusion: "Why does this record have a `NULL` but this other one has an empty string? Is there a difference, or was the data just entered inconsistently?" And "How do I get all the records that have a blank value—should I look for both `NULL` records and empty strings, or do I select only the ones with empty strings?"

To help avoid such ambiguity, Django's automatically generated `CREATE TABLE` statements (which were covered in Chapter 5) add an explicit `NOT NULL` to each column definition. For example, here's the generated statement for our `Author` model, from Chapter 5:

```
CREATE TABLE "books_author" (
    "id" serial NOT NULL PRIMARY KEY,
    "first_name" varchar(30) NOT NULL,
    "last_name" varchar(40) NOT NULL,
    "email" varchar(75) NOT NULL
)
;
```

In most cases, this default behavior is optimal for your application and will save you from data-inconsistency headaches. And it works nicely with the rest of Django, such as the Django admin site, which inserts an empty string (*not* a `NULL` value) when you leave a character field blank.

But there's an exception with database column types that do not accept empty strings as valid values—such as dates, times, and numbers. If you try to insert an empty string into a date or an integer column, you'll likely get a database error, depending on which database you're using. (PostgreSQL, which is strict, will raise an exception here; MySQL might accept it or might not, depending on the version you're using, the time of day, and the phase of the moon.) In this case, `NULL` is the only way to specify an empty value. In Django models, you can specify that `NULL` is allowed by adding `null=True` to a field.

In short, if you want to allow blank values in a date field (e.g., `DateField`, `TimeField`, `DateTimeField`) or numeric field (e.g., `IntegerField`, `DecimalField`, `FloatField`), you'll need to use both `null=True` *and* `blank=True`.

For the sake of example, let's change our `Book` model to allow a blank `publication_date`. Here's the revised code:

```
class Book(models.Model):
    title = models.CharField(max_length=100)
    authors = models.ManyToManyField(Author)
    publisher = models.ForeignKey(Publisher)
    publication_date = models.DateField(blank=True, null=True)
```

Adding `null=True` is more complicated than adding `blank=True`, because `null=True` changes the semantics of the database—that is, it changes the `CREATE TABLE` statement to remove the `NOT NULL` from the `publication_date` field. To complete this change, we'll need to update the database.

For a number of reasons, Django does not attempt to automate changes to database schemas, so it's your own responsibility to execute the appropriate `ALTER TABLE` statement whenever you make such a change to a model. Recall that you can use `manage.py dbshell` to enter your database server's shell. Here's how to remove the `NOT NULL` in this particular case:

```
ALTER TABLE books_book ALTER COLUMN publication_date DROP NOT NULL;
```

(Note that this SQL syntax is specific to PostgreSQL.) We'll cover schema changes in more depth in Chapter 10.

Bringing this back to the admin site, now the Add Book edit form should allow for empty publication-date values.

Customizing Field Labels

On the admin site's edit forms, each field's label is generated from its model field name. The algorithm is simple: Django just replaces underscores with spaces and capitalizes the first character, so, for example, the `Book` model's `publication_date` field has the label Publication Date.

However, field names don't always lend themselves to nice admin field labels, so in some cases you might want to customize a label. You can do this by specifying `verbose_name` in the appropriate model field.

For example, here's how we can change the label of the `Author.email` field to "e-mail," with a hyphen:

```
class Author(models.Model):
    first_name = models.CharField(max_length=30)
    last_name = models.CharField(max_length=40)
    email = models.EmailField(blank=True, verbose_name='e-mail')
```

Make that change and reload the server, and you should see the field's new label on the author edit form.

Note that you shouldn't capitalize the first letter of a `verbose_name` unless it should *always* be capitalized (e.g., `"USA state"`). Django will automatically capitalize it when it needs to, and it will use the exact `verbose_name` value in places that don't require capitalization.

Finally, note that you can pass the verbose_name as a positional argument, for a slightly more compact syntax. This example is equivalent to the previous one:

```
class Author(models.Model):
    first_name = models.CharField(max_length=30)
    last_name = models.CharField(max_length=40)
    email = models.EmailField('e-mail', blank=True)
```

This won't work with ManyToManyField or ForeignKey fields, though, because they require the first argument to be a model class. In those cases, specifying verbose_name explicitly is the way to go.

Custom ModelAdmin Classes

The changes we've made so far—blank=True, null=True, and verbose_name—are really model-level changes, not admin-level changes. That is, these changes are fundamentally a part of the model and just so happen to be used by the admin site; there's nothing admin-specific about them.

Beyond these, the Django admin site offers a wealth of options that let you customize how the admin site works for a particular model. Such options live in ModelAdmin classes, which are classes that contain configuration for a specific model in a specific admin site instance.

Customizing Change Lists

Let's dive into admin customization by specifying the fields that are displayed on the change list for our Author model. By default, the change list displays the result of __unicode__() for each object. In Chapter 5 we defined the __unicode__() method for Author objects to display the first name and last name together:

```
class Author(models.Model):
    first_name = models.CharField(max_length=30)
    last_name = models.CharField(max_length=40)
    email = models.EmailField(blank=True, verbose_name='e-mail')

    def __unicode__(self):
        return u'%s %s' % (self.first_name, self.last_name)
```

As a result, the change list for Author objects displays each author's first name and last name together, as you can see in Figure 6-7.

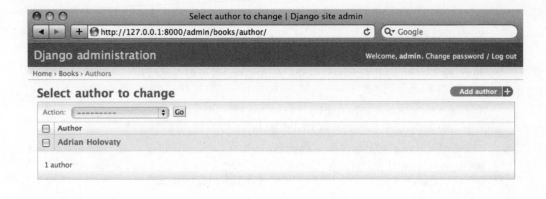

Figure 6-7. *The author change-list page*

We can improve on this default behavior by adding a few other fields to the change-list display. It'd be handy, for example, to see each author's e-mail address in this list, and it'd be nice to be able to sort by first and last name.

To make this happen, we'll define a ModelAdmin class for the Author model. This class is the key to customizing the admin, and one of the most basic things it lets you do is specify the list of fields to display on change-list pages. Edit admin.py to make these changes:

```
from django.contrib import admin
from mysite.books.models import Publisher, Author, Book

class AuthorAdmin(admin.ModelAdmin):
    list_display = ('first_name', 'last_name', 'email')

admin.site.register(Publisher)
admin.site.register(Author, AuthorAdmin)
admin.site.register(Book)
```

Here's what we've done:

- We created the class `AuthorAdmin`. This class, which subclasses `django.contrib.admin.ModelAdmin`, holds custom configuration for a specific admin model. We've specified only one customization—`list_display`, which is set to a tuple of field names to display on the change-list page. These field names must exist in the model, of course.

- We altered the `admin.site.register()` call to add `AuthorAdmin` after `Author`. You can read this as "Register the `Author` model with the `AuthorAdmin` options."

  The `admin.site.register()` function takes a `ModelAdmin` subclass as an optional second argument. If you don't specify a second argument (as is the case for `Publisher` and `Book`), Django will use the default admin options for that model.

With that tweak made, reload the author change-list page, and you'll see it's now displaying three columns—the first name, last name, and e-mail address. In addition, each of those columns is sortable by clicking on the column header. (See Figure 6-8.)

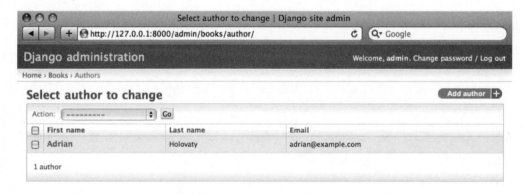

Figure 6-8. *The author change-list page after list_display*

Next let's add a simple search bar. Add `search_fields` to `AuthorAdmin`, like so:

```
class AuthorAdmin(admin.ModelAdmin):
    list_display = ('first_name', 'last_name', 'email')
    search_fields = ('first_name', 'last_name')
```

Reload the page in your browser, and you should see a search bar at the top. (See Figure 6-9.) We've just told the admin change-list page to include a search bar that searches against the `first_name` and `last_name` fields. As a user might expect, this is case insensitive and searches both fields, so searching for the string "bar" would find both an author with the first name Barney and an author with the last name Hobarson.

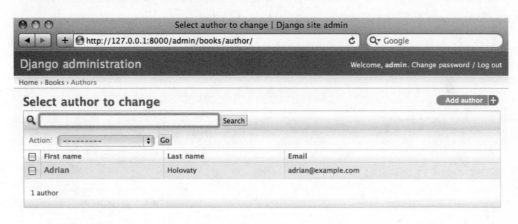

Figure 6-9. *The author change-list page after search_fields*

Next let's add some date filters to our `Book` model's change-list page:

```
from django.contrib import admin
from mysite.books.models import Publisher, Author, Book

class AuthorAdmin(admin.ModelAdmin):
    list_display = ('first_name', 'last_name', 'email')
    search_fields = ('first_name', 'last_name')
```

```
class BookAdmin(admin.ModelAdmin):
    list_display = ('title', 'publisher', 'publication_date')
    list_filter = ('publication_date',)

admin.site.register(Publisher)
admin.site.register(Author, AuthorAdmin)
admin.site.register(Book, BookAdmin)
```

Here, because we're dealing with a different set of options, we created a separate ModelAdmin class—BookAdmin. First we defined a list_display just to make the change list look a bit nicer. Then we used list_filter, which is set to a tuple of fields to use to create filters along the right side of the change-list page. For date fields, Django provides short-cuts to filter the list to "Today," "Past 7 days," "This month," and "This year"—shortcuts that Django's developers have found hit the common cases for filtering by date. Figure 6-10 shows what that looks like.

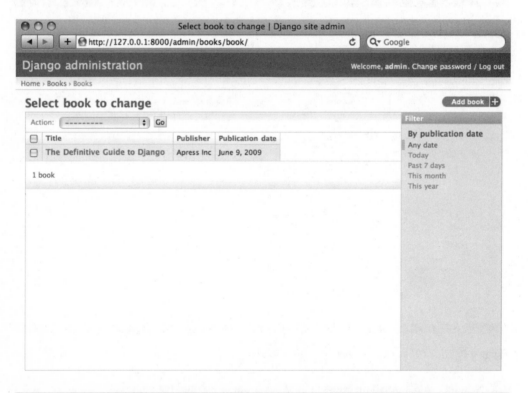

Figure 6-10. *The book change-list page after list_filter*

list_filter also works on fields of other types, not just DateField. (Try it with BooleanField and ForeignKey fields, for example.) The filters show up as long as there are at least two values to choose from.

Another way to offer date filters is to use the `date_hierarchy` admin option, like this:

```
class BookAdmin(admin.ModelAdmin):
    list_display = ('title', 'publisher', 'publication_date')
    list_filter = ('publication_date',)
    date_hierarchy = 'publication_date'
```

With this in place, the change-list page gets a date drill-down navigation bar at the top of the list, as shown in Figure 6-11. It starts with a list of available years, then drills down into months and individual days.

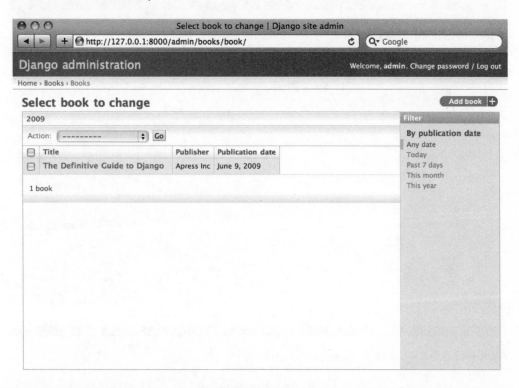

Figure 6-11. *The book change-list page after date_hierarchy*

Note that `date_hierarchy` takes a *string*, not a tuple, because only one date field can be used to make the hierarchy.

Finally, let's change the default ordering so that books on the change-list page are always ordered descending by their publication date. By default, the change list orders objects according to their model's `ordering` within `class Meta` (which we covered in Chapter 5)—but if you haven't specified this `ordering` value, then the ordering is undefined.

```
class BookAdmin(admin.ModelAdmin):
    list_display = ('title', 'publisher', 'publication_date')
    list_filter = ('publication_date',)
    date_hierarchy = 'publication_date'
    ordering = ('-publication_date',)
```

This admin `ordering` option works exactly as the `ordering` in a model's `class Meta`, except that it uses only the first field name in the list. Just pass a list or tuple of field names, and add a minus sign to a field to use descending sort order.

Reload the book change list to see this in action. Note that the Publication Date header now includes a small arrow that indicates which way the records are sorted. (See Figure 6-12.)

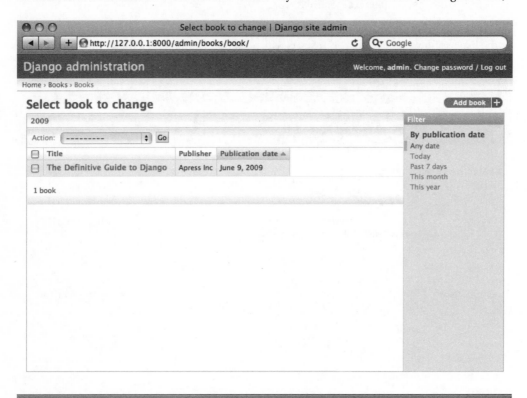

Figure 6-12. *The book change-list page after ordering*

We've covered the main change-list options here. Using these options, you can make a very powerful, production-ready, data-editing interface with only a few lines of code.

Customizing Edit Forms

Just as the change list can be customized, edit forms can be customized in many ways.

First, let's customize the way fields are ordered. By default, the order of fields in an edit form corresponds to the order in which they're defined in the model. We can change that using the `fields` option in our `ModelAdmin` subclass:

```
class BookAdmin(admin.ModelAdmin):
    list_display = ('title', 'publisher', 'publication_date')
    list_filter = ('publication_date',)
    date_hierarchy = 'publication_date'
    ordering = ('-publication_date',)
    fields = ('title', 'authors', 'publisher', 'publication_date')
```

After this change, the edit form for books will use the given ordering for fields. It's slightly more natural to have the authors after the book title. Of course, the field order should depend on your data-entry workflow. Every form is different.

Another useful thing the `fields` option lets you do is to *exclude* certain fields from being edited. Just leave out the field(s) you want to exclude. You might use this if your admin users are trusted to edit only a certain segment of your data, or if parts of your fields are changed by some outside, automated process. For example, in our book database, we could prevent the publication_date field from being editable:

```
class BookAdmin(admin.ModelAdmin):
    list_display = ('title', 'publisher', 'publication_date')
    list_filter = ('publication_date',)
    date_hierarchy = 'publication_date'
    ordering = ('-publication_date',)
    fields = ('title', 'authors', 'publisher')
```

As a result, the edit form for books doesn't offer a way to specify the publication date. This could be useful if, say, you're an editor who prefers that his authors not push back publication dates. (This is purely a hypothetical example, of course.)

When a user employs this incomplete form to add a new book, Django will simply set the publication_date to None—so make sure that field has null=True.

Another commonly used edit-form customization has to do with many-to-many fields. As we've seen on the edit form for books, the admin site represents each ManyToManyField as a multiple-select box, which is the most logical HTML input widget to utilize—but multiple-select boxes can be difficult to use. If you want to select multiple items, you have to hold down the Control key, or Command on a Mac. The admin site helpfully inserts a bit of text that explains this, but, still, it gets unwieldy when your field contains hundreds of options.

The admin site's solution is `filter_horizontal`. Let's add that to BookAdmin and see what it does.

```
class BookAdmin(admin.ModelAdmin):
    list_display = ('title', 'publisher', 'publication_date')
    list_filter = ('publication_date',)
    date_hierarchy = 'publication_date'
    ordering = ('-publication_date',)
    filter_horizontal = ('authors',)
```

(If you're following along, note that we've also removed the `fields` option to restore all the fields in the edit form.)

Reload the edit form for books, and you'll see that the Authors section now uses a fancy JavaScript filter interface that lets you search through the options dynamically and move specific authors from Available Authors to the Chosen Authors box, and vice versa.

Figure 6-13. *The book edit form after adding filter_horizontal*

We'd highly recommend using `filter_horizontal` for any `ManyToManyField` that has more than ten items. It's far easier to use than a simple multiple-select widget. Also, note you can use `filter_horizontal` for multiple fields—just specify each name in the tuple.

`ModelAdmin` classes also support a `filter_vertical` option. This works exactly as `filter_horizontal`, but the resulting JavaScript interface stacks the two boxes vertically instead of horizontally. It's a matter of personal taste.

`filter_horizontal` and `filter_vertical` work on only `ManyToManyField` fields, not `ForeignKey` fields. By default, the admin site uses simple `<select>` boxes for `ForeignKey` fields, but, as for `ManyToManyField`, sometimes you don't want to incur the overhead of having to select all the related objects to display in the drop-down. For example, if our book database grows to include thousands of publishers, the Add Book form could take a while to load, because it would have to load every publisher for display in the `<select>` box.

You can fix this with an option called raw_id_fields. Set this to a tuple of ForeignKey field names, and those fields will be displayed in the admin with a simple text-input box (<input type="text">) instead of a <select>. See Figure 6-14.

```
class BookAdmin(admin.ModelAdmin):
    list_display = ('title', 'publisher', 'publication_date')
    list_filter = ('publication_date',)
    date_hierarchy = 'publication_date'
    ordering = ('-publication_date',)
    filter_horizontal = ('authors',)
    raw_id_fields = ('publisher',)
```

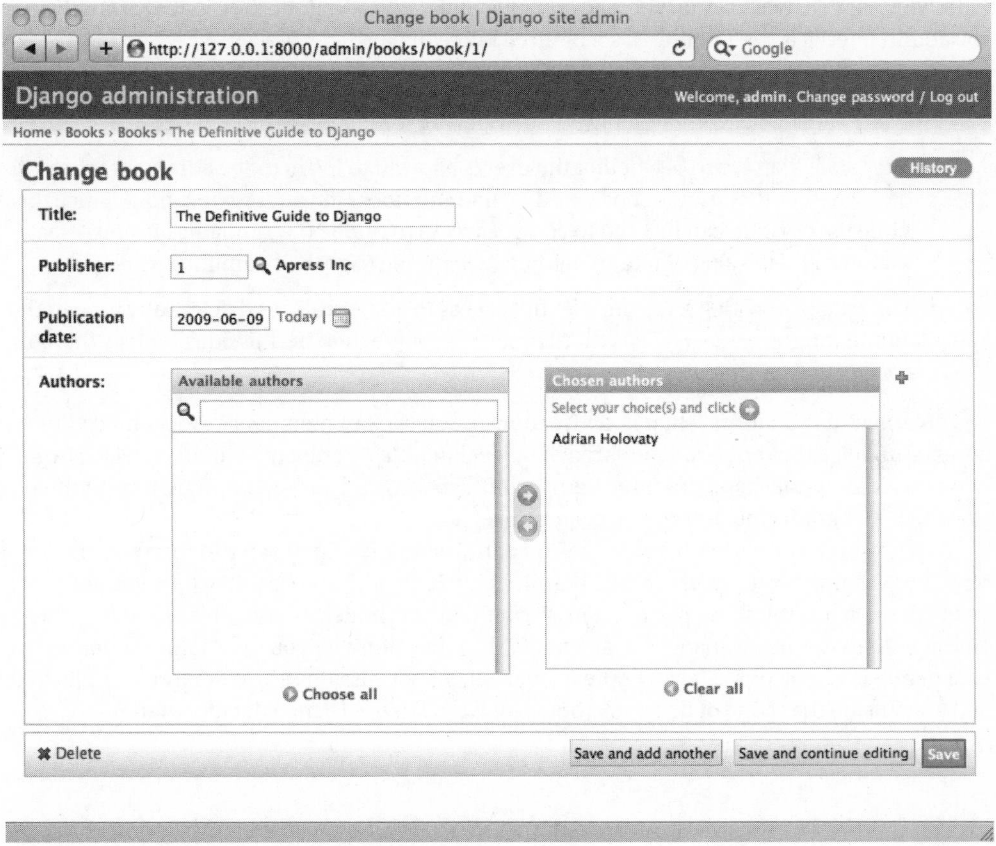

Figure 6-14. *The book edit form after adding raw_id_fields*

What do you enter in this input box? The database ID of the publisher. Given that humans don't normally memorize database IDs, there's a magnifying-glass icon that you can click to pull up a pop-up window from which you can select the publisher.

Users, Groups, and Permissions

Because you're logged in as a superuser, you have access to create, edit, and delete any object. Naturally, different environments require different permission systems—not everybody can or should be a superuser. Django's admin site uses a permissions system that you can use to give specific users access to only the portions of the interface that they need.

These user accounts are meant to be generic enough to be used outside of the admin interface, but we'll just treat them as admin user accounts for now. In Chapter 14 we'll cover how to integrate user accounts with the rest of your site (i.e., not just the admin site).

You can edit users and permissions through the admin interface just like any other object. We saw this earlier in this chapter, when we played around with the User and Group sections of the admin. User objects have the standard username, password, e-mail, and real-name fields you might expect, along with a set of fields that define what the user is allowed to do in the admin interface. First, there's a set of three Boolean flags:

- The "active" flag controls whether the user is active at all. If this flag is off and the user tries to log in, he won't be allowed in, even with a valid password.

- The "staff" flag controls whether the user is allowed to log in to the admin interface (i.e., whether that user is considered a "staff member" in your organization). Since this same user system can be used to control access to public (i.e., nonadmin) sites—see Chapter 14—this flag differentiates between public users and administrators.

- The "superuser" flag gives the user full access to add, create, and delete any item in the admin interface. If a user has this flag set, then all regular permissions (or lack thereof) are ignored for that user.

"Normal" admin users—that is, active, nonsuperuser staff members—are granted admin access through assigned permissions. Each object editable through the admin interface (e.g., books, authors, publishers) has three permissions: *create*, *edit*, and *delete*. Assigning permissions to a user grants the user the associated level of access.

When you create a user, that user has no permissions; it's up to you to assign specific ones. For example, you can give a user permission to add and change publishers but not to delete them. Note that these permissions are defined per model, not per object—so they let you say, "John can make changes to any book," but they don't let you say, "John can make changes to any book published by Apress." Per-object permissions are a bit more complicated and are outside the scope of this book (but are covered in the Django documentation).

■**Note** Access to edit users and permissions is also controlled by this permissions system. If you give someone permission to edit users, she will be able to edit her own permissions, which might not be what you want! Giving a user permission to edit other users is essentially turning a user into a superuser.

You can also assign users to groups. A *group* is simply a set of permissions to apply to all members of that group. Groups are useful for granting identical permissions to a subset of users.

When and Why to Use the Admin Interface— And When Not To

After having worked through this chapter, you should have a good idea of how to use Django's admin site. But we want to make a point of covering *when* and *why* you might want to use it— and when *not* to use it.

Django's admin site especially shines when nontechnical users need to be able to enter data; that's the purpose behind the feature, after all. At the newspaper where Django was first developed, creation of a typical online feature—say, a special report on water quality in the municipal supply—would go something like this:

1. The reporter responsible for the project meets with one of the developers and describes the available data.

2. The developer designs Django models to fit this data and then opens up the admin site to the reporter.

3. The reporter inspects the admin site to point out any missing or extraneous fields— better now than later. The developer changes the models iteratively.

4. When the models are agreed upon, the reporter begins entering data using the admin site. At the same time, the programmer can focus on developing the publicly accessible views/templates (the fun part!).

In other words, the raison d'être of Django's admin interface is to facilitate the simultaneous work of content producers and programmers.

However, beyond these obvious data-entry tasks, the admin site is useful in a few other cases:

- *Inspecting data models*: Once you've defined a few models, it can be quite useful to call them up in the admin interface and enter some dummy data. In some cases, this might reveal data-modeling mistakes or other problems with your models.

- *Managing acquired data*: For applications that rely on data coming from external sources (e.g., users or Web crawlers), the admin site gives you an easy way to inspect or edit this data. You can think of it as a less powerful but more convenient version of your database's command-line utility.

- *Quick and dirty data-management apps*: You can use the admin site to build a very lightweight data-management app—say, to keep track of expenses. If you're just building something for your own needs, not for public consumption, the admin site can take you a long way. In this sense, you can think of it as a beefed-up, relational version of a spreadsheet.

One final point we want to make clear is that the admin site is not an end-all-be-all. Over the years, we've seen it hacked and chopped up to serve a variety of functions it wasn't intended to serve. It's not intended to be a *public* interface to data, nor is it intended to allow for sophisticated sorting and searching of your data. As we said early in this chapter, it's for trusted site administrators. Keeping this sweet spot in mind is the key to effective admin-site usage.

What's Next?

So far we've created a few models and configured a top-notch interface for editing data. In the next chapter we'll move on to the real "meat and potatoes" of Web development: form creation and processing.

CHAPTER 7

■ ■ ■

Forms

HTML forms are the backbone of interactive Web sites, from the simplicity of Google's single search box to ubiquitous blog comment-submission forms to complex custom data-entry interfaces. This chapter covers how you can use Django to access user-submitted form data, validate it, and do something with it. Along the way, we'll cover HttpRequest and Form objects.

Getting Data from the Request Object

We introduced HttpRequest objects in Chapter 3 when we first covered view functions, but we didn't have much to say about them at the time. Recall that each view function takes an HttpRequest object as its first parameter, as in our hello() view:

```
from django.http import HttpResponse

def hello(request):
    return HttpResponse("Hello world")
```

HttpRequest objects, such as the variable request here, have a number of interesting attributes and methods that you should familiarize yourself with so that you know what's possible. You can use these attributes to get information about the current request (i.e., the user/Web browser that's loading the current page on your Django-powered site) at the time the view function is executed.

Information About the URL

HttpRequest objects contain several pieces of information about the currently requested URL, as Table 7-1 shows.

Table 7-1. *HttpRequest Attributes and Methods*

Attribute/Method	Description	Example
request.path	The full path, not including the domain but including the leading slash	"/hello/"
request.get_host()	The host (i.e., the "domain," in common parlance)	"127.0.0.1:8000" or "www.example.com"
request.get_full_path()	The path, plus a query string (if available)	"/hello/?print=true"
request.is_secure()	True if the request was made via HTTPS; otherwise, False	True or False

Always use the attributes/methods outlined in Table 7-1 instead of hard-coding URLs in your views. This makes for more flexible code that can be reused in other places. Here's a simplistic example:

```
# BAD!
def current_url_view_bad(request):
    return HttpResponse("Welcome to the page at /current/")
```

```
# GOOD
def current_url_view_good(request):
    return HttpResponse("Welcome to the page at %s" % request.path)
```

Other Information About the Request

request.META is a Python dictionary containing all available HTTP headers for the given request—including the user's IP address and user agent (generally the name and version of the Web browser). Note that the full list of available headers depends on which headers the user sent and which headers your Web server sets. The following are some commonly available keys in this dictionary:

- HTTP_REFERER: The referring URL, if any. (Note the misspelling of REFERER.)

- HTTP_USER_AGENT: The user-agent string (if any) of the user's browser. This looks something like the following:

  "Mozilla 5.0 (X11; U; Linux i686) Gecko/20080829 Firefox/2.0.0.17"

- REMOTE_ADDR: The IP address of the client—for instance, "12.345.67.89". (If the request has passed through any proxies, then this might be a comma-separated list of IP addresses, such as "12.345.67.89,23.456.78.90".)

Note that because request.META is just a basic Python dictionary, you'll get a KeyError exception if you try to access a key that doesn't exist. (Because HTTP headers are *external* data—that is, they're submitted by your users' browsers—they shouldn't be trusted, and you should always design your application to fail gracefully if a particular header is empty or doesn't exist.) You should either use a try/except clause or the get() method to handle the case of undefined keys, as in this example:

```python
# BAD!
def ua_display_bad(request):
    ua = request.META['HTTP_USER_AGENT']  # Might raise KeyError!
    return HttpResponse("Your browser is %s" % ua)

# GOOD (VERSION 1)
def ua_display_good1(request):
    try:
        ua = request.META['HTTP_USER_AGENT']
    except KeyError:
        ua = 'unknown'
    return HttpResponse("Your browser is %s" % ua)

# GOOD (VERSION 2)
def ua_display_good2(request):
    ua = request.META.get('HTTP_USER_AGENT', 'unknown')
    return HttpResponse("Your browser is %s" % ua)
```

We encourage you to write a small view that displays all of the request.META data so you can get to know what's available. Here's what that view might look like:

```python
def display_meta(request):
    values = request.META.items()
    values.sort()
    html = []
    for k, v in values:
        html.append('<tr><td>%s</td><td>%s</td></tr>' % (k, v))
    return HttpResponse('<table>%s</table>' % '\n'.join(html))
```

As an exercise, see whether you can convert this view to use Django's template system instead of hard-coding the HTML. Also try adding request.path and the other HttpRequest methods from the previous section.

Information About Submitted Data

Beyond basic metadata about the request, HttpRequest objects have two attributes that contain user-submitted information: request.GET and request.POST. Both of these are dictionary-like objects that give you access to GET and POST data.

POST data generally is submitted from an HTML <form>, while GET data can come from a <form> or the query string in the page's URL.

A Simple Form-Handling Example

Continuing this book's ongoing example of books, authors, and publishers, let's create a simple view that lets users search our book database by title.

Generally, there are two parts to developing a form: the HTML user interface and the back-end view code that processes the submitted data. The first part is easy; let's just set up a view that displays a search form:

```
from django.shortcuts import render_to_response

def search_form(request):
    return render_to_response('search_form.html')
```

As you learned in Chapter 3, this view can live anywhere on your Python path. For this example, put it in `books/views.py`.

The accompanying template, `search_form.html`, could look like this:

```html
<html>
<head>
    <title>Search</title>
</head>
<body>
    <form action="/search/" method="get">
        <input type="text" name="q">
        <input type="submit" value="Search">
    </form>
</body>
</html>
```

The URLpattern in `urls.py` could look like this:

```python
from mysite.books import views

urlpatterns = patterns('',
    # ...
    (r'^search-form/$', views.search_form),
    # ...
)
```

Note that we're importing the views module directly, instead of something like from mysite.views import search_form, because the former is less verbose. We'll cover this importing approach in more detail in Chapter 8.

Now, if you run the runserver and visit http://127.0.0.1:8000/search-form/, you'll see the search interface. Simple enough.

Try submitting the form, though, and you'll get a Django 404 error. The form points to the URL /search/, which hasn't yet been implemented. Let's fix that with a second view function:

```
# urls.py

urlpatterns = patterns('',
    # ...
    (r'^search-form/$', views.search_form),
    (r'^search/$', views.search),
    # ...
)
```

```
# views.py

def search(request):
    if 'q' in request.GET:
        message = 'You searched for: %r' % request.GET['q']
    else:
        message = 'You submitted an empty form.'
    return HttpResponse(message)
```

For the moment, this merely displays the user's search term so we can make sure the data is being submitted to Django properly and so you can get a feel for how the search term flows through the system. In short, here's what happens:

1. The HTML <form> defines a variable q. When it's submitted, the value of q is sent via GET (method="get") to the URL /search/.

2. The Django view that handles the URL /search/ (search()) has access to the q value in request.GET.

Note that we explicitly check that 'q' exists in request.GET. As we pointed out in the request.META discussion earlier in this chapter, you shouldn't trust anything submitted by users or even assume that they've submitted anything in the first place. If we didn't add this check, any submission of an empty form would raise KeyError in the view:

```
# BAD!
def bad_search(request):
    # The following line will raise KeyError if 'q' hasn't
    # been submitted!
    message = 'You searched for: %r' % request.GET['q']
    return HttpResponse(message)
```

POST data works the same way as GET data—just use request.POST instead of request.GET. What's the difference between GET and POST? Use GET when the act of submitting the form is just a request to "get" data. Use POST whenever the act of submitting the form will have some side effect—*changing* data or sending an e-mail, or something else that's beyond simple *display* of data. In our book-search example, we're using GET because the query doesn't change any data on our server. (See http://www.w3.org/2001/tag/doc/whenToUseGet.html if you want to learn more about GET and POST.)

Now that we've verified request.GET is being passed in properly, let's hook the user's search query into our book database (again, in views.py):

```
from django.http import HttpResponse
from django.shortcuts import render_to_response
from mysite.books.models import Book

def search(request):
    if 'q' in request.GET and request.GET['q']:
        q = request.GET['q']
        books = Book.objects.filter(title__icontains=q)
        return render_to_response('search_results.html',
            {'books': books, 'query': q})
    else:
        return HttpResponse('Please submit a search term.')
```

Some notes on what we did here:

- In addition to checking that 'q' exists in request.GET, we made sure that request.GET['q'] is a nonempty value before passing it to the database query.

- We used Book.objects.filter(title__icontains=q) to query our book table for all books whose title includes the given submission. The icontains is a lookup type (as explained in Chapter 5 and Appendix B), and the statement can be roughly translated as "Get the books whose title contains q, without being case-sensitive."

  This is a very simple way to do a book search. We wouldn't recommend using a simple icontains query on a large production database, as it can be slow. (In the real world, you'd want to use a custom search system of some sort. Search the Web for *open-source full-text search* to get an idea of the possibilities.)

- We passed books, a list of Book objects, to the template. The template code for search_results.html might include something like this:

```
<p>You searched for: <strong>{{ query }}</strong></p>

{% if books %}
    <p>Found {{ books|length }} book{{ books|pluralize }}.</p>
    <ul>
        {% for book in books %}
        <li>{{ book.title }}</li>
        {% endfor %}
    </ul>
{% else %}
    <p>No books matched your search criteria.</p>
{% endif %}
```

Note the usage of the `pluralize` template filter, which outputs an "s" if appropriate, based on the number of books found.

Improving Our Simple Form-Handling Example

As in previous chapters, we've shown you the simplest thing that could possibly work. Now we'll point out some problems and show you how to improve it.

First, our `search()` view's handling of an empty query is poor—we're just displaying a `"Please submit a search term."` message, requiring the user to hit the browser's Back button. This is horrid and unprofessional, and if you ever actually implement something like this in the wild, your Django privileges will be revoked.

It would be much better to redisplay the form, with an error above it, so that the user can try again immediately. The easiest way to do that would be to render the template again, like this:

```
from django.http import HttpResponse
from django.shortcuts import render_to_response
from mysite.books.models import Book

def search_form(request):
    return render_to_response('search_form.html')

def search(request):
    if 'q' in request.GET and request.GET['q']:
        q = request.GET['q']
        books = Book.objects.filter(title__icontains=q)
        return render_to_response('search_results.html',
            {'books': books, 'query': q})
    else:
        return render_to_response('search_form.html', {'error': True})
```

(Note that we've included `search_form()` here so you can see both views in one place.)

Here we've improved `search()` to render the `search_form.html` template again if the query is empty. And because we need to display an error message in that template, we pass a template variable. Now we can edit `search_form.html` to check for the error variable:

```
<html>
<head>
    <title>Search</title>
</head>
<body>
    {% if error %}
        <p style="color: red;">Please submit a search term.</p>
    {% endif %}
    <form action="/search/" method="get">
        <input type="text" name="q">
        <input type="submit" value="Search">
    </form>
</body>
</html>
```

We can still use this template from our original view, search_form(), because search_
form() doesn't pass error to the template—so the error message won't show up in that case.

With this change in place, it's a better application but it now begs the question: is a dedicated search_form() view really necessary? As it stands, a request to the URL /search/ (without
any GET parameters) will display the empty form (but with an error). We can remove the
search_form() view, along with its associated URLpattern, as long as we change search() to
hide the error message when somebody visits /search/ with no GET parameters:

```
def search(request):
    error = False
    if 'q' in request.GET:
        q = request.GET['q']
        if not q:
            error = True
        else:
            books = Book.objects.filter(title__icontains=q)
            return render_to_response('search_results.html',
                {'books': books, 'query': q})
    return render_to_response('search_form.html',
        {'error': error})
```

In this updated view, if a user visits /search/ with no GET parameters, he'll see the search
form with no error message. If a user submits the form with an empty value for 'q', he'll see
the search form *with* an error message. And, finally, if a user submits the form with a nonempty value for 'q', he'll see the search results.

We can make one final improvement to this application, to remove a bit of redundancy.
Now that we've rolled the two views and URLs into one and /search/ handles both search-
form display and result display, the HTML <form> in search_form.html doesn't have to
hard-code a URL. Instead of this

```
<form action="/search/" method="get">
```

it can be changed to this:

```
<form action="" method="get">
```

The action="" means "Submit the form to the same URL as the current page." With this change in place, you won't have to remember to change the action if you ever hook the search() view to another URL.

Simple Validation

Our search example is still reasonably simple, particularly in terms of its data validation; we're merely checking to make sure the search query isn't empty. Many HTML forms include a level of validation that's more complex than making sure the value is nonempty. We've all seen the following error messages on Web sites:

- "Please enter a valid e-mail address. 'foo' is not an e-mail address."
- "Please enter a valid five-digit U.S. ZIP code. '123' is not a ZIP code."
- "Please enter a valid date in the format YYYY-MM-DD."
- "Please enter a password that is at least 8 characters long and contains at least one number."

A NOTE ON JAVASCRIPT VALIDATION

JavaScript validation is beyond the scope of this book, but you can use JavaScript to validate data on the client side, directly in the browser. Be warned, however: even if you do this, you *must* validate data on the server side. Some people have JavaScript turned off, and some malicious users might submit raw, unvalidated data directly to your form handler to see whether they can cause mischief.

There's nothing you can do about this, other than to *always* validate user-submitted data server-side (i.e., in your Django views). You should think of JavaScript validation as a bonus usability feature, not as your only means of validating.

Let's tweak our search() view so it validates that the search term is less than or equal to 20 characters long. (For this example, let's say anything longer than that might make the query too slow.) How might we do that? The simplest thing would be to embed the logic directly in the view, like this:

```
def search(request):
    error = False
    if 'q' in request.GET:
        q = request.GET['q']
        if not q:
            error = True
        elif len(q) > 20:
            error = True
        else:
            books = Book.objects.filter(title__icontains=q)
            return render_to_response('search_results.html',
                {'books': books, 'query': q})
```

```
    return render_to_response('search_form.html',
        {'error': error})
```

Now if you try submitting a search query greater than 20 characters long, you'll get an error message. But that error message in search_form.html currently says, "Please submit a search term."—so we'll have to change it to be accurate for both cases (an empty search term or a search term that's too long).

```
<html>
<head>
    <title>Search</title>
</head>
<body>
    {% if error %}
        <p style="color: red;">
            Please submit a search term
            20 characters or shorter.
        </p>
    {% endif %}
    <form action="/search/" method="get">
        <input type="text" name="q">
        <input type="submit" value="Search">
    </form>
</body>
</html>
```

There's something ugly about this. Our one-size-fits-all error message is potentially confusing. Why should the error message for an empty form submission mention anything about a 20-character limit? Error messages should be specific and clear.

The problem is that we're using a simple Boolean value for error, whereas we should be using a *list* of error-message strings. Here's how we might fix that:

```
def search(request):
    errors = []
    if 'q' in request.GET:
        q = request.GET['q']
        if not q:
            errors.append('Enter a search term.')
        elif len(q) > 20:
            errors.append('Please enter at most 20 characters.')
        else:
            books = Book.objects.filter(title__icontains=q)
            return render_to_response('search_results.html',
                {'books': books, 'query': q})
    return render_to_response('search_form.html',
        {'errors': errors})
```

Then we need to make a small tweak to the search_form.html template to reflect that it's now passed an errors list instead of an error Boolean value:

```
<html>
<head>
    <title>Search</title>
</head>
<body>
    {% if errors %}
        <ul>
            {% for error in errors %}
            <li>{{ error }}</li>
            {% endfor %}
        </ul>
    {% endif %}
    <form action="/search/" method="get">
        <input type="text" name="q">
        <input type="submit" value="Search">
    </form>
</body>
</html>
```

Making a Contact Form

Although we iterated over the book-search-form example several times and improved it nicely, it's still fundamentally simple: just a single field, 'q'. Because it's so simple, we didn't even use Django's form library to deal with it. But more complex forms call for more complex treatment—and now we'll develop something more complex: a site contact form that lets site users submit a bit of feedback, along with an optional e-mail return address. After the form is submitted and the data is validated, we'll automatically send the message via e-mail to the site staff.

We'll start with our template, contact_form.html.

```
<html>
<head>
    <title>Contact us</title>
</head>
<body>
    <h1>Contact us</h1>

    {% if errors %}
        <ul>
            {% for error in errors %}
            <li>{{ error }}</li>
            {% endfor %}
        </ul>
    {% endif %}
```

```
    <form action="/contact/" method="post">
        <p>Subject: <input type="text" name="subject"></p>
        <p>Your e-mail (optional): <input type="text" name="e-mail"></p>
        <p>Message: <textarea name="message" rows="10" cols="50"></textarea></p>
        <input type="submit" value="Submit">
    </form>
</body>
</html>
```

We've defined three fields: the subject, e-mail address, and message. The second is optional, but the other two fields are required. Note we're using `method="post"` here instead of `method="get"` because this form submission has a side effect—it sends an e-mail. Also, we copied the error-displaying code from our previous template `search_form.html`.

If we continue down the road established by our `search()` view from the previous section, a naive version of our `contact()` view might look like this:

```python
from django.core.mail import send_mail
from django.http import HttpResponseRedirect
from django.shortcuts import render_to_response

def contact(request):
    errors = []
    if request.method == 'POST':
        if not request.POST.get('subject', ''):
            errors.append('Enter a subject.')
        if not request.POST.get('message', ''):
            errors.append('Enter a message.')
        if request.POST.get('e-mail') and '@' not in request.POST['e-mail']:
            errors.append('Enter a valid e-mail address.')
        if not errors:
            send_mail(
                request.POST['subject'],
                request.POST['message'],
                request.POST.get('e-mail', 'noreply@example.com'),
                ['siteowner@example.com'],
            )
            return HttpResponseRedirect('/contact/thanks/')
    return render_to_response('contact_form.html',
        {'errors': errors})
```

■**Note** You may be wondering whether to put this view in the `books/views.py` file. It doesn't have anything to do with the books application, so should it live elsewhere? It's up to you; Django doesn't care, as long as you're able to point to the view from your URLconf. Our personal preference would be to create a separate directory, `contact`, at the same level in the directory tree as `books`. This would contain an empty `__init__.py` and `views.py`.

Several new things are happening here:

- We're checking that `request.method` is `'POST'`. This will be true only in the case of a form submission; it won't be true if somebody is merely viewing the contact form. (In the latter case, `request.method` will be set to `'GET'` because in normal Web browsing, browsers use GET, not POST.) This makes it a nice way to isolate the "form display" case from the "form processing" case.

- Instead of `request.GET`, we're using `request.POST` to access the submitted form data. This is necessary because the HTML `<form>` in `contact_form.html` uses `method="post"`. If this view is accessed via POST, then `request.GET` will be empty.

- We have *two* required fields, `subject` and `message`, so we have to validate both. Note that we're using `request.POST.get()` and providing a blank string as the default value; this is a nice, short way of handling both the cases of missing keys and missing data.

- Although the `e-mail` field is not required, we still validate it if it is indeed submitted. Our validation algorithm here is fragile—we're just checking that the string contains an @ character. In the real world, you'd want more robust validation (and Django provides it, which we'll show you in the "Your First Form Class" section later in this chapter).

- We're using the function `django.core.mail.send_mail` to send an e-mail. This function has four required arguments: the e-mail subject, the e-mail body, the "from" address, and a list of recipient addresses. `send_mail` is a convenient wrapper around Django's `E-mailMessage` class, which provides advanced features such as attachments, multipart e-mails, and full control over e-mail headers.

  Note that in order to send e-mail using `send_mail()`, your server must be configured to send mail, and Django must be told about your outbound e-mail server. See `http://docs.djangoproject.com/en/dev/topics/e-mail/` for the specifics.

- After the e-mail is sent, we redirect to a "success" page by returning an `HttpResponseRedirect` object. We'll leave the implementation of that "success" page up to you (it's a simple view/URLconf/template), but we'll explain why we initiate a redirect instead of, for example, simply calling `render_to_response()` with a template right there.

  The reason: if a user hits Refresh on a page that was loaded via POST, that request will be repeated. This can often lead to undesired behavior, such as a duplicate record being added to the database—or, in our example, the e-mail being sent twice. If the user is redirected to another page after the POST, then there's no chance of repeating the request.

  You should *always* issue a redirect for successful POST requests. It's a Web-development best practice.

This view works, but those validation functions are kind of crufty. Imagine processing a form with a dozen fields; would you really want to have to write all of those `if` statements?

Another problem is *form redisplay*. In the case of validation errors, it's best practice to redisplay the form with the previously submitted data already filled in so the user can see what he did wrong (and doesn't have to re-enter data in fields that were submitted correctly). We *could* manually pass the POST data back to the template, but we'd have to edit each HTML field to insert the proper value in the proper place:

```python
# views.py

def contact(request):
    errors = []
    if request.method == 'POST':
        if not request.POST.get('subject', ''):
            errors.append('Enter a subject.')
        if not request.POST.get('message', ''):
            errors.append('Enter a message.')
        if request.POST.get('e-mail') and '@' not in request.POST['e-mail']:
            errors.append('Enter a valid e-mail address.')
        if not errors:
            send_mail(
                request.POST['subject'],
                request.POST['message'],
                request.POST.get('e-mail', 'noreply@example.com'),
                ['siteowner@example.com'],
            )
            return HttpResponseRedirect('/contact/thanks/')
    return render_to_response('contact_form.html', {
        'errors': errors,
        'subject': request.POST.get('subject', ''),
        'message': request.POST.get('message', ''),
        'e-mail': request.POST.get('e-mail', ''),
    })
```

```html
# contact_form.html

<html>
<head>
    <title>Contact us</title>
</head>
<body>
    <h1>Contact us</h1>

    {% if errors %}
        <ul>
            {% for error in errors %}
            <li>{{ error }}</li>
            {% endfor %}
        </ul>
    {% endif %}

    <form action="/contact/" method="post">
        <p>Subject: <input type="text" name="subject" value="{{ subject }}"></p>
        <p>Your e-mail (optional):
            <input type="text" name="e-mail" value="{{ e-mail }}">
```

```
        </p>
        <p>Message:
            <textarea name="message" rows="10" cols="50">
                **{{ message }}**
            </textarea>
        </p>
        <input type="submit" value="Submit">
    </form>
</body>
</html>
```

This is a lot of cruft, and it introduces a lot of opportunities for human error. We hope you're starting to see the opportunity for some higher-level library that handles form- and validation-related tasks.

Your First Form Class

Django comes with a form library, called `django.forms`, that handles many of the issues we've been exploring in this chapter—from HTML form display to validation. Let's dive in and rework our contact-form application using the Django forms framework.

DJANGO'S "NEWFORMS" LIBRARY

Throughout the Django community, you might see chatter about something called `django.newforms`. When people speak of `django.newforms`, they're talking about what is now `django.forms`—the library covered in this chapter.

When Django was first released to the public, it had a complicated, confusing forms system, `django.forms`. It was completely rewritten, and the new version was called `django.newforms` so that people could still use the old system. When Django 1.0 was released, the old `django.forms` went away, and `django.newforms` became `django.forms`.

The primary way to use the forms framework is to define a `Form` class for each HTML `<form>` you're dealing with. In our case, we only have one `<form>`, so we'll have one `Form` class. This class can live anywhere you want—including directly in your `views.py` file—but community convention is to keep `Form` classes in a separate file called `forms.py`. Create this file in the same directory as your `views.py`, and enter the following:

```
from django import forms

class ContactForm(forms.Form):
    subject = forms.CharField()
    e-mail = forms.EmailField(required=False)
    message = forms.CharField()
```

This is pretty intuitive, and it's similar to Django's model syntax. Each field in the form is represented by a type of `Field` class—`CharField` and `EmailField` are the only types of fields used here—as attributes of a `Form` class. Each field is required by default, so to make e-mail optional, we specify `required=False`.

Let's hop into the Python interactive interpreter and see what this class can do. The first thing it can do is display itself as HTML:

```
>>> from contact.forms import ContactForm
>>> f = ContactForm()
>>> print f
<tr><th><label for="id_subject">Subject:</label></th><td>
<input type="text" name="subject" id="id_subject" /></td></tr>
<tr><th><label for="id_e-mail">E-mail:</label></th><td>
<input type="text" name="e-mail" id="id_e-mail" /></td></tr>
<tr><th><label for="id_message">Message:</label></th><td>
<input type="text" name="message" id="id_message" /></td></tr>
```

Django adds a label to each field, along with `<label>` tags for accessibility. The idea is to make the default behavior as optimal as possible.

This default output is in the format of an HTML `<table>`, but there are a few other built-in outputs:

```
>>> print f.as_ul()
<li><label for="id_subject">Subject:</label>
<input type="text" name="subject" id="id_subject" /></li>
<li><label for="id_e-mail">E-mail:</label>
<input type="text" name="e-mail" id="id_e-mail" /></li>
<li><label for="id_message">Message:</label>
<input type="text" name="message" id="id_message" /></li>
>>> print f.as_p()
<p><label for="id_subject">Subject:</label>
<input type="text" name="subject" id="id_subject" /></p>
<p><label for="id_e-mail">E-mail:</label>
<input type="text" name="e-mail" id="id_e-mail" /></p>
<p><label for="id_message">Message:</label>
<input type="text" name="message" id="id_message" /></p>
```

Note that the opening and closing `<table>`, `<ul>`, and `<form>` tags aren't included in the output, so you can add any additional rows and customization if necessary.

These methods are just shortcuts for the common case of "display the entire form." You can also display the HTML for a particular field:

```
>>> print f['subject']
<input type="text" name="subject" id="id_subject" />
>>> print f['message']
<input type="text" name="message" id="id_message" />
```

The second thing `Form` objects can do is validate data. To do this, create a new `Form` object and pass it a dictionary of data that maps field names to data:

```
>>> f = ContactForm({'subject': 'Hello', 'e-mail': 'adrian@example.com',
… 'message': 'Nice site!'})
```

Once you've associated data with a Form instance, you've created a *bound* Form:

```
>>> f.is_bound
True
```

Call the is_valid() method on any bound Form to find out whether its data is valid. We've passed a valid value for each field, so the Form in its entirety is valid:

```
>>> f.is_valid()
True
```

If we don't pass the e-mail field, it's still valid, because we've specified required=False for that field:

```
>>> f = ContactForm({'subject': 'Hello', 'message': 'Nice site!'})
>>> f.is_valid()
True
```

But if we leave off either subject or message, the Form is no longer valid:

```
>>> f = ContactForm({'subject': 'Hello'})
>>> f.is_valid()
False
>>> f = ContactForm({'subject': 'Hello', 'message': ''})
>>> f.is_valid()
False
```

You can drill down to get field-specific error messages:

```
>>> f = ContactForm({'subject': 'Hello', 'message': ''})
>>> f['message'].errors
[u'This field is required.']
>>> f['subject'].errors
[]
>>> f['e-mail'].errors
[]
```

Each bound Form instance has an errors attribute that gives you a dictionary mapping field names to error-message lists:

```
>>> f = ContactForm({'subject': 'Hello', 'message': ''})
>>> f.errors
{'message': [u'This field is required.']}
```

Finally, for Form instances whose data has been found to be valid, a cleaned_data attribute is available. This is a dictionary of the submitted data, "cleaned up." Django's forms framework not only validates data, but cleans it up by converting values to the appropriate Python types, as shown here:

```
>>> f = ContactForm({'subject': 'Hello', 'e-mail': 'adrian@example.com',
...  'message': 'Nice site!'})
>>> f.is_valid()
True
>>> f.cleaned_data
{'message': u'Nice site!', 'e-mail': u'adrian@example.com', 'subject': u'Hello'}
```

Our contact form deals only with strings, which are "cleaned" into Unicode objects—but if we were to use an `IntegerField` or a `DateField`, the forms framework would ensure that `cleaned_data` used proper Python integers or `datetime.date` objects for the given fields.

Tying Form Objects into Views

Now that you have some basic knowledge about `Form` classes, you might see how we can use this infrastructure to replace some of the cruft in our `contact()` view. Here's how we can rewrite `contact()` to use the forms framework:

```python
# views.py

from django.shortcuts import render_to_response
from mysite.contact.forms import ContactForm

def contact(request):
    if request.method == 'POST':
        form = ContactForm(request.POST)
        if form.is_valid():
            cd = form.cleaned_data
            send_mail(
                cd['subject'],
                cd['message'],
                cd.get('e-mail', 'noreply@example.com'),
                ['siteowner@example.com'],
            )
            return HttpResponseRedirect('/contact/thanks/')
    else:
        form = ContactForm()
    return render_to_response('contact_form.html', {'form': form})

# contact_form.html

<html>
<head>
    <title>Contact us</title>
</head>
<body>
    <h1>Contact us</h1>
```

```
{% if form.errors %}
    <p style="color: red;">
        Please correct the error{{ form.errors|pluralize }} below.
    </p>
{% endif %}

<form action="" method="post">
    <table>
        {{ form.as_table }}
    </table>
    <input type="submit" value="Submit">
</form>
</body>
</html>
```

Look at how much cruft we've been able to remove! Django's forms framework handles the HTML display, the validation, data cleanup, and form redisplay-with-errors.

Try running this locally. Load the form, submit it with none of the fields filled out, submit it with an invalid e-mail address, then finally submit it with valid data. (Of course, depending on your mail-server configuration, you might get an error when send_mail() is called, but that's another issue.)

Changing How Fields Are Rendered

Probably the first thing you'll notice when you render this form locally is that the message field is displayed as an <input type="text">, and it ought to be a <textarea>. We can fix that by setting the field's *widget*:

```
from django import forms

class ContactForm(forms.Form):
    subject = forms.CharField()
    e-mail = forms.EmailField(required=False)
    message = forms.CharField(widget=forms.Textarea)
```

The forms framework separates out the presentation logic for each field into a set of widgets. Each field type has a default widget, but you can easily override the default or provide a custom widget of your own.

Think of the Field classes as representing *validation logic*, while widgets represent *presentation logic*.

Setting a Maximum Length

One of the most common validation needs is to check that a field is of a certain size. For good measure, we should improve our ContactForm to limit the subject to 100 characters. To do that, just supply a max_length to the CharField, like this:

```
from django import forms

class ContactForm(forms.Form):
    subject = forms.CharField(max_length=100)
    e-mail = forms.EmailField(required=False)
    message = forms.CharField(widget=forms.Textarea)
```

An optional `min_length` argument is also available.

Setting Initial Values

As an improvement to this form, let's add an *initial value* for the `subject` field: `"I love your site!"` (A little power of suggestion can't hurt.) To do this, we can use the `initial` argument when we create a `Form` instance:

```
def contact(request):
    if request.method == 'POST':
        form = ContactForm(request.POST)
        if form.is_valid():
            cd = form.cleaned_data
            send_mail(
                cd['subject'],
                cd['message'],
                cd.get('e-mail', 'noreply@example.com'),
                ['siteowner@example.com'],
            )
            return HttpResponseRedirect('/contact/thanks/')
    else:
        form = ContactForm(
            initial={'subject': 'I love your site!'}
        )
    return render_to_response('contact_form.html', {'form': form})
```

Now the `subject` field will be displayed prepopulated with that kind statement.

Note that there is a difference between passing *initial* data and passing data that *binds* the form. If you're just passing *initial* data, then the form will be *unbound*, which means it won't have any error messages.

Adding Custom Validation Rules

Imagine we've launched our feedback form, and the e-mails have started tumbling in. There's just one problem: some of the submitted messages are just one or two words, which isn't long enough for us to make sense of. We decide to adopt a new validation policy: four words or more, please.

There are various ways to hook custom validation into a Django form. If our rule is something we will reuse again and again, we can create a custom field type. Most custom validations are one-off affairs, though, and can be tied directly to the `Form` class.

We want additional validation on the `message` field, so we add a `clean_message()` method to our `Form` class:

```
from django import forms

class ContactForm(forms.Form):
    subject = forms.CharField(max_length=100)
    e-mail = forms.EmailField(required=False)
    message = forms.CharField(widget=forms.Textarea)

    def clean_message(self):
        message = self.cleaned_data['message']
        num_words = len(message.split())
        if num_words < 4:
            raise forms.ValidationError("Not enough words!")
        return message
```

Django's form system automatically looks for any method whose name starts with `clean_` and ends with the name of a field. If any such method exists, it's called during validation.

Specifically, the `clean_message()` method will be called *after* the default validation logic for a given field (in this case, the validation logic for a required `CharField`). Because the field data has already been partially processed, we pull it out of `self.cleaned_data`. Also, we don't have to worry about checking that the value exists and is nonempty; the default validator does that.

We naively use a combination of `len()` and `split()` to count the number of words. If the user has entered too few words, we raise a `forms.ValidationError`. The string attached to this exception will be displayed to the user as an item in the error list.

It's important that we explicitly return the cleaned value for the field at the end of the method. This allows us to modify the value (or convert it to a different Python type) within our custom validation method. If we forget the return statement, then `None` will be returned and the original value will be lost.

Specifying Labels

By default, the labels on Django's autogenerated form HTML are created by replacing underscores with spaces and capitalizing the first letter—so the label for the `e-mail` field is `"E-mail"`. (Sound familiar? It's the same simple algorithm that Django's models use to calculate default `verbose_name` values for fields, which we covered in Chapter 5.)

But, as with Django's models, we can customize the label for a given field. Just use `label`, like so:

```
class ContactForm(forms.Form):
    subject = forms.CharField(max_length=100)
    e-mail = forms.EmailField(required=False, label='Your e-mail address')
    message = forms.CharField(widget=forms.Textarea)
```

Customizing Form Design

Our `contact_form.html` template uses `{{ form.as_table }}` to display the form, but we can display the form in other ways to get more granular control over the display.

The quickest way to customize forms' presentation is with CSS. Error lists, in particular, could do with some visual enhancement, and the autogenerated error lists use <ul class= "errorlist"> precisely so that you can target them with CSS. The following CSS really makes our errors stand out:

```
<style type="text/css">
    ul.errorlist {
        margin: 0;
        padding: 0;
    }
    .errorlist li {
        background-color: red;
        color: white;
        display: block;
        font-size: 10px;
        margin: 0 0 3px;
        padding: 4px 5px;
    }
</style>
```

Although it's convenient to have our form's HTML generated for us, in many cases you'll want to override the default rendering. {{ form.as_table }} and friends are useful shortcuts while you develop your application, but everything about the way a form is displayed can be overridden, mostly within the template itself, and you'll likely override the defaults often.

Each field's widget (<input type="text">, <select>, <textarea>, etc.) can be rendered individually by accessing {{ form.fieldname }} in the template, and any errors associated with a field are available as {{ form.fieldname.errors }}. With this in mind, we can construct a custom template for our contact form with the following template code:

```
<html>
<head>
    <title>Contact us</title>
</head>
<body>
    <h1>Contact us</h1>

    {% if form.errors %}
        <p style="color: red;">
            Please correct the error{{ form.errors|pluralize }} below.
        </p>
    {% endif %}

    <form action="" method="post">
        <div class="field">
            {{ form.subject.errors }}
            <label for="id_subject">Subject:</label>
            {{ form.subject }}
        </div>
```

```
        <div class="field">
            {{ form.e-mail.errors }}
            <label for="id_e-mail">Your e-mail address:</label>
            {{ form.e-mail }}
        </div>
        <div class="field">
            {{ form.message.errors }}
            <label for="id_message">Message:</label>
            {{ form.message }}
        </div>
        <input type="submit" value="Submit">
    </form>
</body>
</html>
```

`{{ form.message.errors }}` displays a `<ul class="errorlist">` if errors are present and
a blank string if the field is valid (or the form is unbound). We can also treat `form.message.`
`errors` as a Boolean or even iterate over it as a list. Consider this example:

```
<div class="field{% if form.message.errors %} errors{% endif %}">
    {% if form.message.errors %}
        <ul>
        {% for error in form.message.errors %}
            <li><strong>{{ error }}</strong></li>
        {% endfor %}
        </ul>
    {% endif %}
    <label for="id_message">Message:</label>
    {{ form.message }}
</div>
```

In the case of validation errors, this will add an errors class to the containing `<div>` and
display the list of errors in an unordered list.

What's Next?

This chapter concludes the introductory material in this book—the so-called "core curriculum." The next section of the book, Chapters 8 to 12, goes into more detail about advanced
Django usage, including how to deploy a Django application (Chapter 12).

After these first seven chapters, you should know enough to start writing your own Django
projects. The rest of the material in this book will help fill in the missing pieces. We'll start in
Chapter 8 by doubling back and taking a closer look at views and URLconfs (introduced first in
Chapter 3).

PART 2

■ ■ ■

Advanced Usage

CHAPTER 8

■ ■ ■

Advanced Views and URLconfs

In Chapter 3, we explained the basics of Django view functions and URLconfs. This chapter goes into more detail about advanced functionality in those two pieces of the framework.

URLconf Tricks

There's nothing "special" about URLconfs—like anything else in Django, they're just Python code. You can take advantage of this in several ways, as described in the sections that follow.

Streamlining Function Imports

Consider this URLconf, which builds on the example in Chapter 3:

```
from django.conf.urls.defaults import *
from mysite.views import hello, current_datetime, hours_ahead

urlpatterns = patterns('',
    (r'^hello/$', hello),
    (r'^time/$', current_datetime),
    (r'^time/plus/(\d{1,2})/$', hours_ahead),
)
```

As explained in Chapter 3, each entry in the URLconf includes its associated view function, passed directly as a function object. This means it's necessary to import the view functions at the top of the module.

But as a Django application grows in complexity, its URLconf grows, too, and keeping those imports can be tedious to manage. (For each new view function, you have to remember to import it, and the `import` statement tends to get overly long if you use this approach.) It's possible to avoid that tedium by importing the `views` module itself. This example URLconf is equivalent to the previous one:

```
from django.conf.urls.defaults import *
from mysite import views

urlpatterns = patterns('',
    (r'^hello/$', views.hello),
    (r'^time/$', views.current_datetime),
    (r'^time/plus/(d{1,2})/$', views.hours_ahead),
)
```

Django offers another way of specifying the view function for a particular pattern in the URLconf: you can pass a string containing the module name and function name rather than the function object itself. Continuing the ongoing example:

```
from django.conf.urls.defaults import *

urlpatterns = patterns('',
    (r'^hello/$', 'mysite.views.hello'),
    (r'^time/$', 'mysite.views.current_datetime'),
    (r'^time/plus/(d{1,2})/$', 'mysite.views.hours_ahead'),
)
```

(Note the quotes around the view names. We're using 'mysite.views.current_datetime'—with quotes—instead of mysite.views.current_datetime.)

Using this technique, it's no longer necessary to import the view functions; Django automatically imports the appropriate view function the first time it's needed, according to the string describing the name and path of the view function.

A further shortcut you can take when using the string technique is to factor out a common "view prefix." In our URLconf example, each of the view strings starts with 'mysite.views', which is redundant to type. We can factor out that common prefix and pass it as the first argument to patterns(), like this:

```
from django.conf.urls.defaults import *

urlpatterns = patterns('mysite.views',
    (r'^hello/$', 'hello'),
    (r'^time/$', 'current_datetime'),
    (r'^time/plus/(d{1,2})/$', 'hours_ahead'),
)
```

Note that you don't put a trailing dot (".") in the prefix, nor do you put a leading dot in the view strings. Django puts those in automatically.

With these two approaches in mind, which is better? It really depends on your personal coding style and needs.

Advantages of the string approach are as follows:

- It's more compact, because it doesn't require you to import the view functions.

- It results in more readable and manageable URLconfs if your view functions are spread across several different Python modules.

Advantages of the function object approach are as follows:

- It allows for easy "wrapping" of view functions. See the section "Wrapping View Functions" later in this chapter.

- It's more "Pythonic"—that is, it's more in line with Python traditions, such as passing functions as objects.

Both approaches are valid, and you can even mix them within the same URLconf. The choice is yours.

Using Multiple View Prefixes

In practice, if you use the string technique, you'll probably end up mixing views to the point where the views in your URLconf won't have a common prefix. However, you can still take advantage of the view prefix shortcut to remove duplication. Just add multiple patterns() objects together, like this:

Old:

```
from django.conf.urls.defaults import *

urlpatterns = patterns('',
    (r'^hello/$', 'mysite.views.hello'),
    (r'^time/$', 'mysite.views.current_datetime'),
    (r'^time/plus/(\d{1,2})/$', 'mysite.views.hours_ahead'),
    (r'^tag/(\w+)/$', 'weblog.views.tag'),
)
```

New:

```
from django.conf.urls.defaults import *

urlpatterns = patterns('mysite.views',
    (r'^hello/$', 'hello'),
    (r'^time/$', 'current_datetime'),
    (r'^time/plus/(\d{1,2})/$', 'hours_ahead'),
)

urlpatterns += patterns('weblog.views',
    (r'^tag/(\w+)/$', 'tag'),
)
```

All the framework cares about is that there's a module-level variable called urlpatterns. This variable can be constructed dynamically, as we do in this example. We should specifically point out that the objects returned by patterns() can be added together, which is something you might not have expected.

Special-Casing URLs in Debug Mode

Speaking of constructing urlpatterns dynamically, you might want to take advantage of this technique to alter your URLconf's behavior while in Django's debug mode. To do this, just check the value of the DEBUG setting at runtime, like so:

```
from django.conf import settings
from django.conf.urls.defaults import *
from mysite import views

urlpatterns = patterns('',
    (r'^$', views.homepage),
    (r'^(\d{4})/([a-z]{3})/$', views.archive_month),
)

if settings.DEBUG:
    urlpatterns += patterns('',
        (r'^debuginfo/$', views.debug),
    )
```

In this example, the URL /debuginfo/ will be available only if your DEBUG setting is set to True.

Using Named Groups

In all of our URLconf examples so far, we've used simple, *non-named* regular expression groups—that is, we put parentheses around parts of the URL we wanted to capture, and Django passes that captured text to the view function as a positional argument. In more advanced usage, it's possible to use *named* regular expression groups to capture URL bits and pass them as *keyword* arguments to a view.

KEYWORD ARGUMENTS VS. POSITIONAL ARGUMENTS

A Python function can be called using keyword arguments or positional arguments—and, in some cases, both at the same time. In a keyword argument call, you specify the names of the arguments along with the values you're passing. In a positional argument call, you simply pass the arguments without explicitly specifying which argument matches which value; the association is implicit in the arguments' order.

For example, consider this simple function:

```
def sell(item, price, quantity):
    print "Selling %s unit(s) of %s at %s" % (quantity, item, price)
```

To call it with positional arguments, you specify the arguments in the order in which they're listed in the function definition:

```
sell('Socks', '$2.50', 6)
```

To call it with keyword arguments, you specify the names of the arguments along with the values. The following statements are equivalent:

```
sell(item='Socks', price='$2.50', quantity=6)
sell(item='Socks', quantity=6, price='$2.50')
sell(price='$2.50', item='Socks', quantity=6)
sell(price='$2.50', quantity=6, item='Socks')
sell(quantity=6, item='Socks', price='$2.50')
sell(quantity=6, price='$2.50', item='Socks')
```

Finally, you can mix keyword and positional arguments, as long as all positional arguments are listed before keyword arguments. The following statements are equivalent to the previous examples:

```
sell('Socks', '$2.50', quantity=6)
sell('Socks', price='$2.50', quantity=6)
sell('Socks', quantity=6, price='$2.50')
```

In Python regular expressions, the syntax for named regular expression groups is (?P<name>pattern), where name is the name of the group and pattern is some pattern to match.

Here's an example URLconf that uses non-named groups:

```
from django.conf.urls.defaults import *
from mysite import views

urlpatterns = patterns('',
    (r'^articles/(\d{4})/$', views.year_archive),
    (r'^articles/(\d{4})/(\d{2})/$', views.month_archive),
)
```

Here's the same URLconf, rewritten to use named groups:

```
from django.conf.urls.defaults import *
from mysite import views

urlpatterns = patterns('',
    (r'^articles/(?P<year>\d{4})/$', views.year_archive),
    (r'^articles/(?P<year>\d{4})/(?P<month>\d{2})/$', views.month_archive),
)
```

This accomplishes exactly the same thing as the previous example, with one subtle difference: the captured values are passed to view functions as keyword arguments rather than positional arguments.

For example, with non-named groups, a request to /articles/2006/03/ would result in a function call equivalent to this:

```
month_archive(request, '2006', '03')
```

With named groups, though, the same request would result in this function call:

```
month_archive(request, year='2006', month='03')
```

In practice, using named groups makes your URLconfs slightly more explicit and less prone to argument-order bugs—and you can reorder the arguments in your views' function definitions. Following the preceding example, if we wanted to change the URLs to include the month *before* the year, and we were using non-named groups, we'd have to remember to change the order of arguments in the month_archive view. If we were using named groups, changing the order of the captured parameters in the URL would have no effect on the view.

Of course, the benefits of named groups come at the cost of brevity; some developers find the named-group syntax ugly and too verbose. Still, another advantage of named groups is readability, especially by those who aren't intimately familiar with regular expressions or your particular Django application. It's easier to see what's happening, at a glance, in a URLconf that uses named groups.

Understanding the Matching/Grouping Algorithm

A caveat with using named groups in a URLconf is that a single URLconf pattern cannot contain both named and non-named groups. If you do this, Django won't throw any errors, but you'll probably find that your URLs aren't matching as you expect. Specifically, here's the algorithm the URLconf parser follows, with respect to named groups vs. non-named groups in a regular expression:

- If there are any named arguments, it will use those, ignoring non-named arguments.

- Otherwise, it will pass all non-named arguments as positional arguments.

- In both cases, it will pass any extra options as keyword arguments. See the next section for more information.

Passing Extra Options to View Functions

Sometimes you'll find yourself writing view functions that are quite similar, with only a few small differences. For example, say you have two views whose contents are identical except for the templates they use:

```
# urls.py

from django.conf.urls.defaults import *
from mysite import views

urlpatterns = patterns('',
    (r'^foo/$', views.foo_view),
    (r'^bar/$', views.bar_view),
)

# views.py

from django.shortcuts import render_to_response
from mysite.models import MyModel
```

```python
def foo_view(request):
    m_list = MyModel.objects.filter(is_new=True)
    return render_to_response('template1.html', {'m_list': m_list})

def bar_view(request):
    m_list = MyModel.objects.filter(is_new=True)
    return render_to_response('template2.html', {'m_list': m_list})
```

We're repeating ourselves in this code, and that's inelegant. At first, you may think to remove the redundancy by using the same view for both URLs, putting parentheses around the URL to capture it, and checking the URL within the view to determine the template, like so:

```python
# urls.py

from django.conf.urls.defaults import *
from mysite import views

urlpatterns = patterns('',
    (r'^(foo)/$', views.foobar_view),
    (r'^(bar)/$', views.foobar_view),
)
```

```python
# views.py

from django.shortcuts import render_to_response
from mysite.models import MyModel

def foobar_view(request, url):
    m_list = MyModel.objects.filter(is_new=True)
    if url == 'foo':
        template_name = 'template1.html'
    elif url == 'bar':
        template_name = 'template2.html'
    return render_to_response(template_name, {'m_list': m_list})
```

The problem with that solution, though, is that it couples your URLs to your code. If you decide to rename /foo/ to /fooey/, you'll have to remember to change the view code.

The elegant solution involves an optional URLconf parameter. Each pattern in a URLconf may include a third item: a dictionary of keyword arguments to pass to the view function.

With this in mind, we can rewrite our ongoing example like this:

```python
# urls.py

from django.conf.urls.defaults import *
from mysite import views

urlpatterns = patterns('',
    (r'^foo/$', views.foobar_view, {'template_name': 'template1.html'}),
    (r'^bar/$', views.foobar_view, {'template_name': 'template2.html'}),
)
```

```
# views.py

from django.shortcuts import render_to_response
from mysite.models import MyModel

def foobar_view(request, template_name):
    m_list = MyModel.objects.filter(is_new=True)
    return render_to_response(template_name, {'m_list': m_list})
```

As you can see, the URLconf in this example specifies `template_name` in the URLconf. The view function treats it as just another parameter.

This extra URLconf options technique is a nice way of sending additional information to your view functions with minimal fuss. As such, it's used by a couple of Django's bundled applications, most notably its generic views system, which we cover in Chapter 11.

The following sections contain a couple of ideas on how you can use the extra URLconf options technique in your own projects.

Faking Captured URLconf Values

Say you have a set of views that match a pattern, along with another URL that doesn't fit the pattern but whose view logic is the same. In this case, you can "fake" the capturing of URL values by using extra URLconf options to handle that extra URL with the same view.

For example, you might have an application that displays some data for a particular day, with URLs such as these:

```
/mydata/jan/01/
/mydata/jan/02/
/mydata/jan/03/
# ...
/mydata/dec/30/
/mydata/dec/31/
```

This is simple enough to deal with—you can capture those in a URLconf like this (using named group syntax):

```
urlpatterns = patterns('',
    (r'^mydata/(?P<month>\w{3})/(?P<day>\d\d)/$', views.my_view),
)
```

And the view function signature would look like this:

```
def my_view(request, month, day):
    # ....
```

This approach is straightforward—it's nothing you haven't seen before. The trick comes in when you want to add another URL that uses `my_view` but whose URL doesn't include a `month` and/or `day`.

For example, you might want to add another URL, `/mydata/birthday/`, which would be equivalent to `/mydata/jan/06/`. You can take advantage of extra URLconf options like so:

```
urlpatterns = patterns('',
    (r'^mydata/birthday/$', views.my_view, {'month': 'jan', 'day': '06'}),
    (r'^mydata/(?P<month>\w{3})/(?P<day>\d\d)/$', views.my_view),
)
```

The cool thing here is that you don't have to change your view function at all. The view function only cares that it *gets* month and day parameters—it doesn't matter whether they come from the URL capturing itself or extra parameters.

Making a View Generic

It's good programming practice to "factor out" commonalities in code. For example, with these two Python functions:

```
def say_hello(person_name):
    print 'Hello, %s' % person_name

def say_goodbye(person_name):
    print 'Goodbye, %s' % person_name
```

we can factor out the greeting to make it a parameter:

```
def greet(person_name, greeting):
    print '%s, %s' % (greeting, person_name)
```

You can apply this same philosophy to your Django views by using extra URLconf parameters.

With this in mind, you can start making higher-level abstractions of your views. Instead of thinking to yourself, "This view displays a list of Event objects," and "That view displays a list of BlogEntry objects," realize they're both specific cases of "A view that displays a list of objects, where the type of object is variable."

Take this code, for example:

```
# urls.py

from django.conf.urls.defaults import *
from mysite import views

urlpatterns = patterns('',
    (r'^events/$', views.event_list),
    (r'^blog/entries/$', views.entry_list),
)

# views.py

from django.shortcuts import render_to_response
from mysite.models import Event, BlogEntry

def event_list(request):
    obj_list = Event.objects.all()
    return render_to_response('mysite/event_list.html', {'event_list': obj_list})
```

```
def entry_list(request):
    obj_list = BlogEntry.objects.all()
    return render_to_response('mysite/blogentry_list.html',
        {'entry_list': obj_list})
```

The two views do essentially the same thing: they display a list of objects. So let's factor out the type of object they're displaying:

```
# urls.py

from django.conf.urls.defaults import *
from mysite import models, views

urlpatterns = patterns('',
    (r'^events/$', views.object_list, {'model': models.Event}),
    (r'^blog/entries/$', views.object_list, {'model': models.BlogEntry}),
)
```

```
# views.py

from django.shortcuts import render_to_response

def object_list(request, model):
    obj_list = model.objects.all()
    template_name = 'mysite/%s_list.html' % model.__name__.lower()
    return render_to_response(template_name, {'object_list': obj_list})
```

With those small changes, we suddenly have a reusable, model-agnostic view! From now on, anytime we need a view that lists a set of objects, we can simply reuse this object_list view rather than writing view code. Here are a couple of notes about what we did:

- We passed the model classes directly, as the model parameter. The dictionary of extra URLconf options can pass any type of Python object—not just strings.

- The model.objects.all() line is an example of *duck typing*: "If it walks like a duck and talks like a duck, we can treat it like a duck." Note the code doesn't know what type of object model is; the only requirement is that model have an objects attribute, which in turn has an all() method.

- We used model.__name__.lower() in determining the template name. Every Python class has a __name__ attribute that returns the class name. This feature is useful at times like this, when we don't know the type of class until runtime. For example, the BlogEntry class's __name__ is the string 'BlogEntry'.

- In a slight difference between this example and the previous example, we passed the generic variable name object_list to the template. We could easily change this variable name to be blogentry_list or event_list, but we've left that as an exercise for the reader.

Because database-driven Web sites have several common patterns, Django comes with a set of "generic views" that use this exact technique to save you time. We cover Django's built-in generic views in Chapter 11.

Giving a View Configuration Options

If you're distributing a Django application, chances are that your users will want some degree of configuration. In this case, it's a good idea to add hooks to your views for any configuration options you think people may want to change. You can use extra URLconf parameters for this purpose.

A common bit of an application to make configurable is the template name:

```
def my_view(request, template_name):
    var = do_something()
    return render_to_response(template_name, {'var': var})
```

Understanding Precedence of Captured Values vs. Extra Options

When there's a conflict, extra URLconf parameters get precedence over captured parameters. In other words, if your URLconf captures a named-group variable and an extra URLconf parameter includes a variable with the same name, the extra URLconf parameter value will be used.

For example, consider this URLconf:

```
from django.conf.urls.defaults import *
from mysite import views

urlpatterns = patterns('',
    (r'^mydata/(?P<id>\d+)/$', views.my_view, {'id': 3}),
)
```

Here, both the regular expression and the extra dictionary include an id. The hard-coded id gets precedence. That means any request (e.g., /mydata/2/ or /mydata/432432/) will be treated as if id is set to 3, regardless of the value captured in the URL.

Astute readers will note that in this case, it's a waste of time and typing to capture the id in the regular expression, because its value will always be overridden by the dictionary's value. That's correct; we bring this up only to help you avoid making the mistake.

Using Default View Arguments

Another convenient trick is to specify default parameters for a view's arguments. This tells the view which value to use for a parameter by default if none is specified.

Here's an example:

```
# urls.py

from django.conf.urls.defaults import *
from mysite import views
```

```
urlpatterns = patterns('',
    (r'^blog/$', views.page),
    (r'^blog/page(?P<num>\d+)/$', views.page),
)
```

```
# views.py
```

```
def page(request, num='1'):
    # Output the appropriate page of blog entries, according to num.
    # ...
```

Here, both URLpatterns point to the same view—views.page—but the first pattern doesn't capture anything from the URL. If the first pattern matches, the page() function will use its default argument for num, '1'. If the second pattern matches, page() will use whatever num value was captured by the regular expression.

■**Note** We've been careful to set the default argument's value to the *string* '1', not the integer 1. That's for consistency because any captured value for num will always be a string.

It's common to use this technique in conjunction with configuration options, as explained earlier. This example makes a slight improvement to the example in the "Giving a View Configuration Options" section by providing a default value for template_name:

```
def my_view(request, template_name='mysite/my_view.html'):
    var = do_something()
    return render_to_response(template_name, {'var': var})
```

Special-Casing Views

Sometimes you'll have a pattern in your URLconf that handles a large set of URLs, but you'll need to special-case one of them. In this case, take advantage of the linear way a URLconf is processed and put the special case first.

For example, you can think of the "add an object" pages in Django's admin site as represented by a URLpattern like this:

```
urlpatterns = patterns('',
    # ...
    ('^([^/]+)/([^/]+)/add/$', views.add_stage),
    # ...
)
```

This matches URLs such as /myblog/entries/add/ and /auth/groups/add/. However, the "add" page for a user object (/auth/user/add/) is a special case—it doesn't display all of the form fields, it displays two password fields, and so forth. We *could* solve this problem by special-casing in the view, like so:

```
def add_stage(request, app_label, model_name):
    if app_label == 'auth' and model_name == 'user':
        # do special-case code
    else:
        # do normal code
```

but that's inelegant for a reason we've touched on multiple times in this chapter: it puts URL logic in the view. As a more elegant solution, we can take advantage of the fact that URLconfs are processed in order from top to bottom:

```
urlpatterns = patterns('',
    # ...
    ('^auth/user/add/$', views.user_add_stage),
    ('^([^/]+)/([^/]+)/add/$', views.add_stage),
    # ...
)
```

With this in place, a request to /auth/user/add/ will be handled by the user_add_stage view. Although that URL matches the second pattern, it matches the top one first. (This is short-circuit logic.)

Capturing Text in URLs

Each captured argument is sent to the view as a plain Python Unicode string, regardless of what sort of match the regular expression makes. For example, in this URLconf line, the year argument to views.year_archive() will be a string, not an integer, even though \d{4} will only match integer strings:

```
(r'^articles/(?P<year>\d{4})/$', views.year_archive),
```

This is important to keep in mind when you're writing view code. Many built-in Python functions are fussy (and rightfully so) about accepting only objects of a certain type. A common error is to attempt to create a datetime.date object with string values instead of integer values:

```
>>> import datetime
>>> datetime.date('1993', '7', '9')
Traceback (most recent call last):
    ...
TypeError: an integer is required
>>> datetime.date(1993, 7, 9)
datetime.date(1993, 7, 9)
```

Translated to a URLconf and view, the error looks like this:

```
# urls.py

from django.conf.urls.defaults import *
from mysite import views
```

```
urlpatterns = patterns('',
    (r'^articles/(\d{4})/(\d{2})/(\d{2})/$', views.day_archive),
)
```

```
# views.py
```

```
import datetime
```

```
def day_archive(request, year, month, day):
    # The following statement raises a TypeError!
    date = datetime.date(year, month, day)
```

Instead, `day_archive()` can be written correctly like this:

```
def day_archive(request, year, month, day):
    date = datetime.date(int(year), int(month), int(day))
```

Note that `int()` itself raises a `ValueError` when you pass it a string that is not composed solely of digits, but we're avoiding that error in this case because the regular expression in our URLconf has ensured that only strings containing digits are passed to the view function.

Determining What the URLconf Searches Against

When a request comes in, Django tries to match the URLconf patterns against the requested URL, as a Python string. This does not include `GET` or `POST` parameters, or the domain name. It also does not include the leading slash, because every URL has a leading slash.

For example, in a request to `http://www.example.com/myapp/`, Django will try to match `myapp/`. In a request to `http://www.example.com/myapp/?page=3`, Django will try to match `myapp/`.

The request method (e.g., `POST`, `GET`) is *not* taken into account when traversing the URLconf. In other words, all request methods will be routed to the same function for the same URL. It's the responsibility of a view function to perform branching based on the request method.

Higher-Level Abstractions of View Functions

And speaking of branching based on the request method, let's take a look at how we might build a nice way of doing that. Consider this URLconf/view layout:

```
# urls.py
```

```
from django.conf.urls.defaults import *
from mysite import views
```

```
urlpatterns = patterns('',
    # ...
    (r'^somepage/$', views.some_page),
    # ...
)
```

```
# views.py
```

```
from django.http import Http404, HttpResponseRedirect
from django.shortcuts import render_to_response

def some_page(request):
    if request.method == 'POST':
        do_something_for_post()
        return HttpResponseRedirect('/someurl/')
    elif request.method == 'GET':
        do_something_for_get()
        return render_to_response('page.html')
    else:
        raise Http404()
```

In this example, the some_page() view's handling of POST vs. GET requests is quite different. The only thing they have in common is a shared URL: /somepage/. As such, it's kind of inelegant to deal with both POST and GET in the same view function. It would be nice if we could have two separate view functions—one handling GET requests and the other handling POST—and ensuring that each one was called only when appropriate.

We can do that by writing a view function that delegates to other views, either before or after executing some custom logic. Here's an example of how this technique could help simplify our some_page() view:

```
# views.py

from django.http import Http404, HttpResponseRedirect
from django.shortcuts import render_to_response

def method_splitter(request, GET=None, POST=None):
    if request.method == 'GET' and GET is not None:
        return GET(request)
    elif request.method == 'POST' and POST is not None:
        return POST(request)
    raise Http404

def some_page_get(request):
    assert request.method == 'GET'
    do_something_for_get()
    return render_to_response('page.html')

def some_page_post(request):
    assert request.method == 'POST'
    do_something_for_post()
    return HttpResponseRedirect('/someurl/')

# urls.py

from django.conf.urls.defaults import *
from mysite import views
```

```
urlpatterns = patterns('',
    # ...
    (r'^somepage/$', views.method_splitter,
        {'GET': views.some_page_get, 'POST': views.some_page_post}),
    # ...
)
```

Let's go through what this does:

- We wrote a new view, `method_splitter()`, that delegates to other views based on
  `request.method`. It looks for two keyword arguments, `GET` and `POST`, which should be
  view functions. If `request.method` is `'GET'`, it calls the `GET` view. If `request.method` is
  `'POST'`, it calls the `POST` view. If `request.method` is something else (`HEAD`, and so on), or if
  `GET` or `POST` were not supplied to the function, it raises an `Http404`.

- In the URLconf, we point `/somepage/` at `method_splitter()` and pass it extra arguments—
  the view functions to use for `GET` and `POST`, respectively.

- Finally, we split the `some_page()` view into two view functions: `some_page_get()` and
  `some_page_post()`. This is much nicer than shoving all that logic into a single view.

■Note These view functions technically no longer have to check `request.method` because `method_splitter()` does that. (By the time `some_page_post()` is called, for example, we can be confident that `request.method` is `'POST'`.) Still, just to be safe, and also to serve as documentation, we stuck in an `assert`, ensuring that `request.method` is what we expect it to be.

Now we have a nice generic view function that encapsulates the logic of delegating a view
by `request.method`. Nothing about `method_splitter()` is tied to our specific application, of
course, so we can reuse it in other projects.

But there's one way to improve on `method_splitter()`. As it's written, it assumes that the
`GET` and `POST` views take no arguments other than `request`. What if we wanted to use `method_splitter()` with views that, for example, capture text from URLs or take optional keyword
arguments?

To do that, we can use a nice Python feature: variable arguments with asterisks. We'll
show the example first and then explain it:

```
def method_splitter(request, *args, **kwargs):
    get_view = kwargs.pop('GET', None)
    post_view = kwargs.pop('POST', None)
    if request.method == 'GET' and get_view is not None:
        return get_view(request, *args, **kwargs)
    elif request.method == 'POST' and post_view is not None:
        return post_view(request, *args, **kwargs)
    raise Http404
```

Here, we refactored `method_splitter()` to remove the `GET` and `POST` keyword arguments in favor of `*args` and `**kwargs` (note the asterisks). This is a Python feature that allows a function to accept a dynamic arbitrary number of arguments whose names aren't known until runtime. If you put a single asterisk in front of a parameter in a function definition, any *positional* arguments to that function will be rolled up into a single tuple. If you put two asterisks in front of a parameter in a function definition, any *keyword* arguments to that function will be rolled up into a single dictionary.

For example, note this function:

```
def foo(*args, **kwargs):
    print "Positional arguments are:"
    print args
    print "Keyword arguments are:"
    print kwargs
```

Here's how it would work:

```
>>> foo(1, 2, 3)
Positional arguments are:
(1, 2, 3)
Keyword arguments are:
{}
>>> foo(1, 2, name='Adrian', framework='Django')
Positional arguments are:
(1, 2)
Keyword arguments are:
{'framework': 'Django', 'name': 'Adrian'}
```

Bringing this back to `method_splitter()`, you can see we're using `*args` and `**kwargs` to accept *any* arguments to the function and pass them along to the appropriate view. But before we do that, we make two calls to `kwargs.pop()` to get the `GET` and `POST` arguments, if they're available. (We're using `pop()` with a default value of `None` to avoid `KeyError` if one or the other isn't defined.)

Wrapping View Functions

Our final view trick takes advantage of an advanced Python technique. Suppose that you find yourself repeating a bunch of code throughout various views, as in this example:

```
def my_view1(request):
    if not request.user.is_authenticated():
        return HttpResponseRedirect('/accounts/login/')
    # ...
    return render_to_response('template1.html')

def my_view2(request):
    if not request.user.is_authenticated():
        return HttpResponseRedirect('/accounts/login/')
    # ...
    return render_to_response('template2.html')
```

```
def my_view3(request):
    if not request.user.is_authenticated():
        return HttpResponseRedirect('/accounts/login/')
    # ...
    return render_to_response('template3.html')
```

Here, each view starts by checking that `request.user` is authenticated—that is, the current user has successfully logged into the site—and redirects to `/accounts/login/` if not.

■**Note** We haven't yet covered `request.user`—Chapter 14 does—but `request.user` represents the current user, either logged-in or anonymous.

It would be nice if we could remove that bit of repetitive code from each of these views and just mark them as requiring authentication. We can do that by making a view wrapper. Take a moment to study this:

```
def requires_login(view):
    def new_view(request, *args, **kwargs):
        if not request.user.is_authenticated():
            return HttpResponseRedirect('/accounts/login/')
        return view(request, *args, **kwargs)
    return new_view
```

This function, `requires_login`, takes a view function (`view`) and returns a new view function (`new_view`). The new function, `new_view`, is defined *within* `requires_login` and handles the logic of checking `request.user.is_authenticated()` and delegating to the original view (`view`).

Now, we can remove the `if not request.user.is_authenticated()` checks from our views and simply wrap them with `requires_login` in our URLconf:

```
from django.conf.urls.defaults import *
from mysite.views import requires_login, my_view1, my_view2, my_view3

urlpatterns = patterns('',
    (r'^view1/$', requires_login(my_view1)),
    (r'^view2/$', requires_login(my_view2)),
    (r'^view3/$', requires_login(my_view3)),
)
```

This has the same effect as before, but with less code redundancy. Now we've created a nice generic function—`requires_login()` that we can wrap around any view in order to make it require a login.

Including Other URLconfs

If you intend your code to be used on multiple Django-based sites, you should consider arranging your URLconfs in such a way that allows for "including."

At any point, your URLconf can "include" other URLconf modules. This essentially "roots" a set of URLs below other ones. For example, this URLconf includes other URLconfs:

```
from django.conf.urls.defaults import *

urlpatterns = patterns('',
    (r'^weblog/', include('mysite.blog.urls')),
    (r'^photos/', include('mysite.photos.urls')),
    (r'^about/$', 'mysite.views.about'),
)
```

You saw this before in Chapter 6, when we introduced the Django admin site. The admin site has its own URLconf that you merely include() within yours.

There's an important gotcha here: the regular expressions in this example that point to an include() do *not* have a $ (end-of-string match character) but *do* include a trailing slash. Whenever Django encounters include(), it chops off whatever part of the URL matched up to that point and sends the remaining string to the included URLconf for further processing.

Continuing this example, here's the URLconf mysite.blog.urls:

```
from django.conf.urls.defaults import *

urlpatterns = patterns('',
    (r'^(\d\d\d\d)/$', 'mysite.blog.views.year_detail'),
    (r'^(\d\d\d\d)/(\d\d)/$', 'mysite.blog.views.month_detail'),
)
```

With these two URLconfs, here's how a few sample requests would be handled:

- /weblog/2007/: In the first URLconf, the pattern r'^weblog/' matches. Because it is an include(), Django strips all the matching text, which is 'weblog/' in this case. The remaining part of the URL is 2007/, which matches the first line in the mysite.blog.urls URLconf.

- /weblog//2007/ (with two slashes): In the first URLconf, the pattern r'^weblog/' matches. Because it is an include(), Django strips all the matching text, which is 'weblog/' in this case. The remaining part of the URL is /2007/ (with a leading slash), which does not match any of the lines in the mysite.blog.urls URLconf.

- /about/: This matches the view mysite.views.about in the first URLconf, demonstrating that you can mix include() patterns with non-include() patterns.

How Captured Parameters Work with include()

An included URLconf receives any captured parameters from parent URLconfs, for example:

```
# root urls.py

from django.conf.urls.defaults import *

urlpatterns = patterns('',
    (r'^(?P<username>\w+)/blog/', include('foo.urls.blog')),
)
```

```
# foo/urls/blog.py

from django.conf.urls.defaults import *

urlpatterns = patterns('',
    (r'^$', 'foo.views.blog_index'),
    (r'^archive/$', 'foo.views.blog_archive'),
)
```

In this example, the captured `username` variable is passed to the included URLconf and, hence, to *every* view function within that URLconf.

Note that the captured parameters will *always* be passed to *every* line in the included URLconf, regardless of whether the line's view actually accepts those parameters as valid. For this reason, this technique is useful only if you're certain that every view in the included URLconf accepts the parameters you're passing.

How Extra URLconf Options Work with include()

Similarly, you can pass extra URLconf options to `include()`, just as you can pass extra URLconf options to a normal view—as a dictionary. When you do this, *each* line in the included URLconf will be passed the extra options.

For example, the following two URLconf sets are functionally identical.

Set one:

```
# urls.py

from django.conf.urls.defaults import *

urlpatterns = patterns('',
    (r'^blog/', include('inner'), {'blogid': 3}),
)


# inner.py

from django.conf.urls.defaults import *

urlpatterns = patterns('',
    (r'^archive/$', 'mysite.views.archive'),
    (r'^about/$', 'mysite.views.about'),
    (r'^rss/$', 'mysite.views.rss'),
)
```

Set two:

```
# urls.py

from django.conf.urls.defaults import *
```

```
urlpatterns = patterns('',
    (r'^blog/', include('inner')),
)

# inner.py

from django.conf.urls.defaults import *

urlpatterns = patterns('',
    (r'^archive/$', 'mysite.views.archive', {'blogid': 3}),
    (r'^about/$', 'mysite.views.about', {'blogid': 3}),
    (r'^rss/$', 'mysite.views.rss', {'blogid': 3}),
)
```

As is the case with captured parameters (explained in the previous section), extra options will *always* be passed to *every* line in the included URLconf, regardless of whether the line's view actually accepts those options as valid. For this reason, this technique is useful only if you're certain that every view in the included URLconf accepts the extra options you're passing.

What's Next?

This chapter provided many advanced tips and tricks for views and URLconfs. In Chapter 9, we'll give this advanced treatment to Django's template system.

CHAPTER 9

■■■

Advanced Templates

Although most of your interactions with Django's template language will be in the role of template author, you may want to customize and extend the template engine—either to make it do something it doesn't already do, or to make your job easier in some other way.

This chapter delves deep into the guts of Django's template system. It covers what you need to know if you plan to extend the system or if you're just curious about how it works. It also covers the autoescaping feature, a security measure you'll no doubt notice over time as you continue to use Django.

If you're looking to use the Django template system as part of another application (i.e., without the rest of the framework), make sure to read the "Configuring the Template System in Standalone Mode" section later in the chapter.

Template Language Review

First, let's quickly review a number of terms introduced in Chapter 4:

- A *template* is a text document, or a normal Python string, that is marked up using the Django template language. A template can contain template tags and variables.

- A *template tag* is a symbol within a template that does something. This definition is deliberately vague. For example, a template tag can produce content, serve as a control structure (an `if` statement or a `for` loop), grab content from a database, or enable access to other template tags.

  Template tags are surrounded by {% and %}:

```
{% if is_logged_in %}
    Thanks for logging in!
{% else %}
    Please log in.
{% endif %}
```

- A *variable* is a symbol within a template that outputs a value.

  Variable tags are surrounded by {{ and }}:

  ```
  My first name is {{ first_name }}. My last name is {{ last_name }}.
  ```

- A *context* is a name-value mapping (similar to a Python dictionary) that is passed to a template.

- A template *renders* a context by replacing the variable "holes" with values from the context and executing all template tags.

For more details about the basics of these terms, refer back to Chapter 4.

The rest of this chapter discusses ways of extending the template engine. First, though, let's take a quick look at a few internals left out of Chapter 4 for simplicity.

RequestContext and Context Processors

When rendering a template, you need a context. Usually this is an instance of django.template. Context, but Django also comes with a special subclass, django.template.RequestContext, that acts slightly differently. RequestContext adds a bunch of variables to your template context by default—things like the HttpRequest object or information about the currently logged-in user.

Use RequestContext when you don't want to have to specify the same set of variables in a series of templates. For example, consider these two views:

```python
from django.template import loader, Context

def view_1(request):
    # ...
    t = loader.get_template('template1.html')
    c = Context({
        'app': 'My app',
        'user': request.user,
        'ip_address': request.META['REMOTE_ADDR'],
        'message': 'I am view 1.'
    })
    return t.render(c)

def view_2(request):
    # ...
    t = loader.get_template('template2.html')
    c = Context({
        'app': 'My app',
        'user': request.user,
        'ip_address': request.META['REMOTE_ADDR'],
        'message': 'I am the second view.'
    })
    return t.render(c)
```

(Note that we're deliberately *not* using the render_to_response() shortcut in these examples—we're manually loading the templates, constructing the context objects, and rendering the templates. We're "spelling out" all of the steps for the purpose of clarity.)

Each view passes the same three variables—app, user, and ip_address—to its template. Wouldn't it be nice if we could remove that redundancy?

RequestContext and *context processors* were created to solve this problem. Context processors let you specify a number of variables that get set in each context automatically—without you having to specify the variables in each render_to_response() call. The catch is that you have to use RequestContext instead of Context when you render a template.

The most low-level way of using context processors is to create some processors and pass them to RequestContext. Here's how the preceding example could be written with context processors:

```
from django.template import loader, RequestContext

def custom_proc(request):
    "A context processor that provides 'app', 'user' and 'ip_address'."
    return {
        'app': 'My app',
        'user': request.user,
        'ip_address': request.META['REMOTE_ADDR']
    }

def view_1(request):
    # ...
    t = loader.get_template('template1.html')
    c = RequestContext(request, {'message': 'I am view 1.'},
            processors=[custom_proc])
    return t.render(c)

def view_2(request):
    # ...
    t = loader.get_template('template2.html')
    c = RequestContext(request, {'message': 'I am the second view.'},
            processors=[custom_proc])
    return t.render(c)
```

Let's step through this code:

- First, we define a function custom_proc. This is a context processor—it takes an HttpRequest object and returns a dictionary of variables to use in the template context. That's all it does.

- We've changed the two view functions to use RequestContext instead of Context. There are two differences in how the context is constructed. First, RequestContext requires the first argument to be an HttpRequest object—the one that was passed into the view function in the first place (request). Second, RequestContext takes an optional processors argument, which is a list or tuple of context processor functions to use. Here, we pass in custom_proc, the custom processor we defined earlier.

- Each view no longer has to include app, user, or ip_address in its context construction, because those are provided by custom_proc.

- Each view *still* has the flexibility to introduce any custom template variables it might need. In this example, the message template variable is set differently in each view.

In Chapter 4, we introduced the render_to_response() shortcut, which saves you from having to call loader.get_template(), then create a Context, then call the render() method on the template. In order to demonstrate the lower-level workings of context processors, the previous examples didn't use render_to_response(). But it's possible—and preferable—to use context processors with render_to_response(). Do this with the context_instance argument, like so:

```
from django.shortcuts import render_to_response
from django.template import RequestContext

def custom_proc(request):
    "A context processor that provides 'app', 'user' and 'ip_address'."
    return {
        'app': 'My app',
        'user': request.user,
        'ip_address': request.META['REMOTE_ADDR']
    }

def view_1(request):
    # ...
    return render_to_response('template1.html',
        {'message': 'I am view 1.'},
        context_instance=RequestContext(request, processors=[custom_proc]))

def view_2(request):
    # ...
    return render_to_response('template2.html',
        {'message': 'I am the second view.'},
        context_instance=RequestContext(request, processors=[custom_proc]))
```

Here, we've trimmed down each view's template-rendering code to a single (wrapped) line.

This is an improvement, but, evaluating the conciseness of this code, we have to admit we're now almost overdosing on the *other* end of the spectrum. We've removed redundancy in data (our template variables) at the cost of adding redundancy in code (in the processors call). Using context processors doesn't save you much typing if you have to type processors all the time.

For that reason, Django provides support for *global* context processors. The TEMPLATE_ CONTEXT_PROCESSORS setting (in your settings.py) designates which context processors should *always* be applied to RequestContext. This removes the need to specify processors each time you use RequestContext.

By default, `TEMPLATE_CONTEXT_PROCESSORS` is set to the following:

```
TEMPLATE_CONTEXT_PROCESSORS = (
    'django.core.context_processors.auth',
    'django.core.context_processors.debug',
    'django.core.context_processors.i18n',
    'django.core.context_processors.media',
)
```

This setting is a tuple of callables that use the same interface as the preceding `custom_proc` function—functions that take a request object as their argument and return a dictionary of items to be merged into the context. Note that the values in `TEMPLATE_CONTEXT_PROCESSORS` are specified as *strings*, which means the processors are required to be somewhere on your Python path (so you can refer to them from the setting).

Each processor is applied in order. That is, if one processor adds a variable to the context and a second processor adds a variable with the same name, the second will override the first.

Django provides a number of simple context processors, including the ones that are enabled by default.

django.core.context_processors.auth

If `TEMPLATE_CONTEXT_PROCESSORS` contains this processor, every `RequestContext` will contain these variables:

- `user`: A `django.contrib.auth.models.User` instance representing the current logged-in user (or an `AnonymousUser` instance, if the client isn't logged in).

- `messages`: A list of messages (as strings) for the current logged-in user. Behind the scenes, this variable calls `request.user.get_and_delete_messages()` for every request. That method collects the user's messages and deletes them from the database.

- `perms`: An instance of `django.core.context_processors.PermWrapper`, which represents the permissions the current logged-in user has.

See Chapter 14 for more information on users, permissions, and messages.

django.core.context_processors.debug

This processor pushes debugging information down to the template layer. If `TEMPLATE_CONTEXT_PROCESSORS` contains this processor, every `RequestContext` will contain these variables:

- `debug`: The value of your `DEBUG` setting (either `True` or `False`). You can use this variable in templates to test whether you're in debug mode.

- `sql_queries`: A list of `{'sql': ..., 'time': ...}` dictionaries representing every SQL query that has happened so far during the request and how long it took. The list is in the order in which the queries were issued.

Because debugging information is sensitive, this context processor will add variables to the context only if both of the following conditions are true:

- The DEBUG setting is True.

- The request came from an IP address in the INTERNAL_IPS setting.

Astute readers will notice that the debug template variable will never have the value False because if DEBUG is False, the debug template variable won't be populated in the first place.

django.core.context_processors.i18n

If this processor is enabled, every RequestContext will contain these variables:

- LANGUAGES: The value of the LANGUAGES setting.

- LANGUAGE_CODE: request.LANGUAGE_CODE if it exists; otherwise, the value of the LANGUAGE_CODE setting.

Appendix D provides more information about these two settings.

django.core.context_processors.request

If this processor is enabled, every RequestContext will contain a variable request, which is the current HttpRequest object. Note that this processor is not enabled by default; you have to activate it.

You might want to use this if you find your templates needing to access attributes of the current HttpRequest such as the IP address:

```
{{ request.REMOTE_ADDR }}
```

Guidelines for Writing Your Own Context Processors

Here are a few tips for rolling your own:

- Make each context processor responsible for the smallest subset of functionality possible. It's easy to use multiple processors, so you might as well split functionality into logical pieces for future reuse.

- Keep in mind that any context processor in TEMPLATE_CONTEXT_PROCESSORS will be available in *every* template powered by that settings file, so try to pick variable names that are unlikely to conflict with variable names your templates might be using independently. Because variable names are case-sensitive, it's not a bad idea to use all uppercase letters for variables that a processor provides.

- It doesn't matter where on the filesystem the processors live, as long as they're on your Python path so you can point to them from the TEMPLATE_CONTEXT_PROCESSORS setting. With that said, the convention is to save them in a file called context_processors.py within your app or project.

Automatic HTML Escaping

When generating HTML from templates, there's always a risk that a variable will include characters that affect the resulting HTML. For example, consider this template fragment:

```
Hello, {{ name }}.
```

At first, it seems like a harmless way to display a user's name, but consider what would happen if the user entered his name this way:

```
<script>alert('hello')</script>
```

With this name value, the template would be rendered as follows:

```
Hello, <script>alert('hello')</script>
```

This means the browser would display a JavaScript alert box! Similarly, what if the name contained a '<' symbol, like this?

```
<b>username
```

It would result in a rendered template like this:

```
Hello, <b>username
```

This, in turn, would result in the remainder of the Web page being bold!

Clearly, user-submitted data shouldn't be trusted blindly and inserted directly into your Web pages because a malicious user could use this kind of hole to do potentially bad things. This type of security exploit is called a cross-site scripting (XSS) attack.

Tip For more on security, see Chapter 20.

To avoid this problem, you have two options:

- You can make sure to run each untrusted variable through the escape filter, which converts potentially harmful HTML characters to unharmful ones. This was the default solution in Django for its first few years, but the problem is that it puts the onus on *you*, the developer/template author, to ensure that you're escaping everything. It's easy to forget to escape data.

- You can take advantage of Django's automatic HTML escaping. The remainder of this section describes how autoescaping works.

By default, in Django every template automatically escapes the output of every variable tag. Specifically, these five characters are escaped:

< is converted to &lt;

> is converted to &gt;

' (single quote) is converted to &#39;

" (double quote) is converted to &quot;

& is converted to &amp;

Again, we stress that this behavior is on by default. If you're using Django's template system, you're protected.

How to Turn It Off

If you don't want data to be autoescaped on a per-site, per-template, or per-variable level, you can turn it off in several ways.

Why would you want to turn it off? Because sometimes template variables contain data that you *intend* to be rendered as raw HTML, in which case you don't want their contents to be escaped. For example, you might store a blob of trusted HTML in your database and want to embed it directly into your template. Or you might be using Django's template system to produce text that is *not* HTML—like an e-mail message, for instance.

For Individual Variables

To disable autoescaping for an individual variable, use the safe filter:

```
This will be escaped: {{ data }}
This will not be escaped: {{ data|safe }}
```

Think of *safe* as shorthand for *safe from further escaping* or *can be safely interpreted as HTML*. In this example, if data contains '<b>', the output will be the following:

```
This will be escaped: &lt;b&gt;
This will not be escaped: <b>
```

For Template Blocks

To control autoescaping for a template, wrap the template (or just a particular section of the template) in the autoescape tag, like so:

```
{% autoescape off %}
    Hello {{ name }}
{% endautoescape %}
```

The autoescape tag takes either on or off as its argument. At times, you might want to force autoescaping when it would otherwise be disabled. Here is an example template:

```
Autoescaping is on by default. Hello {{ name }}

{% autoescape off %}
    This will not be autoescaped: {{ data }}.

    Nor this: {{ other_data }}
    {% autoescape on %}
        Autoescaping applies again: {{ name }}
    {% endautoescape %}
{% endautoescape %}
```

The autoescaping tag passes its effect on to templates that extend the current one as well as templates included via the include tag, just like all block tags. For example:

```
# base.html

{% autoescape off %}
<h1>{% block title %}{% endblock %}</h1>
{% block content %}
{% endblock %}
{% endautoescape %}

# child.html

{% extends "base.html" %}
{% block title %}This & that{% endblock %}
{% block content %}{{ greeting }}{% endblock %}
```

Because autoescaping is turned off in the base template, it will also be turned off in the child template, resulting in the following rendered HTML when the greeting variable contains the string Hello!:

```
<h1>This & that</h1>
<b>Hello!</b>
```

Notes

Template authors usually don't need to worry about autoescaping very much. Developers on the Python side (people writing views and custom filters) need to think about the cases in which data shouldn't be escaped, and mark data appropriately, so things work in the template.

If you're creating a template that might be used in situations in which you're not sure whether autoescaping is enabled, add an escape filter to any variable that needs escaping. When autoescaping is on, there's no danger of the escape filter *double-escaping* data—the escape filter does not affect autoescaped variables.

Automatic Escaping of String Literals in Filter Arguments

As mentioned earlier, filter arguments can be strings:

```
{{ data|default:"This is a string literal." }}
```

All string literals are inserted *without* any automatic escaping into the template—they act as if they were all passed through the safe filter. The reasoning behind this is that the template author is in control of what goes into the string literal, so they can make sure the text is correctly escaped when the template is written.

This means you would write the following:

```
{{ data|default:"3 &lt; 2" }}
```

instead of the following:

```
{{ data|default:"3 < 2" }}   <-- Bad! Don't do this.
```

This doesn't affect what happens to data coming from the variable itself. The variable's contents are still automatically escaped, if necessary, because they're beyond the control of the template author.

Inside Template Loading

Generally, you'll store templates in files on your filesystem, but you can use custom *template loaders* to load templates from other sources.

Django has two ways to load templates:

- django.template.loader.get_template(template_name): get_template returns the compiled template (a Template object) for the template with the given name. If the template doesn't exist, a TemplateDoesNotExist exception will be raised.

- django.template.loader.select_template(template_name_list): select_template is just like get_template, except it takes a list of template names. Of the list, it returns the first template that exists. If none of the templates exist, a TemplateDoesNotExist exception will be raised.

As covered in Chapter 4, each of these functions by default uses your TEMPLATE_DIRS setting to load templates. Internally, however, these functions actually delegate to a template loader for the heavy lifting.

Some of loaders are disabled by default, but you can activate them by editing the TEMPLATE_LOADERS setting. TEMPLATE_LOADERS should be a tuple of strings, where each string represents a template loader. These template loaders ship with Django:

- django.template.loaders.filesystem.load_template_source: This loader loads templates from the filesystem, according to TEMPLATE_DIRS. It is enabled by default.

- django.template.loaders.app_directories.load_template_source: This loader loads templates from Django applications on the filesystem. For each application in INSTALLED_APPS, the loader looks for a templates subdirectory. If the directory exists, Django looks for templates there.

This means you can store templates with your individual applications, making it easy to distribute Django applications with default templates. For example, if INSTALLED_ APPS contains ('myproject.polls', 'myproject.music'), then get_template('foo. html') will look for templates in this order:

- /path/to/myproject/polls/templates/foo.html

- /path/to/myproject/music/templates/foo.html

Note that the loader performs an optimization when it is first imported: it caches a list of which INSTALLED_APPS packages have a templates subdirectory.

This loader is enabled by default.

- django.template.loaders.eggs.load_template_source: This loader is just like app_ directories, except it loads templates from Python eggs rather than from the filesystem. This loader is disabled by default; you'll need to enable it if you're using eggs to distribute your application. (Python eggs are a way of compressing Python code into a single file.)

Django uses the template loaders in order according to the TEMPLATE_LOADERS setting. It uses each loader until a loader finds a match.

Extending the Template System

Now that you understand a bit more about the internals of the template system, let's look at how to extend the system with custom code.

Most template customization comes in the form of custom template tags and/or filters. Although the Django template language comes with many built-in tags and filters, you'll probably assemble your own libraries of tags and filters that fit your own needs. Fortunately, it's quite easy to define your own functionality.

Creating a Template Library

Whether you're writing custom tags or filters, the first thing to do is to create a *template library*—a small bit of infrastructure Django can hook into.

Creating a template library is a two-step process:

1. First, decide which Django application should house the template library. If you've created an app via manage.py startapp, you can put it in there, or you can create another app solely for the template library. We recommend the latter because your filters might be useful to you in future projects.

   Whichever route you take, make sure to add the app to your INSTALLED_APPS setting. We'll explain this shortly.

2. Second, create a templatetags directory in the appropriate Django application's package. It should be on the same level as models.py, views.py, and so forth. For example:

```
books/
    __init__.py
    models.py
    templatetags/
    views.py
```

Create two empty files in the templatetags directory: an __init__.py file (to indicate to Python that this is a package containing Python code) and a file that will contain your custom tag/filter definitions. The name of the latter file is what you'll use to load the tags later. For example, if your custom tags/filters are in a file called poll_extras.py, you'd write the following in a template:

```
{% load poll_extras %}
```

The {% load %} tag looks at your INSTALLED_APPS setting and only allows the loading of template libraries within installed Django applications. This is a security feature; it allows you to host Python code for many template libraries on a single computer without enabling access to all of them for every Django installation.

If you write a template library that isn't tied to any particular models/views, it's valid and quite normal to have a Django application package that contains only a templatetags package. There's no limit on how many modules you put in the templatetags package. Just keep in mind that a {% load %} statement will load tags/filters for the given Python module name, not the name of the application.

Once you've created that Python module, you'll just have to write a bit of Python code, depending on whether you're writing filters or tags.

To be a valid tag library, the module must contain a module-level variable named register that is an instance of template.Library. This is the data structure in which all the tags and filters are registered. So, near the top of your module, insert the following:

```
from django import template

register = template.Library()
```

■Note For a fine selection of examples, read the source code for Django's default filters and tags. They're in django/template/defaultfilters.py and django/template/defaulttags.py, respectively. Some applications in django.contrib also contain template libraries.

Once you've created this register variable, you'll use it to create template filters and tags.

Writing Custom Template Filters

Custom filters are just Python functions that take one or two arguments:

- The value of the variable (input)

- The value of the argument, which can have a default value or be left out altogether

For example, in the filter {{ var|foo:"bar" }}, the filter foo would be passed the contents of the variable var and the argument "bar".

Filter functions should always return something. They shouldn't raise exceptions, and they should fail silently. If there's an error, they should return either the original input or an empty string, whichever makes more sense.

Here's an example filter definition:

```
def cut(value, arg):
    "Removes all values of arg from the given string"
    return value.replace(arg, '')
```

And here's an example of how that filter would be used to cut spaces from a variable's value:

```
{{ somevariable|cut:" " }}
```

Most filters don't take arguments. In this case, just leave the argument out of your function:

```
def lower(value): # Only one argument.
    "Converts a string into all lowercase"
    return value.lower()
```

When you've written your filter definition, you need to register it with your `Library` instance, to make it available to Django's template language:

```
register.filter('cut', cut)
register.filter('lower', lower)
```

The `Library.filter()` method takes two arguments:

- The name of the filter (a string)

- The filter function itself

If you're using Python 2.4 or above, you can use `register.filter()` as a decorator instead:

```
@register.filter(name='cut')
def cut(value, arg):
    return value.replace(arg, '')


@register.filter
def lower(value):
    return value.lower()
```

If you leave off the `name` argument, as in the second example, Django will use the function's name as the filter name.

Here, then, is a complete template library example, supplying the `cut` filter:

```
from django import template

register = template.Library()

@register.filter(name='cut')
def cut(value, arg):
    return value.replace(arg, '')
```

Writing Custom Template Tags

Tags are more complex than filters, because tags can do nearly anything.

Chapter 4 describes how the template system works in a two-step process: compiling and rendering. To define a custom template tag, you need to tell Django how to manage *both* of these steps when it gets to your tag.

When Django compiles a template, it splits the raw template text into *nodes*. Each node is an instance of `django.template.Node` and has a `render()` method. Thus, a compiled template is simply a list of `Node` objects. For example, consider this template:

```
Hello, {{ person.name }}.

{% ifequal name.birthday today %}
    Happy birthday!
{% else %}
    Be sure to come back on your birthday
    for a splendid surprise message.
{% endifequal %}
```

In compiled template form, this template is represented as this list of nodes:

- Text node: `"Hello,"`

- Variable node: `person.name`

- Text node: `".\n\n"`

- IfEqual node: `name.birthday` and `today`

When you call `render()` on a compiled template, the template calls `render()` on each Node in its node list, with the given context. The results are all concatenated together to form the output of the template. Thus, to define a custom template tag, you specify how the raw template tag is converted into a `Node` (the compilation function) and what the node's `render()` method does.

In the sections that follow, we cover all the steps in writing a custom tag.

Writing the Compilation Function

For each template tag the parser encounters, it calls a Python function with the tag contents and the parser object itself. This function is responsible for returning a `Node` instance based on the contents of the tag.

For example, let's write a template tag, `{% current_time %}`, that displays the current date/time, formatted according to a parameter given in the tag, in `strftime` syntax (see http://www.djangoproject.com/r/python/strftime/). It's a good idea to decide the tag syntax before anything else. In our case, let's say the tag should be used like this:

```
<p>The time is {% current_time "%Y-%m-%d %I:%M %p" %}.</p>
```

■Note Yes, this template tag is redundant—Django's default `{% now %}` tag does the same task with simpler syntax. This template tag is presented here just for example purposes.

The parser for this function should grab the parameter and create a `Node` object:

```
from django import template

register = template.Library()

def do_current_time(parser, token):
    try:
        # split_contents() knows not to split quoted strings.
        tag_name, format_string = token.split_contents()
    except ValueError:
        msg = '%r tag requires a single argument' % token.split_contents()[0]
        raise template.TemplateSyntaxError(msg)
    return CurrentTimeNode(format_string[1:-1])
```

There's a lot going here:

- Each template tag compilation function takes two arguments: `parser` and `token`. `parser` is the template parser object. We don't use it in this example. `token` is the token currently being parsed by the parser.

- `token.contents` is a string of the raw contents of the tag. In our example, it's `'current_time "%Y-%m-%d %I:%M %p"'`.

- The `token.split_contents()` method separates the arguments on spaces while keeping quoted strings together. Avoid using `token.contents.split()` (which just uses Python's standard string-splitting semantics). It's not as robust, as it naively splits on *all* spaces, including those within quoted strings.

- This function is responsible for raising `django.template.TemplateSyntaxError`, with helpful messages, for any syntax error.

- Don't hard-code the tag's name in your error messages, because that couples the tag's name to your function. `token.split_contents()[0]` will *always* be the name of your tag—even when the tag has no arguments.

- The function returns a `CurrentTimeNode` (which we'll create shortly) containing everything the node needs to know about this tag. In this case, it just passes the argument `"%Y-%m-%d %I:%M %p"`. The leading and trailing quotes from the template tag are removed with `format_string[1:-1]`.

- Template tag compilation functions *must* return a `Node` subclass; any other return value is an error.

Writing the Template Node

The second step in writing custom tags is to define a Node subclass that has a render() method. Continuing the preceding example, we need to define CurrentTimeNode:

```
import datetime

class CurrentTimeNode(template.Node):
    def __init__(self, format_string):
        self.format_string = str(format_string)

    def render(self, context):
        now = datetime.datetime.now()
        return now.strftime(self.format_string)
```

These two functions (__init__() and render()) map directly to the two steps in template processing (compilation and rendering). Thus, the initialization function only needs to store the format string for later use, and the render() function does the real work.

Like template filters, these rendering functions should fail silently instead of raising errors. The only time that template tags are allowed to raise errors is at compilation time.

Registering the Tag

Finally, you need to register the tag with your module's Library instance. Registering custom tags is very similar to registering custom filters (as explained previously). Just instantiate a template.Library instance and call its tag() method. For example:

```
register.tag('current_time', do_current_time)
```

The tag() method takes two arguments:

- The name of the template tag (string).
- The compilation function.

As with filter registration, it is also possible to use register.tag as a decorator in Python 2.4 and above:

```
@register.tag(name="current_time")
def do_current_time(parser, token):
    # ...

@register.tag
def shout(parser, token):
    # ...
```

If you leave off the name argument, as in the second example, Django will use the function's name as the tag name.

Setting a Variable in the Context

The previous section's example simply returned a value. Often it's useful to set template variables instead of returning values. That way, template authors can just use the variables that your template tags set.

To set a variable in the context, use dictionary assignment on the context object in the render() method. Here's an updated version of CurrentTimeNode that sets a template variable, current_time, instead of returning it:

```
class CurrentTimeNode2(template.Node):
    def __init__(self, format_string):
        self.format_string = str(format_string)

    def render(self, context):
        now = datetime.datetime.now()
        context['current_time'] = now.strftime(self.format_string)
        return ''
```

■**Note** We'll leave the creation of a do_current_time2 function, plus the registration of that function to a current_time2 template tag, as exercises for you.

Note that render() returns an empty string. render() should always return a string, so if all the template tag does is set a variable, render() should return an empty string.

Here's how you'd use this new version of the tag:

```
{% current_time2 "%Y-%M-%d %I:%M %p" %}
<p>The time is {{ current_time }}.</p>
```

But there's a problem with CurrentTimeNode2: the variable name current_time is hard-coded. This means you'll need to make sure your template doesn't use {{ current_time }} anywhere else, because {% current_time2 %} will blindly overwrite that variable's value.

A cleaner solution is to make the template tag specify the name of the variable to be set, like so:

```
{% get_current_time "%Y-%M-%d %I:%M %p" as my_current_time %}
<p>The current time is {{ my_current_time }}.</p>
```

To do so, you'll need to refactor both the compilation function and the Node class, as follows:

```
import re

class CurrentTimeNode3(template.Node):
    def __init__(self, format_string, var_name):
        self.format_string = str(format_string)
        self.var_name = var_name
```

```python
    def render(self, context):
        now = datetime.datetime.now()
        context[self.var_name] = now.strftime(self.format_string)
        return ''

def do_current_time(parser, token):
    # This version uses a regular expression to parse tag contents.
    try:
        # Splitting by None == splitting by spaces.
        tag_name, arg = token.contents.split(None, 1)
    except ValueError:
        msg = '%r tag requires arguments' % token.contents[0]
        raise template.TemplateSyntaxError(msg)

    m = re.search(r'(.*?) as (\w+)', arg)
    if m:
        fmt, var_name = m.groups()
    else:
        msg = '%r tag had invalid arguments' % tag_name
        raise template.TemplateSyntaxError(msg)

    if not (fmt[0] == fmt[-1] and fmt[0] in ('"', "'")):
        msg = "%r tag's argument should be in quotes" % tag_name
        raise template.TemplateSyntaxError(msg)

    return CurrentTimeNode3(fmt[1:-1], var_name)
```

Now do_current_time() passes the format string and the variable name to CurrentTimeNode3.

Parsing Until Another Template Tag

Template tags can work as blocks containing other tags (such as {% if %}, {% for %}, etc.). To create a template tag like this, use parser.parse() in your compilation function.

Here's how the standard {% comment %} tag is implemented:

```python
def do_comment(parser, token):
    nodelist = parser.parse(('endcomment',))
    parser.delete_first_token()
    return CommentNode()

class CommentNode(template.Node):
    def render(self, context):
        return ''
```

parser.parse() takes a tuple of names of template tags to parse until. It returns an instance of django.template.NodeList, which is a list of all Node objects that the parser encountered *before* it encountered any of the tags named in the tuple.

So in the preceding example, nodelist is a list of all nodes between {% comment %} and {% endcomment %}, not counting {% comment %} and {% endcomment %} themselves.

After `parser.parse()` is called, the parser hasn't yet "consumed" the `{% endcomment %}` tag, so the code needs to explicitly call `parser.delete_first_token()` to prevent that tag from being processed twice.

Then `CommentNode.render()` simply returns an empty string. Anything between `{% comment %}` and `{% endcomment %}` is ignored.

Parsing Until Another Template Tag and Saving Contents

In the previous example, `do_comment()` discarded everything between `{% comment %}` and `{% endcomment %}`. It's also possible to do something with the code between template tags instead.

For example, here's a custom template tag, `{% upper %}`, that capitalizes everything between itself and `{% endupper %}`:

```
{% upper %}
    This will appear in uppercase, {{ user_name }}.
{% endupper %}
```

As in the previous example, we'll use `parser.parse()`. This time, we pass the resulting nodelist to `Node`:

```
def do_upper(parser, token):
    nodelist = parser.parse(('endupper',))
    parser.delete_first_token()
    return UpperNode(nodelist)

class UpperNode(template.Node):
    def __init__(self, nodelist):
        self.nodelist = nodelist

    def render(self, context):
        output = self.nodelist.render(context)
        return output.upper()
```

The only new concept here is `self.nodelist.render(context)` in `UpperNode.render()`. This simply calls `render()` on each `Node` in the node list.

For more examples of complex rendering, see the source code for `{% if %}`, `{% for %}`, `{% ifequal %}`, and `{% ifchanged %}`. They live in `django/template/defaulttags.py`.

Shortcut for Simple Tags

Many template tags take a single argument—a string or a template variable reference—and return a string after doing some processing based solely on the input argument and some external information. For example, the `current_time` tag we wrote earlier is of this variety. We give it a format string, and it returns the time as a string.

To ease the creation of these types of tags, Django provides a helper function, `simple_tag`. This function, which is a method of `django.template.Library`, takes a function that accepts one argument, wraps it in a `render` function and the other necessary bits mentioned previously, and registers it with the template system.

Our earlier `current_time` function could thus be written like this:

```
def current_time(format_string):
    try:
        return datetime.datetime.now().strftime(str(format_string))
    except UnicodeEncodeError:
        return ''
```

```
register.simple_tag(current_time)
```

In Python 2.4, the decorator syntax also works:

```
@register.simple_tag
def current_time(token):
    # ...
```

Notice a couple of things about the `simple_tag` helper function:

- Only the (single) argument is passed into our function.

- Checking for the required number of arguments has already been done by the time our function is called, so we don't need to do that.

- The quotes around the argument (if any) have already been stripped away, so we receive a plain Unicode string.

Inclusion Tags

Another common template tag is the type that displays some data by rendering *another* template. For example, Django's admin interface uses custom template tags to display the buttons along the bottom of the "add/change" form pages. Those buttons always look the same, but the link targets change depending on the object being edited. They're a perfect case for using a small template that is filled with details from the current object.

These sorts of tags are called *inclusion tags*. Writing inclusion tags is probably best demonstrated by example. Let's write a tag that produces a list of books for a given `Author` object. We'll use the tag like this:

```
{% books_for_author author %}
```

The result will be something like this:

```
<ul>
    <li>The Cat In The Hat</li>
    <li>Hop On Pop</li>
    <li>Green Eggs And Ham</li>
</ul>
```

First, we define the function that takes the argument and produces a dictionary of data for the result. Notice that we need to return only a dictionary, not anything more complex. This will be used as the context for the template fragment:

```
def books_for_author(author):
    books = Book.objects.filter(authors__id=author.id)
    return {'books': books}
```

Next, we create the template used to render the tag's output. Following our example, the template is very simple:

```
<ul>
{% for book in books %}
    <li>{{ book.title }}</li>
{% endfor %}
</ul>
```

Finally, we create and register the inclusion tag by calling the inclusion_tag() method on a Library object.

Following our example, if the preceding template is in a file called book_snippet.html, we register the tag like this:

```
register.inclusion_tag('book_snippet.html')(books_for_author)
```

Python 2.4 decorator syntax works as well, so we could have written this instead:

```
@register.inclusion_tag('book_snippet.html')
def books_for_author(author):
    # ...
```

Sometimes, your inclusion tags need access to values from the parent template's context. To solve this, Django provides a takes_context option for inclusion tags. If you specify takes_context in creating an inclusion tag, the tag will have no required arguments, and the underlying Python function will have one argument: the template context as of when the tag was called.

For example, say you're writing an inclusion tag that will always be used in a context that contains home_link and home_title variables that point back to the main page. Here's what the Python function would look like:

```
@register.inclusion_tag('link.html', takes_context=True)
def jump_link(context):
    return {
        'link': context['home_link'],
        'title': context['home_title'],
    }
```

■**Note** The first parameter to the function *must* be called context.

The template link.html might contain the following:

```
Jump directly to <a href="{{ link }}">{{ title }}</a>.
```

Then, anytime you want to use that custom tag, load its library and call it without any arguments, like so:

```
{% jump_link %}
```

Writing Custom Template Loaders

Django's built-in template loaders (described in the "Inside Template Loading" section) will usually cover all your template-loading needs, but it's pretty easy to write your own if you need special loading logic. For example, you could load templates from a database, or directly from a Subversion repository using Subversion's Python bindings, or (as shown shortly) from a ZIP archive.

A template loader—that is, each entry in the TEMPLATE_LOADERS setting—is expected to be a callable object with this interface:

```
load_template_source(template_name, template_dirs=None)
```

The template_name argument is the name of the template to load (as passed to loader. get_template() or loader.select_template()), and template_dirs is an optional list of directories to search instead of TEMPLATE_DIRS.

If a loader is able to successfully load a template, it should return a tuple: (template_ source, template_path). Here, template_source is the template string that will be compiled by the template engine, and template_path is the path the template was loaded from. That path might be shown to the user for debugging purposes, so it should quickly identify where the template was loaded from.

If the loader is unable to load a template, it should raise django.template. TemplateDoesNotExist.

Each loader function should also have an is_usable function attribute. This is a Boolean that informs the template engine whether this loader is available in the current Python installation. For example, the eggs loader (which is capable of loading templates from Python eggs) sets is_usable to False if the pkg_resources module isn't installed, because pkg_resources is necessary to read data from eggs.

An example should help clarify all of this. Here's a template loader function that can load templates from a ZIP file. It uses a custom setting, TEMPLATE_ZIP_FILES, as a search path instead of TEMPLATE_DIRS, and it expects each item on that path to be a ZIP file containing templates:

```
from django.conf import settings
from django.template import TemplateDoesNotExist
import zipfile

def load_template_source(template_name, template_dirs=None):
    "Template loader that loads templates from a ZIP file."

    template_zipfiles = getattr(settings, "TEMPLATE_ZIP_FILES", [])
```

```
    # Try each ZIP file in TEMPLATE_ZIP_FILES.
    for fname in template_zipfiles:
        try:
            z = zipfile.ZipFile(fname)
            source = z.read(template_name)
        except (IOError, KeyError):
            continue
        z.close()
        # We found a template, so return the source.
        template_path = "%s:%s" % (fname, template_name)
        return (source, template_path)

    # If we reach here, the template couldn't be loaded
    raise TemplateDoesNotExist(template_name)

# This loader is always usable (since zipfile is included with Python)
load_template_source.is_usable = True
```

The only step left if we want to use this loader is to add it to the TEMPLATE_LOADERS setting. If we put this code in a package called mysite.zip_loader, then we add mysite.zip_loader. load_template_source to TEMPLATE_LOADERS.

Configuring the Template System in Standalone Mode

■Note This section is only of interest to people trying to use the template system as an output component in another application. If you are using the template system as part of a Django application, the information presented here doesn't apply to you.

Normally, Django loads all the configuration information it needs from its own default configuration file, combined with the settings in the module given in the DJANGO_SETTINGS_ MODULE environment variable. (This was explained in "A Special Python Prompt" in Chapter 4.) But if you're using the template system independent of the rest of Django, the environment variable approach isn't very convenient, because you probably want to configure the template system in line with the rest of your application rather than dealing with settings files and pointing to them via environment variables.

To solve this problem, you need to use the manual configuration option described fully in Appendix D. In a nutshell, you need to import the appropriate pieces of the template system and then, *before* you call any of the template functions, call django.conf.settings.configure() with any settings you wish to specify.

You might want to consider setting at least TEMPLATE_DIRS (if you are going to use template loaders), DEFAULT_CHARSET (although the default of utf-8 is probably fine), and TEMPLATE_DEBUG. All available settings are described in Appendix D, and any setting starting with TEMPLATE_ is of obvious interest.

What's Next?

Continuing this section's theme of advanced topics, the next chapter covers the advanced usage of Django models.

■ ■ ■

## CHAPTER 10

Advanced Models

In Chapter 5 we presented an introduction to Django's database layer—how to define models and how to use the database API to create, retrieve, update, and delete records. In this chapter, we'll introduce you to some more advanced features of this part of Django.

Related Objects

Recall our book models from Chapter 5:

```python
from django.db import models

class Publisher(models.Model):
    name = models.CharField(max_length=30)
    address = models.CharField(max_length=50)
    city = models.CharField(max_length=60)
    state_province = models.CharField(max_length=30)
    country = models.CharField(max_length=50)
    website = models.URLField()

    def __unicode__(self):
        return self.name

class Author(models.Model):
    first_name = models.CharField(max_length=30)
    last_name = models.CharField(max_length=40)
    e-mail = models.E-mailField()

    def __unicode__(self):
        return u'%s %s' % (self.first_name, self.last_name)
```

```
class Book(models.Model):
    title = models.CharField(max_length=100)
    authors = models.ManyToManyField(Author)
    publisher = models.ForeignKey(Publisher)
    publication_date = models.DateField()

    def __unicode__(self):
        return self.title
```

As we explained in Chapter 5, accessing the value for a particular field on a database object is as straightforward as using an attribute. For example, to determine the title of the book with ID 50, we'd do the following:

```
>>> from mysite.books.models import Book
>>> b = Book.objects.get(id=50)
>>> b.title
u'The Django Book'
```

But one thing we didn't mention previously is that related objects—fields expressed as either a ForeignKey or ManyToManyField—act slightly differently.

Accessing Foreign Key Values

When you access a field that's a ForeignKey, you'll get the related model object. Consider this example:

```
>>> b = Book.objects.get(id=50)
>>> b.publisher
<Publisher: Apress Publishing>
>>> b.publisher.website
u'http://www.apress.com/'
```

With ForeignKey fields, API access works in reverse, too, but it's slightly different due to the nonsymmetrical nature of the relationship. To get a list of books for a given publisher, use publisher.book_set.all(), like this:

```
>>> p = Publisher.objects.get(name='Apress Publishing')
>>> p.book_set.all()
[<Book: The Django Book>, <Book: Dive Into Python>, ...]
```

Behind the scenes, book_set is just a QuerySet (as covered in Chapter 5), and it can be filtered and sliced like any other QuerySet. Consider this example:

```
>>> p = Publisher.objects.get(name='Apress Publishing')
>>> p.book_set.filter(name__icontains='django')
[<Book: The Django Book>, <Book: Pro Django>]
```

The attribute name book_set is generated by appending the lowercase model name to _set.

Accessing Many-to-Many Values

Many-to-many values work like foreign-key values, except we deal with QuerySet values instead of model instances. For example, here's how to view the authors for a book:

```
>>> b = Book.objects.get(id=50)
>>> b.authors.all()
[<Author: Adrian Holovaty>, <Author: Jacob Kaplan-Moss>]
>>> b.authors.filter(first_name='Adrian')
[<Author: Adrian Holovaty>]
>>> b.authors.filter(first_name='Adam')
[]
```

It works in reverse, too. To view all of the books for an author, use author.book_set, like this:

```
>>> a = Author.objects.get(first_name='Adrian', last_name='Holovaty')
>>> a.book_set.all()
[<Book: The Django Book>, <Book: Adrian's Other Book>]
```

Here, as with ForeignKey fields, the attribute name book_set is generated by appending the lowercase model name to _set.

Making Changes to a Database Schema

When we introduced the syncdb command in Chapter 5, we noted that syncdb merely creates tables that don't yet exist in your database—it does *not* sync changes in models or perform deletions of models. If you add or change a model's field or if you delete a model, you'll need to make the change in your database manually. This section explains how to do that.

When dealing with schema changes, it's important to keep a few things in mind about how Django's database layer works:

- Django will complain loudly if a model contains a field that has not yet been created in the database table. This will cause an error the first time you use the Django database API to query the given table (i.e., it will happen at code-execution time, not at compilation time).

- Django does *not* care if a database table contains columns that are not defined in the model.

- Django does *not* care if a database contains a table that is not represented by a model.

Making schema changes is a matter of changing the various pieces—the Python code and the database itself—in the right order, as outlined in the following sections.

Adding Fields

When adding a field to a table/model in a production setting, the trick is to take advantage of the fact that Django doesn't care if a table contains columns that aren't defined in the model. The strategy is to add the column in the database, and then update the Django model to include the new field.

However, there's a bit of a chicken-and-egg problem here, because in order to know how the new database column should be expressed in SQL, you need to look at the output of Django's `manage.py sqlall` command, which requires that the field exist in the model. (Note that you're not *required* to create your column with exactly the same SQL that Django would, but it's a good idea to do so, just to be sure everything's in sync.)

The solution to the chicken-and-egg problem is to use a development environment instead of making the changes on a production server. (You *are* using a testing/development environment, right?) The following are the detailed steps to take.

First, take these steps in the development environment (i.e., not on the production server):

1. Add the field to your model.

2. Run `manage.py sqlall [yourapp]` to see the new `CREATE TABLE` statement for the model. Note the column definition for the new field.

3. Start your database's interactive shell (e.g., `psql` or `mysql`, or you can use `manage.py dbshell`). Execute an `ALTER TABLE` statement that adds your new column.

4. Launch the Python interactive shell with `manage.py shell` and verify that the new field was added properly by importing the model and selecting from the table (e.g., `MyModel.objects.all()[:5]`). If you updated the database correctly, the statement should work without errors.

Then, on the production server perform these steps:

1. Start your database's interactive shell.

2. Execute the `ALTER TABLE` statement you used in step 3 of the development-environment steps.

3. Add the field to your model. If you're using source-code revision control and you checked in your change in step 1 of the development-environment part of this process, now is the time to update the code (e.g., `svn update`, with Subversion) on the production server.

4. Restart the Web server for the code changes to take effect.

For example, let's walk through what we'd do if we added a `num_pages` field to the `Book` model from Chapter 5. First we'd alter the model in our development environment to look like this:

```
class Book(models.Model):
    title = models.CharField(max_length=100)
    authors = models.ManyToManyField(Author)
    publisher = models.ForeignKey(Publisher)
    publication_date = models.DateField()
    num_pages = models.IntegerField(blank=True, null=True)

    def __unicode__(self):
        return self.title
```

■Note Read the section "Making Fields Optional" in Chapter 6, plus the sidebar "Adding NOT NULL Columns" later in this chapter for important details on why we included `blank=True` and `null=True`.

Then we'd run the command `manage.py sqlall books` to see the `CREATE TABLE` statement. Depending on your database back-end, it would look something like this:

```
CREATE TABLE "books_book" (
    "id" serial NOT NULL PRIMARY KEY,
    "title" varchar(100) NOT NULL,
    "publisher_id" integer NOT NULL REFERENCES "books_publisher" ("id"),
    "publication_date" date NOT NULL,
    "num_pages" integer NULL
);
```

The new column is represented like this:

```
"num_pages" integer NULL
```

Next we'd start the database's interactive shell for our development database by typing `psql` (for PostgreSQL), and we'd execute the following statement:

```
ALTER TABLE books_book ADD COLUMN num_pages integer;
```

ADDING NOT NULL COLUMNS

There's a subtlety here that deserves mention. When we added the `num_pages` field to our model, we included the `blank=True` and `null=True` options because a database column will contain NULL values when you first create it.

However, it's also possible to add columns that cannot contain NULL values. To do this, you have to create the column as NULL, then populate the column's values using some default(s), and then alter the column to set the NOT NULL modifier. Here's an example:

```
BEGIN;
ALTER TABLE books_book ADD COLUMN num_pages integer;
UPDATE books_book SET num_pages=0;
ALTER TABLE books_book ALTER COLUMN num_pages SET NOT NULL;
COMMIT;
```

If you go down this path, remember that you should leave off `blank=True` and `null=True` in your model.

After the `ALTER TABLE` statement, we'd verify that the change worked properly by starting the Python shell and running this code:

```
>>> from mysite.books.models import Book
>>> Book.objects.all()[:5]
```

If that code didn't cause errors, we'd switch to our production server and execute the `ALTER TABLE` statement on the production database. Then we'd update the model in the production environment and restart the Web server.

Removing Fields

Removing a field from a model is a lot easier than adding one. Just follow these steps:

1. Remove the field's code from your model class and restart the Web server.

2. Remove the column from your database, using a command like this:

```
ALTER TABLE books_book DROP COLUMN num_pages;
```

Be sure to perform the steps in this order. If you remove the column from your database first, Django will immediately begin raising errors.

Removing Many-to-Many Fields

Because many-to-many fields are different from normal fields, the removal process is different:

1. Remove the `ManyToManyField` code from your model class and restart the Web server.

2. Remove the many-to-many table from your database, using a command like this:

```
DROP TABLE books_book_authors;
```

As in the previous section, be sure to perform the steps in this order.

Removing Models

Removing a model entirely is as easy as removing a field. Just follow these steps:

1. Remove the model class from your `models.py` file and restart the Web server.

2. Remove the table from your database, using a command like this:

```
DROP TABLE books_book;
```

Note that you might need to remove any dependent tables from your database first—for instance, any tables that have foreign keys to books_book.

As in the previous sections, be sure to perform the steps in the order shown here.

Managers

In the statement `Book.objects.all()`, `objects` is a special attribute through which you query your database. In Chapter 5 we briefly identified this as the model's *manager*. Now it's time to dive a bit deeper into what managers are and how you can use them.

In short, a model's manager is an object through which Django models perform database queries. Each Django model has at least one manager, and you can create custom managers to customize database access.

There are two reasons you might want to create a custom manager: to add extra manager methods, and/or to modify the initial `QuerySet` the manager returns.

Adding Extra Manager Methods

Adding extra manager methods is the preferred way to add *table-level functionality* to your models. A table-level function is one that acts on multiple instances of models, as opposed to single instances. (For *row-level functionality*—i.e., functions that act on a single instance of a model object—use model methods, which are explained later in this chapter.)

For example, let's give our `Book` model a manager method `title_count()` that takes a keyword and returns the number of books that have a title containing that keyword. (This example is slightly contrived, but it demonstrates how managers work.)

```
# models.py

from django.db import models

# ... Author and Publisher models here ...

class BookManager(models.Manager):
    def title_count(self, keyword):
        return self.filter(title__icontains=keyword).count()

class Book(models.Model):
    title = models.CharField(max_length=100)
    authors = models.ManyToManyField(Author)
    publisher = models.ForeignKey(Publisher)
    publication_date = models.DateField()
    num_pages = models.IntegerField(blank=True, null=True)
    objects = BookManager()

    def __unicode__(self):
        return self.title
```

With this manager in place, we can now use the new methods:

```
>>> Book.objects.title_count('django')
4
>>> Book.objects.title_count('python')
18
```

Here are some notes about the code:

- We've created a BookManager class that extends django.db.models.Manager. This has a single method, title_count(), which does the calculation. Note that the method uses self.filter(), where self refers to the manager itself.

- We've assigned BookManager() to the objects attribute on the model. This replaces the default manager for the model, which is called objects and is automatically created if you don't specify a custom manager. By calling our manager objects rather than something else, we're consistent with automatically created managers.

Why would we want to add a method such as title_count()? To encapsulate commonly executed queries so that we don't have to duplicate code.

Modifying Initial Manager QuerySets

A manager's base QuerySet returns all objects in the system. For example, Book.objects.all() returns all books in the book database.

You can override a manager's base QuerySet by overriding the Manager.get_query_set() method. get_query_set() should return a QuerySet with the properties you require.

For example, the following model has *two* managers—one that returns all objects, and one that returns only the books by Roald Dahl.

```
from django.db import models

# First, define the Manager subclass.
class DahlManager(models.Manager):
    def get_query_set(self):
        return super(DahlManager, self).get_query_set().filter(author='Roald Dahl')

# Then hook it into the Book model explicitly.
class Book(models.Model):
    title = models.CharField(max_length=100)
    author = models.CharField(max_length=50)
    # ...

    objects = models.Manager() # The default manager.
    dahl_objects = DahlManager() # The Dahl-specific manager.
```

With this sample model, Book.objects.all() will return all books in the database, but Book.dahl_objects.all() will return only the ones written by Roald Dahl. Note that we explicitly set objects to a vanilla Manager instance because if we hadn't, the only available manager would be dahl_objects.

Of course, because get_query_set() returns a QuerySet object, you can use filter(), exclude(), and all the other QuerySet methods on it. So these statements are all legal:

```
Book.dahl_objects.all()
Book.dahl_objects.filter(title='Matilda')
Book.dahl_objects.count()
```

This example points out another interesting technique: using multiple managers on the same model. You can attach as many `Manager()` instances to a model as you'd like. This is an easy way to define common filters for your models.

Consider this example:

```
class MaleManager(models.Manager):
    def get_query_set(self):
        return super(MaleManager, self).get_query_set().filter(sex='M')

class FemaleManager(models.Manager):
    def get_query_set(self):
        return super(FemaleManager, self).get_query_set().filter(sex='F')

class Person(models.Model):
    first_name = models.CharField(max_length=50)
    last_name = models.CharField(max_length=50)
    sex = models.CharField(max_length=1, choices=(('M', 'Male'), ('F', 'Female')))
    people = models.Manager()
    men = MaleManager()
    women = FemaleManager()
```

This example allows you to request `Person.men.all()`, `Person.women.all()`, and `Person.people.all()`, yielding predictable results.

If you use custom `Manager` objects, take note that the first `Manager` Django encounters (in the order in which they're defined in the model) has a special status. Django interprets this first `Manager` defined in a class as the default `Manager`, and several parts of Django (though not the admin application) will use that default `Manager` exclusively for that model. As a result, it's a good idea to be careful in your choice of default manager, in order to avoid a situation where overriding `get_query_set()` results in an inability to retrieve objects you'd like to work with.

Model Methods

Model methods allow you to define custom methods on a model to add custom row-level functionality to your objects. Whereas managers are intended to do table-wide things, model methods should act on a particular model instance.

Model methods are valuable for keeping business logic in one place—the model. An example is the easiest way to explain this. Here's a model with a few custom methods:

```
from django.contrib.localflavor.us.models import USStateField
from django.db import models

class Person(models.Model):
    first_name = models.CharField(max_length=50)
    last_name = models.CharField(max_length=50)
    birth_date = models.DateField()
    address = models.CharField(max_length=100)
    city = models.CharField(max_length=50)
    state = USStateField() # Yes, this is US-centric...
```

```
    def baby_boomer_status(self):
        "Returns the person's baby-boomer status."
        import datetime
        if datetime.date(1945, 8, 1) <= self.birth_date \
                and self.birth_date <= datetime.date(1964, 12, 31):
            return "Baby boomer"
        if self.birth_date < datetime.date(1945, 8, 1):
            return "Pre-boomer"
        return "Post-boomer"

    def is_midwestern(self):
        "Returns True if this person is from the Midwest."
        return self.state in ('IL', 'WI', 'MI', 'IN', 'OH', 'IA', 'MO')

    def _get_full_name(self):
        "Returns the person's full name."
        return u'%s %s' % (self.first_name, self.last_name)
    full_name = property(_get_full_name)
```

The last method in this example is a property. (You can read more about properties at http://
www.python.org/download/releases/2.2/descrintro/#property.) Here's an example usage:

```
>>> p = Person.objects.get(first_name='Barack', last_name='Obama')
>>> p.birth_date
datetime.date(1961, 8, 4)
>>> p.baby_boomer_status()
'Baby boomer'
>>> p.is_midwestern()
True
>>> p.full_name  # Note this isn't a method—it's treated as an attribute
u'Barack Obama'
```

Executing Raw SQL Queries

The Django database API can take you only so far, so sometimes you'll want to write custom
SQL queries against your database. You can do this very easily by accessing the object django.
db.connection, which represents the current database connection. To use it, call connection.
cursor() to get a cursor object. Then call cursor.execute(sql, [params]) to execute the SQL
and cursor.fetchone() or cursor.fetchall() to return the resulting rows. Here's an example:

```
>>> from django.db import connection
>>> cursor = connection.cursor()
>>> cursor.execute("""
...     SELECT DISTINCT first_name
...     FROM people_person
...     WHERE last_name = %s""", ['Lennon'])
>>> row = cursor.fetchone()
>>> print row
['John']
```

connection and cursor mostly implement the standard Python Database API, which you can read about at http://www.python.org/peps/pep-0249.html. If you're not familiar with the Python Database API, note that the SQL statement in cursor.execute() uses placeholders, "%s", rather than adding parameters directly within the SQL. If you use this technique, the underlying database library will automatically add quotes and escape characters to your parameter(s) as necessary.

Rather than littering your view code with django.db.connection statements, it's a good idea to put them in custom model methods or manager methods. For instance, the preceding example could be integrated into a custom manager method like this:

```python
from django.db import connection, models

class PersonManager(models.Manager):
    def first_names(self, last_name):
        cursor = connection.cursor()
        cursor.execute("""
            SELECT DISTINCT first_name
            FROM people_person
            WHERE last_name = %s""", [last_name])
        return [row[0] for row in cursor.fetchone()]

class Person(models.Model):
    first_name = models.CharField(max_length=50)
    last_name = models.CharField(max_length=50)
    objects = PersonManager()
```

Here's a sample usage:

```python
>>> Person.objects.first_names('Lennon')
['John', 'Cynthia']
```

What's Next?

In the next chapter we'll show you Django's "generic views" framework, which lets you save time building Web sites that follow common patterns.

CHAPTER 11

■ ■ ■

Generic Views

Here again is a recurring theme of this book: at its worst, Web development is boring and monotonous. So far, we've covered how Django tries to take away some of that monotony at the model and template layers, but Web developers also experience this boredom at the view level.

Django's *generic views* were developed to ease that pain. They take certain common idioms and patterns found in view development and abstract them so that you can quickly write common views of data without having to write too much code. In fact, nearly every view example in the preceding chapters could be rewritten with the help of generic views.

Chapter 8 touched briefly on how you'd go about making a view generic. To review, we can recognize certain common tasks, like displaying a list of objects, and write code that displays a list of *any* object. Then the model in question can be passed as an extra argument to the URLconf.

Django ships with generic views to do the following:

- Perform common "simple" tasks: redirect to a different page or render a given template.

- Display list and detail pages for a single object. The event_list and entry_list views from Chapter 8 are examples of list views. A single event page is an example of what we call a *detail view*.

- Present date-based objects in year/month/day archive pages, associated detail, and "latest" pages. The Django weblog's (http://www.djangoproject.com/weblog/) year, month, and day archives are built with these, as would be a typical newspaper's archives.

Taken together, these views provide easy interfaces to perform the most common tasks developers encounter.

Using Generic Views

All of these views are used by creating configuration dictionaries in your URLconf files and passing those dictionaries as the third member of the URLconf tuple for a given pattern. (See "Passing Extra Options to View Functions" in Chapter 8 for an overview of this technique.)

For example, here's a simple URLconf you could use to present a static "about" page:

```
from django.conf.urls.defaults import *
from django.views.generic.simple import direct_to_template

urlpatterns = patterns('',
    (r'^about/$', direct_to_template, {
        'template': 'about.html'
    })
)
```

Though this might seem a bit "magical" at first glance—look, a view with no code!—it's actually exactly the same as the examples in Chapter 8. The direct_to_template view simply grabs information from the extra-parameters dictionary and uses that information when rendering the view.

Because this generic view—and all the others—is a regular view function like any other, we can reuse it inside our own views. As an example, let's extend our "about" example to map URLs of the form /about/<whatever>/ to statically rendered about/<whatever>.html. We'll do this by first modifying the URLconf to point to a view function:

```
from django.conf.urls.defaults import *
from django.views.generic.simple import direct_to_template
from mysite.books.views import about_pages

urlpatterns = patterns('',
    (r'^about/$', direct_to_template, {
        'template': 'about.html'
    }),
    (r'^about/(\w+)/$', about_pages),
)
```

Next, we'll write the about_pages view:

```
from django.http import Http404
from django.template import TemplateDoesNotExist
from django.views.generic.simple import direct_to_template

def about_pages(request, page):
    try:
        return direct_to_template(request, template="about/%s.html" % page)
    except TemplateDoesNotExist:
        raise Http404()
```

Here we're treating direct_to_template like any other function. Since it returns an HttpResponse, we can simply return it as is. The only slightly tricky business here is dealing with missing templates. We don't want a nonexistent template to cause a server error, so we catch TemplateDoesNotExist exceptions and return 404 errors instead.

IS THERE A SECURITY VULNERABILITY HERE?

Sharp-eyed readers may have noticed a possible security hole: we're constructing the template name using interpolated content from the browser (template="about/%s.html" % page). At first glance, this looks like a classic *directory-traversal* vulnerability (discussed in detail in Chapter 20). But is it really?

Not exactly. Yes, a maliciously crafted value of page could cause directory traversal, but although page *is* taken from the request URL, not every value will be accepted. The key is in the URLconf: we're using the regular expression \w+ to match the page part of the URL, and \w accepts only letters and numbers. Thus, any malicious characters (such as dots and slashes) will be rejected by the URL resolver before they reach the view itself.

Generic Views of Objects

The direct_to_template view certainly is useful, but Django's generic views really shine when it comes to presenting views on your database content. Because it's such a common task, Django comes with a handful of built-in generic views that make generating list and detail views of objects incredibly easy.

Let's take a look at one of these generic views: the "object list" view. We'll be using this Publisher object from Chapter 5:

```
class Publisher(models.Model):
    name = models.CharField(max_length=30)
    address = models.CharField(max_length=50)
    city = models.CharField(max_length=60)
    state_province = models.CharField(max_length=30)
    country = models.CharField(max_length=50)
    website = models.URLField()

    def __unicode__(self):
        return self.name

    class Meta:
        ordering = ['name']
```

To build a list page of all publishers, we'd use a URLconf along these lines:

```
from django.conf.urls.defaults import *
from django.views.generic import list_detail
from mysite.books.models import Publisher

publisher_info = {
    'queryset': Publisher.objects.all(),
}

urlpatterns = patterns('',
    (r'^publishers/$', list_detail.object_list, publisher_info)
)
```

That's all the Python code we need to write. We still need to write a template, however. We can explicitly tell the `object_list` view which template to use by including a `template_name` key in the extra-arguments dictionary:

```
from django.conf.urls.defaults import *
from django.views.generic import list_detail
from mysite.books.models import Publisher

publisher_info = {
    'queryset': Publisher.objects.all(),
    'template_name': 'publisher_list_page.html',
}

urlpatterns = patterns('',
    (r'^publishers/$', list_detail.object_list, publisher_info)
)
```

In the absence of `template_name`, though, the `object_list` generic view will infer one from the object's name. In this case, the inferred template will be `books/publisher_list.html`—the `books` part comes from the name of the app that defines the model, while the `publisher` bit is just the lowercased version of the model's name.

This template will be rendered against a context containing a variable called `object_list` that contains all the `publisher` objects. A very simple template might look like the following:

```
{% extends "base.html" %}

{% block content %}
    <h2>Publishers</h2>
    <ul>
        {% for publisher in object_list %}
            <li>{{ publisher.name }}</li>
        {% endfor %}
    </ul>
{% endblock %}
```

(Note that this assumes the existence of a `base.html` template, as we provided in an example in Chapter 4.)

That's really all there is to it. All the cool features of generic views come from changing the "info" dictionary passed to the generic view. Appendix C documents all the generic views and all their options in detail; the rest of this chapter will consider some of the common ways you might customize and extend generic views.

Extending Generic Views

There's no question that using generic views can speed up development substantially. In most projects, however, there comes a moment when the generic views no longer suffice. Indeed, one of the most common questions asked by new Django developers is how to make generic views handle a wider array of situations.

Luckily, in nearly every one of these cases there are ways to simply extend generic views to handle a larger array of use cases. These situations usually fall into the handful of patterns dealt with in the following sections.

Making "Friendly" Template Contexts

You might have noticed that the sample publisher list template stores all the books in a variable named `object_list`. While this works just fine, it isn't all that friendly to template authors: they have to "just know" that they're dealing with books here. A better name for that variable would be `publisher_list`; that variable's content is pretty obvious.

We can change the name of that variable easily with the `template_object_name` argument:

```
from django.conf.urls.defaults import *
from django.views.generic import list_detail
from mysite.books.models import Publisher

publisher_info = {
    'queryset': Publisher.objects.all(),
    'template_name': 'publisher_list_page.html',
    'template_object_name': 'publisher',
}

urlpatterns = patterns('',
    (r'^publishers/$', list_detail.object_list, publisher_info)
)
```

In the template, the generic view will append `_list` to the `template_object_name` to create the variable name representing the list of items.

Providing a useful `template_object_name` is always a good idea. Your coworkers who design templates will thank you.

Adding Extra Context

Sometimes you might need to present information beyond that provided in the generic view. For example, think of showing a list of all the other publishers on each publisher detail page. The object_detail generic view provides the publisher to the context, but it seems there's no way to get a list of *all* publishers in that template.

But there is: all generic views take an extra optional parameter, extra_context. This is a dictionary of extra objects that will be added to the template's context. So, to provide the list of all publishers on the detail view, we'd use an info dictionary like this:

```
publisher_info = {
    'queryset': Publisher.objects.all(),
    'template_object_name': 'publisher',
    'extra_context': {'book_list': Book.objects.all()}
}
```

This would populate a {{ book_list }} variable in the template context. This pattern can be used to pass any information down into the template for the generic view. It's very handy. However, there's actually a subtle bug here—can you spot it?

The problem has to do with when the queries in extra_context are evaluated. Because this example puts Book.objects.all() in the URLconf, it will be evaluated only once (when the URLconf is first loaded). Once you add or remove publishers, you'll notice that the generic view doesn't reflect those changes until you reload the Web server (see "Caching and QuerySets" in Appendix B for more information about when QuerySet objects are cached and evaluated).

■**Note** This problem doesn't apply to the queryset generic view argument. Since Django knows that particular QuerySet should *never* be cached, the generic view takes care of clearing the cache when each view is rendered.

The solution is to use a *callback* in extra_context instead of a value. Any callable (i.e., a function) that's passed to extra_context will be evaluated when the view is rendered (instead of only once). You could do this with an explicitly defined function:

```
def get_books():
    return Book.objects.all()

publisher_info = {
    'queryset': Publisher.objects.all(),
    'template_object_name': 'publisher',
    'extra_context': {'book_list': get_books}
}
```

Or you could use a less obvious but shorter version that relies on the fact that Book.objects.all is itself a callable:

```
publisher_info = {
    'queryset': Publisher.objects.all(),
    'template_object_name': 'publisher',
    'extra_context': {'book_list': Book.objects.all}
}
```

Notice the lack of parentheses after Book.objects.all. This references the function without actually calling it (which the generic view will do later).

Viewing Subsets of Objects

Now let's take a closer look at this queryset key we've been using all along. Most generic views take one of these queryset arguments—it's how the view knows which set of objects to display (see "Selecting Objects" in Chapter 5 for an introduction to QuerySet objects, and see Appendix B for the complete details).

Suppose, for example, that you want to order a list of books by publication date, with the most recent first:

```
book_info = {
    'queryset': Book.objects.order_by('-publication_date'),
}

urlpatterns = patterns('',
    (r'^publishers/$', list_detail.object_list, publisher_info),
    (r'^books/$', list_detail.object_list, book_info),
)
```

That's a pretty simple example, but it illustrates the idea nicely. Of course, you'll usually want to do more than just reorder objects. If you want to present a list of books by a particular publisher, you can use the same technique:

```
apress_books = {
    'queryset': Book.objects.filter(publisher__name='Apress Publishing'),
    'template_name': 'books/apress_list.html'
}

urlpatterns = patterns('',
    (r'^publishers/$', list_detail.object_list, publisher_info),
    (r'^books/apress/$', list_detail.object_list, apress_books),
)
```

Notice that along with a filtered queryset, we're also using a custom template name. If we didn't, the generic view would use the same template as the "vanilla" object list, which might not be what we want.

Also notice that this isn't a very elegant way of doing publisher-specific books. If we want to add another publisher page, we'd need another handful of lines in the URLconf, and more than a few publishers would get unreasonable. We'll deal with this problem in the next section.

Complex Filtering with Wrapper Functions

Another common need is to filter the objects given in a list page by some key in the URL. Earlier we hard-coded the publisher's name in the URLconf, but what if we wanted to write a view that displayed all the books by some arbitrary publisher? The solution is to "wrap" the object_list generic view to avoid writing a lot of code by hand. As usual, we'll start by writing a URLconf:

```
urlpatterns = patterns('',
    (r'^publishers/$', list_detail.object_list, publisher_info),
    (r'^books/(\w+)/$', books_by_publisher),
)
```

Next we'll write the books_by_publisher view itself:

```
from django.shortcuts import get_object_or_404
from django.views.generic import list_detail
from mysite.books.models import Book, Publisher

def books_by_publisher(request, name):

    # Look up the publisher (and raise a 404 if it can't be found).
    publisher = get_object_or_404(Publisher, name__iexact=name)

    # Use the object_list view for the heavy lifting.
    return list_detail.object_list(
        request,
        queryset = Book.objects.filter(publisher=publisher),
        template_name = 'books/books_by_publisher.html',
        template_object_name = 'book',
        extra_context = {'publisher': publisher}
    )
```

This works because there's really nothing special about generic views—they're just Python functions. Like any view function, generic views expect a certain set of arguments and return HttpResponse objects. Thus, it's incredibly easy to wrap a small function around a generic view that does additional work before (or after; see the next section) handing things off to the generic view.

■**Note** Notice that in the preceding example we passed the current publisher being displayed in the extra_context. This is usually a good idea in wrappers of this nature; it lets the template know which "parent" object is currently being browsed.

Performing Extra Work

The last common pattern we'll look at involves doing some extra work before or after calling the generic view.

Imagine we had a `last_accessed` field on our `Author` object that we were using to keep track of the last time anybody looked at that author. The generic `object_detail` view, of course, wouldn't know anything about this field, but once again we could easily write a custom view to keep that field updated.

First, we'd need to add an `author_detail` bit in the URLconf to point to a custom view:

```
from mysite.books.views import author_detail

urlpatterns = patterns('',
    # ...
    (r'^authors/(?P<author_id>\d+)/$', author_detail),
    # ...
)
```

Then we'd write our wrapper function:

```
import datetime
from django.shortcuts import get_object_or_404
from django.views.generic import list_detail
from mysite.books.models import Author

def author_detail(request, author_id):
    # Delegate to the generic view and get an HttpResponse.
    response = list_detail.object_detail(
        request,
        queryset = Author.objects.all(),
        object_id = author_id,
    )

    # Record the last accessed date. We do this *after* the call
    # to object_detail(), not before it, so that this won't be called
    # unless the Author actually exists. (If the author doesn't exist,
    # object_detail() will raise Http404, and we won't reach this point.)
    now = datetime.datetime.now()
    Author.objects.filter(id=author_id).update(last_accessed=now)

    return response
```

Note This code won't work unless you add a `last_accessed` field to your `Author` model and create a `books/author_detail.html` template.

We can use a similar idiom to alter the response returned by the generic view. If we wanted to provide a downloadable plain-text version of the list of authors, we could use a view like this:

```
def author_list_plaintext(request):
    response = list_detail.object_list(
        request,
        queryset = Author.objects.all(),
        mimetype = 'text/plain',
        template_name = 'books/author_list.txt'
    )
    response["Content-Disposition"] = "attachment; filename=authors.txt"
    return response
```

This works because the generic views return simple HttpResponse objects that can be treated like dictionaries to set HTTP headers. This Content-Disposition business, by the way, instructs the browser to download and save the page instead of displaying it in the browser.

What's Next?

In this chapter we looked at only a couple of the generic views Django ships with, but the general ideas presented here should apply pretty closely to any generic view. Appendix C covers all the available views in detail, and it's recommended reading if you want to get the most out of this powerful feature.

This concludes the section of this book devoted to "advanced usage." In the next chapter we cover deployment of Django applications.

■ ■ ■

## CHAPTER 12

Deploying Django

This chapter covers the last essential step of building a Django application: deploying it to a production server.

If you've been following along with our ongoing examples, you probably used the `runserver`, which makes things very easy (you don't have to worry about Web server setup). But `runserver` is intended only for development on your local machine, not for exposure on the public Web. To deploy your Django application, you'll need to hook it into an industrial-strength Web server such as Apache. In this chapter, we'll show you how to do that, but first we'll give you a checklist of things to do in your codebase before you go live.

Preparing Your Codebase for Production

Fortunately, the `runserver` approximates a "real" Web server closely enough that not very many changes need to be made to a Django application in order to make it production-ready. But there are a few *essential things* you should do before you turn the switch.

Turning Off Debug Mode

When we created a project in Chapter 2, the command `django-admin.py startproject` created a `settings.py` file with `DEBUG` set to `True`. Many internal parts of Django check this setting and change their behavior if `DEBUG` mode is on. For example, if `DEBUG` is set to `True`, then:

- All database queries will be saved in memory as the object `django.db.connection.queries`. As you can imagine, this eats up memory!

- Any 404 error will be rendered by Django's special 404 error page (covered in Chapter 3) instead of returning a proper 404 response. This page contains potentially sensitive information and should *not* be exposed to the public Internet.

- Any uncaught exception in your Django application—from basic Python syntax errors to database errors to template syntax errors—will be rendered by the Django pretty error page that you've likely come to know and love. This page contains even *more* sensitive information than the 404 page and should *never* be exposed to the public.

In short, setting DEBUG to True tells Django to assume that only trusted developers are using your site. The Internet is full of untrustworthy hooligans, and the first thing you should do when you're preparing your application for deployment is set DEBUG to False.

Turning Off Template Debug Mode

Similarly, you should set TEMPLATE_DEBUG to False in production. If True, this setting tells Django's template system to save some extra information about every template for use on the pretty error pages.

Implementing a 404 Template

If DEBUG is True, Django displays the useful 404 error page. But if DEBUG is False, it does something different: it renders a template called 404.html in your root template directory. So, when you're ready to deploy, you'll need to create this template and put a useful "Page not found" message in it.

Here's a sample 404.html you can use as a starting point. It assumes that you're using template inheritance and have defined a base.html with blocks called title and content:

```
{% extends "base.html" %}

{% block title %}Page not found{% endblock %}

{% block content %}
<h1>Page not found</h1>

<p>Sorry, but the requested page could not be found.</p>
{% endblock %}
```

To test that your 404.html is working, just change DEBUG to False and visit a nonexistent URL. (This works on the runserver just as well as it works on a production server.)

Implementing a 500 Template

Similarly, if DEBUG is False, then Django no longer displays its useful error/traceback pages in case of an unhandled Python exception. Instead, it looks for a template called 500.html and renders it. Like 404.html, this template should live in your root template directory.

There's one slightly tricky thing about 500.html. You can never be sure *why* this template is being rendered, so it shouldn't do anything that requires a database connection or relies on any potentially broken part of your infrastructure. (For example, it should not use custom template tags.) If it uses template inheritance, then the parent template(s) shouldn't rely on potentially broken infrastructure, either. Therefore, the best approach is to avoid template inheritance and use something very simple. Here's an example 500.html as a starting point:

```
<!DOCTYPE html PUBLIC "-//W3C//DTD HTML 4.01//EN"
    "http://www.w3.org/TR/html4/strict.dtd">
<html lang="en">
<head>
    <title>Page unavailable</title>
</head>
```

```
<body>
    <h1>Page unavailable</h1>

    <p>Sorry, but the requested page is unavailable due to a
    server hiccup.</p>

    <p>Our engineers have been notified, so check back later.</p>
</body>
</html>
```

Setting Up Error Alerts

When your Django-powered site is running and an exception is raised, you'll want to know about it, so you can fix it. By default, Django is configured to send an e-mail to the site developers whenever your code raises an unhandled exception—but you need to do two things to set it up.

First, change your ADMINS setting to include your e-mail address, along with the e-mail addresses of any other people who need to be notified. This setting takes (name, email) tuples, like this:

```
ADMINS = (
    ('John Lennon', 'jlennon@example.com'),
    ('Paul McCartney', 'pmacca@example.com'),
)
```

Second, make sure that your server is configured to send e-mail. Setting up postfix, sendmail, or any other mail server is outside the scope of this book, but on the Django side of things, you'll want to make sure that your EMAIL_HOST setting is set to the proper hostname for your mail server. It's set to 'localhost' by default, which works out of the box for most shared-hosting environments. You might also need to set EMAIL_HOST_USER, EMAIL_HOST_PASSWORD, EMAIL_PORT, or EMAIL_USE_TLS, depending on the complexity of your arrangement.

Also, you can set EMAIL_SUBJECT_PREFIX to control the prefix Django uses in front of its error e-mail. It is set to '[Django]' by default.

Setting Up Broken Link Alerts

If you have the CommonMiddleware installed (e.g., if your MIDDLEWARE_CLASSES setting includes 'django.middleware.common.CommonMiddleware', which it does by default), you have the option of receiving an e-mail any time somebody visits a page on your Django-powered site that raises 404 with a non-empty referrer—that is, every broken link. If you want to activate this feature, set SEND_BROKEN_LINK_EMAILS to True (it's False by default) and set your MANAGERS setting to a person or people who will receive this broken-link e-mail. MANAGERS uses the same syntax as ADMINS. For example:

```
MANAGERS = (
    ('George Harrison', 'gharrison@example.com'),
    ('Ringo Starr', 'ringo@example.com'),
)
```

Note that error e-mail can get annoying; they're not for everybody.

Using Different Settings for Production

So far in this book, we've dealt with only a single settings file: the settings.py generated by django-admin.py startproject. But as you get ready to deploy, you'll likely find yourself needing multiple settings files to keep your development environment isolated from your production environment. (For example, you probably won't want to change DEBUG from False to True whenever you want to test code changes on your local machine.) Django makes this very easy by allowing you to use multiple settings files.

If you want to organize your settings files into "production" and "development" settings, you can accomplish it in three ways:

- Set up two full-blown, independent settings files.

- Set up a "base" settings file (say, for development) and a second (say, production) settings file that merely imports from the first one and defines whatever overrides it needs to define.

- Use only a single settings file that has Python logic to change the settings based on context.

We'll take these one at a time.

First, the most basic approach is to define two separate settings files. If you're following along, you've already got settings.py. Now, just make a copy of it called settings_production.py. (We made this name up; you can call it whatever you want.) In this new file, change DEBUG, and so on.

The second approach is similar, but cuts down on redundancy. Instead of having two settings files whose contents are mostly similar, you can treat one as the "base" file and create another file that imports from it. For example:

```python
# settings.py

DEBUG = True
TEMPLATE_DEBUG = DEBUG

DATABASE_ENGINE = 'postgresql_psycopg2'
DATABASE_NAME = 'devdb'
DATABASE_USER = ''
DATABASE_PASSWORD = ''
DATABASE_PORT = ''

# ...

# settings_production.py

from settings import *

DEBUG = TEMPLATE_DEBUG = False
DATABASE_NAME = 'production'
DATABASE_USER = 'app'
DATABASE_PASSWORD = 'letmein'
```

Here, settings_production.py imports everything from settings.py and just redefines the settings that are particular to production. In this case, DEBUG is set to False, but we also set different database access parameters for the production setting. (The latter goes to show that you can redefine *any* setting, not just the basic ones such as DEBUG.)

Finally, the most concise way of accomplishing two settings environments is to use a single settings file that branches based on the environment. One way to do this is to check the current hostname. For example:

```
# settings.py

import socket

if socket.gethostname() == 'my-laptop':
    DEBUG = TEMPLATE_DEBUG = True
else:
    DEBUG = TEMPLATE_DEBUG = False


# ...
```

Here, we import the socket module from Python's standard library and use it to check the current system's hostname. We can check the hostname to determine whether the code is being run on the production server.

A core lesson here is that settings files are *just Python code*. They can import from other files, they can execute arbitrary logic, and so on. Just make sure that if you go down this road, the Python code in your settings files is bulletproof. If it raises any exceptions, Django will likely crash badly.

RENAMING SETTINGS.PY

Feel free to rename your settings.py to settings_dev.py, or settings/dev.py, or foobar.py— Django doesn't care, as long as you tell it what settings file you're using.

But if you *do* rename the settings.py file that is generated by django-admin.py startproject, you'll find that manage.py will give you an error message saying that it can't find the settings. That's because it tries to import a module called settings. You can fix this either by editing manage.py to change settings to the name of your module, or by using django-admin.py instead of manage.py. In the latter case, you'll need to set the DJANGO_SETTINGS_MODULE environment variable to the Python path to your settings file (e.g., 'mysite.settings').

DJANGO_SETTINGS_MODULE

With those code changes out of the way, the next part of this chapter will focus on deployment instructions for specific environments, such as Apache. The instructions are different for each environment, but one thing remains the same: in each case, you have to tell the Web server your DJANGO_SETTINGS_MODULE. This is the entry point into your Django application. The DJANGO_SETTINGS_MODULE points to your settings file, which points to your ROOT_URLCONF, which points to your views, and so on.

DJANGO_SETTINGS_MODULE is the Python path to your settings file. For example, assuming that the mysite directory is on your Python path, the DJANGO_SETTINGS_MODULE for our ongoing example is 'mysite.settings'.

Using Django with Apache and mod_python

Apache with mod_python historically has been the suggested setup for using Django on a production server.

mod_python (http://www.djangoproject.com/r/mod_python/) is an Apache plug-in that embeds Python within Apache and loads Python code into memory when the server starts. Code stays in memory throughout the life of an Apache process, which leads to significant performance gains over other server arrangements.

Django requires Apache 2.x and mod_python 3.x.

Note Configuring Apache is *well* beyond the scope of this book, so we'll simply mention details as needed. Luckily, many great resources are available if you need to learn more about Apache. A few of them we like are the following.

- The free online Apache documentation, available via http://www.djangoproject.com/r/apache/docs/

- *Pro Apache, Third Edition* by Peter Wainwright (Apress, 2004), available via http://www.djangoproject.com/r/books/pro-apache/

- *Apache: The Definitive Guide, Third Edition* by Ben Laurie and Peter Laurie (O'Reilly, 2002), available via http://www.djangoproject.com/r/books/pro-apache/

Basic Configuration

To configure Django with mod_python, first make sure you have Apache installed with the mod_python module activated. This usually means having a LoadModule directive in your Apache configuration file. It will look something like this:

```
LoadModule python_module /usr/lib/apache2/modules/mod_python.so
```

Then, edit your Apache configuration file and add a <Location> directive that ties a specific URL path to a specific Django installation. For example:

```
<Location "/">
    SetHandler python-program
    PythonHandler django.core.handlers.modpython
    SetEnv DJANGO_SETTINGS_MODULE mysite.settings
    PythonDebug Off
</Location>
```

Make sure to replace `mysite.settings` with the appropriate `DJANGO_SETTINGS_MODULE` for your site.

This tells Apache, "Use mod_python for any URL at or under '/', using the Django mod_python handler." It passes the value of `DJANGO_SETTINGS_MODULE` so mod_python knows which settings to use.

Note that we're using the `<Location>` directive, not the `<Directory>` directive. The latter is used for pointing at places on your filesystem, whereas `<Location>` points at places in the URL structure of a Web site. `<Directory>` would be meaningless here.

Apache likely runs as a different user than your normal login and may have a different path and `sys.path`. You may need to tell mod_python how to find your project and Django itself.

```
PythonPath "['/path/to/project', '/path/to/django'] + sys.path"
```

You can also add directives such as `PythonAutoReload Off` for performance. See the mod_python documentation for a full list of options.

Note that you should set `PythonDebug Off` on a production server. If you leave `PythonDebug On`, your users will see ugly (and revealing) Python tracebacks if something goes wrong within mod_python.

Restart Apache, and any request to your site (or virtual host if you've put this directive inside a `<VirtualHost>` block) will be served by Django.

Running Multiple Django Installations on the Same Apache Instance

It's entirely possible to run multiple Django installations on the same Apache instance. You might want to do this if you're an independent Web developer with multiple clients but only a single server.

To accomplish this, just use `VirtualHost` like so:

```
NameVirtualHost *

<VirtualHost *>
    ServerName www.example.com
    # ...
    SetEnv DJANGO_SETTINGS_MODULE mysite.settings
</VirtualHost>

<VirtualHost *>
    ServerName www2.example.com
    # ...
    SetEnv DJANGO_SETTINGS_MODULE mysite.other_settings
</VirtualHost>
```

If you need to put two Django installations within the same `VirtualHost`, you'll need to take a special precaution to ensure mod_python's code cache doesn't mess things up. Use the `PythonInterpreter` directive to give different `<Location>` directives separate interpreters:

```
<VirtualHost *>
    ServerName www.example.com
    # ...
    <Location "/something">
        SetEnv DJANGO_SETTINGS_MODULE mysite.settings
        PythonInterpreter mysite
    </Location>

    <Location "/otherthing">
        SetEnv DJANGO_SETTINGS_MODULE mysite.other_settings
        PythonInterpreter mysite_other
    </Location>
</VirtualHost>
```

The values of `PythonInterpreter` don't really matter, as long as they're different between the two `Location` blocks.

Running a Development Server with mod_python

Because mod_python caches loaded Python code, when deploying Django sites on mod_python you'll need to restart Apache each time you make changes to your code. This can be a hassle, so here's a quick trick to avoid it: just add `MaxRequestsPerChild 1` to your config file to force Apache to reload everything for each request. But don't do that on a production server, or we'll revoke your Django privileges.

If you're the type of programmer who debugs using scattered `print` statements (we are), note that `print` statements have no effect in mod_python; they don't appear in the Apache log, as you might expect. If you have the need to print debugging information in a mod_python setup, you'll probably want to use Python's standard logging package. More information is available at `http://docs.python.org/lib/module-logging.html`.

Serving Django and Media Files from the Same Apache Instance

Django should not be used to serve media files itself; leave that job to whichever Web server you choose. We recommend using a separate Web server (i.e., one that's not also running Django) for serving media. For more information, see the "Scaling" section.

If, however, you have no option but to serve media files on the same Apache `VirtualHost` as Django, here's how you can turn off mod_python for a particular part of the site:

```
<Location "/media/">
    SetHandler None
</Location>
```

Change `Location` to the root URL of your media files.

You can also use `<LocationMatch>` to match a regular expression. For example, this sets up Django at the site root but explicitly disables Django for the `media` subdirectory and any URL that ends with `.jpg`, `.gif`, or `.png`:

```
<Location "/">
    SetHandler python-program
    PythonHandler django.core.handlers.modpython
    SetEnv DJANGO_SETTINGS_MODULE mysite.settings
</Location>

<Location "/media/">
    SetHandler None
</Location>

<LocationMatch "\.(jpg|gif|png)$">
    SetHandler None
</LocationMatch>
```

In all of these cases, you'll need to set the `DocumentRoot` directive so Apache knows where to find your static files.

Error Handling

When you use Apache/mod_python, errors will be caught by Django—in other words, they won't propagate to the Apache level and won't appear in the Apache `error_log`.

The exception to this is if something is really messed up in your Django setup. In that case, you'll see an ominous "Internal Server Error" page in your browser and the full Python traceback in your Apache `error_log` file. The `error_log` traceback is spread over multiple lines. (Yes, this is ugly and rather hard to read, but it's how mod_python does things.)

Handling a Segmentation Fault

Sometimes, Apache segfaults when you install Django. When this happens, it's almost *always* one of two causes mostly unrelated to Django itself:

- It may be that your Python code is importing the `pyexpat` module (used for XML parsing), which may conflict with the version embedded in Apache. For full information, see "Expat Causing Apache Crash" at `http://www.djangoproject.com/r/articles/expat-apache-crash/`.

- It may be because you're running mod_python and mod_php in the same Apache instance, with MySQL as your database back-end. In some cases, this causes a known mod_python issue due to version conflicts in PHP and the Python MySQL back-end. There's full information in a mod_python FAQ entry, accessible via `http://www.djangoproject.com/r/articles/php-modpython-faq/`.

If you continue to have problems setting up mod_python, a good thing to do is get a bare-bones mod_python site working, without the Django framework. This is an easy way to isolate mod_python-specific problems. The article "Getting mod_python Working" details this procedure: `http://www.djangoproject.com/r/articles/getting-modpython-working/`.

The next step should be to edit your test code and add an import of any Django-specific code you're using—your views, your models, your URLconf, your RSS configuration, and so forth. Put these imports in your test handler function and access your test URL in a browser. If this causes a crash, you've confirmed it's the importing of Django code that causes the problem. Gradually reduce the set of imports until it stops crashing, so as to find the specific module that causes the problem. Drop down further into modules and look into their imports as necessary. For more help, system tools like `ldconfig` on Linux, `otool` on Mac OS, and `ListDLLs` (from SysInternals) on Windows can help you identify shared dependencies and possible version conflicts.

An Alternative: mod_wsgi

As an alternative to mod_python, you might consider using mod_wsgi (`http://code.google.com/p/modwsgi/`), which has been developed more recently than mod_python and is getting some traction in the Django community. A full overview is outside the scope of this book, but see the official Django documentation for more information.

Using Django with FastCGI

Although Django under Apache and mod_python is the most robust deployment setup, many people use shared hosting, on which FastCGI is the only available deployment option.

Additionally, in some situations, FastCGI allows better security and possibly better performance than mod_python. For small sites, FastCGI can also be more lightweight than Apache.

FastCGI Overview

FastCGI is an efficient way of letting an external application serve pages to a Web server. The Web server delegates the incoming Web requests (via a socket) to FastCGI, which executes the code and passes the response back to the Web server, which, in turn, passes it back to the client's Web browser.

Like mod_python, FastCGI allows code to stay in memory, allowing requests to be served with no startup time. Unlike mod_python, a FastCGI process doesn't run inside the Web server process, but in a separate, persistent process.

WHY RUN CODE IN A SEPARATE PROCESS?

The traditional mod_* arrangements in Apache embed various scripting languages (most notably PHP, Python/mod_python, and Perl/mod_perl) inside the process space of your Web server. Although this lowers startup time (because code doesn't have to be read off disk for every request), it comes at the cost of memory use.

Each Apache process gets a copy of the Apache engine, complete with all the features of Apache that Django simply doesn't take advantage of. FastCGI processes, on the other hand, only have the memory overhead of Python and Django.

Due to the nature of FastCGI, it's also possible to have processes that run under a different user account than the Web server process. That's a nice security benefit on shared systems, because it means you can secure your code from other users.

Before you can start using FastCGI with Django, you'll need to install `flup`, a Python library for dealing with FastCGI. Some users have reported stalled pages with older `flup` versions, so you may want to use the latest SVN version. Get `flup` at `http://www.djangoproject.com/r/flup/`.

Running Your FastCGI Server

FastCGI operates on a client/server model, and in most cases you'll be starting the FastCGI server process on your own. Your Web server (be it Apache, lighttpd, or otherwise) contacts your Django-FastCGI process only when the server needs a dynamic page to be loaded. Because the daemon is already running with the code in memory, it's able to serve the response very quickly.

Note If you're on a shared hosting system, you'll probably be forced to use Web server-managed FastCGI processes. If you're in this situation, you should read the section titled "Running Django on a Shared-Hosting Provider with Apache," later in this chapter.

A Web server can connect to a FastCGI server in one of two ways: it can use either a Unix domain socket (a *named pipe* on Win32 systems) or a TCP socket. What you choose is a matter of preference; a TCP socket is usually easier due to permissions issues.

To start your server, first change into the directory of your project (wherever your `manage.py` is), and then run `manage.py` with the `runfcgi` command:

```
./manage.py runfcgi [options]
```

If you specify `help` as the only option after `runfcgi`, a list of all the available options will display.

You'll need to specify either a `socket` or both `host` and `port`. Then, when you set up your Web server, you'll just need to point it at the socket or host/port you specified when starting the FastCGI server.

A few examples should help explain this:

- Running a threaded server on a TCP port:

  ```
  ./manage.py runfcgi method=threaded host=127.0.0.1 port=3033
  ```

- Running a preforked server on a Unix domain socket:

  ```
  ./manage.py runfcgi method=prefork ➥
  socket=/home/user/mysite.sock pidfile=django.pid
  ```

- Running without daemonizing (backgrounding) the process (good for debugging):

  ```
  ./manage.py runfcgi daemonize=false socket=/tmp/mysite.sock
  ```

Stopping the FastCGI Daemon

If you have the process running in the foreground, it's easy enough to stop it: simply press Ctrl+C to stop and quit the FastCGI server. However, when you're dealing with background processes, you'll need to resort to the Unix `kill` command.

If you specify the `pidfile` option to your `manage.py runfcgi`, you can kill the running FastCGI daemon like this:

```
kill 'cat $PIDFILE'
```

where $PIDFILE is the `pidfile` you specified.

To easily restart your FastCGI daemon on Unix, you can use this small shell script:

```bash
#!/bin/bash

# Replace these three settings.
PROJDIR="/home/user/myproject"
PIDFILE="$PROJDIR/mysite.pid"
SOCKET="$PROJDIR/mysite.sock"

cd $PROJDIR
if [ -f $PIDFILE ]; then
    kill 'cat–$PIDFILE'
    rm -f–$PIDFILE
fi

exec /usr/bin/env - \
  PYTHONPATH="../python:.." \
  ./manage.py runfcgi socket=$SOCKET pidfile=$PIDFILE
```

Using Django with Apache and FastCGI

To use Django with Apache and FastCGI, you'll need Apache installed and configured, with mod_fastcgi installed and enabled. Consult the Apache and mod_fastcgi documentation for instructions: http://www.djangoproject.com/r/mod_fastcgi/.

Once you've completed the setup, point Apache at your Django FastCGI instance by editing the `httpd.conf` (Apache configuration) file. You'll need to do two things:

- Use the `FastCGIExternalServer` directive to specify the location of your FastCGI server.

- Use `mod_rewrite` to point URLs at FastCGI as appropriate.

Specifying the Location of the FastCGI Server

The FastCGIExternalServer directive tells Apache how to find your FastCGI server. As the FastCGIExternalServer docs (http://www.djangoproject.com/r/mod_fastcgi/FastCGIExternalServer/) explain, you can specify either a socket or a host. Here are examples of both:

```
# Connect to FastCGI via a socket/named pipe:
FastCGIExternalServer /home/user/public_html/mysite.fcgi ➡
-socket /home/user/mysite.sock

# Connect to FastCGI via a TCP host/port:
FastCGIExternalServer /home/user/public_html/mysite.fcgi -host 127.0.0.1:3033
```

In either case, the directory /home/user/public_html/ should exist, though the file /home/user/public_html/mysite.fcgi doesn't actually have to exist. It's just a URL used by the Web server internally—a hook for signifying which requests at a URL should be handled by FastCGI. (More on this in the next section.)

Using mod_rewrite to Point URLs at FastCGI

The second step is telling Apache to use FastCGI for URLs that match a certain pattern. To do this, use the mod_rewrite module and rewrite URLs to mysite.fcgi (or whatever you specified in the FastCGIExternalServer directive, as explained in the previous section).

In this example, we tell Apache to use FastCGI to handle any request that doesn't represent a file on the filesystem and doesn't start with /media/. This is probably the most common case, if you're using Django's admin site:

```
<VirtualHost 12.34.56.78>
  ServerName example.com
  DocumentRoot /home/user/public_html
  Alias /media /home/user/python/django/contrib/admin/media
  RewriteEngine On
  RewriteRule ^/(media.*)$ /$1 [QSA,L]
  RewriteCond %{REQUEST_FILENAME} !-f
  RewriteRule ^/(.*)$ /mysite.fcgi/$1 [QSA,L]
</VirtualHost>
```

FastCGI and lighttpd

lighttpd (http://www.djangoproject.com/r/lighttpd/) is a lightweight Web server commonly used for serving static files. It supports FastCGI natively and thus is also an ideal choice for serving both static and dynamic pages, if your site doesn't have any Apache-specific needs.

Make sure mod_fastcgi is in your modules list, somewhere after mod_rewrite and mod_access, but not after mod_accesslog. You'll probably want mod_alias as well, for serving admin media.

Add the following to your lighttpd config file:

```
server.document-root = "/home/user/public_html"
fastcgi.server = (
    "/mysite.fcgi" => (
        "main" => (
            # Use host / port instead of socket for TCP fastcgi
            # "host" => "127.0.0.1",
            # "port" => 3033,
            "socket" => "/home/user/mysite.sock",
            "check-local" => "disable",
        )
    ),
)
alias.url = (
    "/media/" => "/home/user/django/contrib/admin/media/",
)

url.rewrite-once = (
    "^(/media.*)$" => "$1",
    "^/favicon\.ico$" => "/media/favicon.ico",
    "^(/.*)$" => "/mysite.fcgi$1",
)
```

Running Multiple Django Sites on One lighttpd Instance

lighttpd lets you use "conditional configuration" to allow configuration to be customized per host. To specify multiple FastCGI sites, just add a conditional block around your FastCGI config for each site:

```
# If the hostname is 'www.example1.com'...
$HTTP["host"] == "www.example1.com" {
    server.document-root = "/foo/site1"
    fastcgi.server = (
        ...
    )
    ...
}

# If the hostname is 'www.example2.com'...
$HTTP["host"] == "www.example2.com" {
    server.document-root = "/foo/site2"
    fastcgi.server = (
        ...
    )
    ...
}
```

You can also run multiple Django installations on the same site simply by specifying multiple entries in the `fastcgi.server` directive. Add one FastCGI host for each.

Running Django on a Shared-Hosting Provider with Apache

Many shared-hosting providers don't allow you to run your own server daemons or edit the `httpd.conf` file. In these cases, it's still possible to run Django using Web server-spawned processes.

■**Note** If you're using Web server-spawned processes, as explained in this section, there's no need for you to start the FastCGI server on your own. Apache will spawn a number of processes, scaling as it needs to.

In your Web root directory, add this to a file named `.htaccess`:

```
AddHandler fastcgi-script .fcgi
RewriteEngine On
RewriteCond %{REQUEST_FILENAME} !-f
RewriteRule ^(.*)$ mysite.fcgi/$1 [QSA,L]
```

Then, create a small script that tells Apache how to spawn your FastCGI program. Create a file, `mysite.fcgi`, and place it in your Web directory, and be sure to make it executable:

```
#!/usr/bin/python
import sys, os

# Add a custom Python path.
sys.path.insert(0, "/home/user/python")

# Switch to the directory of your project. (Optional.)
# os.chdir("/home/user/myproject")

# Set the DJANGO_SETTINGS_MODULE environment variable.
os.environ['DJANGO_SETTINGS_MODULE'] = "myproject.settings"

from django.core.servers.fastcgi import runfastcgi
runfastcgi(method="threaded", daemonize="false")
```

Restarting the Spawned Server

If you change any Python code on your site, you'll need to tell FastCGI the code has changed. But there's no need to restart Apache in this case. Rather, just reupload `mysite.fcgi`—or edit the file—so that the timestamp on the file changes. When Apache sees the file has been updated, it will restart your Django application for you.

If you have access to a command shell on a Unix system, you can accomplish this easily by using the `touch` command:

```
touch mysite.fcgi
```

Scaling

Now that you know how to get Django running on a single server, let's look at how you can scale out a Django installation. This section walks through how a site might scale from a single server to a large-scale cluster that could serve millions of hits an hour.

It's important to note, however, that nearly every large site is large in different ways, so scaling is anything but a one-size-fits-all operation. The following coverage should suffice to show the general principle, and whenever possible we'll try to point out where different choices could be made.

First off, we'll make a pretty big assumption and exclusively talk about scaling under Apache and mod_python. Though we know of a number of successful medium- to large-scale FastCGI deployments, we're much more familiar with Apache.

Running on a Single Server

Most sites start out running on a single server, with an architecture that looks something like Figure 12-1.

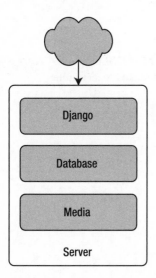

Figure 12-1. *A single-server Django setup*

This works just fine for small- to medium-sized sites, and it's relatively cheap—you can put together a single-server site designed for Django for well under $3,000.

However, as traffic increases you'll quickly run into *resource contention* between the different pieces of software. Database servers and Web servers *love* to have the entire server to themselves, so when run on the same server they often end up "fighting" over the same resources (RAM, CPU) that they'd prefer to monopolize.

This is solved easily by moving the database server to a second machine, as explained in the following section.

Separating Out the Database Server

As far as Django is concerned, the process of separating out the database server is extremely easy: you'll simply need to change the DATABASE_HOST setting to the IP or DNS name of your database server. It's probably a good idea to use the IP if at all possible, as relying on DNS for the connection between your Web server and database server isn't recommended.

With a separate database server, our architecture now looks like Figure 12-2.

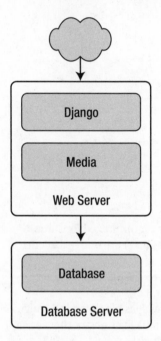

Figure 12-2. *Moving the database onto a dedicated server*

Here we're starting to move into what's usually called *n-tier* architecture. Don't be scared by the buzzword—it just refers to the fact that different "tiers" of the Web stack get separated out onto different physical machines.

At this point, if you anticipate ever needing to grow beyond a single database server, it's probably a good idea to start thinking about connection pooling and/or database replication. Unfortunately, there's not nearly enough space to do those topics justice in this book, so you'll need to consult your database's documentation and/or community for more information.

Running a Separate Media Server

We still have a big problem left over from the single-server setup: the serving of media from the same box that handles dynamic content.

Those two activities perform best under different circumstances, and by smashing them together on the same box you end up with neither performing particularly well. So the next step is to separate out the media—that is, anything *not* generated by a Django view—onto a dedicated server (see Figure 12-3).

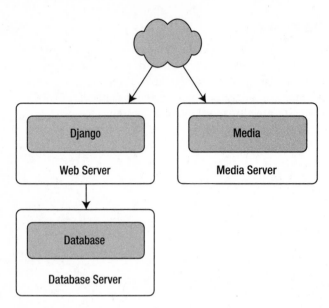

Figure 12-3. *Separating out the media server*

Ideally, this media server should run a stripped-down Web server optimized for static media delivery. lighttpd and tux (http://www.djangoproject.com/r/tux/) are both excellent choices here, but a heavily stripped down Apache could work, too.

For sites heavy in static content (photos, videos, etc.), moving to a separate media server is doubly important and should likely be the *first* step in scaling up.

This step can be slightly tricky, however. If your application involves file uploads, Django needs to be able to write uploaded media to the media server. If media lives on another server, you'll need to arrange a way for that write to happen across the network.

Implementing Load Balancing and Redundancy

At this point, we've broken things down as much as possible. This three-server setup should handle a very large amount of traffic—we served around 10 million hits a day from an architecture of this sort—so if you grow further, you'll need to start adding redundancy.

This is a good thing, actually. One glance at Figure 12-3 shows you that if even a single one of your three servers fails, you'll bring down your entire site. So as you add redundant servers, not only do you increase capacity, but you also increase reliability.

For the sake of this example, let's assume that the Web server hits capacity first. It's relatively easy to get multiple copies of a Django site running on different hardware—just copy all the code onto multiple machines, and start Apache on all of them.

However, you'll need another piece of software to distribute traffic over your multiple servers: a *load balancer*. You can buy expensive and proprietary hardware load balancers, but there are a few high-quality open source software load balancers out there.

Apache's mod_proxy is one option, but we've found Perlbal (http://www.djangoproject.com/r/perlbal/) to be fantastic. It's a load balancer and reverse proxy written by the same folks who wrote Memcached (see Chapter 15).

■Note If you're using FastCGI, you can accomplish this same distribution/load-balancing step by separating your front-end Web servers and back-end FastCGI processes onto different machines. The front-end server essentially becomes the load balancer, and the back-end FastCGI processes replace the Apache/mod_python/Django servers.

With the Web servers now clustered, our evolving architecture starts to look more complex, as shown in Figure 12-4.

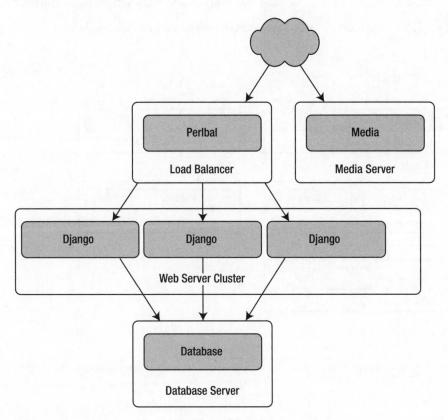

Figure 12-4. *A load-balanced, redundant server setup*

Notice that in the diagram the Web servers are referred to as a "cluster" to indicate that the number of servers is basically variable. Once you have a load balancer out front, you can easily add and remove back-end Web servers without a second of downtime.

Going Big

At this point, the next few steps are pretty much derivatives of the last one:

- As you need more database performance, you might want to add replicated database servers. MySQL includes built-in replication; PostgreSQL users should look into Slony (http://www.djangoproject.com/r/slony/) and pgpool (http://www.djangoproject.com/r/pgpool/) for replication and connection pooling, respectively.

- If the single load balancer isn't enough, you can add more load balancer machines out front and distribute among them using round-robin DNS.

- If a single media server doesn't suffice, you can add more media servers and distribute the load with your load-balancing cluster.

- If you need more cache storage, you can add dedicated cache servers.

- At any stage, if a cluster isn't performing well, you can add more servers to the cluster.

After a few of these iterations, a large-scale architecture might look like Figure 12-5.

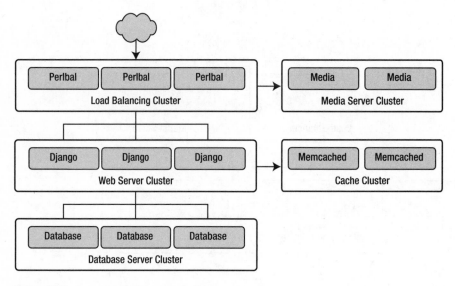

Figure 12-5. *An example large-scale Django setup*

Though we've shown only two or three servers at each level, there's no fundamental limit to how many you can add.

Performance Tuning

If you have a huge amount of money, you can just keep throwing hardware at scaling problems. For the rest of us, though, performance tuning is a must.

■Note Incidentally, if anyone with monstrous gobs of cash is actually reading this book, please consider a substantial donation to the Django Foundation. We accept uncut diamonds and gold ingots, too.

Unfortunately, performance tuning is much more of an art than a science, and it is even more difficult to write about than scaling. If you're serious about deploying a large-scale Django application, you should spend a great deal of time learning how to tune each piece of your stack.

The following sections, though, present a few Django-specific tuning tips we've discovered over the years.

There's No Such Thing As Too Much RAM

Even the really expensive RAM is relatively affordable these days. Buy as much RAM as you can possibly afford, and then buy a little bit more.

Faster processors won't improve performance all that much; most Web servers spend up to 90% of their time waiting on disk I/O. As soon as you start swapping, performance will just die. Faster disks might help slightly, but they're much more expensive than RAM, such that it doesn't really matter.

If you have multiple servers, the first place to put your RAM is in the database server. If you can afford it, get enough RAM to get fit your entire database into memory. This shouldn't be too hard; we've developed a site with more than half a million newspaper articles, and it took under 2GB of space.

Next, max out the RAM on your Web server. The ideal situation is one where neither server swaps—ever. If you get to that point, you should be able to withstand most normal traffic.

Turn Off Keep-Alive

`Keep-Alive` is a feature of HTTP that allows multiple HTTP requests to be served over a single TCP connection, avoiding the TCP setup/teardown overhead.

This looks good at first glance, but it can kill the performance of a Django site. If you're properly serving media from a separate server, each user browsing your site will only request a page from your Django server every ten seconds or so. This leaves HTTP servers waiting around for the next keep-alive request, and an idle HTTP server just consumes RAM that an active one should be using.

Use Memcached

Although Django supports a number of different cache back-ends, none of them even come *close* to being as fast as Memcached. If you have a high-traffic site, don't even bother with the other back-ends—go straight to Memcached.

Use Memcached Often

Of course, selecting Memcached does you no good if you don't actually use it. Chapter 15 is your best friend here: learn how to use Django's cache framework, and use it everywhere possible. Aggressive, preemptive caching is usually the only thing that will keep a site up under major traffic.

Join the Conversation

Each piece of the Django stack—from Linux to Apache to PostgreSQL or MySQL—has an awesome community behind it. If you really want to get that last 1% out of your servers, join the open source communities behind your software and ask for help. Most free-software community members will be happy to help.

And also be sure to join the Django community. Your humble authors are only two members of an incredibly active, growing group of Django developers. Our community has a huge amount of collective experience to offer.

What's Next?

The remaining chapters focus on other Django features that you might or might not need, depending on your application. Feel free to read them in any order you choose.

## PART 3

Other Django Features

■ ■ ■

Generating Non-HTML Content

Usually when we talk about developing Web sites, we're talking about producing HTML. Of course, there's a lot more to the Web than HTML; we use the Web to distribute data in all sorts of formats: RSS, PDFs, images, and so forth.

So far, we've focused on the common case of HTML production, but in this chapter we'll take a detour and look at using Django to produce other types of content.

Django has convenient built-in tools that you can use to produce some common non-HTML content:

- RSS/Atom syndication feeds

- Sitemaps (an XML format originally developed by Google that gives hints to search engines)

We'll examine each of those tools a little later, but first we'll cover the basic principles.

The Basics: Views and MIME Types

Recall from Chapter 3 that a view function is simply a Python function that takes a Web request and returns a Web response. This response can be the HTML contents of a Web page, or a redirect, or a 404 error, or an XML document, or an image . . . or anything, really.

More formally, a Django view function *must*

- Accept an `HttpRequest` instance as its first argument

- Return an `HttpResponse` instance

The key to returning non-HTML content from a view lies in the `HttpResponse` class, specifically the `mimetype` argument. By tweaking the MIME type, we can indicate to the browser that we've returned a response of a different format.

For example, let's look at a view that returns a PNG image. To keep things simple, we'll just read the file off the disk:

```
from django.http import HttpResponse

def my_image(request):
    image_data = open("/path/to/my/image.png", "rb").read()
    return HttpResponse(image_data, mimetype="image/png")
```

That's it! If you replace the image path in the open() call with a path to a real image, you can use this very simple view to serve an image, and the browser will display it correctly.

The other important thing to keep in mind is that HttpResponse objects implement Python's standard "filelike object" API. This means that you can use an HttpResponse instance in any place Python (or a third-party library) expects a file.

For an example of how that works, let's take a look at producing CSV with Django.

Producing CSV

CSV is a simple data format usually used by spreadsheet software. It's basically a series of table rows, with each cell in the row separated by a comma (CSV stands for *comma-separated values*). For example, here's some data on "unruly" airline passengers in CSV format:

```
Year,Unruly Airline Passengers
1995,146
1996,184
1997,235
1998,200
1999,226
2000,251
2001,299
2002,273
2003,281
2004,304
2005,203
2006,134
2007,147
```

■**Note** The preceding listing contains real numbers! They come from the US Federal Aviation Administration.

Though CSV looks simple, its formatting details haven't been universally agreed upon. Different pieces of software produce and consume different variants of CSV, making it a bit tricky to use. Luckily, Python comes with a standard CSV library, csv, that is pretty much bulletproof.

Because the csv module operates on filelike objects, it's a snap to use an HttpResponse instead:

```
import csv
from django.http import HttpResponse

# Number of unruly passengers each year 1995 - 2007. In a real application
# this would likely come from a database or some other back-end data store.
UNRULY_PASSENGERS = [146,184,235,200,226,251,299,273,
281,304,203, 134, 147]
```

```
def unruly_passengers_csv(request):
    # Create the HttpResponse object with the appropriate CSV header.
    response = HttpResponse(mimetype='text/csv')
    response['Content-Disposition'] = 'attachment; filename=unruly.csv'

    # Create the CSV writer using the HttpResponse as the "file."
    writer = csv.writer(response)
    writer.writerow(['Year', 'Unruly Airline Passengers'])
    for (year, num) in zip(range(1995, 2006), UNRULY_PASSENGERS):
        writer.writerow([year, num])

    return response
```

The code and comments should be pretty clear, but a few things deserve special mention:

- The response is given the text/csv MIME type (instead of the default text/html). This tells browsers that the document is a CSV file.

- The response gets an additional Content-Disposition header, which contains the name of the CSV file. This header (well, the "attachment" part) will instruct the browser to prompt for a location to save the file instead of just displaying it. This file name is arbitrary; call it whatever you want. Browsers will use it in the Save As dialog.

- To assign a header on an HttpResponse, just treat the HttpResponse as a dictionary and set a key/value.

- Hooking into the CSV-generation API is easy: just pass response as the first argument to csv.writer. The csv.writer function expects a filelike object, and HttpResponse objects fit the bill.

- For each row in your CSV file, call writer.writerow, passing it an iterable object such as a list or a tuple.

- The CSV module takes care of quoting for you, so you don't have to worry about escaping strings with quotes or commas in them. Just pass information to writerow(), and it will do the right thing.

This is the general pattern you'll use any time you need to return non-HTML content: create an HttpResponse response object (with a special MIME type), pass it to something expecting a file, and then return the response.

Let's look at a few more examples.

Generating PDFs

Portable Document Format (PDF) is a format developed by Adobe that's used to represent printable documents, complete with pixel-perfect formatting, embedded fonts, and 2D vector graphics. You can think of a PDF document as the digital equivalent of a printed document; indeed, PDFs are often used to distribute documents for printing.

You can easily generate PDFs with Python and Django thanks to the excellent open source ReportLab library (http://www.reportlab.org/rl_toolkit.html). The advantage of generating PDF files dynamically is that you can create customized PDFs for different purposes—say, for different users or different pieces of content.

For example, your humble authors used Django and ReportLab at KUsports.com to generate customized, printer-ready NCAA tournament brackets.

Installing ReportLab

Before you do any PDF generation, however, you'll need to install ReportLab. It's usually simple: just download and install the library from `http://www.reportlab.org/downloads.html`.

■Note If you're using a modern Linux distribution, you might want to check your package-management utility before installing ReportLab. Most package repositories have added ReportLab. For example, if you're using Ubuntu, a simple `apt-get install python-reportlab` will do the trick nicely.

The user guide (naturally available only as a PDF file) at `http://www.reportlab.org/rsrc/userguide.pdf` has additional installation instructions.

Test your installation by importing it in the Python interactive interpreter:

```
>>> import reportlab
```

If that command doesn't raise any errors, the installation worked.

Writing Your View

Like CSV, generating PDFs dynamically with Django is easy because the ReportLab API acts on filelike objects.

Here's a "Hello World" example:

```
from reportlab.pdfgen import canvas
from django.http import HttpResponse

def hello_pdf(request):
    # Create the HttpResponse object with the appropriate PDF headers.
    response = HttpResponse(mimetype='application/pdf')
    response['Content-Disposition'] = 'attachment; filename=hello.pdf'

    # Create the PDF object, using the response object as its "file."
    p = canvas.Canvas(response)

    # Draw things on the PDF. Here's where the PDF generation happens.
    # See the ReportLab documentation for the full list of functionality.
    p.drawString(100, 100, "Hello world.")

    # Close the PDF object cleanly, and we're done.
    p.showPage()
    p.save()
    return response
```

A few notes are in order:

- Here we use the application/pdf MIME type. This tells browsers that the document is a PDF file, rather than an HTML file. If you leave off this information, browsers will probably interpret the response as HTML, which will result in scary gobbledygook in the browser window.

- Hooking into the ReportLab API is easy: just pass response as the first argument to canvas.Canvas. The Canvas class expects a filelike object, and HttpResponse objects fit the bill.

- All subsequent PDF-generation methods are called on the PDF object (in this case, p), not on response.

- Finally, it's important to call showPage() and save() on the PDF file—or else you'll end up with a corrupted PDF file.

Complex PDFs

If you're creating a complex PDF document (or any large data blob), consider using the cStringIO library as a temporary holding place for your PDF file. The cStringIO library provides a filelike object interface that is written in C for maximum efficiency.

Here's the previous "Hello World" example rewritten to use cStringIO:

```
from cStringIO import StringIO
from reportlab.pdfgen import canvas
from django.http import HttpResponse

def hello_pdf(request):
    # Create the HttpResponse object with the appropriate PDF headers.
    response = HttpResponse(mimetype='application/pdf')
    response['Content-Disposition'] = 'attachment; filename=hello.pdf'

    temp = StringIO()

    # Create the PDF object, using the StringIO object as its "file."
    p = canvas.Canvas(temp)

    # Draw things on the PDF. Here's where the PDF generation happens.
    # See the ReportLab documentation for the full list of functionality.
    p.drawString(100, 100, "Hello world.")

    # Close the PDF object cleanly.
    p.showPage()
    p.save()

    # Get the value of the StringIO buffer and write it to the response.
    response.write(temp.getvalue())
    return response
```

Other Possibilities

There's a whole host of other types of content you can generate in Python. Here are a few more ideas and some pointers to libraries you could use to implement them:

- *ZIP files*: Python's standard library ships with the `zipfile` module, which can both read and write compressed ZIP files. You could use it to provide on-demand archives of a bunch of files, or perhaps compress large documents when requested. You could similarly produce TAR files using the standard library's `tarfile` module.

- *Dynamic images*: The Python Imaging Library (PIL; `http://www.pythonware.com/products/pil/`) is a fantastic toolkit for producing images (PNG, JPEG, GIF, and a whole lot more). You could use it to automatically scale down images into thumbnails, composite multiple images into a single frame, or even do Web-based image processing.

- *Plots and charts*: There is a number of powerful Python plotting and charting libraries you could use to produce on-demand maps, charts, plots, and graphs. We can't possibly list them all, so here are two of the highlights:

  - `matplotlib` (`http://matplotlib.sourceforge.net/`) can be used to produce the type of high-quality plots usually generated with MatLab or Mathematica.

  - `pygraphviz` (`http://networkx.lanl.gov/pygraphviz/`), an interface to the Graphviz graph layout toolkit (`http://graphviz.org/`), can be used for generating structured diagrams of graphs and networks.

In general, any Python library capable of writing to a file can be hooked into Django. The possibilities are immense.

Now that we've looked at the basics of generating non-HTML content, let's step up a level of abstraction. Django ships with some pretty nifty built-in tools for generating some common types of non-HTML content.

The Syndication-Feed Framework

Django comes with a high-level syndication-feed-generating framework that makes creating RSS and Atom feeds easy.

WHAT'S RSS? WHAT'S ATOM?

RSS and Atom are both XML-based formats you can use to provide automatically updating "feeds" of your site's content. Read more about RSS at `http://www.whatisrss.com/`, and get information on Atom at `http://www.atomenabled.org/`.

To create any syndication feed, all you have to do is write a short Python class. You can create as many feeds as you want.

The high-level syndication-feed-generating framework is a view that's hooked to /feeds/ by convention. Django uses the remainder of the URL (everything after /feeds/) to determine which feed to return.

To create a feed, you'll write a Feed class and point to it in your URLconf.

Initialization

To activate syndication feeds on your Django site, add this URLconf:

```
(r'^feeds/(?P<url>.*)/$', 'django.contrib.syndication.views.feed',
    {'feed_dict': feeds}
),
```

This line tells Django to use the RSS framework to handle all URLs starting with feeds/. (You can change that feeds/prefix to fit your own needs.)

This URLconf line has an extra argument: {'feed_dict': feeds}. Use this extra argument to pass the syndication framework the feeds that should be published under that URL.

Specifically, feed_dict should be a dictionary that maps a feed's slug (short URL label) to its Feed class. You can define the feed_dict in the URLconf itself. Here's a full example URLconf:

```
from django.conf.urls.defaults import *
from mysite.feeds import LatestEntries, LatestEntriesByCategory

feeds = {
    'latest': LatestEntries,
    'categories': LatestEntriesByCategory,
}

urlpatterns = patterns('',
    # ...
    (r'^feeds/(?P<url>.*)/$', 'django.contrib.syndication.views.feed',
        {'feed_dict': feeds}),
    # ...
)
```

The preceding example registers two feeds:

- The feed represented by LatestEntries will live at feeds/latest/.
- The feed represented by LatestEntriesByCategory will live at feeds/categories/.

Once that's set up, you'll need to define the Feed classes themselves.

A Feed class is a simple Python class that represents a syndication feed. A feed can be simple (e.g., a "site news" feed, which is a basic feed displaying the latest entries of a blog) or more complex (e.g., a feed displaying all the blog entries in a particular category, where the category is variable).

Feed classes must subclass django.contrib.syndication.feeds.Feed. They can live anywhere in your code tree.

A Simple Feed

This simple example describes a feed of the latest five blog entries for a given blog:

```
from django.contrib.syndication.feeds import Feed
from mysite.blog.models import Entry

class LatestEntries(Feed):
    title = "My Blog"
    link = "/archive/"
    description = "The latest news about stuff."

    def items(self):
        return Entry.objects.order_by('-pub_date')[:5]
```

The important things to notice here are as follows:

- The class subclasses `django.contrib.syndication.feeds.Feed`.

- `title`, `link`, and `description` correspond to the standard RSS `<title>`, `<link>`, and `<description>` elements, respectively.

- `items()` is simply a method that returns a list of objects that should be included in the feed as `<item>` elements. Although this example returns `Entry` objects using Django's database API, `items()` doesn't have to return model instances.

There's just one more step. In an RSS feed, each `<item>` has a `<title>`, `<link>`, and `<description>`. We need to tell the framework what data to put into those elements.

- To specify the contents of `<title>` and `<description>`, create Django templates called `feeds/latest_title.html` and `feeds/latest_description.html`, where `latest` is the `slug` specified in the URLconf for the given feed. Note that the `.html` extension is required.

  The RSS system renders that template for each item, passing it two template context variables:

  - `obj`: The current object (one of whichever objects you returned in `items()`).

  - `site`: A `django.models.core.sites.Site` object representing the current site. This is useful for `{{ site.domain }}` or `{{ site.name }}`.

  If you don't create a template for either the title or description, the framework will use the template `"{{ obj }}"` by default—that is, the normal string representation of the object. (For model objects, this will be the `__unicode__()` method.)

  You can also change the names of these two templates by specifying `title_template` and `description_template` as attributes of your `Feed` class.

- To specify the contents of `<link>`, you have two options. For each item in `items()`, Django first tries executing a `get_absolute_url()` method on that object. If that method doesn't exist, it tries calling a method `item_link()` in the `Feed` class, passing it a single parameter, `item`, which is the object itself.

  Both `get_absolute_url()` and `item_link()` should return the item's URL as a normal Python string.

- For the previous `LatestEntries` example, we could have very simple feed templates. `latest_title.html` contains

  ```
  {{ obj.title }}
  ```

  and `latest_description.html` contains

  ```
  {{ obj.description }}
  ```

  It's almost *too* easy. . . .

A More Complex Feed

The framework also supports more-complex feeds, via parameters.

For example, say your blog offers an RSS feed for every distinct "tag" you've used to categorize your entries. It would be silly to create a separate `Feed` class for each tag; that would violate the Don't Repeat Yourself (DRY) principle and would couple data to programming logic.

Instead, the syndication framework lets you make generic feeds that return items based on information in the feed's URL.

Your tag-specific feeds could use URLs like this:

- `http://example.com/feeds/tags/python/`: Returns recent entries tagged with "python"

- `http://example.com/feeds/tags/cats/`: Returns recent entries tagged with "cats"

The slug here is `tags`. The syndication framework sees the extra URL bits after the slug—`python` and `cats` and gives you a hook to tell it what those URL bits mean and how they should influence which items get published in the feed.

An example makes this clear. Here's the code for these tag-specific feeds:

```python
from django.core.exceptions import ObjectDoesNotExist
from mysite.blog.models import Entry, Tag

class TagFeed(Feed):
    def get_object(self, bits):
        # In case of "/feeds/tags/cats/dogs/mice/", or other such
        # clutter, check that bits has only one member.
        if len(bits) != 1:
            raise ObjectDoesNotExist
        return Tag.objects.get(tag=bits[0])
```

```
    def title(self, obj):
        return "My Blog: Entries tagged with %s" % obj.tag

    def link(self, obj):
        return obj.get_absolute_url()

    def description(self, obj):
        return "Entries tagged with %s" % obj.tag

    def items(self, obj):
        entries = Entry.objects.filter(tags__id__exact=obj.id)
        return entries.order_by('-pub_date')[:30]
```

Here's the basic algorithm of the RSS framework, given this class and a request to the URL /feeds/tags/python/:

1. The framework gets the URL /feeds/tags/python/ and notices there's an extra bit of URL after the slug. It splits that remaining string by the slash character (/) and calls the Feed class's get_object() method, passing it the bits.

   In this case, bits is [python]. For a request to /feeds/tags/python/django/, bits would be ['python', 'django'].

2. get_object() is responsible for retrieving the given Tag object, from the given bits.

   In this case, it uses the Django database API to retrieve the Tag. Note that get_object() should raise django.core.exceptions.ObjectDoesNotExist if given invalid parameters. There's no try/except around the Tag.objects.get() call, because it's not necessary. That function raises Tag.DoesNotExist on failure, and Tag.DoesNotExist is a subclass of ObjectDoesNotExist. Raising ObjectDoesNotExist in get_object() tells Django to produce a 404 error for that request.

3. To generate the feed's <title>, <link>, and <description>, Django uses the title(), link(), and description() methods. In the previous example, they were simple string class attributes, but this example illustrates that they can be either strings *or* methods. For each of title, link, and description, Django follows this algorithm:

   a. It tries to call a method, passing the obj argument, where obj is the object returned by get_object().

   b. Failing that, it tries to call a method with no arguments.

   c. Failing that, it uses the class attribute.

4. Finally, note that items() in this example also takes the obj argument. The algorithm for items is the same as described in the previous step—first, it tries items(obj), then items(), and then finally an items class attribute (which should be a list).

Full documentation of all the methods and attributes of the Feed classes is always available from the official Django documentation (http://docs.djangoproject.com/en/dev/ref/contrib/syndication/).

Specifying the Type of Feed

By default, the syndication framework produces RSS 2.0. To change that, add a feed_type attribute to your Feed class:

```
from django.utils.feedgenerator import Atom1Feed

class MyFeed(Feed):
    feed_type = Atom1Feed
```

Note that you set feed_type to a class object, not an instance. Currently available feed types are shown in Table 13-1.

Table 13-1. *Feed Types*

Feed Class	Format
django.utils.feedgenerator.Rss201rev2Feed	RSS 2.01 (default)
django.utils.feedgenerator.RssUserland091Feed	RSS 0.91
django.utils.feedgenerator.Atom1Feed	Atom 1.0

Enclosures

To specify enclosures (i.e., media resources associated with a feed item such as MP3 podcast feeds), use the item_enclosure_url, item_enclosure_length, and item_enclosure_mime_type hooks, as in this example:

```
from myproject.models import Song

class MyFeedWithEnclosures(Feed):
    title = "Example feed with enclosures"
    link = "/feeds/example-with-enclosures/"

    def items(self):
        return Song.objects.all()[:30]

    def item_enclosure_url(self, item):
        return item.song_url

    def item_enclosure_length(self, item):
        return item.song_length

    item_enclosure_mime_type = "audio/mpeg"
```

This assumes, of course, that you've created a Song object with song_url and song_length (i.e., the size in bytes) fields.

Language

Feeds created by the syndication framework automatically include the appropriate <language> tag (RSS 2.0) or xml:lang attribute (Atom). This comes directly from your LANGUAGE_CODE setting.

URLs

The link method/attribute can return either an absolute URL (e.g., /blog/) or a URL with the fully qualified domain and protocol (e.g., http://www.example.com/blog/). If link doesn't return the domain, the syndication framework will insert the domain of the current site, according to your SITE_ID setting. (See Chapter 16 for more on SITE_ID and the sites framework.)

Atom feeds require a <link rel="self"> that defines the feed's current location. The syndication framework populates this automatically.

Publishing Atom and RSS Feeds in Tandem

Some developers like to make available both Atom *and* RSS versions of their feeds. That's easy to do with Django: just create a subclass of your Feed class and set the feed_type to something different. Then update your URLconf to add the extra versions. Here's a full example:

```
from django.contrib.syndication.feeds import Feed
from django.utils.feedgenerator import Atom1Feed
from mysite.blog.models import Entry

class RssLatestEntries(Feed):
    title = "My Blog"
    link = "/archive/"
    description = "The latest news about stuff."

    def items(self):
        return Entry.objects.order_by('-pub_date')[:5]

class AtomLatestEntries(RssLatestEntries):
    feed_type = Atom1Feed
```

And here's the accompanying URLconf:

```
from django.conf.urls.defaults import *
from myproject.feeds import RssLatestEntries, AtomLatestEntries

feeds = {
    'rss': RssLatestEntries,
    'atom': AtomLatestEntries,
}
```

```
urlpatterns = patterns('',
    # ...
    (r'^feeds/(?P<url>.*)/$', 'django.contrib.syndication. . views.feed',
        {'feed_dict': feeds}),
    # ...
)
```

The Sitemap Framework

A *sitemap* is an XML file on your Web site that tells search-engine indexers how frequently your pages change and how "important" certain pages are in relation to other pages on your site. This information helps search engines index your site.

For example, here's a piece of the sitemap for Django's Web site (`http://www.djangoproject.com/sitemap.xml`):

```
<?xml version="1.0" encoding="UTF-8"?>
<urlset xmlns="http://www.sitemaps.org/schemas/sitemap/0.9">
  <url>
    <loc>http://www.djangoproject.com/documentation/</loc>
    <changefreq>weekly</changefreq>
    <priority>0.5</priority>
  </url>
  <url>
    <loc>http://www.djangoproject.com/documentation/0_90/</loc>
    <changefreq>never</changefreq>
    <priority>0.1</priority>
  </url>
  ...
</urlset>
```

For more on sitemaps, see `http://www.sitemaps.org/`.

The Django sitemap framework automates the creation of this XML file by letting you express this information in Python code. To create a sitemap, you just need to write a `Sitemap` class and point to it in your URLconf.

Installation

To install the sitemap application, follow these steps:

1. Add `'django.contrib.sitemaps'` to your `INSTALLED_APPS` setting.

2. Make sure `'django.template.loaders.app_directories.load_template_source'` is in your `TEMPLATE_LOADERS` setting. It's in there by default, so you'll need to change this only if you've changed that setting.

3. Make sure you've installed the sites framework (see Chapter 16).

■Note The sitemap application doesn't install any database tables. The only reason it needs to go into INSTALLED_APPS is so the load_template_source template loader can find the default templates.

Initialization

To activate sitemap generation on your Django site, add this line to your URLconf:

```
(r'^sitemap\.xml$', 'django.contrib.sitemaps.views.sitemap', {'sitemaps': sitemaps})
```

This line tells Django to build a sitemap when a client accesses /sitemap.xml. (Note that the dot character in sitemap.xml is escaped with a backslash because dots have a special meaning in regular expressions.)

The name of the sitemap file is not important, but the location is. Search engines will index links in your sitemap for only the current URL level and below. For instance, if sitemap.xml lives in your root directory, it may reference any URL in your site. However, if your sitemap lives at /content/sitemap.xml, it may only reference URLs that begin with /content/.

The sitemap view takes an extra, required argument: {'sitemaps': sitemaps}. sitemaps should be a dictionary that maps a short section label (e.g., blog or news) to its Sitemap class (e.g., BlogSitemap or NewsSitemap). It may also map to an *instance* of a Sitemap class (e.g., BlogSitemap(some_var)).

Sitemap Classes

A Sitemap class is a simple Python class that represents a "section" of entries in your sitemap. For example, one Sitemap class could represent all the entries of your weblog, while another could represent all of the events in your events calendar.

In the simplest case, all these sections get lumped together into one sitemap.xml, but it's also possible to use the framework to generate a sitemap index that references individual sitemap files, one per section (as described shortly).

Sitemap classes must subclass django.contrib.sitemaps.Sitemap. They can live anywhere in your code tree. For example, let's assume you have a blog system, with an Entry model, and you want your sitemap to include all the links to your individual blog entries. Here's how your Sitemap class might look:

```
from django.contrib.sitemaps import Sitemap
from mysite.blog.models import Entry

class BlogSitemap(Sitemap):
    changefreq = "never"
    priority = 0.5

    def items(self):
        return Entry.objects.filter(is_draft=False)

    def lastmod(self, obj):
        return obj.pub_date
```

Declaring a `Sitemap` should look very similar to declaring a `Feed`. That's by design.

Like `Feed` classes, `Sitemap` members can be either methods or attributes. See the steps in the earlier "A More Complex Feed" section for more about how this works.

A `Sitemap` class can define the following methods/attributes:

- `items` *(required)*: Provides a list of objects. The framework doesn't care what *type* of objects they are; all that matters is that these objects get passed to the `location()`, `lastmod()`, `changefreq()`, and `priority()` methods.

- `location` *(optional)*: Gives the absolute URL for a given object. Here, "absolute URL" means a URL that doesn't include the protocol or domain. Here are some examples:

  - *Good*: `'/foo/bar/'`

  - *Bad*: `'example.com/foo/bar/'`

  - *Bad*: `'http://example.com/foo/bar/'`

  If `location` isn't provided, the framework will call the `get_absolute_url()` method on each object as returned by `items()`.

- `lastmod` *(optional)*: The object's "last modification" date, as a Python `datetime` object.

- `changefreq` *(optional)*: How often the object changes. Possible values (as given by the Sitemaps specification) are as follows:

  - `'always'`

  - `'hourly'`

  - `'daily'`

  - `'weekly'`

  - `'monthly'`

  - `'yearly'`

  - `'never'`

- `priority` *(optional)*: A suggested indexing priority between `0.0` and `1.0`. The default priority of a page is `0.5`; see the `http://www.sitemaps.org/` documentation for more about how `priority` works.

Shortcuts

The sitemap framework provides a couple of convenience classes for common cases. These are described in the sections that follow.

FlatPageSitemap

The `django.contrib.sitemaps.FlatPageSitemap` class looks at all flatpages defined for the current site and creates an entry in the sitemap. These entries include only the `location` attribute—not `lastmod`, `changefreq`, or `priority`.

See Chapter 16 for more about flatpages.

GenericSitemap

The GenericSitemap class works with any generic views (see Chapter 11) you already have.

To use it, create an instance, passing in the same info_dict you pass to the generic views. The only requirement is that the dictionary have a queryset entry. It may also have a date_ field entry that specifies a date field for objects retrieved from the queryset. This will be used for the lastmod attribute in the generated sitemap. You may also pass priority and changefreq keyword arguments to the GenericSitemap constructor to specify these attributes for all URLs.

Here's an example of a URLconf using both FlatPageSitemap and GenericSiteMap (with the hypothetical Entry object from earlier):

```
from django.conf.urls.defaults import *
from django.contrib.sitemaps import FlatPageSitemap, GenericSitemap
from mysite.blog.models import Entry

info_dict = {
    'queryset': Entry.objects.all(),
    'date_field': 'pub_date',
}

sitemaps = {
    'flatpages': FlatPageSitemap,
    'blog': GenericSitemap(info_dict, priority=0.6),
}

urlpatterns = patterns('',
    # some generic view using info_dict
    # ...

    # the sitemap
    (r'^sitemap\.xml$',
     'django.contrib.sitemaps.views.sitemap',
     {'sitemaps': sitemaps})
)
```

Creating a Sitemap Index

The sitemap framework also has the ability to create a sitemap index that references individual sitemap files, one per section defined in your sitemaps dictionary. The only differences in usage are as follows:

- You use two views in your URLconf: django.contrib.sitemaps.views.index and django.contrib.sitemaps.views.sitemap.

- The django.contrib.sitemaps.views.sitemap view should take a section keyword argument.

Here is what the relevant URLconf lines would look like for the previous example:

```
(r'^sitemap.xml$',
 'django.contrib.sitemaps.views.index',
 {'sitemaps': sitemaps}),

(r'^sitemap-(?P<section>.+).xml$',
 'django.contrib.sitemaps.views.sitemap',
 {'sitemaps': sitemaps})
```

This will automatically generate a `sitemap.xml` file that references both `sitemap-flatpages.xml` and `sitemap-blog.xml`. The `Sitemap` classes and the `sitemaps` dictionary don't change at all.

Pinging Google

You may want to "ping" Google when your sitemap changes, to let it know to reindex your site. The framework provides a function to do just that: `django.contrib.sitemaps.ping_google()`.

`ping_google()` takes an optional argument, `sitemap_url`, which should be the absolute URL of your site's sitemap (e.g., `'/sitemap.xml'`). If this argument isn't provided, `ping_google()` will attempt to figure out your sitemap by performing a reverse lookup on your URLconf.

`ping_google()` raises the exception `django.contrib.sitemaps.SitemapNotFound` if it cannot determine your sitemap URL.

One useful way to call `ping_google()` is from a model's `save()` method:

```
from django.contrib.sitemaps import ping_google

class Entry(models.Model):
    # ...
    def save(self, *args, **kwargs):
        super(Entry, self).save(*args, **kwargs)
        try:
            ping_google()
        except Exception:
            # Bare 'except' because we could get a variety
            # of HTTP-related exceptions.
            pass
```

A more efficient solution, however, would be to call `ping_google()` from a `cron` script or some other scheduled task. The function makes an HTTP request to Google's servers, so you may not want to introduce that network overhead each time you call `save()`.

Finally, if `'django.contrib.sitemaps'` is in your `INSTALLED_APPS`, then your `manage.py` will include a new command, `ping_google`. This is useful for command-line access to pinging. Here's an example:

```
python manage.py ping_google /sitemap.xml
```

What's Next?

Next we'll continue to dig deeper into Django's built-in tools. Chapter 14 looks at all the tools you need to provide user-customized sites: sessions, users, and authentication.

CHAPTER 14

■ ■ ■

Sessions, Users, and Registration

It's time for a confession: we've been deliberately ignoring an important aspect of Web development prior to this point. So far, we've thought of the traffic visiting our sites as some faceless, anonymous mass hurtling itself against our carefully designed pages.

This isn't true, of course. The browsers hitting our sites have real humans behind them (most of the time, at least). That's a big thing to ignore: the Internet is at its best when it serves to connect *people*, not machines. If we're going to develop truly compelling sites, eventually we're going to have to deal with the bodies behind the browsers.

Unfortunately, it's not all that easy. HTTP is designed to be *stateless*—that is, each and every request happens in a vacuum. There's no persistence between one request and the next, and we can't count on any aspects of a request (IP address, user agent, etc.) to consistently indicate successive requests from the same person.

In this chapter you'll learn how to handle this lack of state. We'll start at the lowest level (*cookies*), and work up to the high-level tools for handling sessions, users, and registration.

Cookies

Browser developers long ago recognized that HTTP's statelessness poses a huge problem for Web developers, and thus *cookies* were born. A cookie is a small piece of information that browsers store on behalf of Web servers. Every time a browser requests a page from a certain server, it gives back the cookie that it initially received.

Let's take a look at how this might work. When you open your browser and type in google.com, your browser sends an HTTP request to Google that starts something like this:

```
GET / HTTP/1.1
Host: google.com
...
```

When Google replies, the HTTP response looks something like the following:

```
HTTP/1.1 200 OK
Content-Type: text/html
Set-Cookie: PREF=ID=5b14f22bdaf1e81c:TM=1167000671:LM=1167000671;
            expires=Sun, 17-Jan-2038 19:14:07 GMT;
            path=/; domain=.google.com
Server: GWS/2.1
...
```

Notice the `Set-Cookie` header. Your browser will store that cookie value (`PREF=ID=`
`5b14f22bdaf1e81c:TM=1167000671:LM=1167000671`) and serve it back to Google every time you
access the site. So the next time you access Google, your browser is going to send a request
like this:

```
GET / HTTP/1.1
Host: google.com
Cookie: PREF=ID=5b14f22bdaf1e81c:TM=1167000671:LM=1167000671
...
```

Google then can use that `Cookie` value to know that you're the same person who accessed
the site earlier. This value might, for example, be a key into a database that stores user information. Google could (and does) use it to display your account's username on the page.

Getting and Setting Cookies

When dealing with persistence in Django, most of the time you'll want to use the higher-level
session and/or user frameworks discussed a little later in this chapter. However, first look at
how to read and write cookies at a low level. This should help you understand how the rest of
the tools discussed in the chapter actually work, and it will come in handy if you ever need to
play with cookies directly.

Reading cookies that are already set is simple. Every `HttpRequest` object has a `COOKIES`
object that acts like a dictionary; you can use it to read any cookies that the browser has sent
to the view:

```
def show_color(request):
    if "favorite_color" in request.COOKIES:
        return HttpResponse("Your favorite color is %s" % \
            request.COOKIES["favorite_color"])
    else:
        return HttpResponse("You don't have a favorite color.")
```

Writing cookies is slightly more complicated. You need to use the `set_cookie()` method
on an `HttpResponse` object. Here's an example that sets the `favorite_color` cookie based on a
`GET` parameter:

```
def set_color(request):
    if "favorite_color" in request.GET:

        # Create an HttpResponse object...
        response = HttpResponse("Your favorite color is now %s" % \
            request.GET["favorite_color"])

        # ... and set a cookie on the response
        response.set_cookie("favorite_color",
                            request.GET["favorite_color"])

        return response

    else:
        return HttpResponse("You didn't give a favorite color.")
```

You can also pass a number of optional arguments to response.set_cookie() that control aspects of the cookie, as shown in Table 14-1.

Table 14-1. *Cookie Options*

Parameter	Default	Description
max_age	None	Age (in seconds) that the cookie should last. If this parameter is None, the cookie will last only until the browser is closed.
expires	None	The actual date/time when the cookie should expire. It needs to be in the format "Wdy, DD-Mth-YY HH:MM:SS GMT". If given, this parameter over-rides the max_age parameter.
path	"/"	The path prefix that this cookie is valid for. Browsers will only pass the cookie back to pages below this path prefix, so you can use this to prevent cookies from being sent to other sections of your site. This is especially useful when you don't control the top level of your site's domain.
domain	None	The domain that this cookie is valid for. You can use this parameter to set a cross-domain cookie. For example, domain=".example.com" will set a cookie that is readable by the domains www.example.com, www2.example.com, and an.other.sub.domain.example.com. If this parameter is set to None, a cookie will only be readable by the domain that set it.
secure	False	If set to True, this parameter instructs the browser to only return this cookie to pages accessed over HTTPS.

The Mixed Blessing of Cookies

You might notice a number of potential problems with the way cookies work. Let's look at some of the more important ones:

- Storage of cookies is voluntary; a client does not have to accept or store cookies. In fact, all browsers enable users to control the policy for accepting cookies. If you want to see just how vital cookies are to the Web, try turning on your browser's "prompt to accept every cookie" option.

  Despite their nearly universal use, cookies are still the definition of unreliability. This means that developers should check that a user actually accepts cookies before relying on them.

- Cookies (especially those not sent over HTTPS) are not secure. Because HTTP data is sent in cleartext, cookies are extremely vulnerable to *snooping* attacks. That is, an attacker snooping on the wire can intercept a cookie and read it. This means you should never store sensitive information in a cookie.

  There's an even more insidious attack, known as a *man-in-the-middle* attack, wherein an attacker intercepts a cookie and uses it to pose as another user. Chapter 20 discusses attacks of this nature in depth, as well as ways to prevent it.

- Cookies aren't even secure from their intended recipients. Most browsers provide easy ways to edit the content of individual cookies, and resourceful users can always use tools like mechanize (`http://wwwsearch.sourceforge.net/mechanize/`) to construct HTTP requests by hand.

  So you can't store data in cookies that might be sensitive to tampering. The canonical mistake in this scenario is storing something like `IsLoggedIn=1` in a cookie when a user logs in. You'd be amazed at the number of sites that make mistakes of this nature; it takes only a second to fool these sites' "security" systems.

Django's Session Framework

With all of these limitations and potential security holes, it's obvious that cookies and persistent sessions are examples of those "pain points" in Web development. Of course, Django's goal is to be an effective painkiller, so it comes with a session framework designed to smooth over these difficulties for you.

This session framework lets you store and retrieve arbitrary data on a per-site visitor basis. It stores data on the server side and abstracts the sending and receiving of cookies. Cookies use only a hashed session ID—not the data itself—thus protecting you from most of the common cookie problems.

Let's look at how to enable sessions and use them in views.

Enabling Sessions

Sessions are implemented via a piece of middleware (see Chapter 17) and a Django model. To enable sessions, you'll need to follow these steps:

1. Edit your `MIDDLEWARE_CLASSES` setting and make sure `MIDDLEWARE_CLASSES` contains `'django.contrib.sessions.middleware.SessionMiddleware'`.

2. Make sure `'django.contrib.sessions'` is in your `INSTALLED_APPS` setting (and run `manage.py syncdb` if you have to add it).

The default skeleton settings created by `startproject` have both of these bits already installed, so unless you've removed them, you probably don't have to change anything to get sessions to work.

If you don't want to use sessions, you might want to remove the `SessionMiddleware` line from `MIDDLEWARE_CLASSES` and `'django.contrib.sessions'` from your `INSTALLED_APPS`. It will save you only a small amount of overhead, but every little bit counts.

Using Sessions in Views

When `SessionMiddleware` is activated, each `HttpRequest` object—the first argument to any Django view function—will have a `session` attribute, which is a dictionary-like object. You can read it and write to it in the same way you'd use a normal dictionary. For example, in a view you could do stuff like this:

```
# Set a session value:
request.session["fav_color"] = "blue"

# Get a session value–this could be called in a different view,
# or many requests later (or both):
fav_color = request.session["fav_color"]

# Clear an item from the session:
del request.session["fav_color"]

# Check if the session has a given key:
if "fav_color" in request.session:
    ...
```

You can also use other dictionary methods like `keys()` and `items()` on `request.session`. There are a couple of simple rules for using Django's sessions effectively:

- Use normal Python strings as dictionary keys on `request.session` (as opposed to integers, objects, etc.).

- Session dictionary keys that begin with an underscore are reserved for internal use by Django. In practice, the framework uses only a small number of underscore-prefixed session variables, but unless you know what they all are (and you are willing to keep up with any changes in Django itself), staying away from underscore prefixes will keep Django from interfering with your application.

  For example, don't use a session key called _fav_color like this:

  ```
  request.session['_fav_color'] = 'blue' # Don't do this!
  ```

- Don't replace `request.session` with a new object, and don't access or set its attributes. Use it like a Python dictionary. Here are a couple of examples:

  ```
  request.session = some_other_object # Don't do this!

  request.session.foo = 'bar' # Don't do this!
  ```

Let's take a look at a few quick examples. This simplistic view sets a has_commented variable to True after a user posts a comment. It's a simple (if not particularly secure) way of preventing a user from posting more than one comment:

```
def post_comment(request):
    if request.method != 'POST':
        raise Http404('Only POSTs are allowed')

    if 'comment' not in request.POST:
        raise Http404('Comment not submitted')

    if request.session.get('has_commented', False):
        return HttpResponse("You've already commented.")

    c = comments.Comment(comment=request.POST['comment'])
    c.save()
    request.session['has_commented'] = True
    return HttpResponse('Thanks for your comment!')
```

This simplistic view logs in a "member" of the site:

```
def login(request):
    if request.method != 'POST':
        raise Http404('Only POSTs are allowed')
    try:
        m = Member.objects.get(username=request.POST['username'])
        if m.password == request.POST['password']:
            request.session['member_id'] = m.id
            return HttpResponseRedirect('/you-are-logged-in/')
    except Member.DoesNotExist:
        return HttpResponse("Your username and password didn't match.")
```

And this one logs out a member who has been logged in via login():

```
def logout(request):
    try:
        del request.session['member_id']
    except KeyError:
        pass
    return HttpResponse("You're logged out.")
```

■Note In practice, this is a lousy way of logging users in. The authentication framework discussed shortly handles this task for you in a much more robust and useful manner. These examples are deliberately simplistic so that you can easily see what's going on.

Setting Test Cookies

As mentioned earlier, you can't rely on every browser accepting cookies. So, as a convenience, Django provides an easy way to test whether a user's browser accepts cookies. Just
call `request.session.set_test_cookie()` in a view, and check `request.session.test_cookie_
worked()` in a subsequent view—not in the same view call.

This awkward split between `set_test_cookie()` and `test_cookie_worked()` is necessary
due to the way cookies work. When you set a cookie, you can't actually tell whether a browser
accepted it until the browser's next request.

It's good practice to use `delete_test_cookie()` to clean up after yourself. Do this after
you've verified that the test cookie worked.

Here's a typical usage example:

```
def login(request):

    # If we submitted the form...
    if request.method == 'POST':

        # Check that the test cookie worked (we set it below):
        if request.session.test_cookie_worked():

            # The test cookie worked, so delete it.
            request.session.delete_test_cookie()

            # In practice, we'd need some logic to check username/password
            # here, but since this is an example...
            return HttpResponse("You're logged in.")

        # The test cookie failed, so display an error message. If this
        # were a real site, we'd want to display a friendlier message.
        else:
            return HttpResponse("Please enable cookies and try again.")

    # If we didn't post, send the test cookie along with the login form.
    request.session.set_test_cookie()
    return render_to_response('foo/login_form.html')
```

■Note Again, the built-in authentication functions handle this check for you.

Using Sessions Outside of Views

Internally, each session is just a normal Django model defined in `django.contrib.sessions.
models`. Each session is identified by a more-or-less random 32-character hash stored in a
cookie. Because it's a normal model, you can access sessions using the normal Django database API:

```
>>> from django.contrib.sessions.models import Session
>>> s = Session.objects.get(pk='2b1189a188b44ad18c35e113ac6ceead')
>>> s.expire_date
datetime.datetime(2005, 8, 20, 13, 35, 12)
```

You'll need to call get_decoded() to get the actual session data. This is necessary because the dictionary is stored in an encoded format:

```
>>> s.session_data
'KGRwMQpTJ19hdXRoX3VzZXJfaWQnCnAyCkkxCnMuMTExY2ZjODI2Yj...'
>>> s.get_decoded()
{'user_id': 42}
```

When Sessions Are Saved

By default, Django only saves to the database if the session has been modified—that is, if any of its dictionary values have been assigned or deleted:

```
# Session is modified.
request.session['foo'] = 'bar'

# Session is modified.
del request.session['foo']

# Session is modified.
request.session['foo'] = {}

# Gotcha: Session is NOT modified, because this alters
# request.session['foo'] instead of request.session.
request.session['foo']['bar'] = 'baz'
```

To change this default behavior, set SESSION_SAVE_EVERY_REQUEST to True. If SESSION_SAVE_EVERY_REQUEST is True, Django will save the session to the database on every single request, even if it wasn't changed.

Note that the session cookie is sent only when a session has been created or modified. If SESSION_SAVE_EVERY_REQUEST is True, the session cookie will be sent on every request. Similarly, the expires part of a session cookie is updated each time the session cookie is sent.

Browser-Length Sessions vs. Persistent Sessions

You might have noticed that the cookie Google sent at the beginning of this chapter contained expires=Sun, 17-Jan-2038 19:14:07 GMT;. Cookies can optionally contain an expiration date that advises the browser on when to remove the cookie. If a cookie doesn't contain an expiration value, the browser will expire it when the user closes his or her browser window. You can control the session framework's behavior in this regard with the SESSION_EXPIRE_AT_BROWSER_CLOSE setting.

By default, `SESSION_EXPIRE_AT_BROWSER_CLOSE` is set to `False`, which means session cookies will be stored in users' browsers for `SESSION_COOKIE_AGE` seconds (which defaults to two weeks, or 1,209,600 seconds). Use this if you don't want people to have to log in every time they open a browser.

If `SESSION_EXPIRE_AT_BROWSER_CLOSE` is set to `True`, Django will use browser-length cookies.

Other Session Settings

Besides the settings already mentioned, a few other settings influence how Django's session framework uses cookies, as shown in Table 14-2.

Table 14-2. *Settings That Influence Cookie Behavior*

Setting	Description	Default
SESSION_COOKIE_DOMAIN	The domain to use for session cookies. Set this to a string such as ".example.com" for cross-domain cookies, or use None for a standard cookie.	None
SESSION_COOKIE_NAME	The name of the cookie to use for sessions. This can be any string.	"sessionid"
SESSION_COOKIE_SECURE	Whether to use a "secure" cookie for the session cookie. If this is set to True, the cookie will be marked as "secure," which means that browsers will ensure that the cookie is only sent via HTTPS.	False

---

TECHNICAL DETAILS

For the curious, here are a few technical notes about the inner workings of the session framework:

- The session dictionary accepts any Python object capable of being "pickled." See the documentation for Python's built-in `pickle` module for information about how this works.

- Session data is stored in a database table named `django_session`.

- Session data is fetched upon demand. If you never access `request.session`, Django won't hit that database table.

- Django sends a cookie only if it needs to. If you don't set any session data, it won't send a session cookie (unless `SESSION_SAVE_EVERY_REQUEST` is set to `True`).

- The Django sessions framework is entirely, and solely, cookie based. It does not fall back to putting session IDs in URLs as a last resort, as some other tools (PHP, JSP) do.

  This is an intentional design decision. Putting sessions in URLs doesn't just make URLs ugly; they also make your site vulnerable to a certain form of session ID theft via the `Referer` header.

  If you're still curious, the source is pretty straightforward; look in `django.contrib.sessions` for more details.

Users and Authentication

Sessions give us a way of persisting data through multiple browser requests; the second part of the equation is using those sessions for user login. Of course, we can't just trust that users are who they say they are, so we need to authenticate them along the way.

Naturally, Django provides tools to handle this common task (and many others). Django's user authentication system handles user accounts, groups, permissions, and cookie-based user sessions. This system is often referred to as an *auth/auth* (authentication and authorization) system. That name recognizes that dealing with users is often a two-step process. We need to

1. Verify (*authenticate*) that a user is who he or she claims to be (usually by checking a username and password against a database of users)

2. Verify that the user is *authorized* to perform some given operation (usually by checking against a table of permissions)

Following these needs, Django's auth/auth system consists of a number of parts:

- *Users*: People registered with your site

- *Permissions*: Binary (yes/no) flags designating whether a user may perform a certain task

- *Groups*: A generic way of applying labels and permissions to more than one user

- *Messages*: A simple way to queue and display system messages to users

If you've used the admin tool (discussed in Chapter 6), you've already seen many of these tools, and if you've edited users or groups in the admin tool, you've actually been editing data in the auth system's database tables.

Enabling Authentication Support

Like the session tools, authentication support is bundled as a Django application in `django.contrib` that needs to be installed. Similar to the session tools, it's also installed by default, but if you've removed it, you'll need to follow these steps to install it:

1. Make sure the session framework is installed as described earlier in this chapter. Keeping track of users obviously requires cookies, and thus builds on the session framework.

2. Put `'django.contrib.auth'` in your `INSTALLED_APPS` setting and run `manage.py syncdb` to install the appropriate database tables.

3. Make sure that `'django.contrib.auth.middleware.AuthenticationMiddleware'` is in your `MIDDLEWARE_CLASSES` setting—*after* `SessionMiddleware`.

With that installation out of the way, we're ready to deal with users in view functions. The main interface you'll use to access users within a view is `request.user`; this is an object that represents the currently logged-in user. If the user isn't logged in, this will instead be an `AnonymousUser` object (see the following section for more details).

You can easily tell if a user is logged in with the is_authenticated() method:

```
if request.user.is_authenticated():
    # Do something for authenticated users.
else:
    # Do something for anonymous users.
```

Using Users

Once you have a User—often from request.user, but possibly through one of the other methods discussed shortly—you have a number of fields and methods available on that object. AnonymousUser objects emulate *some* of this interface, but not all of it, so you should always check user.is_authenticated() before assuming you're dealing with a bona fide user object. Tables 14-3 and 14-4 list the fields and methods, respectively, on User objects.

Table 14-3. *Fields on User Objects*

Field	Description
username	Required; 30 characters or fewer. Alphanumeric characters only (letters, digits, and underscores).
first_name	Optional; 30 characters or fewer.
last_name	Optional; 30 characters or fewer.
email	Optional. E-mail address.
password	Required. A hash of, and metadata about, the password (Django doesn't store the raw password). See the "Passwords" section for more about this value.
is_staff	Boolean. Designates whether this user can access the admin site.
is_active	Boolean. Designates whether this account can be used to log in. Set this flag to False instead of deleting accounts.
is_superuser	Boolean. Designates that this user has all permissions without explicitly assigning them.
last_login	A datetime of the user's last login. This is set to the current date/time by default.
date_joined	A datetime designating when the account was created. This is set to the current date/time by default when the account is created.

Table 14-4. *Methods on User Objects*

Method	Description
is_authenticated()	Always returns True for "real" User objects. This is a way to tell if the user has been authenticated. This does not imply any permissions, and it doesn't check if the user is active. It only indicates that the user has successfully authenticated.
is_anonymous()	Returns True only for AnonymousUser objects (and False for "real" User objects). Generally, you should prefer using is_authenticated() to this method.
get_full_name()	Returns the first_name plus the last_name, with a space in between.

Continued

Table 14-4. *Continued*

Method	Description
set_password(passwd)	Sets the user's password to the given raw string, taking care of the password hashing. This doesn't actually save the User object.
check_password(passwd)	Returns True if the given raw string is the correct password for the user. This takes care of the password hashing in making the comparison.
get_group_permissions()	Returns a list of permission strings that the user has through the groups he or she belongs to.
get_all_permissions()	Returns a list of permission strings that the user has, both through group and user permissions.
has_perm(perm)	Returns True if the user has the specified permission, where perm is in the format "package.codename". If the user is inactive, this method will always return False.
has_perms(perm_list)	Returns True if the user has *all* of the specified permissions. If the user is inactive, this method will always return False.
has_module_perms(app_label)	Returns True if the user has any permissions in the given app_label. If the user is inactive, this method will always return False.
get_and_delete_messages()	Returns a list of Message objects in the user's queue and deletes the messages from the queue.
email_user(subj, msg)	Sends an e-mail to the user. This e-mail is sent from the DEFAULT_FROM_EMAIL setting. You can also pass a third argument, from_email, to override the From address on the e-mail.

Finally, User objects have two many-to-many fields: groups and permissions. User objects can access their related objects in the same way as any other many-to-many field:

```
# Set a user's groups:
myuser.groups = group_list

# Add a user to some groups:
myuser.groups.add(group1, group2,...)

# Remove a user from some groups:
myuser.groups.remove(group1, group2,...)

# Remove a user from all groups:
myuser.groups.clear()

# Permissions work the same way
myuser.permissions = permission_list
myuser.permissions.add(permission1, permission2, ...)
myuser.permissions.remove(permission1, permission2, ...)
myuser.permissions.clear()
```

Logging In and Out

Django provides built-in view functions for handling logging in and out (and a few other nifty tricks), but before we get to those, let's take a look at how to log users in and out "by hand." Django provides two functions to perform these actions in `django.contrib.auth`: `authenticate()` and `login()`.

To authenticate a given username and password, use `authenticate()`. It takes two keyword arguments, `username` and `password`, and it returns a `User` object if the password is valid for the given username. If the password is invalid, `authenticate()` returns `None`:

```
>>> from django.contrib import auth
>>> user = auth.authenticate(username='john', password='secret')
>>> if user is not None:
...     print "Correct!"
... else:
...     print "Invalid password."
```

`authenticate()` only verifies a user's credentials. To log in a user, use `login()`. It takes an `HttpRequest` object and a `User` object and saves the user's ID in the session, using Django's session framework.

This example shows how you might use both `authenticate()` and `login()` within a view function:

```
from django.contrib import auth

def login_view(request):
    username = request.POST.get('username', '')
    password = request.POST.get('password', '')
    user = auth.authenticate(username=username, password=password)
    if user is not None and user.is_active:
        # Correct password, and the user is marked "active"
        auth.login(request, user)
        # Redirect to a success page.
        return HttpResponseRedirect("/account/loggedin/")
    else:
        # Show an error page
        return HttpResponseRedirect("/account/invalid/")
```

To log out a user, use `django.contrib.auth.logout()` within your view. It takes an `HttpRequest` object and has no return value:

```
from django.contrib import auth

def logout_view(request):
    auth.logout(request)
    # Redirect to a success page.
    return HttpResponseRedirect("/account/loggedout/")
```

Note that `auth.logout()` doesn't throw any errors if the user wasn't logged in.

In practice, you usually will not need to write your own login/logout functions; the authentication system comes with a set of views for generically handling logging in and out. The first step in using these authentication views is to wire them up in your URLconf. You'll need to add this snippet:

```
from django.contrib.auth.views import login, logout

urlpatterns = patterns('',
    # existing patterns here...
    (r'^accounts/login/$',  login),
    (r'^accounts/logout/$', logout),
)
```

/accounts/login/ and /accounts/logout/ are the default URLs that Django uses for these views.

By default, the login view renders a template at registration/login.html (you can change this template name by passing an extra view argument , "template_name"). This form needs to contain a username and a password field. A simple template might look like this:

```
{% extends "base.html" %}

{% block content %}

  {% if form.errors %}
    <p class="error">Sorry, that's not a valid username or password</p>
  {% endif %}

  <form action="" method="post">
    <label for="username">User name:</label>
    <input type="text" name="username" value="" id="username">
    <label for="password">Password:</label>
    <input type="password" name="password" value="" id="password">

    <input type="submit" value="login" />
    <input type="hidden" name="next" value="{{ next|escape }}" />
  </form>

{% endblock %}
```

If the user successfully logs in, he or she will be redirected to /accounts/profile/ by default. You can override this by providing a hidden field called next with the URL to redirect to after logging in. You can also pass this value as a GET parameter to the login view and it will be automatically added to the context as a variable called next that you can insert into that hidden field.

The logout view works a little differently. By default it renders a template at registration/logged_out.html (which usually contains a "You've successfully logged out" message). However, you can call the view with an extra argument, next_page, which will instruct the view to redirect after a logout.

Limiting Access to Logged-in Users

Of course, the reason we're going through all this trouble is so we can limit access to parts of our site.

The simple, raw way to limit access to pages is to check `request.user.is_authenticated()` and redirect to a login page:

```
from django.http import HttpResponseRedirect

def my_view(request):
    if not request.user.is_authenticated():
        return HttpResponseRedirect('/accounts/login/?next=%s' % request.path)
    # ...
```

or perhaps display an error message:

```
def my_view(request):
    if not request.user.is_authenticated():
        return render_to_response('myapp/login_error.html')
    # ...
```

As a shortcut, you can use the convenient `login_required` decorator:

```
from django.contrib.auth.decorators import login_required

@login_required
def my_view(request):
    # ...
```

`login_required` does the following:

- If the user isn't logged in, redirect to /accounts/login/, passing the current URL path in the query string as next, for example: /accounts/login/?next=/polls/3/.

- If the user is logged in, execute the view normally. The view code can then assume that the user is logged in.

Limiting Access to Users Who Pass a Test

Limiting access based on certain permissions or some other test, or providing a different location for the login view works essentially the same way.

The raw way is to run your test on `request.user` in the view directly. For example, this view checks to make sure the user is logged in and has the permission `polls.can_vote` (more about how permissions work follows):

```
def vote(request):
    if request.user.is_authenticated() and request.user.has_perm('polls.can_vote')):
        # vote here
    else:
        return HttpResponse("You can't vote in this poll.")
```

Again, Django provides a shortcut called user_passes_test. It takes arguments and generates a specialized decorator for your particular situation:

```
def user_can_vote(user):
    return user.is_authenticated() and user.has_perm("polls.can_vote")

@user_passes_test(user_can_vote, login_url="/login/")
def vote(request):
    # Code here can assume a logged-in user with the correct permission.
    ...
```

user_passes_test takes one required argument: a callable that takes a User object and returns True if the user is allowed to view the page. Note that user_passes_test does not automatically check that the User is authenticated; you should do that yourself.

In this example we're also showing the second (optional) argument, login_url, which lets you specify the URL for your login page (/accounts/login/ by default). If the user doesn't pass the test, the user_passes_test decorator will redirect the user to the login_url.

Because it's a relatively common task to check whether a user has a particular permission, Django provides a shortcut for that case: the permission_required() decorator. Using this decorator, the earlier example can be written as follows:

```
from django.contrib.auth.decorators import permission_required

@permission_required('polls.can_vote', login_url="/login/")
def vote(request):
    # ...
```

Note that permission_required() also takes an optional login_url parameter, which also defaults to '/accounts/login/'.

LIMITING ACCESS TO GENERIC VIEWS

One of the most frequently asked questions on the Django users list deals with limiting access to a generic view. To pull this off, you'll need to write a thin wrapper around the view and point your URLconf to your wrapper instead of the generic view itself:

```
from django.contrib.auth.decorators import login_required
from django.views.generic.date_based import object_detail

@login_required
def limited_object_detail(*args, **kwargs):
    return object_detail(*args, **kwargs)
```

You can, of course, replace login_required with any of the other limiting decorators.

Managing Users, Permissions, and Groups

The easiest way by far to manage the auth system is through the admin interface. Chapter 6 discusses how to use Django's admin site to edit users and control their permissions and access, and most of the time you'll just use that interface.

However, there are low-level APIs you can dive into when you need absolute control, and we discuss these in the sections that follow.

Creating Users

Create users with the create_user helper function:

```
>>> from django.contrib.auth.models import User
>>> user = User.objects.create_user(username='john',
...                                 email='jlennon@beatles.com',
...                                 password='glass onion')
```

At this point, user is a User instance ready to be saved to the database (create_user() doesn't actually call save() itself). You can continue to change its attributes before saving, too:

```
>>> user.is_staff = True
>>> user.save()
```

Changing Passwords

You can change a password with set_password():

```
>>> user = User.objects.get(username='john')
>>> user.set_password('goo goo goo joob')
>>> user.save()
```

Don't set the password attribute directly unless you know what you're doing. The password is actually stored as a *salted hash* and thus can't be edited directly.

More formally, the password attribute of a User object is a string in this format:

hashtype$salt$hash

That's a hash type, the salt, and the hash itself, separated by the dollar sign ($) character.

hashtype is either sha1 (default) or md5, the algorithm used to perform a one-way hash of the password. salt is a random string used to salt the raw password to create the hash, for example:

sha1$a1976$a36cc8cbf81742a8fb52e221aaeab48ed7f58ab4

The User.set_password() and User.check_password() functions handle the setting and checking of these values behind the scenes.

> ### SALTED HASHES
>
> A *hash* is a one-way cryptographic function—that is, you can easily compute the hash of a given value, but it's nearly impossible to take a hash and reconstruct the original value.
>
> If we stored passwords as plain text, anyone who got their hands on the password database would instantly know everyone's password. Storing passwords as hashes reduces the value of a compromised database.
>
> However, an attacker with the password database could still run a *brute-force* attack, hashing millions of passwords and comparing those hashes against the stored values. This takes some time, but less than you might think.
>
> Worse, there are publicly available *rainbow tables*, or databases of pre-computed hashes of millions of passwords. With a rainbow table, an experienced attacker could break most passwords in seconds.
>
> Adding a *salt*—basically an initial random value—to the stored hash adds another layer of difficulty to breaking passwords. Because salts differ from password to password, they also prevent the use of a rainbow table, thus forcing attackers to fall back on a brute-force attack, itself made more difficult by the extra entropy added to the hash by the salt.
>
> While salted hashes aren't absolutely the most secure way of storing passwords, they're a good middle ground between security and convenience.

Handling Registration

We can use these low-level tools to create views that allow users to sign up for new accounts. Different developers implement registration differently, so Django leaves writing a registration view up to you. Luckily, it's pretty easy.

At its simplest, we could provide a small view that prompts for the required user information and creates those users. Django provides a built-in form you can use for this purpose, which we'll use in this example:

```python
from django import forms
from django.contrib.auth.forms import UserCreationForm
from django.http import HttpResponseRedirect
from django.shortcuts import render_to_response

def register(request):
    if request.method == 'POST':
        form = UserCreationForm(request.POST)
        if form.is_valid():
            new_user = form.save()
            return HttpResponseRedirect("/books/")
    else:
        form = UserCreationForm()
    return render_to_response("registration/register.html", {
        'form': form,
    })
```

This form assumes a template named `registration/register.html`. Here's an example of what that template might look like:

```
{% extends "base.html" %}

{% block title %}Create an account{% endblock %}

{% block content %}
  <h1>Create an account</h1>

  <form action="" method="post">
      {{ form.as_p }}
      <input type="submit" value="Create the account">
  </form>
{% endblock %}
```

Using Authentication Data in Templates

The current logged-in user and his or her permissions are made available in the template context when you use `RequestContext` (see Chapter 9).

■**Note** Technically, these variables are only made available in the template context if you use `RequestContext` *and* your `TEMPLATE_CONTEXT_PROCESSORS` setting contains `"django.core.context_processors.auth"`, which is the default. Again, see Chapter 9 for more information.

When using `RequestContext`, the current user (either a `User` instance or an `AnonymousUser` instance) is stored in the template variable `{{ user }}`:

```
{% if user.is_authenticated %}
  <p>Welcome, {{ user.username }}. Thanks for logging in.</p>
{% else %}
  <p>Welcome, new user. Please log in.</p>
{% endif %}
```

This user's permissions are stored in the template variable `{{ perms }}`. This is a template-friendly proxy to a couple of permission methods described shortly.

There are two ways you can use this `perms` object. You can use something like `{% if perms.polls %}` to check whether the user has *any* permissions for some given application, or you can use something like `{% if perms.polls.can_vote %}` to check if the user has a specific permission.

Thus, you can check permissions in template {% if %} statements:

```
{% if perms.polls %}
  <p>You have permission to do something in the polls app.</p>
  {% if perms.polls.can_vote %}
    <p>You can vote!</p>
  {% endif %}
{% else %}
  <p>You don't have permission to do anything in the polls app.</p>
{% endif %}
```

Permissions, Groups, and Messages

There are a few other bits of the authentication framework that we've only dealt with in passing. We'll take a closer look at them in the following sections.

Permissions

Permissions are a simple way to "mark" users and groups as being able to perform some action. They are usually used by the Django admin site, but you can easily use them in your own code.

The Django admin site uses permissions as follows:

- Access to view the "add" form, and add an object is limited to users with the *add* permission for that type of object.

- Access to view the change list, view the "change" form, and change an object is limited to users with the *change* permission for that type of object.

- Access to delete an object is limited to users with the *delete* permission for that type of object.

Permissions are set globally per type of object, not per specific object instance. For example, it's possible to say "Mary may change news stories," but permissions don't let you say "Mary may change news stories, but only the ones she created herself" or "Mary may only change news stories that have a certain status, publication date, or ID."

These three basic permissions—add, change, and delete—are automatically created for each Django model. Behind the scenes, these permissions are added to the auth_permission database table when you run manage.py syncdb.

These permissions will be of the form "<app>.<action>_<object_name>". That is, if you have a polls application with a Choice model, you'll get permissions named "polls.add_choice", "polls.change_choice", and "polls.delete_choice".

Just like users, permissions are implemented in a Django model that lives in `django.contrib.auth.models`. This means that you can use Django's database API to interact directly with permissions if you like.

Groups

Groups are a generic way of categorizing users so you can apply permissions, or some other label, to those users. A user can belong to any number of groups.

A user in a group automatically has the permissions granted to that group. For example, if the group `Site editors` has the permission `can_edit_home_page`, any user in that group will have that permission.

Groups are also a convenient way to categorize users to give them some label, or extended functionality. For example, you could create a group `'Special users'`, and you could write code that could, say, give those users access to a members-only portion of your site, or send them members-only e-mail messages.

Like users, the easiest way to manage groups is through the admin interface. However, groups are also just Django models that live in `django.contrib.auth.models`, so once again you can always use Django's database APIs to deal with groups at a low level.

Messages

The message system is a lightweight way to queue messages for given users. A message is associated with a `User`. There's no concept of expiration or timestamps.

Messages are used by the Django admin interface after successful actions. For example, when you create an object, you'll notice a "The object was created successfully" message at the top of the admin page.

You can use the same API to queue and display messages in your own application. The API is simple:

- To create a new message, use `user.message_set.create(message='message_text')`.

- To retrieve/delete messages, use `user.get_and_delete_messages()`, which returns a list of `Message` objects in the user's queue (if any) and deletes the messages from the queue.

In this example view, the system saves a message for the user after creating a playlist:

```
def create_playlist(request, songs):
    # Create the playlist with the given songs.
    # ...
    request.user.message_set.create(
        message="Your playlist was added successfully."
    )
    return render_to_response("playlists/create.html",
        context_instance=RequestContext(request))
```

When you use RequestContext, the current logged-in user and his or her messages are made available in the template context as the template variable {{ messages }}. Here's an example of template code that displays messages:

```
{% if messages %}
<ul>
    {% for message in messages %}
    <li>{{ message }}</li>
    {% endfor %}
</ul>
{% endif %}
```

Note that RequestContext calls get_and_delete_messages behind the scenes, so any messages will be deleted even if you don't display them.

Finally, note that this messages framework only works with users in the user database. To send messages to anonymous users, use the session framework directly.

What's Next?

The session and authorization system is a lot to absorb. Most of the time, you won't need all the features described in this chapter, but when you need to allow complex interactions between users, it's good to have all that power available.

In the next chapter, we'll take a look at Django's caching infrastructure, which is a convenient way to improve the performance of your application.

CHAPTER 15

■ ■ ■

Caching

A fundamental trade-off in dynamic Web sites is, well, they're dynamic. Each time a user requests a page, the Web server makes all sorts of calculations—from database queries to template rendering to business logic—to create the page that your site's visitor sees. This is a lot more expensive, from a processing-overhead perspective, than your standard read-a-file-off-the-filesystem-server arrangement.

For most Web applications, this overhead isn't a big deal. Most Web applications aren't washingtonpost.com or slashdot.org; they're simply small- to medium-sized sites with so-so traffic. But for medium- to high-traffic sites, it's essential to cut as much overhead as possible.

That's where caching comes in.

To *cache* something is to save the result of an expensive calculation so that you don't have to perform the calculation next time. Here's some pseudocode explaining how this would work for a dynamically generated Web page:

```
given a URL, try finding that page in the cache
if the page is in the cache:
    return the cached page
else:
    generate the page
    save the generated page in the cache (for next time)
    return the generated page
```

Django comes with a robust cache system that lets you save dynamic pages so they don't have to be calculated for each request. For convenience, Django offers different levels of cache granularity: you can cache the output of specific views, you can cache only the pieces that are difficult to produce, or you can cache your entire site.

Django also works well with "upstream" caches, such as Squid (http://www.squid-cache.org/) and browser-based caches. These are the types of caches that you don't directly control but to which you can provide hints (via HTTP headers) about which parts of your site should be cached, and how.

Setting Up the Cache

The cache system requires a small amount of setup. Namely, you have to tell it where your cached data should live—whether in a database, on the filesystem, or directly in memory. This is an important decision that affects your cache's performance; yes, some cache types are faster than others.

Your cache preference goes in the CACHE_BACKEND setting in your settings file. Here's an explanation of all available values for CACHE_BACKEND.

Memcached

By far the fastest, most efficient type of cache available to Django, Memcached is an entirely memory-based cache framework originally developed to handle high loads at LiveJournal.com and subsequently open-sourced by Danga Interactive. It's used by sites such as Facebook and Wikipedia to reduce database access and dramatically increase site performance.

Memcached is available for free at http://danga.com/memcached/. It runs as a daemon and is allotted a specified amount of RAM. All it does is provide a fast interface for adding, retrieving, and deleting arbitrary data in the cache. All data is stored directly in memory, so there's no overhead of database or filesystem usage.

After installing Memcached itself, you'll need to install the Memcached Python bindings, which are not bundled with Django directly. Two versions are available. Choose and install *one* of the following modules:

- The fastest available option is a module called cmemcache, available at http://gijsbert.org/cmemcache/.

- If you can't install cmemcache, you can install python-memcached, available at ftp://ftp.tummy.com/pub/python-memcached/. If that URL is no longer valid, just go to the Memcached Web site (http://www.danga.com/memcached/) and get the Python bindings from the "Client APIs" section.

To use Memcached with Django, set CACHE_BACKEND to memcached://ip:port/, where ip is the IP address of the Memcached daemon and port is the port on which Memcached is running.

In this example, Memcached is running on localhost (127.0.0.1) port 11211:

```
CACHE_BACKEND = 'memcached://127.0.0.1:11211/'
```

One excellent feature of Memcached is its ability to share cache over multiple servers. This means you can run Memcached daemons on multiple machines, and the program will treat the group of machines as a *single* cache, without the need to duplicate cache values on each machine. To take advantage of this feature, include all server addresses in CACHE_BACKEND, separated by semicolons.

In this example, the cache is shared over Memcached instances running on IP addresses 172.19.26.240 and 172.19.26.242, both on port 11211:

```
CACHE_BACKEND = 'memcached://172.19.26.240:11211;172.19.26.242:11211/'
```

In the following example, the cache is shared over Memcached instances running on the IP addresses 172.19.26.240 (port 11211), 172.19.26.242 (port 11212), and 172.19.26.244 (port 11213):

```
CACHE_BACKEND = 'memcached://➥
172.19.26.240:11211;172.19.26.242:11212;172.19.26.244:11213/'
```

A final point about Memcached is that memory-based caching has one disadvantage: because the cached data is stored in memory, the data will be lost if your server crashes. Clearly, memory isn't intended for permanent data storage, so don't rely on memory-based caching as your only data storage. Without a doubt, *none* of the Django caching back-ends should be used for permanent storage—they're all intended to be solutions for caching, not storage—but we point this out here because memory-based caching is particularly temporary.

Database Caching

To use a database table as your cache back-end, first create a cache table in your database by running this command where [cache_table_name] is the name of the database table to create:

```
python manage.py createcachetable [cache_table_name]
```

This name can be whatever you want, as long as it's a valid table name that's not already being used in your database. This command creates a single table in your database that is in the proper format that Django's database-cache system expects.

Once you've created that database table, set your CACHE_BACKEND setting to "db://tablename", where tablename is the name of the database table. In this example, the cache table's name is my_cache_table:

```
CACHE_BACKEND = 'db://my_cache_table'
```

The database caching back-end uses the same database as specified in your settings file. You can't use a different database back-end for your cache table.

Database caching works best if you have a fast, well-indexed database server.

Filesystem Caching

To store cached items on a filesystem, use the "file://" cache type for CACHE_BACKEND. For example, to store cached data in /var/tmp/django_cache, use this setting:

```
CACHE_BACKEND = 'file:///var/tmp/django_cache'
```

Note that there are three forward slashes toward the beginning of that example. The first two are for file://, and the third is the first character of the directory path, /var/tmp/django_cache. If you're on Windows, put the drive letter after the file://, like this:

```
file://c:/foo/bar
```

The directory path should be absolute—that is, it should start at the root of your filesystem. It doesn't matter whether you put a slash at the end of the setting.

Make sure the directory pointed to by this setting exists and is readable and writable by the system user under which your Web server runs. Continuing the preceding example, if your server runs as the user apache, make sure the directory /var/tmp/django_cache exists and is readable and writable by the user apache.

Each cache value will be stored as a separate file whose contents are the cache data saved in a serialized ("pickled") format, using Python's pickle module. Each file's name is the cache key, escaped for safe filesystem use.

Local-Memory Caching

If you want the speed advantages of in-memory caching but don't have the capability of running Memcached, consider the local-memory cache back-end. This cache is multi-process and thread-safe. To use it, set CACHE_BACKEND to "locmem:///". For example:

```
CACHE_BACKEND = 'locmem:///'
```

Note that each process will have its own private cache instance, which means no cross-process caching is possible. This obviously also means the local memory cache isn't particularly memory efficient, so it's probably not a good choice for production environments. It's nice for development.

Dummy Caching (for Development)

Finally, Django comes with a "dummy" cache that doesn't actually cache; it just implements the cache interface without doing anything.

This is useful if you have a production site that uses heavy-duty caching in various places but a development/test environment in which you don't want to cache and don't want to have to change your code to special-case the latter. To activate dummy caching, set CACHE_BACKEND like so:

```
CACHE_BACKEND = 'dummy:///'
```

Using a Custom Cache Back-End

Although Django includes support for a number of cache back-ends out of the box, sometimes you might want to use a customized cache back-end. To use an external cache back-end with Django, use a Python import path as the scheme portion (the part before the initial colon) of the CACHE_BACKEND URI, like so:

```
CACHE_BACKEND = 'path.to.backend://'
```

If you're building your own back-end, you can use the standard cache back-ends as reference implementations. You'll find the code in the django/core/cache/backends/ directory of the Django source.

■**Note** Without a really compelling reason (for example, a host that doesn't support back-ends), you should stick to the cache back-ends included with Django. They've been well-tested and are easy to use.

CACHE_BACKEND Arguments

Each cache back-end may take arguments. They're given in query-string style on the CACHE_ BACKEND setting. Valid arguments are as follows:

- timeout: The default timeout, in seconds, to use for the cache. This argument defaults to 300 seconds (5 minutes).

- max_entries: For the locmem, filesystem, and database back-ends, the maximum number of entries allowed in the cache before old values are deleted. This argument defaults to 300.

- cull_percentage: The percentage of entries that are culled when max_entries is reached. The actual ratio is 1/cull_percentage, so set cull_percentage=2 to cull half of the entries when max_entries is reached.

  A value of 0 for cull_percentage means that the entire cache will be dumped when max_entries is reached. This makes culling *much* faster at the expense of more cache misses.

In this example, timeout is set to 60:

```
CACHE_BACKEND = "memcached://127.0.0.1:11211/?timeout=60"
```

In this example, timeout is 30 and max_entries is 400:

```
CACHE_BACKEND = "locmem:///?timeout=30&max_entries=400"
```

Invalid arguments are silently ignored, as are invalid values of known arguments.

The Per-Site Cache

After the cache is set up, the simplest way to use caching is to cache your entire site. You'll need to add 'django.middleware.cache.UpdateCacheMiddleware' and 'django.middleware. cache.FetchFromCacheMiddleware' to your MIDDLEWARE_CLASSES setting, as in this example:

```
MIDDLEWARE_CLASSES = (
    'django.middleware.cache.UpdateCacheMiddleware',
    'django.middleware.common.CommonMiddleware',
    'django.middleware.cache.FetchFromCacheMiddleware',
)
```

■**Note** No, that's not a typo: the "update" middleware must be first in the list, and the "fetch" middleware must be last. The details are a bit obscure, but see "Order of MIDDLEWARE_CLASSES," at the end of the chapter, if you want the full story.

Then, add the following required settings to your Django settings file:

- `CACHE_MIDDLEWARE_SECONDS`: The number of seconds each page should be cached.

- `CACHE_MIDDLEWARE_KEY_PREFIX`: If the cache is shared across multiple sites using the same Django installation, set this to the name of the site, or some other string that is unique to this Django instance, to prevent key collisions. Use an empty string if you don't care.

The cache middleware caches every page that doesn't have `GET` or `POST` parameters. Optionally, if the `CACHE_MIDDLEWARE_ANONYMOUS_ONLY` setting is `True`, only anonymous requests (i.e., not those made by a logged-in user) will be cached. This is a simple and effective way of disabling caching for any user-specific pages (include Django's admin interface). Note that if you use `CACHE_MIDDLEWARE_ANONYMOUS_ONLY`, you should make sure you've activated `AuthenticationMiddleware`.

Additionally, the cache middleware automatically sets a few headers in each `HttpResponse`:

- Sets the `Last-Modified` header to the current date/time when a fresh (uncached) version of the page is requested.

- Sets the `Expires` header to the current date/time plus the defined `CACHE_MIDDLEWARE_SECONDS`.

- Sets the `Cache-Control` header to give a max age for the page—again, from the `CACHE_MIDDLEWARE_SECONDS` setting.

■Note See Chapter 17 for more on middleware.

If a view sets its own cache expiry time (i.e., it has a `max-age` section in its `Cache-Control` header), the page will be cached until the expiry time instead of `CACHE_MIDDLEWARE_SECONDS`. Using the decorators in `django.views.decorators.cache`, you can easily set a view's expiry time (using the `cache_control` decorator) or disable caching for a view (using the `never_cache` decorator). See the following "Controlling Cache: Using Other Headers" section for more on these decorators.

The Per-View Cache

A more granular way to use the caching framework is by caching the output of individual views. `django.views.decorators.cache` defines a `cache_page` decorator that will automatically cache the view's response for you. It's easy to use:

```
from django.views.decorators.cache import cache_page

def my_view(request):
    # ...

my_view = cache_page(my_view, 60 * 15)
```

Or, using Python 2.4's *decorator* syntax:

```
@cache_page(60 * 15)
def my_view(request):
    # ...
```

cache_page takes a single argument: the cache timeout, in seconds. In the preceding example, the result of the my_view() view will be cached for 15 minutes. (Note that we've written it as 60 * 15 for the purpose of readability. 60 * 15 will be evaluated to 900—that is, 15 minutes multiplied by 60 seconds per minute.)

The per-view cache, like the per-site cache, is keyed off of the URL. If multiple URLs point at the same view, each URL will be cached separately. Continuing the my_view example, if your URLconf looks like this:

```
urlpatterns = ('',
    (r'^foo/(\d{1,2})/$', my_view),
)
```

then requests to /foo/1/ and /foo/23/ will be cached separately, as you may expect. But once a particular URL (e.g., /foo/23/) has been requested, subsequent requests to that URL will use the cache.

Specifying Per-View Cache in the URLconf

The examples in the previous section have hard-coded the fact that the view is cached, because cache_page alters the my_view function in place. This approach couples your view to the cache system, which is not ideal for several reasons. For instance, you might want to reuse the view functions on another, cache-less site, or you might want to distribute the views to people who might want to use them without being cached. The solution to these problems is to specify the per-view cache in the URLconf rather than next to the view functions themselves.

Doing so is easy: simply wrap the view function with cache_page when you refer to it in the URLconf. Here's the old URLconf from earlier:

```
urlpatterns = ('',
    (r'^foo/(\d{1,2})/$', my_view),
)
```

Here's the same thing, with my_view wrapped in cache_page:

```
from django.views.decorators.cache import cache_page

urlpatterns = ('',
    (r'^foo/(\d{1,2})/$', cache_page(my_view, 60 * 15)),
)
```

If you take this approach, don't forget to import cache_page within your URLconf.

Template Fragment Caching

If you're after even more control, you can also cache template fragments using the cache template tag. To give your template access to this tag, put {% load cache %} near the top of your template.

The {% cache %} template tag caches the contents of the block for a given amount of time. It takes at least two arguments: the cache timeout in seconds and the name to give the cache fragment. For example:

```
{% load cache %}
{% cache 500 sidebar %}
    .. sidebar ..
{% endcache %}
```

Sometimes you might want to cache multiple copies of a fragment, depending on some dynamic data that appears inside the fragment. For example, you might want a separate cached copy of the sidebar used in the previous example for every user of your site. Do this by passing additional arguments to the {% cache %} template tag to uniquely identify the cache fragment:

```
{% load cache %}
{% cache 500 sidebar request.user.username %}
    .. sidebar for logged in user ..
{% endcache %}
```

It's perfectly fine to specify more than one argument to identify the fragment. Simply pass as many arguments to {% cache %} as you need.

The cache timeout can be a template variable, as long as the template variable resolves to an integer value. For example, if the template variable my_timeout is set to the value 600, the following two examples are equivalent:

```
{% cache 600 sidebar %} ... {% endcache %}
{% cache my_timeout sidebar %} ... {% endcache %}
```

This feature is useful for avoiding repetition in templates. You can set the timeout in a variable, in one place, and just reuse that value.

The Low-Level Cache API

Sometimes, caching an entire rendered page doesn't gain you very much and is, in fact, inconvenient overkill.

Perhaps, for instance, your site includes a view whose results depend on several expensive queries, the results of which change at different intervals. In this case, it would not be ideal to use the full-page caching that the per-site or per-view cache strategies offer, because you wouldn't want to cache the entire result (since some of the data changes often), but you'd still want to cache the results that rarely change.

For cases like this, Django exposes a simple, low-level cache API. You can use this API to store objects in the cache with any level of granularity you like. You can cache any Python object that can be pickled safely: strings, dictionaries, lists of model objects, and so forth. (Most common Python objects can be pickled; refer to the Python documentation for more information about pickling.)

The cache module, django.core.cache, has a cache object that's automatically created from the CACHE_BACKEND setting:

```
>>> from django.core.cache import cache
```

The basic interface is set(key, value, timeout_seconds) and get(key):

```
>>> cache.set('my_key', 'hello, world!', 30)
>>> cache.get('my_key')
'hello, world!'
```

The timeout_seconds argument is optional and defaults to the timeout argument in the CACHE_BACKEND setting (explained earlier).

If the object doesn't exist in the cache, cache.get() returns None:

```
# Wait 30 seconds for 'my_key' to expire...

>>> cache.get('my_key')
None
```

We advise against storing the literal value None in the cache, because you won't be able to distinguish between your stored None value and a cache miss signified by a return value of None.

cache.get() can take a default argument. This specifies which value to return if the object doesn't exist in the cache:

```
>>> cache.get('my_key', 'has expired')
'has expired'
```

To add a key (only if it doesn't already exist), use the add() method. It takes the same parameters as set(), but it will not attempt to update the cache if the key specified is already present:

```
>>> cache.set('add_key', 'Initial value')
>>> cache.add('add_key', 'New value')
>>> cache.get('add_key')
'Initial value'
```

If you need to know whether add() stored a value in the cache, you can check the return value. It returns True if the value was stored; it returns False otherwise.

There's also a get_many() interface that hits the cache only once: get_many() returns a dictionary with all the keys you asked for that actually exist in the cache (and haven't expired):

```
>>> cache.set('a', 1)
>>> cache.set('b', 2)
>>> cache.set('c', 3)
>>> cache.get_many(['a', 'b', 'c'])
{'a': 1, 'b': 2, 'c': 3}
```

Finally, you can delete keys explicitly with delete(). This is an easy way of clearing the cache for a particular object:

```
>>> cache.delete('a')
```

You can also increment or decrement a key that already exists using the `incr()` or `decr()` methods, respectively. By default, the existing cache value will be incremented or decremented by 1. Other increment/decrement values can be specified by providing an argument to the increment/decrement call. A `ValueError` will be raised if you attempt to increment or decrement a nonexistent cache key:

```
>>> cache.set('num', 1)
>>> cache.incr('num')
2
>>> cache.incr('num', 10)
12
>>> cache.decr('num')
11
>>> cache.decr('num', 5)
6
```

■**Note**   `incr()`/`decr()` methods are not guaranteed to be atomic. On those back-ends that support atomic increment/decrement (most notably, the Memcached back-end), increment and decrement operations will be atomic. However, if the back-end doesn't natively provide an increment/decrement operation, it will be implemented using a two-step retrieve/update.

Upstream Caches

So far, this chapter has focused on caching your *own* data. But another type of caching is relevant to Web development, too: caching performed by "upstream" caches. These are systems that cache pages for users even before the request reaches your Web site.

Here are a few examples of upstream caches:

- Your ISP may cache certain pages, so if you requested a page from http://example.com/, your ISP would send you the page without having to access example.com directly. The maintainers of example.com have no knowledge of this caching; the ISP sits between example.com and your Web browser, handling all of the caching transparently.

- Your Django Web site may sit behind a *proxy cache*, such as Squid Web Proxy Cache (http://www.squid-cache.org/), that caches pages for performance. In this case, each request first would be handled by the proxy, and it would be passed to your application only if needed.

- Your Web browser caches pages, too. If a Web page sends out the appropriate headers, your browser will use the local cached copy for subsequent requests to that page, without even contacting the Web page again to see whether it has changed.

Upstream caching is a nice efficiency boost, but there's a danger to it: many Web pages' contents differ based on authentication and a host of other variables, and cache systems that blindly save pages based purely on URLs could expose incorrect or sensitive data to subsequent visitors to those pages.

For example, say you operate a Web e-mail system, and the contents of the "inbox" page obviously depend on which user is logged in. If an ISP blindly cached your site, then the first user who logged in through that ISP would have his user-specific inbox page cached for subsequent visitors to the site. That's not cool.

Fortunately, HTTP provides a solution to this problem. A number of HTTP headers exist to instruct upstream caches to differ their cache contents depending on designated variables, and to tell caching mechanisms not to cache particular pages. We'll look at some of these headers in the sections that follow.

Using Vary Headers

The Vary header defines which request headers a cache mechanism should take into account when building its cache key. For example, if the contents of a Web page depend on a user's language preference, the page is said to "vary on language."

By default, Django's cache system creates its cache keys using the requested path (e.g., "/stories/2005/jun/23/bank_robbed/"). This means every request to that URL will use the same cached version, regardless of user-agent differences such as cookies or language preferences. However, if this page produces different content based on some difference in request headers—such as a cookie, or a language, or a user-agent—you'll need to use the Vary header to tell caching mechanisms that the page output depends on those things.

To do this in Django, use the convenient vary_on_headers view decorator, like so:

```
from django.views.decorators.vary import vary_on_headers

# Python 2.3 syntax.
def my_view(request):
    # ...
my_view = vary_on_headers(my_view, 'User-Agent')

# Python 2.4+ decorator syntax.
@vary_on_headers('User-Agent')
def my_view(request):
    # ...
```

In this case, a caching mechanism (such as Django's own cache middleware) will cache a separate version of the page for each unique user-agent.

The advantage to using the vary_on_headers decorator rather than manually setting the Vary header (using something like response['Vary'] = 'user-agent') is that the decorator *adds* to the Vary header (which may already exist), rather than setting it from scratch and potentially overriding anything that was already in there.

You can pass multiple headers to vary_on_headers():

```
@vary_on_headers('User-Agent', 'Cookie')
def my_view(request):
    # ...
```

This tells upstream caches to vary on *both*, which means each combination of user-agent and cookie will get its own cache value. For example, a request with the user-agent Mozilla and the cookie value foo=bar will be considered different from a request with the user-agent Mozilla and the cookie value foo=ham.

Because varying on cookie is so common, there's a vary_on_cookie decorator. These two views are equivalent:

```
@vary_on_cookie
def my_view(request):
    # ...
```

```
@vary_on_headers('Cookie')
def my_view(request):
    # ...
```

The headers you pass to vary_on_headers are not case sensitive; "User-Agent" is the same thing as "user-agent".

You can also use a helper function, django.utils.cache.patch_vary_headers, directly. This function sets, or adds to, the Vary header. For example:

```
from django.utils.cache import patch_vary_headers

def my_view(request):
    # ...
    response = render_to_response('template_name', context)
    patch_vary_headers(response, ['Cookie'])
    return response
```

patch_vary_headers takes an HttpResponse instance as its first argument and a list/tuple of case-insensitive header names as its second argument.

Controlling Cache: Using Other Headers

Other problems with caching are the privacy of data and the question of where data should be stored in a cascade of caches.

A user usually faces two kinds of caches: his or her own browser cache (a private cache) and his or her provider's cache (a public cache). A public cache is used by multiple users and controlled by someone else. This poses problems with sensitive data—you don't want, say, your bank account number stored in a public cache. So Web applications need a way to tell caches which data is private and which is public.

The solution is to indicate a page's cache should be "private." To do this in Django, use the cache_control view decorator. Here's an example:

```
from django.views.decorators.cache import cache_control

@cache_control(private=True)
def my_view(request):
    # ...
```

This decorator takes care of sending out the appropriate HTTP header behind the scenes. There are a few other ways to control cache parameters. For example, HTTP allows applications to do the following:

- Define the maximum time a page should be cached.

- Specify whether a cache should always check for newer versions, only delivering the cached content when there are no changes. (Some caches might deliver cached content even if the server page changes, simply because the cache copy isn't yet expired.)

In Django, use the cache_control view decorator to specify these cache parameters. In this example, cache_control tells caches to revalidate the cache on every access and to store cached versions for, at most, 3,600 seconds:

```
from django.views.decorators.cache import cache_control

@cache_control(must_revalidate=True, max_age=3600)
def my_view(request):
    # ...
```

Any valid Cache-Control HTTP directive is valid in cache_control(). Here's a full list:

- public=True

- private=True

- no_cache=True

- no_transform=True

- must_revalidate=True

- proxy_revalidate=True

- max_age=num_seconds

- s_maxage=num_seconds

(Note that the caching middleware already sets the cache header's max-age with the value of the CACHE_MIDDLEWARE_SETTINGS setting. If you use a custom max_age in a cache_control decorator, the decorator will take precedence, and the header values will be merged correctly.)

If you want to use headers to disable caching altogether, django.views.decorators.cache. never_cache is a view decorator that adds headers to ensure that the response won't be cached by browsers or other caches. For example:

```
from django.views.decorators.cache import never_cache

@never_cache
def myview(request):
    # ...
```

Other Optimizations

Django comes with a few other pieces of middleware that can help optimize your apps' performance:

- `django.middleware.http.ConditionalGetMiddleware` adds support for modern browsers to conditionally GET responses based on the `ETag` and `Last-Modified` headers.

- `django.middleware.gzip.GZipMiddleware` compresses responses for all modern browsers, saving bandwidth and transfer time.

Order of MIDDLEWARE_CLASSES

If you use caching middleware, it's important to put each half in the right place within the `MIDDLEWARE_CLASSES` setting. That's because the cache middleware needs to know which headers should be used to vary the cache storage. Middleware always adds something to the `Vary` response header when it can.

`UpdateCacheMiddleware` runs during the response phase (in which middleware is run in reverse order), so an item at the top of the list runs *last* during the response phase. Thus, you need to make sure that `UpdateCacheMiddleware` appears *before* any other middleware that might add something to the `Vary` header. The following middleware modules do so:

- `SessionMiddleware` adds `Cookie`

- `GZipMiddleware` adds `Accept-Encoding`

- `LocaleMiddleware` adds `Accept-Language`

On the other hand, `FetchFromCacheMiddleware` runs during the request phase, during which middleware is applied first to last, so an item at the top of the list runs *first* during the request phase. The `FetchFromCacheMiddleware` also needs to run after other middleware updates the `Vary` header, so `FetchFromCacheMiddleware` must be *after* any item that does so.

What's Next?

Django ships with a number of "contrib" packages—optional features that can make your life easier. We've already covered a few of these: the admin site (discussed in Chapter 6) and the session/user framework (refer to Chapter 14). The next chapter covers more of the "contributed" subframeworks.

CHAPTER 16

■ ■ ■

django.contrib

One of the many strengths of Python is its "batteries included" philosophy: when you install Python, it comes with a large standard library of packages that you can start using immediately, without having to download anything else. Django aims to follow this philosophy, and it includes its own standard library of add-ons useful for common Web-development tasks. This chapter covers that collection of add-ons.

The Django Standard Library

Django's standard library lives in the package `django.contrib`. Within each subpackage is a separate piece of add-on functionality. These pieces are not necessarily related, but some `django.contrib` subpackages may require other ones.

There's no hard requirement for the types of functionality in `django.contrib`. Some of the packages include models (and hence require you to install their database tables into your database), but others consist solely of middleware or template tags.

The single characteristic the `django.contrib` packages have in common is this: if you were to remove the `django.contrib` package entirely, you could still use Django's fundamental features with no problems. When the Django developers add new functionality to the framework, they use this rule of thumb in deciding whether the new functionality should live in `django.contrib` or elsewhere.

`django.contrib` consists of these packages:

- `admin`: The Django admin site. See Chapter 6.

- `admindocs`: autodocumentation for the Django admin site. This book doesn't cover this feature; check the official Django documentation.

- `auth`: Django's authentication framework. See Chapter 14.

- `comments`: A comments application. This book doesn't cover this feature; check the official Django documentation.

- `contenttypes`: A framework for hooking into "types" of content, where each installed Django model is a separate content type. This framework is used internally by other "contrib" applications and is mostly intended for very advanced Django developers. Those developers should find out more about this application by reading the source code in `django/contrib/contenttypes`.

- `csrf`: Protection against cross-site request forgery (CSRF). See the later section titled "CSRF Protection."

- `databrowse`: A Django application that lets you browse your data. This book doesn't cover this feature; check the official Django documentation.

- `flatpages`: A framework for managing simple "flat" HTML content in a database. See the later section titled "Flatpages."

- `formtools`: A number of useful higher-level libraries for dealing with common patterns in forms. This book doesn't cover this feature; check the official Django documentation.

- `gis`: Extensions to Django that provide for GIS (Geographic Information Systems) support. These, for example, allow your Django models to store geographic data and perform geographic queries. This is a large, complex library and isn't covered in this book. See `http://geodjango.org/` for documentation.

- `humanize`: A set of Django template filters useful for adding a "human touch" to data. See the later section titled "Humanizing Data."

- `localflavor`: Assorted pieces of code that are useful for particular countries or cultures. For example, this includes ways to validate US ZIP codes or Icelandic personal identification numbers.

- `markup`: A set of Django template filters that implement a number of common markup languages. See the later section titled "Markup Filters."

- `redirects`: A framework for managing redirects. See the later section titled "Redirects."

- `sessions`: Django's session framework. See Chapter 14.

- `sitemaps`: A framework for generating sitemap XML files. See Chapter 13.

- `sites`: A framework that lets you operate multiple Web sites from the same database and Django installation. See the next section, "Sites."

- `syndication`: A framework for generating syndication feeds in RSS and Atom. See Chapter 13.

- `webdesign`: Django add-ons that are particularly useful to Web *designers* (as opposed to developers). As of this writing, this includes only a single template tag, `{% lorem %}`. Check the Django documentation for more information.

The rest of this chapter goes into detail about a number of `django.contrib` packages that we haven't yet covered in this book.

Sites

Django's sites system is a generic framework that lets you operate multiple Web sites from the same database and Django project. This is an abstract concept, and it can be tricky to understand, so we'll start with a couple of scenarios where it would be useful.

Scenario 1: Reusing Data on Multiple Sites

As we explained in Chapter 1, the Django-powered sites LJWorld.com and Lawrence.com are operated by the same news organization: the *Lawrence Journal-World* newspaper in Lawrence, Kansas. LJWorld.com focuses on news, while Lawrence.com focuses on local entertainment. But sometimes editors want to publish an article on *both* sites.

The brain-dead way of solving the problem would be to use a separate database for each site and to require site producers to publish the same story twice: once for LJWorld.com and again for Lawrence.com. But that's inefficient for site producers, and it's redundant to store multiple copies of the same story in the database.

The better solution? Both sites use the same article database, and an article is associated with one or more sites via a many-to-many relationship. The Django sites framework provides the database table to which articles can be related. It's a hook for associating data with one or more "sites."

Scenario 2: Storing Your Site Name/Domain in One Place

LJWorld.com and Lawrence.com both have e-mail alert functionality, which lets readers sign up to get notifications when news happens. It's pretty basic: a reader signs up on a Web form, and immediately gets an e-mail saying, "Thanks for your subscription."

It would be inefficient and redundant to implement this signup-processing code twice, so the sites use the same code behind the scenes. But the "Thank you for your subscription" notice needs to be different for each site. By using Site objects, we can abstract the thank-you notice to use the values of the current site's name (e.g., LJWorld.com) and domain (e.g., www.ljworld.com).

The Django sites framework provides a place for you to store the name and domain for each site in your Django project, which means you can reuse those values in a generic way.

How to Use the Sites Framework

The sites framework is more a series of conventions than a framework. The whole thing is based on two simple concepts:

- The Site model, found in django.contrib.sites, has domain and name fields.

- The SITE_ID setting specifies the database ID of the Site object associated with that particular settings file.

How you use these two concepts is up to you, but Django uses them in a couple of ways automatically via simple conventions.

To install the sites application, follow these steps:

1. Add 'django.contrib.sites' to your INSTALLED_APPS.

2. Run the command manage.py syncdb to install the django_site table into your database. This will also create a default site object, with the domain example.com.

3. Change the example.com site to your own domain, and add any other Site objects, either through the Django admin site or via the Python API. Create a Site object for each site/domain that this Django project powers.

4. Define the SITE_ID setting in each of your settings files. This value should be the database ID of the Site object for the site powered by that settings file.

The Sites Framework's Capabilities

The sections that follow describe the various things you can do with the sites framework.

Reusing Data on Multiple Sites

To reuse data on multiple sites, as explained in the first scenario, just create a ManyToManyField to Site in your models, as in this example:

```
from django.db import models
from django.contrib.sites.models import Site

class Article(models.Model):
    headline = models.CharField(max_length=200)
    # ...
    sites = models.ManyToManyField(Site)
```

That's the infrastructure you need to associate articles with multiple sites in your database. With that in place, you can reuse the same Django view code for multiple sites. Continuing the Article model example, here's what an article_detail view might look like:

```
from django.conf import settings
from django.shortcuts import get_object_or_404
from mysite.articles.models import Article

def article_detail(request, article_id):
    a = get_object_or_404(Article, id=article_id, sites__id=settings.SITE_ID)
    # ...
```

This view function is reusable because it checks the article's site dynamically, according to the value of the SITE_ID setting.

For example, say LJWorld.com's settings file has a SITE_ID set to 1, and Lawrence.com's settings file has a SITE_ID set to 2. If this view is called when LJWorld.com's settings file is active, then it will limit the article lookup to articles in which the list of sites includes LJWorld.com.

Associating Content with a Single Site

Similarly, you can associate a model to the Site model in a many-to-one relationship using ForeignKey.

For example, if each article is associated with only a single site, you could use a model like this:

```
from django.db import models
from django.contrib.sites.models import Site

class Article(models.Model):
    headline = models.CharField(max_length=200)
    # ...
    site = models.ForeignKey(Site)
```

This has the same benefits as described in the preceding section.

Hooking into the Current Site from Views

On a lower level, you can use the sites framework in your Django views to do particular things based on the site in which the view is being called, as in this example:

```
from django.conf import settings


def my_view(request):
    if settings.SITE_ID == 3:
        # Do something.
    else:
        # Do something else.
```

Of course, it's ugly to hard-code the site IDs like that. A slightly cleaner way of accomplishing the same thing is to check the current site's domain:

```
from django.conf import settings
from django.contrib.sites.models import Site


def my_view(request):
    current_site = Site.objects.get(id=settings.SITE_ID)
    if current_site.domain == 'foo.com':
        # Do something
    else:
        # Do something else.
```

The idiom of retrieving the Site object for the value of settings.SITE_ID is quite common, so the Site model's manager (Site.objects) has a get_current() method. This example is equivalent to the previous one:

```
from django.contrib.sites.models import Site

def my_view(request):
    current_site = Site.objects.get_current()
    if current_site.domain == 'foo.com':
        # Do something
    else:
        # Do something else.
```

Note In this final example, you don't have to import `django.conf.settings`.

Getting the Current Domain for Display

For a DRY (Don't Repeat Yourself) approach to storing your site's name and domain name, as explained in "Scenario 2: Storing Your Site Name/Domain in One Place," just reference the name and domain of the current Site object. Here's an example:

```
from django.contrib.sites.models import Site
from django.core.mail import send_mail

def register_for_newsletter(request):
    # Check form values, etc., and subscribe the user.
    # ...
    current_site = Site.objects.get_current()
    send_mail('Thanks for subscribing to %s alerts' % current_site.name,
        'Thanks for your subscription. We appreciate it.\n\n-The %s team.' % \
        current_site.name,
        'editor@%s' % current_site.domain,
        [user_email])
    # ...
```

Continuing our ongoing example of LJWorld.com and Lawrence.com, on Lawrence.com this e-mail has the subject line "Thanks for subscribing to Lawrence.com alerts." On LJWorld.com, the e-mail has the subject line "Thanks for subscribing to LJWorld.com alerts." This same site-specific behavior is applied to the e-mails' message body.

An even more flexible (but more heavyweight) way of doing this would be to use Django's template system. Assuming Lawrence.com and LJWorld.com have different template directories (TEMPLATE_DIRS), you could simply delegate to the template system like so:

```
from django.core.mail import send_mail
from django.template import loader, Context

def register_for_newsletter(request):
    # Check form values, etc., and subscribe the user.
    # ...
    subject = loader.get_template('alerts/subject.txt').render(Context({}))
    message = loader.get_template('alerts/message.txt').render(Context({}))
    send_mail(subject, message, 'do-not-reply@example.com', [user_email])
    # ...
```

In this case, you have to create subject.txt and message.txt templates in both the LJWorld.com and Lawrence.com template directories. As mentioned previously, that gives you more flexibility, but it's also more complex.

It's a good idea to exploit the Site objects as much as possible to remove unneeded complexity and redundancy.

CurrentSiteManager

If Site objects play a key role in your application, consider using the CurrentSiteManager in your model(s). It's a model manager (see Chapter 10) that automatically filters its queries to include only objects associated with the current Site.

Use CurrentSiteManager by adding it to your model explicitly, as in this example:

```
from django.db import models
from django.contrib.sites.models import Site
from django.contrib.sites.managers import CurrentSiteManager

class Photo(models.Model):
    photo = models.FileField(upload_to='/home/photos')
    photographer_name = models.CharField(max_length=100)
    pub_date = models.DateField()
    site = models.ForeignKey(Site)
    objects = models.Manager()
    on_site = CurrentSiteManager()
```

With this model, Photo.objects.all() will return all Photo objects in the database, but Photo.on_site.all() will return only the Photo objects associated with the current site, according to the SITE_ID setting.

In other words, these two statements are equivalent:

```
Photo.objects.filter(site=settings.SITE_ID)
Photo.on_site.all()
```

How did `CurrentSiteManager` know which field of `Photo` was the `Site`? It defaults to looking for a field called `site`. If your model has a `ForeignKey` or `ManyToManyField` called something *other* than `site`, you need to explicitly pass that as the parameter to `CurrentSiteManager`. The following model, which has a field called `publish_on`, demonstrates this:

```
from django.db import models
from django.contrib.sites.models import Site
from django.contrib.sites.managers import CurrentSiteManager

class Photo(models.Model):
    photo = models.FileField(upload_to='/home/photos')
    photographer_name = models.CharField(max_length=100)
    pub_date = models.DateField()
    publish_on = models.ForeignKey(Site)
    objects = models.Manager()
    on_site = CurrentSiteManager('publish_on')
```

If you attempt to use `CurrentSiteManager` and pass a field name that doesn't exist, Django will raise a `ValueError`.

■**Note** You'll probably want to keep a normal (non-site-specific) `Manager` on your model, even if you use `CurrentSiteManager`. As explained in Appendix B, if you define a manager manually, then Django won't create the automatic `objects = models.Manager()` manager for you.

Also, certain parts of Django—namely, the Django admin site and generic views—use whichever manager is defined *first* in the model, so if you want your admin site to have access to all objects (not just site-specific ones), put `objects = models.Manager()` in your model before you define `CurrentSiteManager`.

How Django Uses the Sites Framework

Although it's not required that you use the sites framework, it's encouraged because Django takes advantage of it in a few places. Even if your Django installation is powering only a single site, you should take a few seconds to create the site object with your `domain` and `name`, and point to its ID in your `SITE_ID` setting.

Here's how Django uses the sites framework:

- In the redirects framework (see the later section "Redirects"), each redirect object is associated with a particular site. When Django searches for a redirect, it takes into account the current `SITE_ID`.

- In the comments framework, each comment is associated with a particular site. When a comment is posted, its `site` is set to the current `SITE_ID`, and when comments are listed via the appropriate template tag, only the comments for the current site are displayed.

- In the flatpages framework (see the later section "Flatpages"), each flatpage is associated with a particular site. When a flatpage is created, you specify its site, and the flatpage middleware checks the current SITE_ID in retrieving flatpages to display.

- In the syndication framework (see Chapter 13), the templates for title and description automatically have access to a variable {{ site }}, which is the Site object representing the current site. Also, the hook for providing item URLs will use the domain from the current Site object if you don't specify a fully qualified domain.

- In the authentication framework (see Chapter 14), the django.contrib.auth.views. login view passes the current Site name to the template as {{ site_name }} and the current Site object as {{ site }}.

Flatpages

Often you'll have a database-driven Web application up and running, but you'll need to add a couple of one-off static pages, such as an About page or a Privacy Policy page. It would be possible to use a standard Web server such as Apache to serve these files as flat HTML files, but that introduces an extra level of complexity into your application, because then you have to worry about configuring Apache, you have to set up access for your team to edit those files, and you can't take advantage of Django's template system to style the pages.

The solution to this problem is Django's flatpages application, which lives in the package django.contrib.flatpages. This application lets you manage such one-off pages via Django's admin site, and it lets you specify templates for them using Django's template system. It uses Django models behind the scenes, which means it stores the pages in a database, just like the rest of your data, and you can access flatpages with the standard Django database API.

Flatpages are keyed by their URL and site. When you create a flatpage, you specify which URL it's associated with, along with which site(s) it's on. (For more on sites, see the "Sites" section.)

Using Flatpages

To install the flatpages application, follow these steps:

1. Add 'django.contrib.flatpages' to your INSTALLED_APPS. django.contrib.flatpages depends on django.contrib.sites, so make sure both packages are in INSTALLED_APPS.

2. Add 'django.contrib.flatpages.middleware.FlatpageFallbackMiddleware' to your MIDDLEWARE_CLASSES setting.

3. Run the command manage.py syncdb to install the two required tables into your database.

The flatpages application creates two tables in your database: django_flatpage and django_flatpage_sites. django_flatpage simply maps a URL to a title and bunch of text content. django_flatpage_sites is a many-to-many table that associates a flatpage with one or more sites.

The application comes with a single FlatPage model, defined in django/contrib/flatpages/ models.py. It looks something like this:

```
from django.db import models
from django.contrib.sites.models import Site

class FlatPage(models.Model):
    url = models.CharField(max_length=100, db_index=True)
    title = models.CharField(max_length=200)
    content = models.TextField(blank=True)
    enable_comments = models.BooleanField()
    template_name = models.CharField(max_length=70, blank=True)
    registration_required = models.BooleanField()
    sites = models.ManyToManyField(Site)
```

Let's examine these fields one at a time:

- url: The URL at which this flatpage lives, excluding the domain name but including the leading slash (e.g., /about/contact/).

- title: The title of the flatpage. The framework doesn't do anything special with this. It's your responsibility to display it in your template.

- content: The content of the flatpage (i.e., the HTML of the page). The framework doesn't do anything special with this. It's your responsibility to display it in the template.

- enable_comments: Whether to enable comments on this flatpage. The framework doesn't do anything special with this. You can check this value in your template and display a comment form if needed.

- template_name: The name of the template to use for rendering this flatpage. This is optional; if it's not given or if this template doesn't exist, the framework will fall back to the template flatpages/default.html.

- registration_required: Whether registration is required for viewing this flatpage. This integrates with Django's authentication/user framework, which is explained further in Chapter 14.

- sites: The sites that this flatpage lives on. This integrates with Django's sites framework, which is explained in the "Sites" section of this chapter.

You can create flatpages through either the Django admin interface or the Django database API. For more information on this, see the section "Adding, Changing, and Deleting Flatpages."

Once you've created flatpages, FlatpageFallbackMiddleware does all of the work. Each time any Django application raises a 404 error, this middleware checks the flatpages database for the requested URL as a last resort. Specifically, it checks for a flatpage with the given URL with a site ID that corresponds to the SITE_ID setting.

If it finds a match, it loads the flatpage's template or flatpages/default.html if the flatpage has not specified a custom template. It passes that template a single context variable, flatpage, which is the FlatPage object. It uses RequestContext in rendering the template.

If `FlatpageFallbackMiddleware` doesn't find a match, the request continues to be processed as usual.

■Note This middleware gets activated for only 404 (page not found) errors—not for 500 (server error) or other error responses. Also note that the order of `MIDDLEWARE_CLASSES` matters. Generally, you can put `FlatpageFallbackMiddleware` at or near the end of the list, because it's a last resort.

Adding, Changing, and Deleting Flatpages

You can add, change, and delete flatpages in two ways.

Via the Admin Interface

If you've activated the automatic Django admin interface, you should see a Flatpages section on the admin index page. Edit flatpages as you would edit any other object in the system.

Via the Python API

As described previously, flatpages are represented by a standard Django model that lives in `django/contrib/flatpages/models.py`. Hence, you can access flatpage objects via the Django database API, as in this example:

```
>>> from django.contrib.flatpages.models import FlatPage
>>> from django.contrib.sites.models import Site
>>> fp = FlatPage.objects.create(
...     url='/about/',
...     title='About',
...     content='<p>About this site...</p>',
...     enable_comments=False,
...     template_name='',
...     registration_required=False,
... )
>>> fp.sites.add(Site.objects.get(id=1))
>>> FlatPage.objects.get(url='/about/')
<FlatPage: /about/--About>
```

Using Flatpage Templates

By default, flatpages are rendered via the template `flatpages/default.html`, but you can override that for a particular flatpage with the `template_name` field on the `FlatPage` object.

Creating the `flatpages/default.html` template is your responsibility. In your template directory, just create a `flatpages` directory containing a `default.html` file.

Flatpage templates are passed a single context variable, flatpage, which is the flatpage object.

Here's a sample flatpages/default.html template:

```
<!DOCTYPE HTML PUBLIC "-//W3C//DTD HTML 4.0 Transitional//EN"
    "http://www.w3.org/TR/REC-html40/loose.dtd">
<html>
<head>
<title>{{ flatpage.title }}</title>
</head>
<body>
{{ flatpage.content|safe }}
</body>
</html>
```

Note that we've used the safe template filter to allow flatpage.content to include raw HTML and bypass autoescaping.

Redirects

Django's redirects framework lets you manage redirects easily by storing them in a database and treating them as any other Django model object. For example, you can use the redirects framework to tell Django, "Redirect any request to /music/ to /sections/arts/music/." This comes in handy when you need to move things around on your site; Web developers should do whatever is necessary to avoid broken links.

Using the Redirects Framework

To install the redirects application, follow these steps:

1. Add 'django.contrib.redirects' to your INSTALLED_APPS.

2. Add 'django.contrib.redirects.middleware.RedirectFallbackMiddleware' to your MIDDLEWARE_CLASSES setting.

3. Run the command manage.py syncdb to install the single required table into your database.

manage.py syncdb creates a django_redirect table in your database. This is a simple lookup table with site_id, old_path, and new_path fields.

You can create redirects through either the Django admin interface or the Django database API. For more, see the section "Adding, Changing, and Deleting Redirects."

Once you've created redirects, the RedirectFallbackMiddleware class does all of the work. Each time any Django application raises a 404 error, this middleware checks the redirects database for the requested URL as a last resort. Specifically, it checks for a redirect with the given old_path with a site ID that corresponds to the SITE_ID setting. (See the earlier section "Sites" for more information on SITE_ID and the sites framework.) Then it follows these steps:

1. If it finds a match and new_path is not empty, it redirects to new_path.

2. If it finds a match and new_path is empty, it sends a 410 ("Gone") HTTP header and an empty (contentless) response.

3. If it doesn't find a match, the request continues to be processed as usual.

■**Note** The middleware gets activated for only 404 errors—not for 500 errors or responses of any other status code. Additionally, the order of MIDDLEWARE_CLASSES matters. Generally, you can put RedirectFallbackMiddleware toward the end of the list, because it's a last resort.

■**Note** If you're using both the redirect and flatpage fallback middleware, consider which one (redirect or flatpage) you'd like checked first. We suggest flatpages before redirects (thus putting the flatpage middleware before the redirect middleware), but you might feel differently.

Adding, Changing, and Deleting Redirects

You can add, change, and delete redirects in two ways.

Via the Admin Interface

If you've activated the automatic Django admin interface, you should see a Redirects section on the admin index page. Edit redirects as you would edit any other object in the system.

Via the Python API

Redirects are represented by a standard Django model that lives in django/contrib/redirects/ models.py. Hence, you can access redirect objects via the Django database API, as in this example:

```
>>> from django.contrib.redirects.models import Redirect
>>> from django.contrib.sites.models import Site
>>> red = Redirect.objects.create(
...     site=Site.objects.get(id=1),
...     old_path='/music/',
...     new_path='/sections/arts/music/',
... )
>>> Redirect.objects.get(old_path='/music/')
<Redirect: /music/ ---> /sections/arts/music/>
```

CSRF Protection

The `django.contrib.csrf` package protects against CSRF (also known as "session riding"), which is a Web site security exploit. It happens when a malicious Web site tricks a user into unknowingly loading a URL from a site at which that user is already authenticated, hence taking advantage of the user's authenticated status. This can be a bit tricky to understand at first, so we walk through two examples in this section.

A Simple CSRF Example

Suppose you're logged in to a Webmail account at `example.com`. This Webmail site has a Log Out button that points to the URL `example.com/logout`—that is, the only action you need to take in order to log out is to visit the page `example.com/logout`.

A malicious site can coerce you to visit the URL `example.com/logout` by including that URL as a hidden `<iframe>` on its own (malicious) page. Thus, if you're logged in to the `example.com` Webmail account and visit the malicious page that has an `<iframe>` to `example.com/logout`, the act of visiting the malicious page will log you out from `example.com`.

Clearly, being logged out of a Webmail site against your will is not a terrifying breach of security, but this same type of exploit can happen to *any* site that trusts users, such as an online banking site or an e-commerce site, where the exploit could be used to initiate an order or payment without the user's knowledge.

A More Complex CSRF Example

In the previous example, `example.com` was partially at fault because it allowed a state change (i.e., logging the user out) to be requested via the HTTP `GET` method. It's much better practice to require an HTTP `POST` for any request that changes state on the server. But even Web sites that require `POST` for state-changing actions are vulnerable to CSRF.

Suppose `example.com` has upgraded its Log Out functionality so that it's a `<form>` button that is requested via `POST` to the URL `example.com/logout`. Furthermore, the logout `<form>` includes this hidden field:

```
<input type="hidden" name="confirm" value="true">
```

This ensures that a simple `POST` to the URL `example.com/logout` won't log out a user; in order for a user to log out, the user must request `example.com/logout` via `POST` *and* send the `confirm` POST variable with a value of `true`.

Well, despite the extra security, this arrangement can still be exploited by CSRF—the malicious page just needs to do a little more work. Attackers can create an entire form targeting your site, hide it in an invisible `<iframe>`, and then use JavaScript to submit that form automatically.

Preventing CSRF

How, then, can your site protect itself from this exploit? The first step is to make sure all `GET` requests are free of side effects. That way, if a malicious site includes one of your pages as an `<iframe>`, it won't have a negative effect.

That leaves POST requests. The second step is to give each POST <form> a hidden field whose value is secret and is generated from the user's session ID. Then, when processing the form on the server side, check for that secret field and raise an error if it doesn't validate.

This is exactly what Django's CSRF prevention layer does, as explained in the sections that follow.

Using the CSRF Middleware

The django.contrib.csrf package contains only one module: middleware.py. This module contains a Django middleware class, CsrfMiddleware, which implements the CSRF protection.

To activate this CSRF protection, add 'django.contrib.csrf.middleware.CsrfMiddleware' to the MIDDLEWARE_CLASSES setting in your settings file. This middleware needs to process the response *after* SessionMiddleware, so CsrfMiddleware must appear *before* SessionMiddleware in the list (because the response middleware is processed last-to-first). Also, it must process the response before the response gets compressed or otherwise mangled, so CsrfMiddleware must come after GZipMiddleware. Once you've added CsrfMiddleware to your MIDDLEWARE_CLASSES setting, you're done. See the section "Order of MIDDLEWARE_CLASSES" in Chapter 15 for more explanation.

In case you're interested, here's how CsrfMiddleware works:

- It modifies outgoing requests by adding a hidden form field to all POST forms, with the name csrfmiddlewaretoken and a value that is a hash of the session ID plus a secret key. The middleware does *not* modify the response if there's no session ID set, so the performance penalty is negligible for requests that don't use sessions.

- On all incoming POST requests that have the session cookie set, it checks that csrfmiddlewaretoken is present and correct. If it isn't, the user will get a 403 HTTP error. The content of the 403 error page is the message "Cross Site Request Forgery detected. Request aborted."

This ensures that only forms originating from your Web site can be used to POST data back.

This middleware deliberately targets only HTTP POST requests (and the corresponding POST forms). As we explained, GET requests ought never to have side effects; it's your own responsibility to ensure this.

POST requests not accompanied by a session cookie are not protected, but they don't *need* to be protected, because a malicious Web site could make these kind of requests anyway.

To avoid altering non-HTML requests, the middleware checks the response's Content-Type header before modifying it. Only pages that are served as text/html or application/xml+xhtml are modified.

Limitations of the CSRF Middleware

CsrfMiddleware requires Django's session framework to work. (See Chapter 14 for more on sessions.) If you're using a custom session or authentication framework that manually manages session cookies, this middleware will not help you.

If your application creates HTML pages and forms in some unusual way (e.g., if it sends fragments of HTML in JavaScript document.write statements), you might bypass the filter that adds the hidden field to the form. In this case, the form submission will always fail. (This happens because CsrfMiddleware uses a regular expression to add the csrfmiddlewaretoken field to your HTML before the page is sent to the client, and the regular expression sometimes cannot handle wacky HTML.) If you suspect this might be happening, just view the source in your Web browser to see whether `csrfmiddlewaretoken` was inserted into your `<form>`.

For more CSRF information and examples, visit `http://en.wikipedia.org/wiki/CSRF`.

Humanizing Data

The package `django.contrib.humanize` holds a set of Django template filters useful for adding a "human touch" to data. To activate these filters, add `'django.contrib.humanize'` to your `INSTALLED_APPS`. Once you've done that, use `{% load humanize %}` in a template, and you'll have access to the filters described in the following sections.

apnumber

For numbers 1 through 9, this filter returns the number spelled out. Otherwise, it returns the numeral. This follows Associated Press style. Here are some examples:

- "1" becomes "one".
- "2" becomes "two".
- "10" remains "10".

You can pass in either an integer or a string representation of an integer.

intcomma

This filter converts an integer to a string containing commas every three digits. Here are some examples:

- "4500" becomes "4,500".
- "45000" becomes "45,000".
- "450000" becomes "450,000".
- "4500000" becomes "4,500,000".

You can pass in either an integer or a string representation of an integer.

intword

This filter converts a large integer to a friendly text representation. It works best for numbers over 1 million. Values up to 1 quadrillion (1,000,000,000,000,000) are supported. Here are some examples:

- "1000000" becomes "1.0 million".
- "1200000" becomes "1.2 million".
- "1200000000" becomes "1.2 billion".

You can pass in either an integer or a string representation of an integer.

ordinal

This filter converts an integer to its ordinal as a string. Here are some examples:

- "1" becomes "1st".
- "2" becomes "2nd".
- "3" becomes "3rd".
- "254" becomes "254th".

You can pass in either an integer or a string representation of an integer.

Markup Filters

The package `django.contrib.markup` includes a handful of Django template filters, each of which implements a common markup language:

- `textile`: Implements Textile (http://en.wikipedia.org/wiki/Textile_%28markup_language%29)
- `markdown`: Implements Markdown (http://en.wikipedia.org/wiki/Markdown)
- `restructuredtext`: Implements reStructured Text (http://en.wikipedia.org/wiki/ReStructuredText)

In each case, the filter expects formatted markup as a string and returns a string representing the marked-up text. For example, the `textile` filter converts text that is marked up in Textile format to HTML:

```
{% load markup %}
{{ object.content|textile }}
```

To activate these filters, add `'django.contrib.markup'` to your `INSTALLED_APPS` setting. Once you've done that, use `{% load markup %}` in a template, and you'll have access to these filters. For more documentation, read the source code in `django/contrib/markup/templatetags/markup.py`.

What's Next?

Many of these contributed frameworks (CSRF, the auth system, etc.) do their magic by providing a piece of *middleware*. Middleware is code that runs before and/or after every request and can modify requests and responses at will to extend the framework. In the next chapter, we'll discuss Django's built-in middleware and explain how you can write your own.

Middleware

On occasion, you'll need to run a piece of code on each and every request that Django handles. This code might need to modify the request before the view handles it, it might need to log information about the request for debugging purposes, and so forth.

You can do this with Django's *middleware* framework, which is a set of hooks into Django's request/response processing. It's a light, low-level "plug-in" system capable of globally altering both Django's input and output.

Each middleware component is responsible for doing some specific function. If you're reading this book straight through, you've seen middleware a number of times already:

- All of the session and user tools that we looked at in Chapter 14 are made possible by a few small pieces of middleware (more specifically, the middleware makes `request.session` and `request.user` available to you in views).

- The sitewide cache discussed in Chapter 15 is actually just a piece of middleware that bypasses the call to your view function if the response for that view has already been cached.

- The flatpages, redirects, and csrf applications from Chapter 16 all do their magic through middleware components.

This chapter dives deeper into exactly what middleware is and how it works, and explains how you can write your own middleware.

What's Middleware?

Let's start with a very simple example.

High-traffic sites often need to deploy Django behind a load-balancing proxy (see Chapter 12). This can cause a few small complications, one of which is that every request's remote IP (`request.META["REMOTE_IP"]`) will be that of the load balancer, not the actual IP making the request. Load balancers deal with this by setting a special header, `X-Forwarded-For`, to the actual requesting IP address.

So here's a small bit of middleware that lets sites running behind a proxy still see the correct IP address in request.META["REMOTE_ADDR"]:

```
class SetRemoteAddrFromForwardedFor(object):
    def process_request(self, request):
        try:
            real_ip = request.META['HTTP_X_FORWARDED_FOR']
        except KeyError:
            pass
        else:
            # HTTP_X_FORWARDED_FOR can be a comma-separated list of IPs.
            # Take just the first one.
            real_ip = real_ip.split(",")[0]
            request.META['REMOTE_ADDR'] = real_ip
```

■**Note** Although the HTTP header is called X-Forwarded-For, Django makes it available as request.META['HTTP_X_FORWARDED_FOR']. With the exception of content-length and content-type, any HTTP headers in the request are converted to request.META keys by converting all characters to uppercase, replacing any hyphens with underscores, and adding an HTTP_ prefix to the name.

If this middleware is installed (see the next section), every request's X-Forwarded-For value will be automatically inserted into request.META['REMOTE_ADDR']. This means your Django applications don't need to be concerned with whether they're behind a load-balancing proxy or not; they can simply access request.META['REMOTE_ADDR'], and that will work whether or not a proxy is being used.

In fact, this is a common enough need that this piece of middleware is a built-in part of Django. It lives in django.middleware.http, and you can read a bit more about it later in this chapter.

Middleware Installation

If you've read this book straight through, you've already seen a number of examples of middleware installation; many of the examples in previous chapters have required certain middleware. For completeness, here's how to install middleware.

To activate a middleware component, add it to the MIDDLEWARE_CLASSES tuple in your settings module. In MIDDLEWARE_CLASSES, each middleware component is represented by a string: the full Python path to the middleware's class name. For example, here's the default MIDDLEWARE_CLASSES created by django-admin.py startproject:

```
MIDDLEWARE_CLASSES = (
    'django.middleware.common.CommonMiddleware',
    'django.contrib.sessions.middleware.SessionMiddleware',
    'django.contrib.auth.middleware.AuthenticationMiddleware',
)
```

A Django installation doesn't require any middleware—MIDDLEWARE_CLASSES can be empty, if you'd like—but we recommend that you activate CommonMiddleware, which we explain shortly.

The order is significant. On the request and view phases, Django applies middleware in the order given in MIDDLEWARE_CLASSES, and on the response and exception phases, Django applies middleware in reverse order. That is, Django treats MIDDLEWARE_CLASSES as a sort of "wrapper" around the view function: on the request it walks down the list to the view, and on the response it walks back up.

Middleware Methods

Now that you know what middleware is and how to install it, let's take a look at all the available methods that middleware classes can define.

Initializer: __init__(self)

Use __init__() to perform systemwide setup for a given middleware class.

For performance reasons, each activated middleware class is instantiated only *once* per server process. This means that __init__() is called only once—at server startup—not for individual requests.

A common reason to implement an __init__() method is to check whether the middleware is indeed needed. If __init__() raises django.core.exceptions.MiddlewareNotUsed, then Django will remove the middleware from the middleware stack. You might use this feature to check for some piece of software that the middleware class requires, or check whether the server is running in debug mode, or any other such environment situation.

If a middleware class defines an __init__() method, the method should take no arguments beyond the standard self.

Request Preprocessor: process_request(self, request)

This method gets called as soon as the request has been received—before Django has parsed the URL to determine which view to execute. It gets passed the HttpRequest object, which you may modify at will.

process_request() should return either None or an HttpResponse object.

- If it returns None, Django will continue processing this request, executing any other middleware and then the appropriate view.

- If it returns an HttpResponse object, Django won't bother calling *any* other middleware (of any type) or the appropriate view. Django will immediately return that HttpResponse.

View Preprocessor: process_view(self, request, view, args, kwargs)

This method gets called after the request preprocessor is called and Django has determined which view to execute, but before that view has actually been executed.

The arguments passed to this view are shown in Table 17-1.

Table 17-1. *Arguments Passed to process_view()*

Argument	Explanation
request	The HttpRequest object.
view	The Python function that Django will call to handle this request. This is the actual function object itself, not the name of the function as a string.
args	The list of positional arguments that will be passed to the view, not including the request argument (which is always the first argument to a view).
kwargs	The dictionary of keyword arguments that will be passed to the view.

Just like process_request(), process_view() should return either None or an HttpResponse object.

- If it returns None, Django will continue processing this request, executing any other middleware and then the appropriate view.

- If it returns an HttpResponse object, Django won't bother calling *any* other middleware (of any type) or the appropriate view. Django will immediately return that HttpResponse.

Response Postprocessor: process_response(self, request, response)

This method gets called after the view function is called and the response is generated. Here, the processor can modify the content of a response. One obvious use case is content compression, such as gzipping of the request's HTML.

The parameters should be pretty self-explanatory: request is the request object, and response is the response object returned from the view.

Unlike the request and view preprocessors, which may return None, process_response() *must* return an HttpResponse object. That response could be the original one passed into the function (possibly modified) or a brand-new one.

Exception Postprocessor: process_exception(self, request, exception)

This method gets called only if something goes wrong and a view raises an uncaught exception. You can use this hook to send error notifications, dump postmortem information to a log, or even try to recover from the error automatically.

The parameters to this function are the same request object we've been dealing with all along, and exception, which is the actual Exception object raised by the view function.

process_exception() should return either None or an HttpResponse object.

- If it returns None, Django will continue processing this request with the framework's built-in exception handling.

- If it returns an HttpResponse object, Django will use that response instead of the framework's built-in exception handling.

> ■**Note** Django ships with a number of middleware classes (discussed in the following section) that make good examples. Reading the code for them should give you a good feel for the power of middleware.
>
> You can also find a number of community-contributed examples on Django's wiki: `http://code.djangoproject.com/wiki/ContributedMiddleware`.

Built-in Middleware

Django comes with some built-in middleware to deal with common problems, which we discuss in the sections that follow.

Authentication Support Middleware

Middleware class: `django.contrib.auth.middleware.AuthenticationMiddleware`.

This middleware enables authentication support. It adds the `request.user` attribute, representing the currently logged-in user, to every incoming `HttpRequest` object.

See Chapter 14 for complete details.

"Common" Middleware

Middleware class: `django.middleware.common.CommonMiddleware`.

This middleware adds a few conveniences for perfectionists:

- *Forbids access to user agents in the* `DISALLOWED_USER_AGENTS` *setting*: If provided, this setting should be a list of compiled regular expression objects that are matched against the user-agent header for each incoming request. Here's an example snippet from a settings file:

```
import re

DISALLOWED_USER_AGENTS = (
    re.compile(r'^OmniExplorer_Bot'),
    re.compile(r'^Googlebot')
)
```

  Note the `import re`, because `DISALLOWED_USER_AGENTS` requires its values to be compiled regexes (i.e., the output of `re.compile()`). The settings file is regular Python, so it's perfectly OK to include Python `import` statements in it.

- *Performs URL rewriting based on the* `APPEND_SLASH` *and* `PREPEND_WWW` *settings*: If `APPEND_SLASH` is `True`, URLs that lack a trailing slash will be redirected to the same URL with a trailing slash, unless the last component in the path contains a period. So `foo.com/bar` is redirected to `foo.com/bar/`, but `foo.com/bar/file.txt` is passed through unchanged.

  If `PREPEND_WWW` is `True`, URLs that lack a leading "www." will be redirected to the same URL with a leading "www.".

Both of these options are meant to normalize URLs. The philosophy is that each URL should exist in one—and only one—place. Technically the URL example.com/bar is distinct from example.com/bar/, which in turn is distinct from www.example.com/bar/. A search-engine indexer would treat these as separate URLs, which is detrimental to your site's search-engine rankings, so it's a best practice to normalize URLs.

- *Handles ETags based on the USE_ETAGS setting.* ETags are an HTTP-level optimization for caching pages conditionally. If USE_ETAGS is set to True, Django will calculate an ETag for each request by MD5-hashing the page content, and it will take care of sending Not Modified responses, if appropriate.

Note that there is also a conditional GET middleware, covered shortly, which handles ETags and does a bit more.

Compression Middleware

Middleware class: django.middleware.gzip.GZipMiddleware.

This middleware automatically compresses content for browsers that understand gzip compression (all modern browsers). This can greatly reduce the amount of bandwidth a Web server consumes. The tradeoff is that it takes a bit of processing time to compress pages.

We usually prefer speed over bandwidth, but if you prefer the reverse, just enable this middleware.

Conditional GET Middleware

Middleware class: django.middleware.http.ConditionalGetMiddleware.

This middleware provides support for conditional GET operations. If the response has a Last-Modified, an ETag, and a header, and if the request has If-None-Match or If-Modified-Since, the response is replaced by a 304 ("Not modified") response. ETag support depends on the use of the USE_ETAGS setting and expects the ETag response header to already be set. As discussed previously, the ETag header is set by the common middleware.

It also removes the content from any response to a HEAD request and sets the Date and Content-Length response headers for all requests.

Reverse Proxy Support (X-Forwarded-For Middleware)

Middleware class: django.middleware.http.SetRemoteAddrFromForwardedFor.

This is the example we examined in the "What's Middleware?" section earlier. It sets request.META['REMOTE_ADDR'] based on request.META['HTTP_X_FORWARDED_FOR'], if the latter is set. This is useful if you're sitting behind a reverse proxy that causes each request's REMOTE_ADDR to be set to 127.0.0.1.

> **Warning** This middleware does *not* validate `HTTP_X_FORWARDED_FOR`.
>
> If you're not behind a reverse proxy that sets `HTTP_X_FORWARDED_FOR` automatically, do not use this middleware. Anybody can spoof the value of `HTTP_X_FORWARDED_FOR`, and because this sets `REMOTE_ADDR` based on `HTTP_X_FORWARDED_FOR`, that means anybody can fake his IP address.
>
> Only use this middleware when you can absolutely trust the value of `HTTP_X_FORWARDED_FOR`.

Session Support Middleware

Middleware class: `django.contrib.sessions.middleware.SessionMiddleware`.

This middleware enables session support. See Chapter 14 for details.

Sitewide Cache Middleware

Middleware classes: `django.middleware.cache.UpdateCacheMiddleware` and `django.middleware.cache.FetchFromCacheMiddleware`.

These classes of middleware work together to cache each Django-powered page. This was discussed in detail in Chapter 15.

Transaction Middleware

Middleware class: `django.middleware.transaction.TransactionMiddleware`.

This middleware binds a database `COMMIT` or `ROLLBACK` to the request/response phase. If a view function runs successfully, a `COMMIT` is issued. If the view raises an exception, a `ROLLBACK` is issued.

The order of this middleware in the stack is important. Middleware modules running outside of it run with commit-on-save—the default Django behavior. Middleware modules running inside it (coming later in the stack) will be under the same transaction control as the view functions.

See Appendix B for more about information about database transactions.

What's Next?

Web developers and database-schema designers don't always have the luxury of starting from scratch. In the next chapter, we'll cover how to integrate with legacy systems, such as database schemas you've inherited from the 1980s.

CHAPTER 18

■ ■ ■

Integrating with Legacy Databases and Applications

Django is best suited for so-called green-field development—that is, starting projects from scratch, as if you were constructing a building on a fresh field of green grass. But despite the fact that Django favors from-scratch projects, it's possible to integrate the framework into legacy databases and applications. This chapter explains a few integration strategies.

Integrating with a Legacy Database

Django's database layer generates SQL schemas from Python code—but with a legacy database, you already have the SQL schemas. In such a case, you'll need to create models for your existing database tables. For this purpose, Django comes with a tool that can generate model code by reading your database table layouts. This tool is called `inspectdb`, and you can call it by executing the command `manage.py inspectdb`.

Using inspectdb

The `inspectdb` utility inspects the database that your settings file points to, determines a Django model representation for each of your tables, and prints the Python model code to standard output.

The following is a walk-through of a typical legacy database–integration process from scratch. The only assumptions are that Django is installed and that you have a legacy database.

1. Create a Django project by running `django-admin.py startproject mysite` (where `mysite` is your project's name).

2. Edit the settings file in that project, `mysite/settings.py`, to tell Django your database-connection parameters and the name of the database. Specifically, provide the `DATABASE_NAME`, `DATABASE_ENGINE`, `DATABASE_USER`, `DATABASE_PASSWORD`, `DATABASE_HOST`, and `DATABASE_PORT` settings. (Note that some of these settings are optional. Refer to Chapter 5 for more information.)

3. Create a Django application within your project by running `python mysite/manage.py startapp myapp` (where `myapp` is your application's name).

4. Run the command `python mysite/manage.py inspectdb`. This will examine the tables in the `DATABASE_NAME` database and print the generated model class for each table. Take a look at the output to get an idea of what `inspectdb` can do.

5. Save the output to the `models.py` file within your application by using standard shell output redirection:

```
python mysite/manage.py inspectdb > mysite/myapp/models.py
```

6. Edit the `mysite/myapp/models.py` file to clean up the generated models and make any necessary customizations. We'll give some hints for this in the next section.

Cleaning Up Generated Models

As you might expect, the database inspection isn't perfect, and you'll need to do some light cleanup of the resulting model code. Here are a few pointers for dealing with the generated models:

- Each database table is converted to a model class (i.e., there is a one-to-one mapping between database tables and model classes). This means that you'll need to refactor the models for any many-to-many join tables into `ManyToManyField` objects.

- Each generated model has an attribute for every field, including `id` primary-key fields. However, recall that Django automatically adds an `id` primary-key field if a model doesn't have a primary key. Thus, you'll want to remove any lines that look like this:

  ```
  id = models.IntegerField(primary_key=True)
  ```

  Not only are these lines redundant, but also they can cause problems if your application will be adding *new* records to these tables.

- Each field's type (e.g., `CharField`, `DateField`) is determined by looking at the database column type (e.g., `VARCHAR`, `DATE`). If `inspectdb` cannot map a column's type to a model field type, it will use `TextField` and will insert the Python comment `'This field type is a guess.'` next to the field in the generated model. Keep an eye out for that, and change the field type accordingly if needed.

  If a field in your database has no good Django equivalent, you can safely leave it off. The Django model layer is not required to include every field in your table(s).

- If a database column name is a Python reserved word (such as `pass`, `class`, or `for`), `inspectdb` will append `_field` to the attribute name and set the `db_column` attribute to the real field name (e.g., `pass`, `class`, or `for`).

  For example, if a table has an `INT` column called `for`, the generated model will have a field like this:

  ```
  for_field = models.IntegerField(db_column='for')
  ```

  `inspectdb` will insert the Python comment `'Field renamed because it was a Python reserved word.'` next to the field.

- If your database contains tables that refer to other tables (as most databases do), you might need to rearrange the order of the generated models so models that refer to other models are ordered properly. For example, if model Book has a ForeignKey to model Author, model Author should be defined before model Book. If you need to create a relationship on a model that has not yet been defined, you can use a string containing the name of the model, rather than the model object itself.

- inspectdb detects primary keys for PostgreSQL, MySQL, and SQLite. That is, it inserts primary_key=True where appropriate. For other databases, you'll need to insert primary_key=True for at least one field in each model, because Django models are required to have a primary_key=True field.

- Foreign-key detection works with only PostgreSQL and certain types of MySQL tables. In other cases, foreign-key fields will be generated as IntegerFields, assuming the foreign-key column was an INT column.

Integrating with an Authentication System

It's possible to integrate Django with an existing authentication system—another source of usernames and passwords or authentication methods.

For example, your company may already have an LDAP setup that stores a username and password for every employee. It would be a hassle for both the network administrator and the users themselves if users had separate accounts in LDAP and the Django-based applications.

To handle situations like this, the Django authentication system lets you plug in other authentication sources. You can override Django's default database-based scheme, or you can use the default system in tandem with other systems.

Specifying Authentication Back-Ends

Behind the scenes, Django maintains a list of authentication back-ends that it checks. When somebody calls django.contrib.auth.authenticate() (as described in Chapter 14), Django tries authenticating across all of its authentication back-ends. If the first authentication method fails, Django tries the second one, and so on, until all back-ends have been attempted.

The list of authentication back-ends to use is specified in the AUTHENTICATION_BACKENDS setting. This should be a tuple of Python path names that point to Python classes that know how to authenticate. These classes can be anywhere on your Python path.

By default, AUTHENTICATION_BACKENDS is set to the following:

```
('django.contrib.auth.backends.ModelBackend',)
```

That's the basic authentication scheme that checks the Django users database.

The order of AUTHENTICATION_BACKENDS matters, so if the same username and password are valid in multiple back-ends, Django will stop processing at the first positive match.

Writing an Authentication Back-End

An authentication back-end is a class that implements two methods: get_user(id) and authenticate(**credentials).

The get_user method takes an id—which could be a username, database ID, or whatever—and returns a User object.

The authenticate method takes credentials as keyword arguments. Most of the time it looks like this:

```
class MyBackend(object):
    def authenticate(self, username=None, password=None):
        # Check the username/password and return a User.
```

But it could also authenticate a token, like so:

```
class MyBackend(object):
    def authenticate(self, token=None):
        # Check the token and return a User.
```

Either way, authenticate should check the credentials it gets, and it should return a User object that matches those credentials, if the credentials are valid. If they're not valid, it should return None.

The Django admin system is tightly coupled to Django's own database-backed User object described in Chapter 14. The best way to deal with this is to create a Django User object for each user that exists for your back-end (e.g., in your LDAP directory, your external SQL database, etc.). Either you can write a script to do this in advance, or your authenticate method can do it the first time a user logs in.

Here's an example back-end that authenticates against a username and password variable defined in your settings.py file and creates a Django User object the first time a user authenticates:

```
from django.conf import settings
from django.contrib.auth.models import User, check_password

class SettingsBackend(object):
    """
    Authenticate against the settings ADMIN_LOGIN and ADMIN_PASSWORD.

    Use the login name, and a hash of the password. For example:

    ADMIN_LOGIN = 'admin'
    ADMIN_PASSWORD = 'sha1$4e987$afbcf42e21bd417fb71db8c66b321e9fc33051de'
    """
    def authenticate(self, username=None, password=None):
        login_valid = (settings.ADMIN_LOGIN == username)
        pwd_valid = check_password(password, settings.ADMIN_PASSWORD)
        if login_valid and pwd_valid:
            try:
                user = User.objects.get(username=username)
```

```
        except User.DoesNotExist:
            # Create a new user. Note that we can set password
            # to anything, because it won't be checked; the password
            # from settings.py will.
            user = User(username=username, password='get from settings.py')
            user.is_staff = True
            user.is_superuser = True
            user.save()
        return user
    return None

def get_user(self, user_id):
    try:
        return User.objects.get(pk=user_id)
    except User.DoesNotExist:
        return None
```

For more on authentication back-ends, see the official Django documentation.

Integrating with Legacy Web Applications

It's possible to run a Django application on the same Web server as an application powered by another technology. The most straightforward way of doing this is to use Apache's configuration file, httpd.conf, to delegate different URL patterns to different technologies. (Note that Chapter 12 covers Django deployment on Apache/mod_python, so it might be worth reading that chapter before attempting this integration.)

The key is that Django will be activated for a particular URL pattern only if your httpd.conf file says so. The default deployment explained in Chapter 12 assumes you want Django to power every page on a particular domain:

```
<Location "/">
    SetHandler python-program
    PythonHandler django.core.handlers.modpython
    SetEnv DJANGO_SETTINGS_MODULE mysite.settings
    PythonDebug On
</Location>
```

Here, the <Location "/"> line means "handle every URL, starting at the root," with Django.

It's perfectly fine to limit this <Location> directive to a certain directory tree. For example, say you have a legacy PHP application that powers most pages on a domain and you want to install a Django admin site at /admin/ without disrupting the PHP code. To do this, just set the <Location> directive to /admin/:

```
<Location "/admin/">
    SetHandler python-program
    PythonHandler django.core.handlers.modpython
    SetEnv DJANGO_SETTINGS_MODULE mysite.settings
    PythonDebug On
</Location>
```

With this in place, only the URLs that start with /admin/ will activate Django. Any other page will use whatever infrastructure already existed.

Note that attaching Django to a qualified URL (such as /admin/ in this section's example) does not affect the Django URL parsing. Django works with the absolute URL (e.g., /admin/people/person/add/), not a "stripped" version of the URL (e.g., /people/person/add/). This means that your root URLconf should include the leading /admin/.

What's Next?

If you're a native English speaker, you might not have noticed one of the coolest features of Django's admin site: it's available in more than 50 languages! This is made possible by Django's internationalization framework (and the hard work of Django's volunteer translators). The next chapter explains how to use this framework to provide localized Django sites.

CHAPTER 19

■ ■ ■

Internationalization

Django was originally developed right in the middle of the United States quite literally because Lawrence, Kansas lies fewer than 40 miles from the geographic center of the continental United States. Like most open source projects, though, Django's community grew to include people from all over the globe. As Django's community became increasingly diverse, *internationalization* and *localization* became increasingly important. Because many developers have at best a fuzzy understanding of these terms, we'll define them briefly.

Internationalization refers to the process of designing programs for the potential use of any locale. This includes marking text such as user interface (UI) elements and error messages for future translation, abstracting the display of dates and times so that different local standards can be observed, providing support for differing time zones, and generally making sure that the code contains no assumptions about the location of its users. You'll often see *internationalization* abbreviated as *I18N* (*18* refers to the number of letters omitted between the initial *I* and the terminal *N*.)

Localization refers to the process of actually translating an internationalized program for use in a particular locale. You'll sometimes see *localization* abbreviated as *L10N*.

Django itself is fully internationalized; all strings are marked for translation, and settings control the display of locale-dependent values such as dates and times. Django also ships with more than 50 different localization files. If you're not a native English speaker, there's a good chance that Django is already translated into your primary language.

The same internationalization framework used for these localizations is available for you to use in your own code and templates.

To use this framework, you'll need to add a minimal number of hooks to your Python code and templates. These hooks are called *translation strings*. They tell Django, "This text should be translated into the end user's language if a translation for this text is available in that language."

Django takes care of using these hooks to translate Web applications on the fly, according to users' language preferences.

Django does two things:

- It lets developers and template authors specify which parts of their applications should be translatable.

- It uses that information to translate Web applications for particular users according to their language preferences.

Note Django's translation machinery uses GNU `gettext` (http://www.gnu.org/software/gettext/) via the standard `gettext` module that comes with Python.

IF YOU DON'T NEED INTERNATIONALIZATION

Django's internationalization hooks are enabled by default, which incurs a small bit of overhead. If you don't use internationalization, you should set `USE_I18N = False` in your settings file. If `USE_I18N` is set to `False`, Django will make some optimizations to avoid loading the internationalization machinery.

You'll probably also want to remove `'django.core.context_processors.i18n'` from your `TEMPLATE_CONTEXT_PROCESSORS` setting.

The three steps for internationalizing your Django application are as follows:

1. Embed translation strings in your Python code and templates.

2. Get translations for those strings, in whichever languages you want to support.

3. Activate the locale middleware in your Django settings.

We'll cover each one of these steps in detail in the following sections.

How to Specify Translation Strings

Translation strings specify that "this text should be translated." These strings can appear in your Python code and templates. It's your responsibility to mark translatable strings; the system can translate only strings it knows about.

In Python Code

Standard Translation

Specify a translation string by using the function `ugettext()`. It's convention to import this as a shorter alias, `_`, to save typing.

In this example, the text "Welcome to my site." is marked as a translation string:

```
from django.utils.translation import ugettext as _

def my_view(request):
    output = _("Welcome to my site.")
    return HttpResponse(output)
```

Obviously, you could code this without using the alias. This example is identical to the previous one:

```
from django.utils.translation import ugettext

def my_view(request):
    output = ugettext("Welcome to my site.")
    return HttpResponse(output)
```

Translation works on computed values. This example is identical to the previous two:

```
def my_view(request):
    words = ['Welcome', 'to', 'my', 'site.']
    output = _(' '.join(words))
    return HttpResponse(output)
```

Translation works on variables. Again, here's an identical example:

```
def my_view(request):
    sentence = 'Welcome to my site.'
    output = _(sentence)
    return HttpResponse(output)
```

■**Caution** The caveat when using variables or computed values, as in the previous two examples, is that Django's translation string–detecting utility, django-admin.py makemessages, can't find these strings. More on makemessages later.

The strings you pass to _() or ugettext() can take placeholders specified with Python's standard named-string interpolation syntax. For example:

```
def my_view(request, m, d):
    output = _('Today is %(month)s %(day)s.') % {'month': m, 'day': d}
    return HttpResponse(output)
```

This technique lets language-specific translations reorder the placeholder text. For example, an English translation may be "Today is November 26.", whereas a Spanish translation may be "Hoy es 26 de Noviembre." Only the placeholders (the month and the day) have their positions swapped.

For this reason, you should use *named-string interpolation* (e.g., %(day)s) instead of *positional interpolation* (e.g., %s or %d) whenever you have more than a single parameter. If you used positional interpolation, translations couldn't reorder placeholder text.

Marking Strings As No-Op

Use the function django.utils.translation.ugettext_noop() to mark a string as a translation string without translating it. The string is later translated from a variable.

Use it if you have constant strings that should be stored in the source language because they are exchanged over systems or users such as strings in a database but should be translated at the last possible point in time, such as when the string is presented to the user.

Lazy Translation

Use the function django.utils.translation.ugettext_lazy() to translate strings lazily when the value is accessed instead of when the ugettext_lazy() function is called.

For example, to translate a model's help_text, do the following:

```
from django.utils.translation import ugettext_lazy

class MyThing(models.Model):
    name = models.CharField(help_text=ugettext_lazy('This is the help text'))
```

In this example, ugettext_lazy() stores a lazy reference to the string, not the actual translation. The translation itself will be done when the string is used in a string context, such as template rendering on the Django admin site.

The result of a ugettext_lazy() call can be used wherever you would use a Unicode string (an object with type unicode) in Python. If you try to use it where a bytestring (a str object) is expected, things will not work as expected because a ugettext_lazy() object doesn't know how to convert itself to a bytestring. You can't use a Unicode string inside a bytestring, either, so this is consistent with normal Python behavior. For example:

```
# This is fine: putting a unicode proxy into a unicode string.
u"Hello %s" % ugettext_lazy("people")

# This will not work, since you cannot insert a unicode object
# into a bytestring (nor can you insert our unicode proxy there)
"Hello %s" % ugettext_lazy("people")
```

If you ever see output that looks like "hello <django.utils.functional...>", you have tried to insert the result of ugettext_lazy() into a bytestring. That's a bug in your code.

If you don't like the verbose name ugettext_lazy, you can just alias it as _ (underscore), like so:

```
from django.utils.translation import ugettext_lazy as _

class MyThing(models.Model):
    name = models.CharField(help_text=_('This is the help text'))
```

Always use lazy translations in Django models. Field names and table names should be marked for translation (otherwise, they won't be translated in the admin interface). This means writing explicit verbose_name and verbose_name_plural options in the Meta class, though, instead of relying on Django's default determination of verbose_name and verbose_name_plural by looking at the model's class name:

```
from django.utils.translation import ugettext_lazy as _

class MyThing(models.Model):
    name = models.CharField(_('name'), help_text=_('This is the help text'))
    class Meta:
        verbose_name = _('my thing')
        verbose_name_plural = _('mythings')
```

Pluralization

Use the function django.utils.translation.ungettext() to specify pluralized messages. For example:

```
from django.utils.translation import ungettext

def hello_world(request, count):
    page = ungettext('there is %(count)d object',
        'there are %(count)d objects', count) % {
            'count': count,
        }
    return HttpResponse(page)
```

ungettext takes three arguments: the singular translation string, the plural translation string, and the number of objects (which is passed to the translation languages as the count variable).

In Template Code

Translation in Django templates uses two template tags and a slightly different syntax than in Python code. To give your template access to these tags, put {% load i18n %} toward the top of your template.

The {% trans %} template tag translates either a constant string (enclosed in single or double quotes) or variable content:

```
<title>{% trans "This is the title." %}</title>
<title>{% trans myvar %}</title>
```

If the noop option is present, variable lookup still takes place, but the translation is skipped. This is useful when "stubbing out" content that will require translation in the future:

```
<title>{% trans "myvar" noop %}</title>
```

It's not possible to mix a template variable inside a string within {% trans %}. If your translations require strings with variables (placeholders), use {% blocktrans %}:

```
{% blocktrans %}This string will have {{ value }} inside.{% endblocktrans %}
```

To translate a template expression (using template filters, for instance), you need to bind the expression to a local variable for use within the translation block:

```
{% blocktrans with value|filter as myvar %}
This will have {{ myvar }} inside.
{% endblocktrans %}
```

If you need to bind more than one expression inside a blocktrans tag, separate the pieces with and:

```
{% blocktrans with book|title as book_t and author|title as author_t %}
This is {{ book_t }} by {{ author_t }}
{% endblocktrans %}
```

To pluralize, specify both the singular and plural forms with the {% plural %} tag, which appears within {% blocktrans %} and {% endblocktrans %}. For example:

```
{% blocktrans count list|length as counter %}
There is only one {{ name }} object.
{% plural %}
There are {{ counter }} {{ name }} objects.
{% endblocktrans %}
```

Internally, all block and inline translations use the appropriate ugettext/ungettext call. Each RequestContext has access to three translation-specific variables:

- LANGUAGES is a list of tuples in which the first element is the language code and the second is the language name (translated into the currently active locale).

- LANGUAGE_CODE is the current user's preferred language as a string. For example: en-us. (See the following section, "How Django Discovers Language Preference.")

- LANGUAGE_BIDI is the current locale's direction. If True, it's a right-to-left language (e.g., Hebrew and Arabic). If False, it's a left-to-right language (e.g., English, French, German, and so on).

If you don't use the RequestContext extension, you can get those values with three tags:

```
{% get_current_language as LANGUAGE_CODE %}
{% get_available_languages as LANGUAGES %}
{% get_current_language_bidi as LANGUAGE_BIDI %}
```

These tags also require a {% load i18n %}.

Translation hooks are also available within any template block tag that accepts constant strings. In those cases, just use _() syntax to specify a translation string:

```
{% some_special_tag _("Page not found") value|yesno:_("yes,no") %}
```

In this case, both the tag and the filter will see the already-translated string, so they don't need to be aware of translations.

Note In this example, the translation infrastructure will be passed the string "yes,no", not the individual strings "yes" and "no". The translated string will need to contain the comma so that the filter parsing code knows how to split up the arguments. For example, a German translator might translate the string "yes,no" as "ja,nein" (keeping the comma intact).

Working with Lazy Translation Objects

Using ugettext_lazy() and ungettext_lazy() to mark strings in models and utility functions is a common operation. When you're working with these objects elsewhere in your code, you should ensure that you don't accidentally convert them to strings because they should be converted as late as possible (so that the correct locale is in effect). This necessitates the use of a couple of helper functions, discussed in the following sections.

Joining Strings: string_concat()

Standard Python string joins (''.join([...])) will not work on lists containing lazy translation objects. Instead, you can use django.utils.translation.string_concat(), which creates a lazy object that concatenates its contents *and* converts them to strings only when the result is included in a string. For example:

```
from django.utils.translation import string_concat
# ...
name = ugettext_lazy(u'John Lennon')
instrument = ugettext_lazy(u'guitar')
result = string_concat([name, ': ', instrument])
```

In this case, the lazy translations in result will be converted to strings only when result itself is used in a string (usually at template-rendering time).

The allow_lazy() Decorator

Django offers many utility functions (particularly in django.utils) that take a string as their first argument and do something to that string. These functions are used by template filters as well as directly in other code.

If you write your own similar functions and deal with translations, you'll face the problem of what to do when the first argument is a lazy translation object. You don't want to convert it to a string immediately because you might be using this function outside of a view (and hence the current thread's locale setting will not be correct).

For cases like these, use the `django.utils.functional.allow_lazy()` decorator. It modifies the function so that *if* it's called with a lazy translation as the first argument, the function evaluation is delayed until it needs to be converted to a string. For example:

```
from django.utils.functional import allow_lazy

def fancy_utility_function(s, ...):
    # Do some conversion on string 's'
    # ...
fancy_utility_function = allow_lazy(fancy_utility_function, unicode)
```

In addition to the function to decorate, the `allow_lazy()` decorator takes a number of extra arguments (`*args`) specifying the type(s) that the original function can return. Usually, it's enough to include `unicode` here and ensure that your function returns only Unicode strings.

Using this decorator means that you can write your function and assume that the input is a proper string; then add support for lazy translation objects at the end.

How to Create Language Files

After you tag your strings for later translation, you need to write (or obtain) the language translations themselves. Here's how that works.

LOCALE RESTRICTIONS

Django does not support localizing your application into a locale for which Django itself has not been translated. In this case, it will ignore your translation files. If you were to try this, and Django supported it, you would inevitably see a mixture of translated strings (from your application) and English strings (from Django itself).

If you want to support a locale for your application that is not already part of Django, you'll need to make at least a minimal translation of the Django core.

Message Files

The first step is to create a *message file* for a new language. A message file is a plain-text file, representing a single language, that contains all available translation strings and how they should be represented in the given language. Message files have a `.po` file extension.

Django comes with a tool, `django-admin.py makemessages`, which automates the creation and upkeep of these files. To create or update a message file, run this command, where `de` is the language code for the message file you want to create:

```
django-admin.py makemessages -l de
```

The language code, in this case, is in locale format. For example, it's pt_BR for Brazilian Portuguese and de_AT for Austrian German.

The script should be run from one of three places:

- The root directory of your Django project.
- The root directory of your Django app.
- The root django directory (not a Subversion checkout, but the one that is linked to via $PYTHONPATH or is located somewhere on that path). This is relevant only when you are creating a translation for Django itself.

This script runs over your project source tree or your application source tree, and pulls out all strings marked for translation. It creates (or updates) a message file in the directory locale/LANG/LC_MESSAGES. In the de example, the file will be locale/de/LC_MESSAGES/django.po.

By default, django-admin.py makemessages examines every file that has the .html file extension. In case you want to override that default, use the --extension or -e option to specify the file extensions to examine:

```
django-admin.py makemessages -l de -e txt
```

Separate multiple extensions with commas and/or use -e or --extension multiple times:

```
django-admin.py makemessages -l de -e html,txt -e xml
```

When creating JavaScript translation catalogs (covered later in this chapter), you need to use the special djangojs domain, not -e js.

NO GETTEXT?

If you don't have the gettext utilities installed, django-admin.py makemessages will create empty files. If that's the case, either install the gettext utilities or just copy the English message file (locale/en/LC_MESSAGES/django.po), if available, and use it as a starting point; it's just an empty translation file.

WORKING ON WINDOWS?

If you're using Windows and need to install the GNU gettext utilities so django-admin makemessages works, see the "gettext on Windows" section for more information.

The format of .po files is straightforward. Each .po file contains a small bit of metadata, such as the translation maintainer's contact information, but the bulk of the file is a list of *messages*—simple mappings between translation strings and the actual translated text for the particular language.

For example, if your Django app contained a translation string for the text "Welcome to my site." like so:

```
_("Welcome to my site.")
```

django-admin.py makemessages will have created a .po file containing the following snippet message:

```
#: path/to/python/module.py:23
msgid "Welcome to my site."
msgstr ""
```

Here's a quick explanation:

- msgid is the translation string that appears in the source. Don't change it.

- msgstr is where you put the language-specific translation. It starts out empty, so it's your responsibility to change it. Make sure to keep the quotes around your translation.

- As a convenience, each message includes, in the form of a comment line prefixed with # and located above the msgid line, the file name and line number from which the translation string was gleaned.

Long messages are a special case. There, the first string directly after the msgstr (or msgid) is an empty string. Then the content itself will be written over the next few lines as one string per line. Those strings are directly concatenated. Don't forget trailing spaces within the strings; otherwise, they'll be tacked together without whitespace!

To reexamine all source code and templates for new translation strings and update all message files for *all* languages, run this:

```
django-admin.py makemessages -a
```

Compiling Message Files

After you create your message file and each time you make changes to it you'll need to compile it into a more efficient form for use by gettext. Do this with the django-admin.py compilemessages utility.

This tool runs over all available .po files and creates .mo files, which are binary files optimized for use by gettext. In the same directory from which you ran django-admin.py makemessages, run django-admin.py compilemessages like this:

```
django-admin.py compilemessages
```

That's it. Your translations are ready for use.

How Django Discovers Language Preference

After you prepare your translations (or if you just want to use the translations that come with Django), you need to activate translation for your app.

Behind the scenes, Django has a very flexible model of deciding which language should be used: installation-wide, for a particular user, or both.

To set an installation-wide language preference, set LANGUAGE_CODE. Django uses this language as the default translation—the final attempt if no other translator finds a translation.

If all you want to do is run Django with your native language, and a language file is available for your language, just set LANGUAGE_CODE.

If you want to let each individual user specify which language he or she prefers, use LocaleMiddleware. LocaleMiddleware enables language selection based on data from the request. It customizes content for each user.

To use LocaleMiddleware, add 'django.middleware.locale.LocaleMiddleware' to your MIDDLEWARE_CLASSES setting. Because middleware order matters, you should follow these guidelines:

- Make sure that it's one of the first middlewares installed.

- It should come after SessionMiddleware because LocaleMiddleware makes use of session data.

- If you use CacheMiddleware, put LocaleMiddleware after it.

For example, your MIDDLEWARE_CLASSES might look like this:

```
MIDDLEWARE_CLASSES = (
    'django.contrib.sessions.middleware.SessionMiddleware',
    'django.middleware.locale.LocaleMiddleware',
    'django.middleware.common.CommonMiddleware',
)
```

(For more on middleware, see Chapter 17.)

LocaleMiddleware tries to determine the user's language preference by following this algorithm:

1. First, it looks for a django_language key in the current user's session.

2. Failing that, it looks for a cookie.

3. Failing that, it looks at the Accept-Language HTTP header. This header is sent by your browser and tells the server which language(s) you prefer, in order by priority. Django tries each language in the header until it finds one with available translations.

4. Failing that, it uses the global LANGUAGE_CODE setting.

Note the following:

- In each of these places, the language preference is expected to be in the standard language format as a string. For example, Brazilian Portuguese is `pt-br`.

- If a base language is available, but the sublanguage specified is not, Django uses the base language. For example, if a user specifies `de-at` (Austrian German) but Django has only `de` available, Django uses `de`.

- Only languages listed in the `LANGUAGES` setting can be selected. If you want to restrict the language selection to a subset of provided languages (because your application doesn't provide all those languages), set `LANGUAGES` to a list of languages. For example:

```
LANGUAGES = (
  ('de', _('German')),
  ('en', _('English')),
)
```

This example restricts languages that are available for automatic selection to German and English (and any sublanguage such as `de-ch` or `en-us`).

- If you define a custom `LANGUAGES` setting, as explained in the previous bullet, it's fine to mark the languages as translation strings but use a "dummy" `ugettext()` function, not the one in `django.utils.translation`. You should *never* import `django.utils.translation` from within your settings file because that module in itself depends on the settings, and that would cause a circular import.

  The solution is to use a "dummy" `ugettext()` function. Here's a sample settings file:

```
ugettext = lambda s: s

LANGUAGES = (
    ('de', ugettext('German')),
    ('en', ugettext('English')),
)
```

  With this arrangement, `django-admin.py makemessages` will still find and mark these strings for translation, but the translation won't happen at runtime. You'll have to remember to wrap the languages in the *real* `ugettext()` in any code that uses `LANGUAGES` at runtime.

- The `LocaleMiddleware` can select only languages for which there is a Django-provided base translation. If you want to provide translations for your application that aren't already in the set of translations in Django's source tree, you'll want to provide at least basic translations for that language. For example, Django uses technical message IDs to translate date formats and time formats, so you need at least those translations for the system to work correctly.

  A good starting point is to copy the English `.po` file and to translate at least the technical messages (maybe the validation messages, too).

Technical message IDs are easily recognized; they're all uppercase. You don't translate the message ID as with other messages; you provide the correct local variant on the provided English value. For example, with DATETIME_FORMAT (or DATE_FORMAT or TIME_FORMAT) this would be the format string that you want to use in your language. The format is identical to the format strings used by the now template tag.

After LocaleMiddleware determines the user's preference, it makes this preference available as request.LANGUAGE_CODE for each HttpRequest. Feel free to read this value in your view code. Here's a simple example:

```
def hello_world(request):
    if request.LANGUAGE_CODE == 'de-at':
        return HttpResponse("You prefer to read Austrian German.")
    else:
        return HttpResponse("You prefer to read another language.")
```

Note that with static (middleware-less) translation the language is in settings.LANGUAGE_CODE, whereas with dynamic (middleware) translation, it's in request.LANGUAGE_CODE.

Using Translations in Your Own Projects

Django looks for translations by following this algorithm:

1. First, it looks for a locale directory in the application directory of the view that's being called. If it finds a translation for the selected language, the translation will be installed.

2. Next, it looks for a locale directory in the project directory. If it finds a translation, the translation will be installed.

3. Finally, it checks the Django-provided base translation in django/conf/locale.

This way, you can write applications that include their own translations, and you can override base translations in your project path. Or you can just build a big project out of several apps and put all translations into one big project message file. The choice is yours.

All message file repositories are structured in the same way:

- $APPPATH/locale/<language>/LC_MESSAGES/django.(po|mo)

- $PROJECTPATH/locale/<language>/LC_MESSAGES/django.(po|mo)

- All paths listed in LOCALE_PATHS in your settings file are searched in that order for <language>/LC_MESSAGES/django.(po|mo)

- $PYTHONPATH/django/conf/locale/<language>/LC_MESSAGES/django.(po|mo)

To create message files, use the same django-admin.py makemessages tool as with the Django message files. You only need to be in the right place: in the directory in which either the conf/locale (in case of the source tree) or the locale/ (in case of app messages or project messages) directory is located. And you use the same django-admin.py compilemessages to produce the binary django.mo files that are used by gettext.

You can also run django-admin.py compilemessages --settings=path.to.settings to make the compiler process all the directories in your LOCALE_PATHS setting.

Application message files are a bit complicated to discover they need the `LocaleMiddleware`. If you don't use the middleware, only the Django message files and project message files will be processed.

Finally, you should give some thought to the structure of your translation files. If your applications need to be delivered to other users and will be used in other projects, you might want to use app-specific translations. But using app-specific translations and project translations could produce weird problems with `makemessages`: `makemessages` will traverse all directories below the current path and so might put message IDs into the project message files that are already in application message files.

The easiest way out is to store applications that are not part of the project (and so carry their own translations) outside the project tree. That way, `django-admin.py makemessages` on the project level will translate only strings that are connected to your explicit project, not strings that are distributed independently.

The set_language Redirect View

As a convenience, Django comes with a view, `django.views.i18n.set_language`, which sets a user's language preference and redirects back to the previous page.

Activate this view by adding the following line to your URLconf:

```
(r'^i18n/', include('django.conf.urls.i18n')),
```

■**Note** This example makes the view available at `/i18n/setlang/`.

The view expects to be called via the `POST` method with a `language` parameter set in the request. If session support is enabled, the view saves the language choice in the user's session. Otherwise, it saves the language choice in a cookie named `django_language` by default. (The name can be changed through the `LANGUAGE_COOKIE_NAME` setting.)

After setting the language choice, Django redirects the user, following this algorithm:

- Django looks for a `next` parameter in the `POST` data.

- If that doesn't exist or is empty, Django tries the URL in the `Referrer` header.

- If that's empty (for example, if a user's browser suppresses that header), the user will be redirected to / (the site root) as a fallback.

Here's an example of HTML template code:

```
<form action="/i18n/setlang/" method="post">
<input name="next" type="hidden" value="/next/page/" />
<select name="language">
    {% for lang in LANGUAGES %}
    <option value="{{ lang.0 }}">{{ lang.1 }}</option>
    {% endfor %}
</select>
<input type="submit" value="Go" />
</form>
```

Translations and JavaScript

Adding translations to JavaScript poses some problems:

- JavaScript code doesn't have access to a gettext implementation.

- JavaScript code doesn't have access to .po or .mo files; they need to be delivered by the server.

- The translation catalogs for JavaScript should be kept as small as possible.

Django provides an integrated solution for these problems: it passes the translations into JavaScript, so you can call gettext, and so on from within JavaScript.

The javascript_catalog View

The main solution to these problems is the javascript_catalog view, which sends out a JavaScript code library with functions that mimic the gettext interface, plus an array of translation strings. Those translation strings are taken from the application, project, or Django core, according to what you specify in either the info_dict or the URL.

You hook it up like this:

```
js_info_dict = {
    'packages': ('your.app.package',),
}

urlpatterns = patterns('',
    (r'^jsi18n/$', 'django.views.i18n.javascript_catalog', js_info_dict),
)
```

Each string in packages should be in Python dotted-package syntax (the same format as the strings in INSTALLED_APPS) and should refer to a package that contains a locale directory. If you specify multiple packages, all those catalogs are merged into one catalog. This is useful if you have JavaScript that uses strings from different applications.

You can make the view dynamic by putting the packages into the URL pattern:

```
urlpatterns = patterns('',
    (r'^jsi18n/(?P<packages>\S+)/$', 'django.views.i18n.javascript_catalog'),
)
```

With this, you specify the packages as a list of package names delimited by + signs in the URL. This is especially useful if your pages use code from different apps and change often, and you don't want to pull in one big catalog file. As a security measure, these values can be only django.conf or any package from the INSTALLED_APPS setting.

Using the JavaScript Translation Catalog

To use the catalog, just pull in the dynamically generated script like this:

```
<script type="text/javascript" src="/path/to/jsi18n/"></script>
```

This is how the admin fetches the translation catalog from the server. When the catalog is loaded, your JavaScript code can use the standard gettext interface to access it:

```
document.write(gettext('this is to be translated'));
```

There is also an ngettext interface:

```
var object_cnt = 1 // or 0, or 2, or 3, ...
s = ngettext('literal for the singular case',
        'literal for the plural case', object_cnt);
```

And even a string interpolation function:

```
function interpolate(fmt, obj, named);
```

The interpolation syntax is borrowed from Python, so the interpolate function supports both positional and named interpolation:

- *Positional interpolation*: obj contains a JavaScript Array object whose elements values are then sequentially interpolated in their corresponding fmt placeholders in the same order they appear. For example:

```
fmts = ngettext('There is %s object. Remaining: %s',
        'There are %s objects. Remaining: %s', 11);
s = interpolate(fmts, [11, 20]);
// s is 'There are 11 objects. Remaining: 20'
```

- *Named interpolation*: This mode is selected by passing the optional Boolean named parameter as true. obj contains a JavaScript object or associative array. For example:

```
d = {
    count: 10
    total: 50
};

fmts = ngettext('Total: %(total)s, there is %(count)s object',
    'there are %(count)s of a total of %(total)s objects', d.count);
s = interpolate(fmts, d, true);
```

You shouldn't go over the top with string interpolation, though; this is still JavaScript, so the code has to make repeated regular-expression substitutions. This isn't as fast as string interpolation in Python, so keep it to those cases where you really need it (for example, in conjunction with ngettext to produce proper pluralizations).

Creating JavaScript Translation Catalogs

You create and update the translation catalogs the same way as with the other Django translation catalogs: with the `django-admin.py makemessages` tool. The only difference is you need to provide a `-d djangojs` parameter, like this:

```
django-admin.py makemessages -d djangojs -l de
```

This creates or updates the translation catalog for JavaScript for German. After updating translation catalogs, just run `django-admin.py compilemessages` the same way as you do with normal Django translation catalogs.

Notes for Users Familiar with gettext

If you know `gettext`, you might note these specialties in the way Django does translation:

- The string domain is `django` or `djangojs`. This string domain is used to differentiate between different programs that store their data in a common message-file library (usually `/usr/share/locale/`). The `django` domain is used for Python and template translation strings, and is loaded into the global translation catalogs. The `djangojs` domain is used only for JavaScript translation catalogs to make sure that they are as small as possible.

- Django doesn't use `xgettext` alone. It uses Python wrappers around `xgettext` and `msgfmt`. This is mostly for convenience.

gettext on Windows

This is needed only for people who either want to extract message IDs or compile message files (`.po`). Translation work itself just involves editing existing files of this type, but if you want to create your own message files, or want to test or compile a changed message file, you need the `gettext` utilities:

1. Download the following ZIP files from `http://sourceforge.net/projects/gettext`:

   - `gettext-runtime-X.bin.woe32.zip`
   - `gettext-tools-X.bin.woe32.zip`
   - `libiconv-X.bin.woe32.zip`

2. Extract the three files in the same folder (`C:\Program Files\gettext-utils`).

3. Update the system `PATH`:

   a. `Control Panel` ➤ `System` ➤ `Advanced` ➤ `Environment Variables`.

   b. In the `System variables` list, click `Path`; then click `Edit`.

   c. Add `;C:\Program Files\gettext-utils\bin` at the end of the `Variable value` field.

You can also use gettext binaries you have obtained elsewhere as long as the xgettext --version command works properly. Some version 0.14.4 binaries have been found to not support this command. Do not attempt to use Django translation utilities with a gettext package if the command xgettext --version entered at a Windows command prompt causes a pop-up window saying "xgettext.exe has generated errors and will be closed by Windows."

What's Next?

The final chapter focuses on security: how you can help secure your sites and your users from malicious attackers.

CHAPTER 20

■ ■ ■

Security

The Internet can be a scary place.

These days, high-profile security gaffes seem to crop up on a daily basis. We've seen viruses spread with amazing speed; swarms of compromised computers wielded as weapons; a never-ending arms race against spammers; and many, many reports of identity theft from hacked Web sites.

As Web developers, we have a duty to do what we can to combat these forces of darkness. Every Web developer needs to treat security as a fundamental aspect of Web programming. Unfortunately, it turns out that implementing security is *hard*—attackers need to find only a single vulnerability, but defenders have to protect every single one.

Django attempts to mitigate this difficulty. It's designed to automatically protect you from many of the common security mistakes that new (and even experienced) Web developers make. Still, it's important to understand what these problems are, how Django protects you, and—most important—the steps you can take to make your code even more secure.

First, though, an important disclaimer: we do not intend to present a definitive guide to every known Web security exploit, so we won't try to explain each vulnerability in a comprehensive manner. Instead, we'll give a short synopsis of security problems as they apply to Django.

The Theme of Web Security

If you learn only one thing from this chapter, let it be this:

Never—under any circumstances—trust data from the browser.

You *never* know who's on the other side of that HTTP connection. It might be one of your users, but it just as easily could be a nefarious cracker looking for an opening.

Any data of any nature that comes from the browser needs to be treated with a healthy dose of paranoia. This includes data that's both "in band" (i.e., submitted from Web forms) and "out of band" (i.e., HTTP headers, cookies, and other request information). It's trivial to spoof the request metadata that browsers usually add automatically.

Every one of the vulnerabilities discussed in this chapter stems directly from trusting data that comes over the wire and then failing to sanitize that data before using it. You should make it a general practice to continuously ask, "Where does this data come from?"

SQL Injection

SQL injection is a common exploit in which an attacker alters Web page parameters (such as GET/POST data or URLs) to insert arbitrary SQL snippets that a naive Web application executes in its database directly. It's probably the most dangerous—and unfortunately one of the most common—vulnerabilities out there.

This vulnerability most commonly crops up when constructing SQL "by hand" from user input. For example, imagine writing a function to gather a list of contact information from a contact search page. To prevent spammers from reading every single e-mail in our system, we'll force the user to type in someone's username before providing her e-mail address:

```
def user_contacts(request):
    user = request.GET['username']
    sql = "SELECT * FROM user_contacts WHERE username = '%s';" % username
    # execute the SQL here...
```

■Note In this example, and in all similar "don't-do-this" examples that follow, we deliberately left out most of the code needed to make the functions actually work. We don't want this code to work if someone accidentally takes it out of context.

Although at first this SQL construction doesn't look dangerous, it really is.

First, our attempt at protecting our entire e-mail list will fail with a cleverly constructed query. Think about what happens if an attacker types "' OR 'a'='a" into the query box. In that case, the query that the string interpolation will construct will be the following:

```
SELECT * FROM user_contacts WHERE username = '' OR 'a' = 'a';
```

Because we allowed unsecured SQL into the string, the attacker's added OR clause ensures that every single row is returned.

However, that's the *least* scary attack. Imagine what will happen if the attacker submits "'; DELETE FROM user_contacts WHERE 'a' = 'a". We'll end up with this complete query (comprising two statements):

```
SELECT * FROM user_contacts WHERE username = '';
DELETE FROM user_contacts WHERE 'a' = 'a';
```

Yikes! Our entire contact list would be deleted instantly.

The Solution

Although this problem is insidious and sometimes hard to spot, the solution is simple: *never* trust user-submitted data, and *always* escape it when passing it into SQL.

The Django database API does this for you. It automatically escapes all special SQL parameters, according to the quoting conventions of the database server you're using (e.g., PostgreSQL or MySQL).

For example, in this API call:

```
foo.get_list(bar__exact="' OR 1=1")
```

Django will escape the input accordingly, resulting in a statement like this:

```
SELECT * FROM foos WHERE bar = '\' OR 1=1'
```

Completely harmless.

This applies to the entire Django database API, with a couple of exceptions:

- The `where` argument to the `extra()` method. That parameter accepts raw SQL by design.

- Queries done "by hand" using the lower-level database API (see Chapter 10).

In each of these cases, it's easy to keep yourself protected. In each case, avoid string interpolation in favor of passing in *bind parameters*. That is, the example we started this section with should be written as follows:

```
from django.db import connection

def user_contacts(request):
    user = request.GET['username']
    sql = "SELECT * FROM user_contacts WHERE username = %s"
    cursor = connection.cursor()
    cursor.execute(sql, [user])
    # ... do something with the results
```

The low-level `execute` method takes a SQL string with `%s` placeholders and automatically escapes and inserts parameters from the list passed as the second argument. You should *always* construct custom SQL this way.

Unfortunately, you can't use bind parameters everywhere in SQL; they're not allowed as identifiers (i.e., table or column names). Thus, if you need to dynamically construct a list of tables from a `POST` variable, for example, you'll need to escape that name in your code. Django provides a function, `django.db.connection.ops.quote_name`, which will escape the identifier according to the current database's quoting scheme.

Cross-Site Scripting (XSS)

Cross-site scripting (XSS) is found in Web applications that fail to escape user-submitted content properly before rendering it into HTML. This allows an attacker to insert arbitrary HTML into your Web page, usually in the form of `<script>` tags.

Attackers often use XSS attacks to steal cookie and session information, or to trick users into giving private information to the wrong person (aka *phishing*).

This type of attack can take a number of different forms and has an almost infinite number of permutations, so we'll just look at a typical example. Consider this extremely simple "Hello, World" view:

```
from django.http import HttpResponse
```

```
def say_hello(request):
    name = request.GET.get('name', 'world')
    return HttpResponse('<h1>Hello, %s!</h1>' % name)
```

This view simply reads a name from a `GET` parameter and passes that name into the generated HTML. So if we accessed `http://example.com/hello/?name=Jacob`, the page would contain this:

```
<h1>Hello, Jacob!</h1>
```

But wait—what happens if we access `http://example.com/hello/?name=<i>Jacob</i>`? We get this:

```
<h1>Hello, <i>Jacob</i>!</h1>
```

Of course, an attacker wouldn't use something as benign as `<i>` tags; he could include a whole set of HTML that hijacked your page with arbitrary content. This type of attack has been used to trick users into entering data into what looks like their bank's Web site, but in fact is an XSS-hijacked form that submits their back account information to an attacker.

The problem gets worse if you store this data in the database and later display it on your site. For example, MySpace was once found to be vulnerable to an XSS attack of this nature. A user inserted JavaScript into his profile that automatically added him as your friend when you visited his profile page. Within a few days, he had millions of friends.

Now this may sound relatively benign, but keep in mind that this attacker managed to get *his* code—not MySpace's—running on *your* computer. This violates the assumed trust that all the code on MySpace is actually written by MySpace.

MySpace was extremely lucky that this malicious code didn't automatically delete viewers' accounts, change their passwords, flood the site with spam, or create any of the other nightmare scenarios this vulnerability unleashes.

The Solution

The solution is simple: *always* escape *any* content that might have come from a user before inserting it into HTML.

To guard against this, Django's template system automatically escapes all variable values. Let's see what happens if we rewrite our example using the template system:

```
# views.py
```

```
from django.shortcuts import render_to_response
```

```
def say_hello(request):
    name = request.GET.get('name', 'world')
    return render_to_response('hello.html', {'name': name})

# hello.html

<h1>Hello, {{ name }}!</h1>
```

With this in place, a request to `http://example.com/hello/name=<i>Jacob</i>` will result in the following page:

```
<h1>Hello, &lt;i&gt;Jacob&lt;/i&gt;!</h1>
```

We covered Django's auto-escaping back in Chapter 4, along with ways to turn it off. But even if you're using this feature, you should *still* get in the habit of asking yourself at all times, "Where does this data come from?" No automatic solution will ever protect your site from XSS attacks 100% of the time.

Cross-Site Request Forgery

Cross-site request forgery (CSRF) happens when a malicious Web site tricks users into unknowingly loading a URL from a site at which they're already authenticated—hence taking advantage of their authenticated status.

Django has built-in tools to protect from this kind of attack. (The attack itself and those tools are covered in great detail in Chapter 16.)

Session Forging/Hijacking

This isn't a specific attack; it's a general class of attacks on a user's session data. It can take a number of different forms:

- A *man-in-the-middle* attack, in which an attacker snoops on session data as it travels over the wire (or wireless) network.

- *Session forging*, in which an attacker uses a session ID (perhaps obtained through a man-in-the-middle attack) to pretend to be another user.

  An example of these first two is an attacker in a coffee shop using the shop's wireless network to capture a session cookie. She could then use that cookie to impersonate the original user.

- A *cookie-forging* attack, in which an attacker overrides the supposedly read-only data stored in a cookie. Chapter 14 explains in detail how cookies work; one of the salient points is that it's trivial for browsers and malicious users to change cookies without your knowledge.

  There's a long history of Web sites that have stored a cookie such as `IsLoggedIn=1` or even `LoggedInAsUser=jacob`. It's dead simple to exploit these types of cookies.

  On a more subtle level, though, it's never a good idea to trust anything stored in cookies. You never know who's been poking at them.

- *Session fixation*, in which an attacker tricks a user into setting or resetting the user's session ID.

  For example, PHP allows session identifiers to be passed in the URL (e.g., `http://example.com/?PHPSESSID=fa90197ca25f6ab40bb1374c510d7a32`). An attacker who tricks a user into clicking a link with a hard-coded session ID will cause the user to pick up that session.

  Session fixation has been used in phishing attacks to trick users into entering personal information into an account the attacker owns. He can later log into that account and retrieve the data.

- *Session poisoning*, in which an attacker injects potentially dangerous data into a user's session—usually through a Web form that the user submits to set session data.

  A canonical example is a site that stores a simple user preference (such as a page's background color) in a cookie. An attacker could trick a user into clicking a link to submit a "color" that actually contains an XSS attack. If that color isn't escaped, the user could again inject malicious code into the user's environment.

The Solution

There are a number of general principles that can protect you from these attacks:

- Never allow session information to be contained in the URL.

  Django's session framework (see Chapter 14) simply doesn't allow sessions to be contained in the URL.

- Don't store data in cookies directly. Instead, store a session ID that maps to session data stored on the back-end.

  If you use Django's built-in session framework (i.e., `request.session`), this is handled automatically for you. The only cookie that the session framework uses is a single session ID; all the session data is stored in the database.

- Remember to escape session data if you display it in the template. See the earlier XSS section, and remember that it applies to any user-created content as well as any data from the browser. You should treat session information as being user created.

- Prevent attackers from spoofing session IDs whenever possible.

  Although it's nearly impossible to detect someone who's hijacked a session ID, Django does have built-in protection against a brute-force session attack. Session IDs are stored as hashes (instead of sequential numbers), which prevents a brute-force attack, and a user will always get a new session ID if she tries a nonexistent one, which prevents session fixation.

Notice that none of those principles and tools prevents man-in-the-middle attacks, which are nearly impossible to detect. If your site allows logged-in users to see any sort of sensitive data, you should *always* serve that site over HTTPS. Additionally, if you have an SSL-enabled site, you should set the `SESSION_COOKIE_SECURE` setting to `True`; this will make Django only send session cookies over HTTPS.

E-mail Header Injection

SQL injection's less well-known sibling, *e-mail header injection*, hijacks Web forms that send e-mail. An attacker can use this technique to send spam via your mail server. Any form that constructs e-mail headers from Web form data is vulnerable to this kind of attack.

Let's look at the canonical contact form found on many sites. Usually this sends a message to a hard-coded e-mail address, so it doesn't appear vulnerable to spam abuse at first glance.

However, most of these forms also allow the user to type in his own subject for the e-mail (along with a "from" address, a body, and sometimes a few other fields). This subject field is used to construct the "subject" header of the e-mail message.

If that header is unescaped when building the e-mail message, an attacker could submit something like "hello\nccc:spamvictim@example.com" (where "\n" is a newline character). That would make the constructed e-mail headers turn into this:

```
To: hardcoded@example.com
Subject: hello
cc: spamvictim@example.com
```

Like SQL injection, if we trust the subject line given by the user, we'll allow him to construct a malicious set of headers, and he can use our contact form to send spam.

The Solution

We can prevent this attack in the same way we prevent SQL injection: always escape or validate user-submitted content.

Django's built-in mail functions (in django.core.mail) simply do not allow newlines in any fields used to construct headers (the "from" and "to" addresses, plus the subject). If you try to use django.core.mail.send_mail with a subject that contains newlines, Django will raise a BadHeaderError exception.

If you do not use Django's built-in mail functions to send e-mail, you'll need to make sure that newlines in headers either cause an error or are stripped. You may want to examine the SafeMIMEText class in django.core.mail to see how Django does this.

Directory Traversal

Directory traversal is another injection-style attack, in which a malicious user tricks filesystem code into reading and/or writing files that the Web server shouldn't have access to.

An example might be a view that reads files from the disk without carefully sanitizing the file name:

```
def dump_file(request):
    filename = request.GET["filename"]
    filename = os.path.join(BASE_PATH, filename)
    content = open(filename).read()

    # ...
```

Though it looks like that view restricts file access to files beneath BASE_PATH (by using os.path.join), if the attacker passes in a filename containing .. (two periods, a shorthand for "the parent directory"), she can access files "above" BASE_PATH. It's only a matter of time before she can discover the correct number of dots to successfully access ../../../../../etc/passwd, for example.

Anything that reads files without proper escaping is vulnerable to this problem. Views that *write* files are just as vulnerable, but the consequences are doubly dire.

Another permutation of this problem lies in code that dynamically loads modules based on the URL or other request information. A well-publicized example came from the world of Ruby on Rails. Prior to mid-2006, Rails used URLs such as http://example.com/person/poke/1 directly to load modules and call methods. The result was that a carefully constructed URL could automatically load arbitrary code, including a database reset script!

The Solution

If your code ever needs to read or write files based on user input, you need to sanitize the requested path very carefully to ensure that an attacker can't escape from the base directory you're restricting access to.

■**Note** Needless to say, you should *never* write code that can read from any area of the disk!

A good example of how to do this escaping lies in Django's built-in static content-serving view (in django.views.static). Here's the relevant code:

```
import os
import posixpath

# ...

path = posixpath.normpath(urllib.unquote(path))
newpath = ''
for part in path.split('/'):
    if not part:
        # strip empty path components
        continue

    drive, part = os.path.splitdrive(part)
    head, part = os.path.split(part)
    if part in (os.curdir, os.pardir):
        # strip '.' and '..' in path
        continue

    newpath = os.path.join(newpath, part).replace('\\', '/')
```

Django doesn't read files (unless you use the static.serve function, but that's protected with the code just shown), so this vulnerability doesn't affect the core code much.

In addition, the use of the URLconf abstraction means that Django will *never* load code you've not explicitly told it to load. There's no way to create a URL that causes Django to load something not mentioned in a URLconf.

Exposed Error Messages

During development, being able to see tracebacks and errors live in your browser is extremely useful. Django has "pretty" and informative debug messages specifically to make debugging easier.

However, if these errors get displayed after the site goes live, they can reveal aspects of your code or configuration that could aid an attacker.

Furthermore, errors and tracebacks aren't at all useful to end users. Django's philosophy is that site visitors should never see application-related error messages. If your code raises an unhandled exception, a site visitor should not see the full traceback—or *any* hint of code snippets or Python (programmer-oriented) error messages. Instead, the visitor should see a friendly "This page is unavailable" message.

Naturally, of course, developers need to see tracebacks to debug problems in their code. So the framework should hide all error messages from the public, but it should display them to the trusted site developers.

The Solution

As we covered in Chapter 12, Django's DEBUG setting controls the display of these error messages. Make sure to set this to False when you're ready to deploy.

Users deploying Apache and mod_python (also in Chapter 12) should also make sure they have PythonDebug Off in their Apache conf files; this will suppress any errors that occur before Django has had a chance to load.

A Final Word on Security

We hope all this talk of security problems isn't too intimidating. It's true that the Web can be a wild world, but with a little bit of foresight, you can have a secure Web site.

Keep in mind that Web security is a constantly changing field; if you're reading the dead-tree version of this book, be sure to check more up-to-date security resources for any new vulnerabilities that have been discovered. In fact, it's always a good idea to spend some time each week or month researching and keeping current on the state of Web application security. It's a small investment to make, but the protection you'll get for your site and your users is priceless.

What's Next?

You've reached the end of our regularly scheduled program. The following appendixes all contain reference material that you might need as you work on your Django projects.

We wish you the best of luck in running your Django site, whether it's a little toy for you and a few friends, or the next Google.

PART 4

■■■

Appendixes

APPENDIX A

■■■

Model Definition Reference

Chapter 5 explains the basics of defining models, and we use them throughout the rest of the book. There is, however, a *huge* range of model options available not covered elsewhere. This appendix explains each model definition option.

Note that although these APIs are considered stable, the Django developers consistently add new shortcuts and conveniences to the model definition. It's a good idea to always check the latest documentation online at http://docs.djangoproject.com/.

Fields

The most important part of a model—and the only required part of a model—is the list of database fields it defines.

FIELD NAME RESTRICTIONS

Django places only two restrictions on model field names:

- A field name cannot be a Python reserved word because that would result in a Python syntax error. For example:

```
class Example(models.Model):
    pass = models.IntegerField() # 'pass' is a reserved word!
```

- A field name cannot contain more than one underscore in a row because of the way Django's query lookup syntax works. For example:

```
class Example(models.Model):
    foo__bar = models.IntegerField() # 'foo__bar' has two underscores!
```

These limitations can be worked around, though, because your field name doesn't necessarily have to match your database column name. (See the "db_column" section later in this appendix.)

SQL reserved words, such as `join`, `where`, or `select`, *are* allowed as model field names because Django escapes all database table names and column names in every underlying SQL query. It uses the quoting syntax of your particular database engine.

Each field in your model should be an instance of the appropriate `Field` class. Django uses the field class types to determine a few things:

- The database column type (e.g., `INTEGER`, `VARCHAR`)
- The widget to use in Django's forms and admin site if you care to use it (e.g., `<input type="text">`, `<select>`)
- The minimal validation requirements, which are used in Django's admin interface and by forms

A complete list of field classes follows, sorted alphabetically. Note that relationship fields (`ForeignKey`, etc.) are handled in the next section.

AutoField

An `IntegerField` that automatically increments according to available IDs. You usually won't need to use this directly; a primary key field will automatically be added to your model if you don't specify otherwise.

BooleanField

A true/false field.

MYSQL USERS...

A Boolean field in MySQL is stored as a `TINYINT` column with a value of either 0 or 1 (most databases have a proper `BOOLEAN` type instead). So, for MySQL only, when a `BooleanField` is retrieved from the database and stored on a model attribute, it will have the values of 1 or 0 instead of `True` or `False`.

Normally this shouldn't be a problem because Python guarantees that `1 == True` and `0 == False` are both true. Just be careful if you're writing something `obj is True` when `obj` is a value from a Boolean attribute on a model. If that model was constructed using the `mysql` back-end, the `is` test will fail. Prefer an equality test (using `==`) in cases like this.

CharField

A string field for small- to large-sized strings. (For very large amounts of text, use `TextField`.)

`CharField` has one extra required argument: `max_length`. This is the maximum length (in characters) of the field. The `max_length` is enforced at the database level and in Django's validation.

CommaSeparatedIntegerField

A field of integers separated by commas. As in `CharField`, the `max_length` argument is required.

DateField

A date represented in Python by a `datetime.date` instance.

DateTimeField

A date and time represented in Python by a `datetime.datetime` instance.

DecimalField

A fixed-precision decimal number represented in Python by a `decimal.Decimal` instance. It has two required arguments:

- `max_digits` is the maximum number of digits allowed in the number.
- `decimal_place` is the number of decimal places to store with the number.

For example, to store numbers up to 999 with a resolution of 2 decimal places, you'd use this:

```
models.DecimalField(..., max_digits=5, decimal_places=2)
```

And to store numbers up to approximately one billion with a resolution of ten decimal places, use this:

```
models.DecimalField(..., max_digits=19, decimal_places=10)
```

When assigning to a `DecimalField`, use either a `decimal.Decimal` object or a string, not a Python float.

EmailField

A `CharField` that checks that the value is a valid e-mail address.

FileField

A file-upload field.

■**Note** The `primary_key` and `unique` arguments are not supported; they create a `TypeError` if used.

Has one *required* argument:

`upload_to`

A local filesystem path that will be appended to your `MEDIA_ROOT` setting to determine the value of the `django.core.files.File.url` attribute.

This path may contain *strftime formatting* (see the Python docs for the `time` standard library module), which will be replaced using the date/time of the file upload (so that uploaded files don't fill up the given directory).

It can also be a callable, such as a function, which will be called to obtain the upload path, including the file name. This callable must be able to accept two arguments and return a Unix-style path (with forward slashes) to be passed along to the storage system. The two arguments that will be passed are shown in Table A-1.

Table A-1. *Arguments Passed to Callable upload_to argument*

Argument	Description
instance	An instance of the model where the FileField is defined. More specifically, this is the particular instance where the current file is being attached.
	In most cases, this object will not have been saved to the database yet, so if it uses the default AutoField, *it might not yet have a value for its primary key field.*
filename	The file name that was originally given to the file. It may or may not be taken into account when determining the final destination path.

It also has one optional argument:

storage

Optional: a storage object that handles the storage and retrieval of your files.

Using a FileField or an ImageField (see the ImageField section) in a model takes a few steps:

1. In your settings file, you'll need to define MEDIA_ROOT as the full path to a directory in which you want Django to store uploaded files. (For performance, these files are not stored in the database.) Define MEDIA_URL as the base public URL of that directory. Make sure that this directory is writable by the Web server's user account.

2. Add the FileField or ImageField to your model, making sure to define the upload_to option to tell Django to which subdirectory of MEDIA_ROOT it should upload files.

3. All that will be stored in your database is a path to the file (relative to MEDIA_ROOT). You'll most likely want to use the convenience url function provided by Django. For example, if your ImageField is called mug_shot, you can get the absolute URL to your image in a template with {{ object.mug_shot.url }}.

For example, say your MEDIA_ROOT is set to '/home/media', and upload_to is set to 'photos/%Y/%m/%d'. The '%Y/%m/%d' part of upload_to is strftime formatting; '%Y' is the four-digit year, '%m' is the two-digit month, and '%d' is the two-digit day. If you upload a file on January 15, 2007, it will be saved in the directory /home/media/photos/2007/01/15.

If you want to retrieve the upload file's on-disk file name, a URL that refers to that file, or the file's size, you can use the name, url, and size attributes, respectively.

Note that whenever you deal with uploaded files, you should pay close attention to where you're uploading them, and what type of files they are, to avoid security holes. Be sure to validate all uploaded files so that you're sure the files are what you think they are. For example, if you blindly let somebody upload files without validation to a directory that's within your Web server's document root, somebody could upload a CGI or PHP script and execute that script by visiting its URL on your site. Don't allow that to happen.

By default, FileField instances are created as varchar(100) columns in your database. As with other fields, you can change the maximum length using the max_length argument.

FilePathField

A `CharField` whose choices are limited to the file names in a certain directory on the filesystem. It has three special arguments, of which the first is *required*:

path

Required. The absolute filesystem path to a directory from which this `FilePathField` should get its choices. For example: `"/home/images"`.

match

Optional. A regular expression, as a string, that `FilePathField` will use to filter file names. Note that the regex will be applied to the base file name, not the full path. For example: `"foo.*\.txt$"`, which will match a file called `foo23.txt` but not `bar.txt` or `foo23.gif`.

recursive

Optional. Either `True` or `False`. Default is `False`. Specifies whether all subdirectories of `path` should be included.

Of course, these arguments can be used together.

The one potential gotcha is that `match` applies to the base file name, not the full path. So this example will match `/home/images/bar/foo.gif`, but not `/home/images/foo/bar.gif` because the `match` applies to the base file name (`foo.gif` and `bar.gif`):

```
FilePathField(path="/home/images", match="foo.*", recursive=True)
```

By default, `FilePathField` instances are created as `varchar(100)` columns in your database. As with other fields, you can change the maximum length using the `max_length` argument.

FloatField

A floating-point number represented in Python by a `float` instance.

ImageField

Similar to `FileField`, but validates that the uploaded object is a valid image. It has two extra optional arguments:

height_field

The name of a model field that will be autopopulated with the height of the image each time the model instance is saved.

width_field

The name of a model field that will be autopopulated with the width of the image each time the model instance is saved.

In addition to the special attributes that are available for `FileField`, an `ImageField` also has `height` and `width` attributes, both of which correspond to the image's height and width in pixels.

It requires the Python Imaging Library, available at http://www.pythonware.com/products/pil/.

By default, ImageField instances are created as varchar(100) columns in your database. As with other fields, you can change the maximum length using the max_length argument.

IntegerField

An integer.

IPAddressField

An IP address in string format (e.g., '192.0.2.30').

NullBooleanField

Similar to a BooleanField, but allows NULL as one of the options. Use this instead of a BooleanField with null=True.

PositiveIntegerField

Similar to an IntegerField, but must be positive.

PositiveSmallIntegerField

Similar to a PositiveIntegerField, but allows only values under a certain (database-dependent) point.

SlugField

Slug, which is a newspaper term, is a short label for something, containing only letters, numbers, underscores, or hyphens. Slugs are generally used in URLs.

Like a CharField, you can specify max_length. If max_length is not specified, Django will use a default length of 50.

It implies setting db_index to True.

SmallIntegerField

Similar to an IntegerField, but allows only values under a certain (database-dependent) point.

TextField

A large text field.

Also see CharField for storing smaller bits of text.

TimeField

A time represented in Python by a datetime.time instance. Accepts the same autopopulation options as DateField.

URLField

A `CharField` for a URL; it has one extra optional argument:

`verify_exists`

If `True` (the default), the URL given will be checked for existence (i.e., the URL actually loads and doesn't give a 404 response). It should be noted that when using the single-threaded development server, validating a URL being served by the same server will hang. This should not be a problem for multithreaded servers.

Like all `CharField` subclasses, `URLField` takes the optional `max_length` argument. If you don't specify `max_length`, a default of 200 is used.

XMLField

A `TextField` that checks whether the value is valid XML that matches a given schema. Takes one required argument:

`schema_path`

The filesystem path to a RelaxNG schema against which to validate the field. For more on RelaxNG, see `http://www.relaxng.org/`.

Universal Field Options

The following arguments are available to all field types. All are optional.

null

If `True`, Django will store empty values as `NULL` in the database. If `False`, saving empty values will likely result in a database error. The default is `False`.

Note that empty string values will always get stored as empty strings, not as `NULL`. Use `null=True` only for nonstring fields such as integers, Booleans, and dates. For both types of fields, you will also need to set `blank=True` if you want to permit empty values in forms because the `null` parameter affects only database storage (see `blank`).

Avoid using `null` on string-based fields such as `CharField` and `TextField` unless you have an excellent reason. If a string-based field has `null=True`, that means it has two possible values for "no data": `NULL` and the empty string. In most cases, it's redundant to have two possible values for "no data"; Django's convention is to use the empty string, not `NULL`.

■**Note** When using the Oracle database back-end, the `null=True` option will be coerced for string-based fields that have the empty string as a possible value, and the value `NULL` will be stored to denote the empty string.

For more on this, refer to the section "Making Date and Numeric Fields Optional" in Chapter 6.

blank

If True, the field is allowed to be blank. The default is False.

Note that this is different from null. null is purely database-related, whereas blank is validation-related. If a field has blank=True, validation on Django's admin site will allow entry of an empty value. If a field has blank=False, the field will be required.

choices

An iterable (e.g., a list or tuple) of two-tuples to use as choices for this field.

A choices list looks like this:

```
YEAR_IN_SCHOOL_CHOICES = (
    ('FR', 'Freshman'),
    ('SO', 'Sophomore'),
    ('JR', 'Junior'),
    ('SR', 'Senior'),
    ('GR', 'Graduate'),
)
```

The first element in each tuple is the actual value to be stored. The second element is the human-readable name for the option.

The choices list can be defined as part of your model class:

```
class Foo(models.Model):
    GENDER_CHOICES = (
        ('M', 'Male'),
        ('F', 'Female'),
    )
    gender = models.CharField(max_length=1, choices=GENDER_CHOICES)
```

It can also be defined outside your model class altogether:

```
GENDER_CHOICES = (
    ('M', 'Male'),
    ('F', 'Female'),
)
class Foo(models.Model):
    gender = models.CharField(max_length=1, choices=GENDER_CHOICES)
```

You can also collect your available choices into named groups that can be used for organizational purposes in a form:

```
MEDIA_CHOICES = (
    ('Audio', (
            ('vinyl', 'Vinyl'),
            ('cd', 'CD'),
        )
    ),
```

```
('Video', (
        ('vhs', 'VHS Tape'),
        ('dvd', 'DVD'),
    )
),
('unknown', 'Unknown'),
)
```

The first element in each tuple is the name to apply to the group. The second element is an iterable of two-tuples, with each two-tuple containing a value and a human-readable name for an option. Grouped options can be combined with ungrouped options within a single list (such as the *unknown* option in this example).

Finally, note that choices can be any iterable object—not necessarily a list or tuple. This lets you construct choices dynamically. But if you find yourself hacking choices to be dynamic, you're probably better off using a proper database table with a ForeignKey. choices is meant for static data that doesn't change much, if ever.

db_column

The name of the database column to use for this field. If it isn't given, Django will use the field's name.

If your database column name is an SQL-reserved word or contains characters that aren't allowed in Python variable names—notably, the hyphen—that's okay. Django quotes column and table names behind the scenes.

db_index

If True, django-admin.py sqlindexes will output a CREATE INDEX statement for this field.

db_tablespace

The name of the database tablespace to use for this field's index if this field is indexed. The default is the project's DEFAULT_INDEX_TABLESPACE setting, if set; or the db_tablespace of the model, if any. If the back-end doesn't support tablespaces, this option is ignored.

default

The default value for the field; it can be a value or a callable object. If callable, it will be called every time a new object is created.

editable

If False, the field will not be editable in the admin or via forms automatically generated from the model class. Default is True.

help_text

Extra "help" text to be displayed under the field on the object's admin form. It's useful for documentation even if your object doesn't have an admin form.

Note that this value is *not* HTML-escaped when it's displayed in the admin interface. This lets you include HTML in help_text if you so desire. For example:

```
help_text="Please use the following format: <em>YYYY-MM-DD</em>."
```

Alternatively, you can use plain text and django.utils.html.escape() to escape any HTML special characters.

primary_key

If True, this field is the primary key for the model.

If you don't specify primary_key=True for any fields in your model, Django will automatically add an AutoField to hold the primary key, so you don't need to set primary_key=True on any of your fields unless you want to override the default primary key behavior.

primary_key=True implies null=False and unique=True. Only one primary key is allowed on an object.

unique

If True, this field must be unique throughout the table.

This is enforced at the database level and at the level of forms created with ModelForm (including forms in the Django admin site). If you try to save a model with a duplicate value in a unique field, an IntegrityError will be raised by the model's save method.

This option is valid on all field types except ManyToManyField, FileField, and ImageField.

unique_for_date

Set this to the name of a DateField or DateTimeField to require that this field be unique for the value of the date field.

For example, if you have a field title that has unique_for_date="pub_date", Django wouldn't allow the entry of two records with the same title and pub_date.

This is enforced at the level of forms created with ModelForm (including forms in the Django admin site), but not at the database level.

unique_for_month

Similar to unique_for_date, but requires the field to be unique with respect to the month.

unique_for_year

Similar to unique_for_date and unique_for_month.

verbose_name

A human-readable name for the field. If the verbose name isn't given, Django will automatically create it using the field's attribute name, converting underscores to spaces.

Relationships

Clearly, the power of relational databases lies in relating tables to each other. Django offers ways to define the three most common types of database relationships: many-to-one, many-to-many, and one-to-one.

ForeignKey

A many-to-one relationship. Requires a positional argument: the class to which the model is related.

To create a recursive relationship—an object that has a many-to-one relationship with itself—use models.ForeignKey('self').

If you need to create a relationship on a model that has not yet been defined, you can use the name of the model instead of the model object itself:

```
class Car(models.Model):
    manufacturer = models.ForeignKey('Manufacturer')
    # ...

class Manufacturer(models.Model):
    # ...
```

Note, however, that this refers only to models in the same models.py file. To refer to models defined in another application, you must instead explicitly specify the application label. For example, if the Manufacturer model is defined in another application called production, you'd need to use the following:

```
class Car(models.Model):
    manufacturer = models.ForeignKey('production.Manufacturer')
```

Behind the scenes, Django appends "_id" to the field name to create its database column name. In the preceding example, the database table for the Car model will have a manufacturer_id column. (You can change it explicitly by specifying db_column.) However, your code should never have to deal with the database column name unless you write custom SQL. You'll always deal with the field names of your model object.

ForeignKey accepts an extra set of arguments—all optional—which define the details of how the relation works.

limit_choices_to

A dictionary of lookup arguments and values that limit the available admin choices for this object. Use this with functions from the Python datetime module to limit choices of objects by date. For example, the following allows only the choice of related objects with a pub_date before the current date/time to be chosen:

```
limit_choices_to = {'pub_date__lte': datetime.now}
```

limit_choices_to has no effect on the inline FormSets that are created to display related objects in the admin.

`related_name`

The name to use for the relation from the related object back to this one.

`to_field`

The field on the related object that the relation is to. By default, Django uses the primary key of the related object.

ManyToManyField

A many-to-many relationship. Requires a positional argument: the class to which the model is related. This works exactly the same as it does for `ForeignKey`, including all the options regarding recursive relationships and lazy relationships.

Behind the scenes, Django creates an intermediary join table to represent the many-to-many relationship. By default, this table name is generated using the names of the two tables being joined. Because some databases don't support table names above a certain length, these table names will be automatically truncated to 64 characters, and a uniqueness hash will be used. This means you might see table names such as `author_books_9cdf4`; this is perfectly normal. You can manually provide the name of the join table using the `db_table` option.

`ManyToManyField` accepts an extra set of arguments—all optional—that control how the relationship functions:

`related_name`

Same as `related_name` in `ForeignKey`.

`limit_choices_to`

Same as `limit_choices_to` in `ForeignKey`.

`limit_choices_to` has no effect when used on a `ManyToManyField` with a custom intermediate table specified using the `through` parameter.

`symmetrical`

Only used in the definition of `ManyToManyField` on `self`. Consider the following model:

```
class Person(models.Model):
    friends = models.ManyToManyField("self")
```

When Django processes this model, it identifies that it has a `ManyToManyField` on itself, so it doesn't add a `person_set` attribute to the `Person` class. Instead, the `ManyToManyField` is assumed to be symmetrical (if I am your friend, you are my friend).

If you do not want symmetry in many-to-many relationships with `self`, set `symmetrical` to `False`. This will force Django to add the descriptor for the reverse relationship, allowing `ManyToManyField` relationships to be nonsymmetrical.

`through`

Django will automatically generate a table to manage many-to-many relationships. However, if you want to manually specify the intermediary table, you can use the `through` option to specify the Django model that represents the intermediate table that you want to use.

The most common use for this option is when you want to associate extra data with a many-to-many relationship.

db_table

The name of the table to create for storing the many-to-many data. If it is not provided, Django will assume a default name based on the names of the two tables being joined.

OneToOneField

A one-to-one relationship. Conceptually, this is similar to a ForeignKey with unique=True, but the "reverse" side of the relation will directly return a single object.

This is most useful as the primary key of a model that "extends" another model in some way; multitable inheritance is implemented by adding an implicit one-to-one relationship from the child model to the parent model, for example.

One positional argument is required: the class to which the model will be related. This works exactly the same as it does for ForeignKey, including all the options regarding recursive relationships and lazy relationships.

Additionally, OneToOneField accepts all the extra arguments accepted by ForeignKey, plus one extra argument:

parent_link

When True and used in a model that inherits from another (concrete) model, indicates that this field should be used as the link back to the parent class instead of the extra OneToOneField, which would normally be implicitly created by subclassing.

Model Metadata Options

Model-specific metadata lives in a class Meta defined in the body of your model class:

```
class Book(models.Model):
    title = models.CharField(maxlength=100)

    class Meta:
        # model metadata options go here
        ...
```

Model metadata is "anything that's not a field," such as ordering options and so forth.

The sections that follow present a list of all possible Meta options. No options are required. Adding class Meta to a model is completely optional.

abstract

If True, this model will be an abstract base class. See the Django documentation for more on abstract base classes.

db_table

The name of the database table to use for the model:

```
db_table = 'music_album'
```

Table names

To save time, Django automatically derives the name of the database table from the name of the model class and the app that contains it. A model's database table name is constructed by joining the model's *app label*—the name you used in `manage.py startapp`—to the model's class name, with an underscore between them.

For example, if you have an app `bookstore` (as created by `manage.py startapp bookstore`), a model defined as `class Book` will have a database table named `bookstore_book`.

To override the database table name, use the `db_table` parameter in `class Meta`.

If your database table name is an SQL-reserved word or contains characters that aren't allowed in Python variable names—notably, the hyphen—that's okay. Django quotes column and table names behind the scenes.

db_tablespace

The name of the database tablespace to use for the model. If the back-end doesn't support tablespaces, this option is ignored.

get_latest_by

The name of a `DateField` or `DateTimeField` in the model. This specifies the default field to use in the model `Manager` `latest` method.

For example:

```
get_latest_by = "order_date"
```

managed

Defaults to `True`, meaning that Django will create the appropriate database tables in `django-admin.py syncdb` and remove them as part of a `reset` management command. That is, Django *manages* the database tables' life cycles.

If `False`, no database table creation or deletion operations will be performed for this model. This is useful if the model represents an existing table or a database view that has been created by some other means. This is the *only* difference when `managed` is `False`. All other aspects of model handling are exactly the same as normal, including the following:

- Adding an automatic primary key field to the model if you don't declare it. To avoid confusion for later code readers, it's recommended that you specify all the columns from the database table you are modeling when using unmanaged models.

- If a model with managed=False contains a ManyToManyField that points to another unmanaged model, the intermediary table for the many-to-many join will also not be created. However, the intermediary table between one managed and one unmanaged model *will* be created.

  If you need to change this default behavior, create the intermediary table as an explicit model (with managed set as needed) and use the through attribute to make the relation use your custom model.

For tests involving models with managed=False, it's up to you to ensure the correct tables are created as part of the test setup.

If you're interested in changing the Python-level behavior of a model class, you *could* use managed=False and create a copy of an existing model. However, there's a better approach for that situation: proxy models.

ordering

The default ordering for the object, for use when obtaining lists of objects:

```
ordering = ['-order_date']
```

This is a tuple or list of strings. Each string is a field name with an optional - prefix, which indicates descending order. Fields without a leading - will be ordered ascending. Use the string ? to order randomly.

■**Note** Regardless of how many fields are in ordering, the admin site uses only the first field.

For example, to order by a pub_date field ascending, use this:

```
ordering = ['pub_date']
```

To order by pub_date descending, use this:

```
ordering = ['-pub_date']
```

To order by pub_date descending and then by author ascending, use this:

```
ordering = ['-pub_date', 'author']
```

proxy

If set to True, a model that subclasses another model will be treated as a proxy model. For more on proxy models, see the Django documentation.

unique_together

Sets of field names that, when taken together, must be unique:

```
unique_together = (("driver", "restaurant"),)
```

This is a list of lists of fields that must be unique when considered together. It's used by ModelForm forms (including forms in the Django admin site) and is enforced at the database level (i.e., the appropriate UNIQUE statements are included in the CREATE TABLE statement).

For convenience, unique_together can be a single sequence when dealing with a single set of fields:

```
unique_together = ("driver", "restaurant")
```

verbose_name

A human-readable name for the object, singular:

```
verbose_name = "pizza"
```

If this isn't given, Django will use a munged version of the class name: CamelCase becomes camel case.

verbose_name_plural

The plural name for the object:

```
verbose_name_plural = "stories"
```

If this isn't given, Django will use verbose_name + "s".

APPENDIX B

■ ■ ■

Database API Reference

Django's database API is the other half of the model API discussed in Appendix A. Once you've defined a model, you'll use this API any time you need to access the database. You've seen examples of this API in use throughout the book; this appendix explains all the various options in detail.

Like the model APIs discussed in Appendix A, although these APIs are considered very stable, the Django developers consistently add new shortcuts and conveniences. It's a good idea to always check the latest documentation online, available at http://docs.djangoproject.com/.

Throughout this reference, we'll refer to the following models, which might form a simple blog application:

```python
from django.db import models

class Blog(models.Model):
    name = models.CharField(max_length=100)
    tagline = models.TextField()

    def __unicode__(self):
        return self.name

class Author(models.Model):
    name = models.CharField(max_length=50)
    email = models.EmailField()

    def __unicode__(self):
        return self.name

class Entry(models.Model):
    blog = models.ForeignKey(Blog)
    headline = models.CharField(max_length=255)
    body_text = models.TextField()
    pub_date = models.DateTimeField()
    authors = models.ManyToManyField(Author)

    def __unicode__(self):
        return self.headline
```

Creating Objects

To create an object, instantiate it using keyword arguments to the model class, and then call save() to save it to the database:

```
>>> from mysite.blog.models import Blog
>>> b = Blog(name='Beatles Blog', tagline='All the latest Beatles news.')
>>> b.save()
```

This performs an INSERT SQL statement behind the scenes. Django doesn't hit the database until you explicitly call save(). The save() method has no return value.

To create an object and save it all in one step, see the create manager method.

What Happens When You Save?

When you save an object, Django performs the following steps:

1. *Emit a pre_save signal*: This provides a notification that an object is about to be saved. You can register a listener that will be invoked whenever this signal is emitted. Check the online documentation for more on signals.

2. *Preprocess the data*: Each field on the object is asked to perform any automated data modification that the field may need to perform.

   Most fields do *no* preprocessing—the field data is kept as is. Preprocessing is used only on fields that have special behavior, like file fields.

3. *Prepare the data for the database*: Each field is asked to provide its current value in a data type that can be written to the database.

   Most fields require no data preparation. Simple data types, such as integers and strings, are "ready to write" as a Python object. However, more-complex data types often require some modification. For example, DateFields use a Python datetime object to store data. Databases don't store datetime objects, so the field value must be converted into an ISO-compliant date string for insertion into the database.

4. *Insert the data into the database*: The preprocessed, prepared data is composed into an SQL statement for insertion into the database.

5. *Emit a post_save signal*: As with the pre_save signal, this is used to provide notification that an object has been saved successfully.

Autoincrementing Primary Keys

For convenience, each model is given an autoincrementing primary-key field named id unless you explicitly specify primary_key=True on a field (see the section titled "AutoField" in Appendix A).

If your model has an `AutoField`, that autoincremented value will be calculated and saved as an attribute on your object the first time you call `save()`:

```
>>> b2 = Blog(name='Cheddar Talk', tagline='Thoughts on cheese.')
>>> b2.id     # Returns None, because b doesn't have an ID yet.
None

>>> b2.save()
>>> b2.id     # Returns the ID of your new object.
14
```

There's no way to tell what the value of an ID will be before you call `save()`, because that value is calculated by your database, not by Django.

If a model has an `AutoField` but you want to define a new object's ID explicitly when saving, define it explicitly before saving, rather than relying on the autoassignment of the ID:

```
>>> b3 = Blog(id=3, name='Cheddar Talk', tagline='Thoughts on cheese.')
>>> b3.id
3
>>> b3.save()
>>> b3.id
3
```

If you assign auto–primary-key values manually, make sure not to use an existing primary-key value! If you create a new object with an explicit primary-key value that already exists in the database, Django will assume you're changing the existing record rather than creating a new one.

Given the preceding `'Cheddar Talk'` blog example, this example would override the previous record in the database:

```
>>> b4 = Blog(id=3, name='Not Cheddar', tagline='Anything but cheese.')
>>> b4.save()  # Overrides the previous blog with ID=3!
```

Explicitly specifying auto–primary-key values is mostly useful for bulk-saving objects, when you're confident you won't have primary-key collision.

Saving Changes to Objects

To save changes to an object that's already in the database, use `save()`.

Given a `Blog` instance `b5` that has already been saved to the database, this example changes its name and updates its record in the database:

```
>>> b5.name = 'New name'
>>> b5.save()
```

This performs an `UPDATE` SQL statement behind the scenes. Again, Django doesn't hit the database until you explicitly call `save()`.

> ### HOW DJANGO KNOWS WHEN TO UPDATE AND WHEN TO INSERT
>
> You may have noticed that Django database objects use the same `save()` method for creating and changing objects. Django abstracts the need to use `INSERT` or `UPDATE` SQL statements. Specifically, when you call `save()`, Django follows this algorithm:
>
> - If the object's primary-key attribute is set to a value that evaluates to `True` (i.e., a value other than `None` or the empty string), Django executes a `SELECT` query to determine whether a record with the given primary key already exists.
>
> - If the record with the given primary key does already exist, Django executes an `UPDATE` query.
>
> - If the object's primary-key attribute is *not* set or if it's set but a record doesn't exist, Django executes an `INSERT`.
>
> You should be careful not to specify a primary-key value explicitly when saving new objects if you cannot guarantee the primary-key value is unused.

Updating `ForeignKey` fields works exactly the same way; simply assign an object of the right type to the field in question:

```
>>> joe = Author.objects.create(name="Joe")
>>> entry.author = joe
>>> entry.save()
```

Django will complain if you try to assign an object of the wrong type.

Retrieving Objects

Throughout this book you've seen objects retrieved using code like the following:

```
>>> blogs = Blog.objects.filter(author__name__contains="Joe")
```

There are quite a few "moving parts" behind the scenes here: when you retrieve objects from the database, you're actually constructing a `QuerySet` using the model's `Manager`. This `QuerySet` knows how to execute SQL and return the requested objects.

Appendix A looked at both `QuerySet` and `Manager` from a model-definition point of view; now we'll look at how they operate.

A `QuerySet` represents a collection of objects from your database. It can have zero, one, or many *filters*—criteria that narrow down the collection based on given parameters. In SQL terms, a `QuerySet` equates to a `SELECT` statement, and a filter is a `WHERE`.

You get a `QuerySet` by using your model's `Manager`. Each model has at least one `Manager`, and it's called `objects` by default. Access it directly via the model class, like so:

```
>>> Blog.objects
<django.db.models.manager.Manager object at 0x137d00d>
```

Managers are accessible only via model classes, rather than from model instances, to enforce a separation between table-level operations and record-level operations:

```
>>> b = Blog(name='Foo', tagline='Bar')
>>> b.objects
Traceback (most recent call last):
  File "<stdin>", line 1, in <module>
AttributeError: Manager isn't accessible via Blog instances.
```

The Manager is the main source of QuerySets for a model. It acts as a "root" QuerySet that describes all objects in the model's database table. For example, Blog.objects is the initial QuerySet that contains all Blog objects in the database.

Caching and QuerySets

Each QuerySet contains a cache to minimize database access. To write the most efficient code, it's important to understand how QuerySet caching works.

In a newly created QuerySet, the cache is empty. The first time a QuerySet is evaluated— and, hence, a database query happens—Django saves the query results in the QuerySet's cache and returns the results that have been explicitly requested (e.g., the next element, if the QuerySet is being iterated over). Subsequent evaluations of the QuerySet reuse the cached results.

Keep this caching behavior in mind, because it may bite you if you don't use your QuerySets correctly. For example, the following will create two QuerySets, evaluate them, and throw them away:

```
print [e.headline for e in Entry.objects.all()]
print [e.pub_date for e in Entry.objects.all()]
```

That means the same database query will be executed twice, effectively doubling your database load. Also, there's a possibility the two lists may not include the same database records, because an Entry may have been added or deleted in the split second between the two requests.

To avoid this problem, simply save the QuerySet and reuse it:

```
queryset = Poll.objects.all()
print [p.headline for p in queryset] # Evaluate the query set.
print [p.pub_date for p in queryset] # Reuse the cache from the evaluation.
```

Filtering Objects

The simplest way to retrieve objects from a table is to get all of them. To do this, use the all() method on a Manager:

```
>>> Entry.objects.all()
```

The all() method returns a QuerySet of all the objects in the database.

Usually, though, you'll need to select only a subset of the complete set of objects. To create such a subset, you refine the initial QuerySet, adding filter conditions. You'll usually do this using the filter() and/or exclude() methods:

```
>>> ·y2006 = Entry.objects.filter(pub_date__year=2006)
>>> not2006 = Entry.objects.exclude(pub_date__year=2006)
```

filter() and exclude() both take *field lookup* arguments, which are discussed in detail in the "Field Lookups" section of this appendix.

Chaining Filters

The result of refining a QuerySet is itself a QuerySet, so it's possible to chain refinements together, as in this example:

```
>>> qs = Entry.objects.filter(headline__startswith='What')
>>> qs = qs.exclude(pub_date__gte=datetime.datetime.now())
>>> qs = qs.filter(pub_date__gte=datetime.datetime(2005, 1, 1))
```

This takes the initial QuerySet of all entries in the database, adds a filter, then an exclusion, and then another filter. The final result is a QuerySet containing all entries with a headline that starts with "What" that were published between January 1, 2005, and the current day.

It's important to point out here that QuerySets are lazy—the act of creating a QuerySet doesn't involve any database activity. In fact, the three preceding lines don't make *any* database calls; you can chain filters together all day long and Django won't actually run the query until the QuerySet is *evaluated*.

You can evaluate a QuerySet in any of the following ways:

- *Iterating*: A QuerySet is iterable, and it executes its database query the first time you iterate over it. For example, the following QuerySet isn't evaluated until it's iterated over in the for loop:

  ```
  qs = Entry.objects.filter(pub_date__year=2006)
  qs = qs.filter(headline__icontains="bill")
  for e in qs:
      print e.headline
  ```

  This prints all headlines from 2006 that contain "bill" but causes only one database hit.

- *Printing*: A QuerySet is evaluated when you call repr() on it. This is for convenience in the Python interactive interpreter, so you can immediately see your results when using the API interactively.

- *Slicing*: As explained in the upcoming "Limiting QuerySets" section, a QuerySet can be sliced using Python's array-slicing syntax. Usually slicing a QuerySet returns another (unevaluated) QuerySet, but Django will execute the database query if you use the step parameter of Python's slice syntax.

- *Converting to a list*: You can force evaluation of a QuerySet by calling list() on it, as in this example:

  ```
  >>> entry_list = list(Entry.objects.all())
  ```

Be warned, though, that this could have a large memory overhead, because Django will load each element of the list into memory. In contrast, iterating over a QuerySet will take advantage of your database to load data and instantiate objects only as you need them.

FILTERED QUERYSETS ARE UNIQUE

Each time you refine a QuerySet, you get a brand-new QuerySet that is in no way bound to the previous one. Each refinement creates a separate and distinct QuerySet that can be stored, used, and reused:

```
q1 = Entry.objects.filter(headline__startswith="What")
q2 = q1.exclude(pub_date__gte=datetime.now())
q3 = q1.filter(pub_date__gte=datetime.now())
```

These three QuerySets are separate. The first is a base QuerySet containing all entries that have a headline starting with "What." The second is a subset of the first, with an additional criterion that excludes records whose pub_date is later than the current date. The third is a subset of the first, with an additional criterion that selects only the records whose pub_date is later than the current date. The initial QuerySet (q1) is unaffected by the refinement process.

Limiting QuerySets

Use Python's array-slicing syntax to limit your QuerySet to a certain number of results. This is the equivalent of SQL's LIMIT and OFFSET clauses.

For example, this returns the first five entries (LIMIT 5):

```
>>> Entry.objects.all()[:5]
```

This returns the sixth through tenth entries (OFFSET 5 LIMIT 5):

```
>>> Entry.objects.all()[5:10]
```

Generally, slicing a QuerySet returns a new QuerySet—it doesn't evaluate the query. An exception is if you use the step parameter of Python's slice syntax. For example, this would execute the query to return a list of every *second* object of the first ten:

```
>>> Entry.objects.all()[:10:2]
```

To retrieve a *single* object rather than a list (e.g., SELECT foo FROM bar LIMIT 1), use a simple index instead of a slice. For example, the following code returns the first Entry in the database, after ordering Entry objects alphabetically by headline:

```
>>> Entry.objects.order_by('headline')[0]
```

This is roughly equivalent to the following:

```
>>> Entry.objects.order_by('headline')[0:1].get()
```

Note, however, that the first of these will raise IndexError while the second will raise DoesNotExist if no objects match the given criteria.

Query Methods That Return New QuerySets

Django provides a range of QuerySet refinement methods that modify either the types of results returned by the QuerySet or the way its SQL query is executed. These methods are described in the sections that follow. Some of the methods take field-lookup arguments, which are discussed in detail in the "Field Lookups" section a bit later on.

filter(**lookup)

This method returns a new QuerySet containing objects that match the given lookup parameters.

exclude(**lookup)

The exclude(**lookup) method returns a new QuerySet containing objects that do *not* match the given lookup parameters.

order_by(*fields)

By default, results returned by a QuerySet are ordered by the ordering tuple given by the ordering option in the model's metadata (see Appendix A). You can override this for a particular query using the order_by() method:

```
>> Entry.objects.filter(pub_date__year=2005).order_by('-pub_date', 'headline')
```

This result will be ordered by descending pub_date, then by ascending headline. The minus sign in -pub_date indicates *descending* order. Ascending order is assumed if the - is absent. To order randomly, use ?, like so:

```
>>> Entry.objects.order_by('?')
```

Ordering randomly incurs a performance penalty, though, so you shouldn't use it for anything with heavy load.

If no ordering is specified in a model's class Meta and a QuerySet from that model doesn't include order_by(), then ordering will be undefined and may differ from query to query.

distinct()

This returns a new QuerySet that uses SELECT DISTINCT in its SQL query, eliminating duplicate rows from the query results.

By default, a QuerySet will not eliminate duplicate rows. In practice this is rarely a problem, because simple queries such as Blog.objects.all() don't introduce the possibility of duplicate result rows. However, if your query spans multiple tables, it's possible to get duplicate results when a QuerySet is evaluated. That's when you'd use distinct().

values(*fields)

The values(*fields) method returns a special QuerySet that evaluates to a list of dictionaries instead of model-instance objects. Each of those dictionaries represents an object, with the keys corresponding to the attribute names of model objects:

```
# This list contains a Blog object.
>>> Blog.objects.filter(name__startswith='Beatles')
[Beatles Blog]

# This list contains a dictionary.
>>> Blog.objects.filter(name__startswith='Beatles').values()
[{'id': 1, 'name': 'Beatles Blog', 'tagline': 'All the latest Beatles news.'}]
```

values() takes optional positional arguments, *fields, which specify field names to which the SELECT should be limited. If you specify the fields, each dictionary will contain only the field keys/values for the fields you specify. If you don't specify the fields, each dictionary will contain a key and value for every field in the database table:

```
>>> Blog.objects.values()
[{'id': 1, 'name': 'Beatles Blog', 'tagline': 'All the latest Beatles news.'}],
>>> Blog.objects.values('id', 'name')
[{'id': 1, 'name': 'Beatles Blog'}]
```

This method is useful when you know you're going to need values from only a small number of the available fields and you won't need the functionality of a model-instance object. It's more efficient to select only the fields you need to use.

dates(field, kind, order)

This method returns a special QuerySet that evaluates to a list of datetime.datetime objects representing all available dates of a particular kind within the contents of the QuerySet.

The field argument must be the name of a DateField or DateTimeField of your model. The kind argument must be "year", "month", or "day". Each datetime.datetime object in the result list is truncated to the given type:

- "year" returns a list of all distinct year values for the field.
- "month" returns a list of all distinct year/month values for the field.
- "day" returns a list of all distinct year/month/day values for the field.

order, which defaults to 'ASC', should be either 'ASC' or 'DESC'. This specifies how to order the results—ascending or descending. Here are a few examples:

```
>>> Entry.objects.dates('pub_date', 'year')
[datetime.datetime(2005, 1, 1)]

>>> Entry.objects.dates('pub_date', 'month')
[datetime.datetime(2005, 2, 1), datetime.datetime(2005, 3, 1)]
```

```
>>> Entry.objects.dates('pub_date', 'day')
[datetime.datetime(2005, 2, 20), datetime.datetime(2005, 3, 20)]

>>> Entry.objects.dates('pub_date', 'day', order='DESC')
[datetime.datetime(2005, 3, 20), datetime.datetime(2005, 2, 20)]

>>> Entry.objects.filter(headline__contains='Lennon').dates('pub_date', 'day')
[datetime.datetime(2005, 3, 20)]
```

select_related()

The select_related() method returns a QuerySet that will automatically "follow" foreign-key relationships, selecting that additional related-object data when it executes its query. This is a performance booster that results in (sometimes much) larger queries but means later use of foreign-key relationships won't require database queries.

The following examples illustrate the difference between plain lookups and select_related() lookups. Here's a standard lookup:

```
# Hits the database.
>>> e = Entry.objects.get(id=5)

# Hits the database again to get the related Blog object.
>>> b = e.blog
```

And here's a select_related lookup:

```
# Hits the database.
>>> e = Entry.objects.select_related().get(id=5)

# Doesn't hit the database, because e.blog has been prepopulated
# in the previous query.
>>> b = e.blog
```

select_related() follows foreign keys as far as possible. If you have the following models

```
class City(models.Model):
    # ...

class Person(models.Model):
    # ...
    hometown = models.ForeignKey(City)

class Book(models.Model):
    # ...
    author = models.ForeignKey(Person)
```

then a call to Book.objects.select_related().get(id=4) will cache the related Person *and* the related City:

```
>>> b = Book.objects.select_related().get(id=4)
>>> p = b.author          # Doesn't hit the database.
>>> c = p.hometown        # Doesn't hit the database.

>>> b = Book.objects.get(id=4) # No select_related() in this example.
>>> p = b.author          # Hits the database.
>>> c = p.hometown        # Hits the database.
```

Note that select_related() does not follow foreign keys that have null=True.

Usually, using select_related() can vastly improve performance because your application can avoid many database calls. However, in situations with deeply nested sets of relationships, select_related() can sometimes end up following too many relationships and can generate queries so large that they end up being slow.

QuerySet Methods That Do Not Return QuerySets

The following QuerySet methods evaluate the QuerySet and return something *other than* a QuerySet—a single object, a value, and so forth.

get(**lookup)

This returns the object matching the given lookup parameters, which should be in the format described in the "Field Lookups" section. This raises AssertionError if more than one object is found.

get() raises a DoesNotExist exception if an object isn't found for the given parameters. The DoesNotExist exception is an attribute of the model class. Consider this example:

```
>>> Entry.objects.get(id='foo') # raises Entry.DoesNotExist
```

The DoesNotExist exception inherits from django.core.exceptions.ObjectDoesNotExist, so you can target multiple DoesNotExist exceptions:

```
>>> from django.core.exceptions import ObjectDoesNotExist
>>> try:
...     e = Entry.objects.get(id=3)
...     b = Blog.objects.get(id=1)
... except ObjectDoesNotExist:
...     print "Either the entry or blog doesn't exist."
```

create(**kwargs)

This is a convenience method for creating an object and saving it all in one step. It lets you compress two common steps

```
>>> p = Person(first_name="Bruce", last_name="Springsteen")
>>> p.save()
```

into a single line:

```
>>> p = Person.objects.create(first_name="Bruce", last_name="Springsteen")
```

get_or_create(**kwargs)

This is a convenience method for looking up an object and creating one if it doesn't exist. It returns a tuple of (object, created), where object is the retrieved or created object and created is a Boolean specifying whether a new object was created.

This method is meant as a shortcut to boilerplate code and is mostly useful for data-import scripts. Here's an example:

```
try:
    obj = Person.objects.get(first_name='John', last_name='Lennon')
except Person.DoesNotExist:
    obj = Person(first_name='John', last_name='Lennon', birthday=date(1940, 10, 9))
    obj.save()
```

This pattern gets quite unwieldy as the number of fields in a model increases. The previous example can be rewritten using get_or_create() like so:

```
obj, created = Person.objects.get_or_create(
    first_name = 'John',
    last_name  = 'Lennon',
    defaults   = {'birthday': date(1940, 10, 9)}
)
```

Any keyword arguments passed to get_or_create()—*except* an optional one called defaults—will be used in a get() call. If an object is found, get_or_create() returns a tuple of that object and False. If an object is *not* found, get_or_create() will instantiate and save a new object, returning a tuple of the new object and True. The new object will be created according to this algorithm:

```
defaults = kwargs.pop('defaults', {})
params = dict([(k, v) for k, v in kwargs.items() if '__' not in k])
params.update(defaults)
obj = self.model(**params)
obj.save()
```

In English, that means you should start with any non-'defaults' keyword argument that doesn't contain a double underscore (which would indicate an inexact lookup). Then add the contents of defaults, overriding any keys if necessary, and use the result as the keyword arguments to the model class.

If you have a field named defaults and want to use it as an exact lookup in get_or_create(), just use 'defaults__exact' like so:

```
Foo.objects.get_or_create(
    defaults__exact = 'bar',
    defaults={'defaults': 'bar'}
)
```

■Note As mentioned earlier, `get_or_create()` is mostly useful in scripts that need to parse data and create new records if existing ones aren't available. But if you need to use `get_or_create()` in a view, please make sure to use it only in POST requests unless you have a good reason not to. GET requests shouldn't have any effect on data; use POST whenever a request to a page has a side effect on your data.

---

count()

`count()` returns an integer representing the number of objects in the database matching the QuerySet. `count()` never raises exceptions. Here's an example:

```
# Returns the total number of entries in the database.
>>> Entry.objects.count()
4

# Returns the number of entries whose headline contains 'Lennon'
>>> Entry.objects.filter(headline__contains='Lennon').count()
1
```

`count()` performs a `SELECT COUNT(*)` behind the scenes, so you should always use `count()` rather than loading all of the records into Python objects and calling `len()` on the result.

Depending on which database you're using (e.g., PostgreSQL or MySQL), `count()` may return a long integer instead of a normal Python integer. This is an underlying implementation quirk that shouldn't pose any real-world problems.

in_bulk(id_list)

This method takes a list of primary-key values and returns a dictionary mapping each primary-key value to an instance of the object with the given ID, as in this example:

```
>>> Blog.objects.in_bulk([1])
{1: Beatles Blog}
>>> Blog.objects.in_bulk([1, 2])
{1: Beatles Blog, 2: Cheddar Talk}
>>> Blog.objects.in_bulk([])
{}
```

IDs of objects that don't exist are silently dropped from the result dictionary. If you pass `in_bulk()` an empty list, you'll get an empty dictionary.

latest(field_name=None)

This returns the latest object in the table, by date, using the `field_name` provided as the date field. This example returns the latest `Entry` in the table, according to the `pub_date` field:

```
>>> Entry.objects.latest('pub_date')
```

If your model's `Meta` specifies get_latest_by, you can leave off the field_name argument to latest(). Django will use the field specified in get_latest_by by default.

Like `get()`, `latest()` raises `DoesNotExist` if an object doesn't exist with the given parameters.

Field Lookups

Field lookups are how you specify the meat of an SQL `WHERE` clause. They're specified as keyword arguments to the `QuerySet` methods `filter()`, `exclude()`, and `get()`.

Basic lookup keyword arguments take the form field__lookuptype=value (note the double underscore). This example

```
>>> Entry.objects.filter(pub_date__lte='2006-01-01')
```

translates (roughly) into the following SQL:

```
SELECT * FROM blog_entry WHERE pub_date <= '2006-01-01';
```

If you pass an invalid keyword argument, a lookup function will raise `TypeError`.
The supported lookup types follow.

exact

exact performs an exact match:

```
>>> Entry.objects.get(headline__exact="Man bites dog")
```

This matches any object with the exact headline *"Man bites dog"*.

If you don't provide a lookup type—that is, if your keyword argument doesn't contain a double underscore—the lookup type is assumed to be exact. For example, the following two statements are equivalent:

```
>>> Blog.objects.get(id__exact=14) # Explicit form
>>> Blog.objects.get(id=14) # __exact is implied
```

This is for convenience, because exact lookups are the common case.

iexact

This method performs a case-insensitive exact match:

```
>>> Blog.objects.get(name__iexact='beatles blog')
```

This will match 'Beatles Blog', 'beatles blog', 'BeAtLes BLoG', and so forth.

contains

This method performs a case-sensitive containment test:

```
Entry.objects.get(headline__contains='Lennon')
```

This will match the headline 'Today Lennon honored' but not 'today lennon honored'.
SQLite doesn't support case-sensitive `LIKE` statements; when using SQLite, contains acts like icontains.

ESCAPING PERCENT SIGNS AND UNDERSCORES IN LIKE STATEMENTS

The field lookups that equate to `LIKE` SQL statements (`iexact`, `contains`, `icontains`, `startswith`, `istartswith`, `endswith`, and `iendswith`) will automatically escape the two special characters used in `LIKE` statements—the percent sign and the underscore. (In a `LIKE` statement, the percent sign signifies a multiple-character wildcard and the underscore signifies a single-character wildcard.)

This means things should work intuitively, so the abstraction doesn't leak. For example, to retrieve all the entries that contain a percent sign, just use the percent sign as any other character:

```
Entry.objects.filter(headline__contains='%')
```

Django takes care of the quoting for you. The resulting SQL will look something like this:

```
SELECT ... WHERE headline LIKE '%\%%';
```

The same goes for underscores. Both percent signs and underscores are handled for you transparently.

icontains

This performs a case-insensitive containment test:

```
>>> Entry.objects.get(headline__icontains='Lennon')
```

Unlike `contains`, `icontains` *will* match `'today lennon honored'`.

gt, gte, lt, and lte

These represent greater than, greater than or equal to, less than, and less than or equal to:

```
>>> Entry.objects.filter(id__gt=4)
>>> Entry.objects.filter(id__lt=15)
>>> Entry.objects.filter(id__lte=3)
>>> Entry.objects.filter(id__gte=0)
```

These queries return any object with an ID greater than 4, an ID less than 15, and an ID greater than or equal to 1, respectively.

You'll usually use these on numeric fields. Be careful with character fields since character order isn't always what you'd expect (i.e., the string "4" sorts *after* the string "10").

in

The `in` method filters where a value is on a given list:

```
Entry.objects.filter(id__in=[1, 3, 4])
```

This returns all objects with the ID 1, 3, or 4.

startswith

startswith performs a case-sensitive search based on the starting characters:

```
>>> Entry.objects.filter(headline__startswith='Will')
```

This will return the headlines "Will he run?" and "Willbur named judge," but not "Who is Will?" or "will found in crypt."

istartswith

This method performs a case-insensitive search based on the starting characters:

```
>>> Entry.objects.filter(headline__istartswith='will')
```

This will return the headlines "Will he run?" "Willbur named judge," and "will found in crypt," but not "Who is Will?"

endswith and iendswith

These methods perform case-sensitive and case-insensitive, respectively, searches based on the ending characters, similar to startswith and istartswith:

```
>>> Entry.objects.filter(headline__endswith='cats')
>>> Entry.objects.filter(headline__iendswith='cats')
```

range

range performs an inclusive range check:

```
>>> start_date = datetime.date(2005, 1, 1)
>>> end_date = datetime.date(2005, 3, 31)
>>> Entry.objects.filter(pub_date__range=(start_date, end_date))
```

You can use range anywhere you can use BETWEEN in SQL—for dates, numbers, and even characters.

year, month, and day

For date/datetime fields, these methods perform exact year, month, or day matches:

```
# Return all entries published in 2005
>>>Entry.objects.filter(pub_date__year=2005)

# Return all entries published in December
>>> Entry.objects.filter(pub_date__month=12)

# Return all entries published on the 3rd of the month
>>> Entry.objects.filter(pub_date__day=3)

# Combination: return all entries on Christmas of any year
>>> Entry.objects.filter(pub_date__month=12, pub_date_day=25)
```

isnull

This method takes either `True` or `False`, which correspond to SQL queries of `IS NULL` and `IS NOT NULL`, respectively:

```
>>> Entry.objects.filter(pub_date__isnull=True)
```

search

`search` is a Boolean full-text search that takes advantage of full-text indexing. This is like `contains` but is significantly faster due to full-text indexing.

   Note this is available only in MySQL and requires direct manipulation of the database to add the full-text index.

The pk Lookup Shortcut

For convenience, Django provides a `pk` lookup type, which stands for "primary_key."

   In the example `Blog` model, the primary key is the `id` field, so these three statements are equivalent:

```
>>> Blog.objects.get(id__exact=14) # Explicit form
>>> Blog.objects.get(id=14) # __exact is implied
>>> Blog.objects.get(pk=14) # pk implies id__exact
```

   The use of `pk` isn't limited to `__exact` queries—any query term can be combined with `pk` to perform a query on a model's primary key:

```
# Get blogs entries  with id 1, 4, and 7
>>> Blog.objects.filter(pk__in=[1,4,7])

# Get all blog entries with id > 14
>>> Blog.objects.filter(pk__gt=14)
```

   `pk` lookups also work across joins. For example, these three statements are equivalent:

```
>>> Entry.objects.filter(blog__id__exact=3) # Explicit form
>>> Entry.objects.filter(blog__id=3) # __exact is implied
>>> Entry.objects.filter(blog__pk=3) # __pk implies __id__exact
```

   The point of `pk` is to give you a generic way to refer to the primary key when you're not sure whether the model's primary key is called `id`.

Complex Lookups with Q Objects

Keyword argument queries—in `filter()` and so on—are ANDed together. If you need to execute more-complex queries (e.g., queries with OR statements), you can use Q objects.

   A Q object (`django.db.models.Q`) is an object used to encapsulate a collection of keyword arguments. These keyword arguments are specified as explained in the "Field Lookups" section.

For example, this Q object encapsulates a single LIKE query:

```
Q(question__startswith='What')
```

Q objects can be combined using the & and | operators. When an operator is used on two Q objects, it yields a new Q object. For example, this statement yields a single Q object that represents the OR of two "question__startswith" queries:

```
Q(question__startswith='Who') | Q(question__startswith='What')
```

This is equivalent to the following SQL WHERE clause:

```
WHERE question LIKE 'Who%' OR question LIKE 'What%'
```

You can compose statements of arbitrary complexity by combining Q objects with the & and | operators. You can also use parenthetical grouping.

Each lookup function that takes keyword arguments (e.g., filter(), exclude(), get()) can also be passed one or more Q objects as positional (not-named) arguments. If you provide multiple Q object arguments to a lookup function, the arguments will be ANDed together, as in this example:

```
Poll.objects.get(
    Q(question__startswith='Who'),
    Q(pub_date=date(2005, 5, 2)) | Q(pub_date=date(2005, 5, 6))
)
```

This roughly translates into the following SQL:

```
SELECT * from polls WHERE question LIKE 'Who%'
    AND (pub_date = '2005-05-02' OR pub_date = '2005-05-06')
```

Lookup functions can mix the use of Q objects and keyword arguments. All arguments provided to a lookup function (be they keyword arguments or Q objects) are ANDed together. However, if a Q object is provided, it must precede the definition of any keyword arguments. For example, the following

```
Poll.objects.get(
    Q(pub_date=date(2005, 5, 2)) | Q(pub_date=date(2005, 5, 6)),
    question__startswith='Who')
```

would be a valid query, equivalent to the previous example, but this would not be valid:

```
# INVALID QUERY
Poll.objects.get(
    question__startswith='Who',
    Q(pub_date=date(2005, 5, 2)) | Q(pub_date=date(2005, 5, 6)))
```

You can find some examples online at http://www.djangoproject.com/documentation/models/or_lookups/.

Related Objects

When you define a relationship in a model (i.e., a ForeignKey, OneToOneField, or ManyToManyField), instances of that model will have a convenient API to access the related object(s).

For example, an Entry object e can get its associated Blog object by accessing the blog attribute e.blog.

Django also creates API accessors for the "other" side of the relationship—the link from the related model to the model that defines the relationship. For example, a Blog object b has access to a list of all related Entry objects via the entry_set attribute: b.entry_set.all().

All examples in this section use the sample Blog, Author, and Entry models defined at the start of this appendix.

Lookups That Span Relationships

Django offers a powerful and intuitive way to "follow" relationships in lookups, taking care of the SQL JOINs for you automatically behind the scenes. To span a relationship, just use the field name of related fields across models, separated by double underscores, until you get to the field you want.

This example retrieves all Entry objects with a Blog whose name is 'Beatles Blog':

```
>>> Entry.objects.filter(blog__name__exact='Beatles Blog')
```

This spanning can be as deep as you'd like.

It works backward, too. To refer to a "reverse" relationship (see the section "'Reverse' Foreign-Key Relationships"), just use the lowercase name of the model.

This example retrieves all Blog objects that have at least one Entry whose headline contains 'Lennon':

```
>>> Blog.objects.filter(entry__headline__contains='Lennon')
```

Foreign-Key Relationships

If a model has a ForeignKey, instances of that model will have access to the related (foreign) object via a simple attribute of the model, as in this example:

```
e = Entry.objects.get(id=2)
e.blog # Returns the related Blog object.
```

You can get and set foreign-key values via a foreign-key attribute. As you may expect, changes to the foreign key aren't saved to the database until you call save(), as in this example:

```
e = Entry.objects.get(id=2)
e.blog = some_blog
e.save()
```

If a ForeignKey field has null=True set (i.e., it allows NULL values), you can set it to NULL by assigning None to it and saving:

```
e = Entry.objects.get(id=2)
e.blog = None
e.save() # "UPDATE blog_entry SET blog_id = NULL ...;"
```

Forward access to one-to-many relationships is cached the first time the related object is accessed. Subsequent accesses to the foreign key on the same object instance are cached, as in this example:

```
e = Entry.objects.get(id=2)
print e.blog  # Hits the database to retrieve the associated Blog.
print e.blog  # Doesn't hit the database; uses cached version.
```

Note that the select_related() QuerySet method recursively prepopulates the cache of all one-to-many relationships:

```
e = Entry.objects.select_related().get(id=2)
print e.blog  # Doesn't hit the database; uses cached version.
print e.blog  # Doesn't hit the database; uses cached version.
```

select_related() is documented in the "select_related()" section earlier in this appendix.

"Reverse" Foreign-Key Relationships

Foreign-key relationships are automatically symmetrical—a reverse relationship is inferred from the presence of a ForeignKey pointing to another model.

If a model has a ForeignKey, instances of the foreign-key model will have access to a Manager that returns all instances of the first model that relate to that object. By default, this Manager is named FOO_set, where FOO is the source model name, lowercased. This Manager returns QuerySets, which can be filtered and manipulated as described in the "Retrieving Objects" section earlier in this appendix.

Here's an example:

```
b = Blog.objects.get(id=1)
b.entry_set.all() # Returns all Entry objects related to Blog.

# b.entry_set is a Manager that returns QuerySets.
b.entry_set.filter(headline__contains='Lennon')
b.entry_set.count()
```

You can override the FOO_set name by setting the related_name parameter in the ForeignKey() definition. For example, if the Entry model was altered to blog = ForeignKey(Blog, related_name='entries'), the preceding example code would look like this:

```
b = Blog.objects.get(id=1)
b.entries.all() # Returns all Entry objects related to Blog.

# b.entries is a Manager that returns QuerySets.
b.entries.filter(headline__contains='Lennon')
b.entries.count()
```

related_name is particularly useful if a first model has two foreign keys to the same second model.

You cannot access a reverse ForeignKey Manager from the class; it must be accessed from an instance:

```
Blog.entry_set # Raises AttributeError: "Manager must be accessed via instance".
```

In addition to the QuerySet methods defined in the earlier "Retrieving Objects" section, the ForeignKey Manager has these methods:

- add(obj1, obj2, ...): Adds the specified model objects to the related object set, for example

```
b = Blog.objects.get(id=1)
e = Entry.objects.get(id=234)
b.entry_set.add(e) # Associates Entry e with Blog b.
```

- create(**kwargs): Creates a new object, saves it, and puts it in the related object set. It returns the newly created object:

```
b = Blog.objects.get(id=1)
e = b.entry_set.create(headline='Hello', body_text='Hi',
        pub_date=datetime.date(2005, 1, 1))
# No need to call e.save() at this point—it's already been saved.
```

This is equivalent to (but much simpler than) the following:

```
b = Blog.objects.get(id=1)
e = Entry(blog=b, headline='Hello', body_text='Hi',
        pub_date=datetime.date(2005, 1, 1))
e.save()
```

Note that there's no need to specify the keyword argument of the model that defines the relationship. In the preceding example, we don't pass the parameter blog to create(). Django figures out that the new Entry object's blog field should be set to b.

- remove(obj1, obj2, ...): Removes the specified model objects from the related object set:

```
b = Blog.objects.get(id=1)
e = Entry.objects.get(id=234)
b.entry_set.remove(e) # Disassociates Entry e from Blog b.
```

To prevent database inconsistency, this method exists only on ForeignKey objects where null=True. If the related field can't be set to None (NULL), then an object can't be removed from a relation without being added to another. In the preceding example, removing e from b.entry_set() is equivalent to doing e.blog = None, and because the blog ForeignKey doesn't have null=True, this is invalid.

- clear(): Removes all objects from the related object set:

```
b = Blog.objects.get(id=1)
b.entry_set.clear()
```

Note that this doesn't delete the related objects—it just disassociates them.

Just like remove(), clear() is available only on ForeignKeys where null=True.

To assign the members of a related set in one fell swoop, just assign to it from any iterable object, as in this example:

```
b = Blog.objects.get(id=1)
b.entry_set = [e1, e2]
```

If the clear() method is available, any pre-existing objects will be removed from the entry_set before all objects in the iterable (in this case, a list) are added to the set. If the clear() method is *not* available, all objects in the iterable will be added without removing any existing elements.

Each "reverse" operation described in this section has an immediate effect on the database. Every addition, creation, and deletion is immediately and automatically saved to the database.

Many-to-Many Relationships

Both ends of a many-to-many relationship get automatic API access to the other end. The API works just as a "reverse" one-to-many relationship (described in the previous section). The only difference is in the attribute naming: the model that defines the ManyToManyField uses the attribute name of that field itself, whereas the "reverse" model uses the lowercased model name of the original model, plus '_set' (just like reverse one-to-many relationships).

An example makes this concept easier to understand:

```
e = Entry.objects.get(id=3)
e.authors.all() # Returns all Author objects for this Entry.
e.authors.count()
e.authors.filter(name__contains='John')

a = Author.objects.get(id=5)
a.entry_set.all() # Returns all Entry objects for this Author.
```

Like `ForeignKey`, `ManyToManyField` can specify `related_name`. In the preceding example, if the `ManyToManyField` in `Entry` had specified `related_name='entries'`, then each `Author` instance would have an `entries` attribute instead of `entry_set`.

HOW ARE THE REVERSE RELATIONSHIPS POSSIBLE?

Some object-relational mappers require you to define relationships on both sides. The Django developers believe this is a violation of the DRY (Don't Repeat Yourself) principle, so Django requires you to define the relationship on only one end. But how is this possible, given that a model class doesn't know which other model classes are related to it until those other model classes are loaded?

The answer lies in the `INSTALLED_APPS` setting. The first time any model is loaded, Django iterates over every model in `INSTALLED_APPS` and creates the reverse relationships in memory as needed. Essentially, one of the functions of `INSTALLED_APPS` is to tell Django the entire model domain.

Queries over Related Objects

Queries involving related objects follow the same rules as queries involving normal value fields. When specifying the value for a query to match, you may use either an object instance itself or the primary-key value for the object.

For example, if you have a `Blog` object `b` with `id=5`, the following three queries would be identical:

```
Entry.objects.filter(blog=b) # Query using object instance
Entry.objects.filter(blog=b.id) # Query using id from instance
Entry.objects.filter(blog=5) # Query using id directly
```

Deleting Objects

The deletion method, conveniently, is named `delete()`. This method immediately deletes the object and has no return value:

```
e.delete()
```

You can also delete objects in bulk. Every `QuerySet` has a `delete()` method, which deletes all members of that `QuerySet`. For example, this deletes all `Entry` objects with a `pub_date` year of 2005:

```
Entry.objects.filter(pub_date__year=2005).delete()
```

When Django deletes an object, it emulates the behavior of the SQL constraint `ON DELETE CASCADE`—in other words, any objects that had foreign keys pointing at the object to be deleted will be deleted along with it. Here's an example:

```
b = Blog.objects.get(pk=1)
# This will delete the Blog and all of its Entry objects.
b.delete()
```

Note that delete() is the only QuerySet method that is not exposed on a Manager itself. This is a safety mechanism to prevent you from accidentally requesting Entry.objects. delete() and deleting *all* the entries. If you *do* want to delete all the objects, then you have to explicitly request a complete query set:

```
Entry.objects.all().delete()
```

Shortcuts

As you develop views, you will discover a number of common idioms in the way you use the database API. Django encodes some of these idioms as shortcuts that can be used to simplify the process of writing views. These functions are in the django.shortcuts module.

get_object_or_404()

One common idiom is to use get() and raise Http404 if the object doesn't exist. This idiom is captured by get_object_or_404(). This function takes a Django model as its first argument and an arbitrary number of keyword arguments, which it passes to the default manager's get() function. It raises Http404 if the object doesn't exist. Consider this example:

```
# Get the Entry with a primary key of 3
e = get_object_or_404(Entry, pk=3)
```

When you provide a model to this shortcut function, the default manager is used to execute the underlying get() query. If you don't want to use the default manager or if you want to search a list of related objects, you can provide get_object_or_404() with a Manager object instead:

```
# Get the author of blog instance e with a name of 'Fred'
a = get_object_or_404(e.authors, name='Fred')

# Use a custom manager 'recent_entries' in the search for an
# entry with a primary key of 3
e = get_object_or_404(Entry.recent_entries, pk=3)
```

get_list_or_404()

get_list_or_404 behaves the same way as get_object_or_404(), except that it uses filter() instead of get(). It raises Http404 if the list is empty.

Falling Back to Raw SQL

If you find yourself needing to write an SQL query that is too complex for Django's database mapper to handle, you can fall back into raw SQL-statement mode.

The preferred way to do this is by giving your model custom methods or custom manager methods that execute queries. Although there's nothing in Django that *requires* database queries to live in the model layer, this approach keeps all your data-access logic in one place, which is smart from a code-organization standpoint. For instructions, see Appendix A.

Finally, it's important to note that the Django database layer is merely an interface to your database. You can access your database via other tools, programming languages, or database frameworks—there's nothing Django-specific about your database.

■■■

Generic View Reference

Chapter 11 introduced generic views but leaves out some of the gory details. This appendix describes each generic view along with all the options each view can take. Be sure to read Chapter 11 before trying to understand the reference material that follows. You might want to refer to the Book, Publisher, and Author objects defined in that chapter; the examples that follow use these models.

Common Arguments to Generic Views

Most of these views take a large number of arguments that can change the generic view's behavior. Many of these arguments work the same across a large number of views. Table C-1 describes each of these common arguments; any time you see one of these arguments in a generic view's argument list, it will work as described in the table.

Table C-1. *Common Arguments to Generic Views*

Argument	Description
allow_empty	A Boolean specifying whether to display the page if no objects are available. If this is False and no objects are available, the view will raise a 404 error instead of displaying an empty page. By default, this is True.
context_processors	A list of additional template-context processors (besides the defaults) to apply to the view's template. See Chapter 9 for information on template context processors.
extra_context	A dictionary of values to add to the template context. By default, this is an empty dictionary. If a value in the dictionary is callable, the generic view will call it just before rendering the template.
mimetype	The MIME type to use for the resulting document. It defaults to the value of the DEFAULT_MIME_TYPE setting, which is text/html if you haven't changed it.
queryset	A QuerySet (i.e., something like Author.objects.all()) to read objects from. See Appendix B for more information about QuerySet objects. Most generic views require this argument.

Continued

Table C-1. *Continued*

Argument	Description
template_loader	The template loader to use when loading the template. By default, it's `django.template.loader`. See Chapter 9 for information on template loaders.
template_name	The full name of a template to use in rendering the page. This lets you override the default template name derived from the QuerySet.
template_object_name	The name of the template variable to use in the template context. By default, this is `'object'`. Views that list more than one object (i.e., object_list views and various objects-for-date views) will append `'_list'` to the value of this parameter.

"Simple" Generic Views

The module `django.views.generic.simple` contains simple views that handle a couple of common cases: rendering a template when no view logic is needed and issuing a redirect.

Rendering a Template

View function: `django.views.generic.simple.direct_to_template`

This view renders a given template, passing it a `{{ params }}` template variable, which is a dictionary of the parameters captured in the URL.

Example

Given the following URLconf, a request to /foo/ would render the template foo_index.html, and a request to /foo/15/ would render foo_detail.html with a context variable `{{ params.id }}` that is set to 15:

```
from django.conf.urls.defaults import *
from django.views.generic.simple import direct_to_template

urlpatterns = patterns('',
    (r'^foo/$',              direct_to_template, {'template': 'foo_index.html'}),
    (r'^foo/(?P<id>\d+)/$', direct_to_template, {'template': 'foo_detail.html'}),
)
```

Required Arguments

- `template`: The full name of a template to use.

Redirecting to Another URL

View function: `django.views.generic.simple.redirect_to`

This view redirects to another URL. The given URL may contain dictionary-style string formatting, which will be interpolated against the parameters captured in the URL.

If the given URL is None, Django will return an HTTP 410 ("Gone") message.

Example

This URLconf redirects from /foo/<id>/ to /bar/<id>/:

```
from django.conf.urls.defaults import *
from django.views.generic.simple import redirect_to

urlpatterns = patterns('django.views.generic.simple',
    ('^foo/(?p<id>\d+)/$', redirect_to, {'url': '/bar/%(id)s/'}),
)
```

This example returns a "Gone" response for requests to /bar/:

```
from django.views.generic.simple import redirect_to

urlpatterns = patterns('django.views.generic.simple',
    ('^bar/$', redirect_to, {'url': None}),
)
```

Required Arguments

- url: The URL to redirect to, as a string. Or None to return a 410 ("Gone") HTTP response.

List/Detail Generic Views

The list/detail generic views (in the module `django.views.generic.list_detail`) handle the common case of displaying a list of items at one view and individual "detail" views of those items at another.

Lists of Objects

View function: `django.views.generic.list_detail.object_list`

Use this view to display a page representing a list of objects.

Example

Given the Author object from Chapter 5, we can use the object_list view to show a simple list of all authors, given the following URLconf snippet:

```
from mysite.books.models import Author
from django.conf.urls.defaults import *
from django.views.generic import list_detail
```

```
author_list_info = {
    'queryset':  Author.objects.all(),
}

urlpatterns = patterns('',
    (r'authors/$', list_detail.object_list, author_list_info)
)
```

Required Arguments

- queryset: A QuerySet of objects to list (refer to Table C-1).

Optional Arguments

- paginate_by: An integer specifying how many objects should be displayed per page. If this is given, the view will paginate objects with paginate_by objects per page. The view will expect either a page query string parameter (via GET) containing a zero-indexed page number or a page variable specified in the URLconf. (See the following "A Note on Pagination" sidebar.)

Additionally, this view may take any of these common arguments (described in Table C-1):

- allow_empty
- context_processors
- extra_context
- mimetype
- template_loader
- template_name
- template_object_name

Template Name

If template_name isn't specified, this view will use the template <app_label>/<model_name>_list.html by default. Both the application label and the model name are derived from the queryset parameter. The application label is the name of the application that the model is defined in, and the model name is the lowercased version of the name of the model class.

In the previous example using Author.objects.all() as the queryset, the application label would be books and the model name would be author. This means the default template would be books/author_list.html.

Template Context

In addition to extra_context, the template's context will contain the following:

- object_list: The list of objects. This variable's name depends on the template_object_name parameter, which is 'object' by default. If template_object_name is 'foo', this variable's name will be foo_list.

- is_paginated: A Boolean representing whether the results are paginated. Specifically, this is set to False if the number of available objects is less than or equal to paginate_by.

If the results are paginated, the context will contain these extra variables:

- results_per_page: The number of objects per page (this is the same as the paginate_by parameter).

- has_next: A Boolean representing whether there's a next page.

- has_previous: A Boolean representing whether there's a previous page.

- page: The current page number as an integer. This is 1-based.

- next: The next page number, as an integer. If there's no next page, this will still be an integer representing the theoretical next-page number. This is 1-based.

- previous: The previous page number, as an integer. This is 1-based.

- pages: The total number of pages, as an integer.

- hits: The total number of objects across *all* pages, not just this page.

A NOTE ON PAGINATION

If paginate_by is specified, Django will paginate the results. You can specify the page number in the URL in one of two ways:

- Use the page parameter in the URLconf. For example, this is what your URLconf might look like:

```
(r'^objects/page(?P<page>[0-9]+)/$', 'object_list', dict(info_dict))
```

- Pass the page number via the page query-string parameter. For example, a URL would look like this:

```
/objects/?page=3
```

In both cases, page is 1-based, not 0-based, so the first page would be represented as page 1.

Detail Views

View function: `django.views.generic.list_detail.object_detail`
This view provides a "detail" view of a single object.

Example

Continuing the previous `object_list` example, we could add a detail view for a given author by modifying the URLconf:

```
from mysite.books.models import Author
from django.conf.urls.defaults import *
from django.views.generic import list_detail

author_list_info = {
    'queryset' :    Author.objects.all(),
}
author_detail_info = {
    "queryset" : Author.objects.all(),
    "template_object_name" : "author",
}

urlpatterns = patterns('',
    (r'authors/$', list_detail.object_list, author_list_info),
    (r'^authors/(?P<object_id>d+)/$', list_detail.object_detail,
        author_detail_info),
)
```

Required Arguments

- queryset: A QuerySet that will be searched for the object (refer to Table C-1).

You'll also need either:

- object_id: The value of the primary-key field for the object.

or

- slug: The slug of the given object. If you pass this field, the slug_field argument (see the following section) is also required.

Optional Arguments

- slug_field: The name of the field on the object containing the slug. This is required if you are using the slug argument, but it must be absent if you're using the object_id argument.
- template_name_field: The name of a field on the object whose value is the template name to use. This lets you store template names in your data.

In other words, if your object has a field 'the_template' that contains a string 'foo.html', and you set template_name_field to 'the_template', the generic view for this object will use the template 'foo.html'.

If the template named by template_name_field doesn't exist, the one named by template_name is used instead. It's a bit of a brain-bender, but it's useful in some cases.

This view may also take these common arguments (refer to Table C-1):

- context_processors
- extra_context
- mimetype
- template_loader
- template_name
- template_object_name

Template Name

If template_name and template_name_field aren't specified, this view will use the template `<app_label>/<model_name>_detail.html` by default.

Template Context

In addition to extra_context, the template's context will be as follows:

- object: The object. This variable's name depends on the template_object_name parameter, which is 'object' by default. If template_object_name is 'foo', this variable's name will be foo.

Date-Based Generic Views

Date-based generic views are generally used to provide a set of "archive" pages for dated material. Think year/month/day archives for a newspaper, or a typical blog archive.

Tip By default, these views ignore objects with dates in the future. This means that if you try to visit an archive page in the future, Django will automatically show a 404 ("Page not found") error, even if there are objects published that day. Thus, you can publish postdated objects that don't appear publicly until their desired publication date. However, for different types of date-based objects, this isn't appropriate (e.g., a calendar of upcoming events). For these views, setting the allow_future option to True will make the future objects appear (and allow users to visit "future" archive pages).

Archive Index

View function: django.views.generic.date_based.archive_index

This view provides a top-level index page showing the "latest" (i.e., most recent) objects by date.

Example

Say a typical book publisher wants a page of recently published books. Given some Book object with a publication_date field, we can use the archive_index view for this common task:

```
from mysite.books.models import Book
from django.conf.urls.defaults import *
from django.views.generic import date_based

book_info = {
    "queryset"   : Book.objects.all(),
    "date_field" : "publication_date"
}

urlpatterns = patterns('',
    (r'^books/$', date_based.archive_index, book_info),
)
```

Required Arguments

- date_field: The name of the DateField or DateTimeField in the QuerySet's model that the date-based archive should use to determine the objects on the page.

- queryset: A QuerySet of objects for which the archive serves.

Optional Arguments

- allow_future: A Boolean specifying whether to include "future" objects on this page, as described in the previous note.

- num_latest: The number of latest objects to send to the template context. By default, it's 15.

This view may also take these common arguments (refer to Table C-1):

- allow_empty

- context_processors

- extra_context

- mimetype

- template_loader

- template_name

Template Name

If `template_name` isn't specified, this view will use the template `<app_label>/<model_name>_archive.html` by default.

Template Context

In addition to `extra_context`, the template's context will be as follows:

- `date_list`: A list of `datetime.date` objects representing all years that have objects available according to `queryset`. These are ordered in reverse.

  For example, if you have blog entries from 2003 through 2006, this list will contain four `datetime.date` objects: one for each of those years.

- `latest`: The `num_latest` objects in the system, in descending order by `date_field`. For example, if `num_latest` is 10, then `latest` will be a list of the latest 10 objects in `queryset`.

Year Archives

View function: `django.views.generic.date_based.archive_year`

Use this view for yearly archive pages. These pages have a list of months in which objects exist and they can optionally display all the objects published in a given year.

Example

Extending the `archive_index` example from earlier, we'll add a way to view all the books published in a given year:

```
from mysite.books.models import Book
from django.conf.urls.defaults import *
from django.views.generic import date_based

book_info = {
    "queryset"   : Book.objects.all(),
    "date_field" : "publication_date"
}

urlpatterns = patterns('',
    (r'^books/$', date_based.archive_index, book_info),
    (r'^books/(?P<year>\d{4})/?$', date_based.archive_year, book_info),
)
```

Required Arguments

- `date_field`: As for `archive_index` (refer to the previous section).
- `queryset`: A QuerySet of objects for which the archive serves.
- `year`: The four-digit year for which the archive serves (as in our example, this is usually taken from a URL parameter).

Optional Arguments

- `make_object_list`: A Boolean specifying whether to retrieve the full list of objects for this year and pass those to the template. If `True`, this list of objects will be made available to the template as `object_list`. (The name `object_list` may be different; see the information about `object_list` in the following "Template Context" section.) By default, this is `False`.

- `allow_future`: A Boolean specifying whether to include "future" objects on this page.

This view may also take these common arguments (refer to Table C-1):

- `allow_empty`
- `context_processors`
- `extra_context`
- `mimetype`
- `template_loader`
- `template_name`
- `template_object_name`

Template Name

If `template_name` isn't specified, this view will use the template `<app_label>/<model_name>_archive_year.html` by default.

Template Context

In addition to `extra_context`, the template's context will be as follows:

- `date_list`: A list of `datetime.date` objects representing all months that have objects available in the given year, according to `queryset`, in ascending order.

- `year`: The given year, as a four-character string.

- `object_list`: If the `make_object_list` parameter is `True`, this will be set to a list of objects available for the given year, ordered by the date field. This variable's name depends on the `template_object_name` parameter, which is `'object'` by default. If `template_object_name` is `'foo'`, this variable's name will be `foo_list`.

  If `make_object_list` is `False`, `object_list` will be passed to the template as an empty list.

Month Archives

View function: `django.views.generic.date_based.archive_month`
This view provides monthly archive pages showing all objects for a given month.

Example

Continuing with our example, adding month views should look familiar:

```
urlpatterns = patterns('',
    (r'^books/$', date_based.archive_index, book_info),
    (r'^books/(?P<year>d{4})/?$', date_based.archive_year, book_info),
    (
        r'^(?P<year>d{4})/(?P<month>[a-z]{3})/$',
        date_based.archive_month,
        book_info
    ),
)
```

Required Arguments

- year: The four-digit year for which the archive serves (a string).

- month: The month for which the archive serves, formatted according to the month_ format argument.

- queryset: A QuerySet of objects for which the archive serves.

- date_field: The name of the DateField or DateTimeField in the QuerySet's model that the date-based archive should use to determine the objects on the page.

Optional Arguments

- month_format: A format string that regulates what format the month parameter uses. This should be in the syntax accepted by Python's time.strftime. (See Python's strftime documentation at http://docs.python.org/library/time.html#time. strftime.) It's set to "%b" by default, which is a three-letter month abbreviation (i.e., "jan," "feb," etc.). To change it to use numbers, use "%m".

- allow_future: A Boolean specifying whether to include "future" objects on this page, as described in the previous note.

This view may also take these common arguments (refer to Table C-1):

- allow_empty

- context_processors

- extra_context

- mimetype

- template_loader

- template_name

- template_object_name

Template Name

If template_name isn't specified, this view will use the template <app_label>/<model_name>_archive_month.html by default.

Template Context

In addition to extra_context, the template's context will be as follows:

- month: A datetime.date object representing the given month.

- next_month: A datetime.date object representing the first day of the next month. If the next month is in the future, this will be None.

- previous_month: A datetime.date object representing the first day of the previous month. Unlike next_month, this will never be None.

- object_list: A list of objects available for the given month. This variable's name depends on the template_object_name parameter, which is 'object' by default. If template_object_name is 'foo', this variable's name will be foo_list.

Week Archives

View function: django.views.generic.date_based.archive_week
    This view shows all objects in a given week.

■**Note** For the sake of consistency with Python's built-in date/time handling, Django assumes that the first day of the week is Sunday.

Example

```
urlpatterns = patterns('',
    # ...
    (
        r'^(?P<year>d{4})/(?P<week>d{2})/$',
        date_based.archive_week,
        book_info
    ),
)
```

Required Arguments

- `year`: The four-digit year for which the archive serves (a string).
- `week`: The week of the year for which the archive serves (a string).
- `queryset`: A QuerySet of objects for which the archive serves.
- `date_field`: The name of the DateField or DateTimeField in the QuerySet's model that the date-based archive should use to determine the objects on the page.

Optional Arguments

- `allow_future`: A Boolean specifying whether to include "future" objects on this page, as described in the previous note.

This view may also take these common arguments (refer to Table C-1):

- `allow_empty`
- `context_processors`
- `extra_context`
- `mimetype`
- `template_loader`
- `template_name`
- `template_object_name`

Template Name

If `template_name` isn't specified, this view will use the template `<app_label>/<model_name>_archive_week.html` by default.

Template Context

In addition to `extra_context`, the template's context will be as follows:

- `week`: A datetime.date object representing the first day of the given week.
- `object_list`: A list of objects available for the given week. This variable's name depends on the `template_object_name` parameter, which is `'object'` by default. If `template_object_name` is `'foo'`, this variable's name will be `foo_list`.

Day Archives

View function: `django.views.generic.date_based.archive_day`
   This view generates all objects in a given day.

Example

```
urlpatterns = patterns('',
    # ...
    (
        r'^(?P<year>d{4})/(?P<month>[a-z]{3})/(?P<day>d{2})/$',
        date_based.archive_day,
        book_info
    ),
)
```

Required Arguments

- `year`: The four-digit year for which the archive serves (a string).

- `month`: The month for which the archive serves, formatted according to the `month_format` argument.

- `day`: The day for which the archive serves, formatted according to the `day_format` argument.

- `queryset`: A `QuerySet` of objects for which the archive serves.

- `date_field`: The name of the `DateField` or `DateTimeField` in the `QuerySet`'s model that the date-based archive should use to determine the objects on the page.

Optional Arguments

- `month_format`: A format string that regulates what format the `month` parameter uses. See the detailed explanation in the preceding "Month Archives" section.

- `day_format`: Like `month_format`, but for the `day` parameter. It defaults to `"%d"` (the day of the month as a decimal number, 01-31).

- `allow_future`: A Boolean specifying whether to include "future" objects on this page, as described in the previous note.

This view may also take these common arguments (refer to Table C-1):

- `allow_empty`

- `context_processors`

- `extra_context`

- `mimetype`
- `template_loader`
- `template_name`
- `template_object_name`

Template Name

If `template_name` isn't specified, this view will use the template `<app_label>/<model_name>_archive_day.html` by default.

Template Context

In addition to `extra_context`, the template's context will be as follows:

- `day`: A `datetime.date` object representing the given day.
- `next_day`: A `datetime.date` object representing the next day. If the next day is in the future, this will be `None`.
- `previous_day`: A `datetime.date` object representing the previous day. Unlike `next_day`, this will never be `None`.
- `object_list`: A list of objects available for the given day. This variable's name depends on the `template_object_name` parameter, which is `'object'` by default. If `template_object_name` is `'foo'`, this variable's name will be `foo_list`.

Archive for Today

The `django.views.generic.date_based.archive_today` view shows all objects for *today*. This is exactly the same as `archive_day`, except the `year`/`month`/`day` arguments are not used, and today's date is used instead.

Example

```
urlpatterns = patterns('',
    # ...
    (r'^books/today/$', date_based.archive_today, book_info),
)
```

Date-Based Detail Pages

View function: `django.views.generic.date_based.object_detail`

Use this view for a page representing an individual object.

This has a different URL from the `object_detail` view; the `object_detail` view uses URLs such as `/entries/<slug>/`, whereas this one uses URLs such as `/entries/2006/aug/27/<slug>/`.

■**Note** If you're using date-based detail pages with slugs in the URLs, you probably also want to use the `unique_for_date` option on the slug field to validate that slugs aren't duplicated in a single day. See Appendix A for details on `unique_for_date`.

Example

This one differs (slightly) from all the other date-based examples in that we need to provide either an object ID or a slug so that Django can look up the object in question.

Since the object we're using doesn't have a slug field, we'll use ID-based URLs. It's considered a best practice to use a slug field, but in the interest of simplicity we'll let it go.

```
urlpatterns = patterns('',
    # ...
    (
        r'^(?P<year>d{4})/(?P<month>[a-z]{3})/(?P<day>d{2})/(?P<object_id>[w-]+)/$',
        date_based.object_detail,
        book_info
    ),
)
```

Required Arguments

- year: The object's four-digit year (a string).
- month: The object's month, formatted according to the `month_format` argument.
- day: The object's day, formatted according to the `day_format` argument.
- queryset: A `QuerySet` that contains the object.
- date_field: The name of the `DateField` or `DateTimeField` in the `QuerySet`'s model that the generic view should use to look up the object according to year, month, and day.

You'll also need either:

- object_id: The value of the primary-key field for the object.

or:

- slug: The slug of the given object. If you pass this field, then the `slug_field` argument (described in the following section) is also required.

Optional Arguments

- `allow_future`: A Boolean specifying whether to include "future" objects on this page, as described in the previous note.

- `day_format`: Like `month_format`, but for the day parameter. It defaults to "%d" (the day of the month as a decimal number, 01-31).

- `month_format`: A format string that regulates what format the `month` parameter uses. See the detailed explanation in the "Month Archives" section.

- `slug_field`: The name of the field on the object containing the slug. This is required if you are using the `slug` argument, but it must be absent if you're using the `object_id` argument.

- `template_name_field`: The name of a field on the object whose value is the template name to use. This lets you store template names in the data. In other words, if your object has a field `'the_template'` that contains a string `'foo.html'`, and you set `template_name_field` to `'the_template'`, the generic view for this object will use the template `'foo.html'`.

This view may also take these common arguments (refer to Table C-1):

- `context_processors`
- `extra_context`
- `mimetype`
- `template_loader`
- `template_name`
- `template_object_name`

Template Name

If `template_name` and `template_name_field` aren't specified, this view will use the template `<app_label>/<model_name>_detail.html` by default.

Template Context

In addition to `extra_context`, the template's context will be as follows:

- `object`: The object. This variable's name depends on the `template_object_name` parameter, which is `'object'` by default. If `template_object_name` is `'foo'`, this variable's name will be foo.

APPENDIX D

■■■

Settings

Your Django settings file contains all the configuration of your Django installation. This appendix explains how settings work and which settings are available.

The Basics of Settings Files

A *settings file* is just a Python module with module-level variables.

Here are a couple of example settings:

```
DEBUG = False
DEFAULT_FROM_EMAIL = 'webmaster@example.com'
TEMPLATE_DIRS = ('/home/templates/mike', '/home/templates/john')
```

Because a settings file is a Python module, the following apply to it:

- It must be valid Python code; syntax errors aren't allowed.

- It can assign settings dynamically using normal Python syntax, for example

  ```
  MY_SETTING = [str(i) for i in range(30)]
  ```

- It can import values from other settings files.

Default Settings

A Django settings file doesn't have to define any settings if it doesn't need to. Each setting has a sensible default value. These defaults live in the file `django/conf/global_settings.py`.

Here are the steps Django uses in compiling settings:

1. Load settings from `global_settings.py`.

2. Load settings from the specified settings file, overriding the global settings as necessary.

Note that a settings file should *not* import from `global_settings.py`, because that's redundant.

Seeing Which Settings You've Changed

There's an easy way to view which of your settings deviate from the default settings. The command `manage.py diffsettings` displays differences between the current settings file and Django's default settings.

`manage.py` is described in more detail in Appendix F.

Using Settings in Python Code

In your Django applications, use settings by importing the object `django.conf.settings`, as in this example:

```
from django.conf import settings

if settings.DEBUG:
    # Do something
```

Note that `django.conf.settings` isn't a module; it's an object. So importing individual settings is not possible:

```
from django.conf.settings import DEBUG  # This won't work.
```

Also note that your code should *not* import from either `global_settings` or your own settings file. `django.conf.settings` abstracts the concepts of default settings and site-specific settings; it presents a single interface. It also decouples the code that uses settings from the location of your settings.

Altering Settings at Runtime

You shouldn't alter settings in your applications at runtime. For example, don't do this in a view:

```
from django.conf import settings

settings.DEBUG = True    # Don't do this!
```

The only place that settings should be defined in is a settings file.

Security

Because a settings file contains sensitive information, such as the database password, you should make every attempt to limit access to it. For example, change its file permissions so that only you and your Web server's users can read it. This is especially important in a shared-hosting environment.

Creating Your Own Settings

There's nothing stopping you from creating your own settings for your own Django applications. Just follow these conventions:

- Use all uppercase for setting names.
- For settings that are sequences, use tuples instead of lists. Settings should be considered immutable and shouldn't be changed once they're defined.
- Don't reinvent an existing setting.

Designating the Settings: DJANGO_SETTINGS_MODULE

When you use Django, you have to tell it which settings you're using. Do this by using the environment variable DJANGO_SETTINGS_MODULE.

The value of DJANGO_SETTINGS_MODULE should be in Python path syntax (e.g., mysite.settings). Note that the settings module should be on the Python import search path (PYTHONPATH).

Tip A good guide to PYTHONPATH can be found at http://diveintopython.org/getting_to_know_python/everything_is_an_object.html.

The django-admin.py Utility

When using django-admin.py (see Appendix F), you can either set the environment variable once or explicitly pass in the settings module each time you run the utility.

Here's an example using the Unix Bash shell:

```
export DJANGO_SETTINGS_MODULE=mysite.settings
django-admin.py runserver
```

Here's an example using the Windows shell:

```
set DJANGO_SETTINGS_MODULE=mysite.settings
django-admin.py runserver
```

Use the --settings command-line argument to specify the settings manually:

```
django-admin.py runserver --settings=mysite.settings
```

The manage.py utility created by startproject as part of the project skeleton sets DJANGO_SETTINGS_MODULE automatically; see Appendix F for more about manage.py.

On the Server (mod_python)

In your live server environment, you'll need to tell Apache/mod_python which settings file to use. Do that with `SetEnv`:

```
<Location "/mysite/">
    SetHandler python-program
    PythonHandler django.core.handlers.modpython
    SetEnv DJANGO_SETTINGS_MODULE mysite.settings
</Location>
```

For more information, read the Django mod_python documentation online at `http://docs.djangoproject.com/en/dev/howto/deployment/modpython/`.

Using Settings Without Setting DJANGO_SETTINGS_MODULE

In some cases, you might want to bypass the `DJANGO_SETTINGS_MODULE` environment variable. For example, if you're using the template system by itself, you likely don't want to have to set up an environment variable pointing to a settings module.

In these cases, you can configure Django's settings manually. Do this by calling `django.conf.settings.configure()`. Here's an example:

```
from django.conf import settings

settings.configure(
    DEBUG = True,
    TEMPLATE_DEBUG = True,
    TEMPLATE_DIRS = [
        '/home/web-apps/myapp',
        '/home/web-apps/base',
    ]
)
```

Pass `configure()` as many keyword arguments as you'd like, with each keyword argument representing a setting and its value. Each argument name should be all uppercase, with the same name as the settings described earlier. If a particular setting is not passed to `configure()` and is needed at some later point, Django will use the default setting value.

Configuring Django in this fashion is necessary mostly—and, indeed, recommended—when you're using a piece of the framework inside a larger application. Consequently, when configured via `settings.configure()`, Django will not make any modifications to the process environment variables. (See the explanation of `TIME_ZONE` later in this appendix to find out why this would normally occur.) It's assumed that you're already in full control of your environment in these cases.

Custom Default Settings

If you'd like default values to come from somewhere other than django.conf.global_settings, you can pass in a module or class that provides the default settings as the default_settings argument (or as the first positional argument) in the call to configure().

In this example, default settings are taken from myapp_defaults, and the DEBUG setting is set to True, regardless of its value in myapp_defaults:

```
from django.conf import settings
from myapp import myapp_defaults

settings.configure(default_settings=myapp_defaults, DEBUG=True)
```

The following example, which uses myapp_defaults as a positional argument, is equivalent:

```
settings.configure(myapp_defaults, DEBUG = True)
```

Normally, you will not need to override the defaults in this fashion. The Django defaults are sufficiently tame that you can safely use them. Be aware that if you do pass in a new default module, it entirely *replaces* the Django defaults, so you must specify a value for every possible setting that might be used in that code you are importing. Check django.conf.settings.global_settings for the full list.

Either configure() or DJANGO_SETTINGS_MODULE Is Required

If you're not setting the DJANGO_SETTINGS_MODULE environment variable, you *must* call configure() at some point before using any code that reads settings.

If you don't set DJANGO_SETTINGS_MODULE and don't call configure(), Django will raise an EnvironmentError exception the first time a setting is accessed. If you set DJANGO_SETTINGS_MODULE, access settings values, and *then* call configure(), Django will raise an EnvironmentError stating that settings have already been configured.

Also, it's an error to call configure() more than once or to call configure() after any setting has been accessed.

It boils down to this: use exactly one of either configure() or DJANGO_SETTINGS_MODULE, and use it only once.

Available Settings

The following sections consist of a list of the main available settings, in alphabetical order, and their default values.

ABSOLUTE_URL_OVERRIDES

Default: {} (empty dictionary)

This is a dictionary mapping "app_label.model_name" strings to functions that take a model object and return its URL. This is a way of overriding get_absolute_url() methods on a per-installation basis. Here's an example:

```
ABSOLUTE_URL_OVERRIDES = {
    'blogs.weblog': lambda o: "/blogs/%s/" % o.slug,
    'news.story': lambda o: "/stories/%s/%s/" % (o.pub_year, o.slug),
}
```

Note that the model name used in this setting should be all lowercase, regardless of the case of the actual model class name.

ADMIN_MEDIA_PREFIX

Default: `'/media/'`

This setting is the URL prefix for admin media: CSS, JavaScript, and images. Make sure to use a trailing slash.

ADMINS

Default: `()` (empty tuple)

This is a tuple that lists people who get code-error notifications. When `DEBUG=False` and a view raises an exception, Django will e-mail these people with the full exception information. Each member of the tuple should be a tuple of (Full name, e-mail address), for example:

```
(('John', 'john@example.com'), ('Mary', 'mary@example.com'))
```

Note that Django will e-mail *all* of these people whenever an error happens.

ALLOWED_INCLUDE_ROOTS

Default: `()` (empty tuple)

This is a tuple of strings representing allowed prefixes for the `{% ssi %}` template tag. This is a security measure so that template authors can't access files that they shouldn't be accessing.

For example, if `ALLOWED_INCLUDE_ROOTS` is `('/home/html', '/var/www')`, then `{% ssi /home/html/foo.txt %}` would work, but `{% ssi /etc/passwd %}` wouldn't.

APPEND_SLASH

Default: `True`

This setting indicates whether to append trailing slashes to URLs. This is used only if `CommonMiddleware` is installed (see Chapter 17). See also `PREPEND_WWW`.

CACHE_BACKEND

Default: `'locmem://'`

This is the cache back-end to use (see Chapter 15).

CACHE_MIDDLEWARE_KEY_PREFIX

Default: `''` (empty string)

This is the cache key prefix that the cache middleware should use (see Chapter 15).

DATABASE_ENGINE

Default: `''` (empty string)

This setting indicates which database back-end to use, (e.g., `'postgresql_psycopg2'` or `'mysql'`).

DATABASE_HOST

Default: ' ' (empty string)

This setting indicates which host to use when connecting to the database. An empty string means `localhost`. This is not used with SQLite.

If this value starts with a forward slash ('/') and you're using MySQL, MySQL will connect via a Unix socket to the specified socket:

```
DATABASE_HOST = '/var/run/mysql'
```

If you're using MySQL and this value *doesn't* start with a forward slash, then this value is assumed to be the host.

DATABASE_NAME

Default: ' ' (empty string)

This is the name of the database to use. For SQLite, it's the full path to the database file.

DATABASE_OPTIONS

Default: {} (empty dictionary)

This specifies extra parameters to use when connecting to the database. Consult the back-end module's document for available keywords.

DATABASE_PASSWORD

Default: ' ' (empty string)

This setting is the password to use when connecting to the database. It is not used with SQLite.

DATABASE_PORT

Default: ' ' (empty string)

This is the port to use when connecting to the database. An empty string means the default port. It is not used with SQLite.

DATABASE_USER

Default: ' ' (empty string)

This setting is the username to use when connecting to the database. It is not used with SQLite.

DATE_FORMAT

Default: 'N j, Y' (e.g., Feb. 4, 2003)

This is the default formatting to use for date fields on Django admin change-list pages—and, possibly, by other parts of the system. It accepts the same format as the `now` tag (see Appendix E, Table E-2).

See also `DATETIME_FORMAT`, `TIME_FORMAT`, `YEAR_MONTH_FORMAT`, and `MONTH_DAY_FORMAT`.

DATETIME_FORMAT

Default: `'N j, Y, P'` (e.g., `Feb. 4, 2003, 4 p.m.`)

This is the default formatting to use for datetime fields on Django admin change-list pages—and, possibly, by other parts of the system. It accepts the same format as the `now` tag (see Appendix E, Table E-2).

See also `DATE_FORMAT`, `TIME_FORMAT`, `YEAR_MONTH_FORMAT`, and `MONTH_DAY_FORMAT`.

DEBUG

Default: `False`

This setting is a Boolean that turns debug mode on and off.

If you define custom settings, `django/views/debug.py` has a `HIDDEN_SETTINGS` regular expression that will hide from the `DEBUG` view anything that contains `SECRET`, `PASSWORD`, or `PROFANITIES`. This allows untrusted users to be able to provide backtraces without seeing sensitive (or offensive) settings.

Still, note that there are always going to be sections of your debug output that are inappropriate for public consumption. File paths, configuration options, and the like all give attackers extra information about your server. Never deploy a site with `DEBUG` turned on.

DEFAULT_CHARSET

Default: `'utf-8'`

This is the default charset to use for all `HttpResponse` objects if a MIME type isn't specified manually. It is used with `DEFAULT_CONTENT_TYPE` to construct the `Content-Type` header. See Appendix G for more about `HttpResponse` objects.

DEFAULT_CONTENT_TYPE

Default: `'text/html'`

This is the default content type to use for all `HttpResponse` objects if a MIME type isn't manually specified. It is used with `DEFAULT_CHARSET` to construct the `Content-Type` header. See Appendix G for more about `HttpResponse` objects.

DEFAULT_FROM_EMAIL

Default: `'webmaster@localhost'`

This is the default e-mail address to use for various automated correspondence from the site manager(s).

DISALLOWED_USER_AGENTS

Default: () (empty tuple)

This is a list of compiled regular-expression objects representing user-agent strings that are not allowed to visit any page, systemwide. Use this for bad robots/crawlers. This is used only if `CommonMiddleware` is installed (see Chapter 17).

EMAIL_HOST

Default: `'localhost'`

This is the host to use for sending e-mail. See also `EMAIL_PORT`.

EMAIL_HOST_PASSWORD

Default: `' '` (empty string)

This is the password to use for the SMTP server defined in `EMAIL_HOST`. This setting is used in conjunction with `EMAIL_HOST_USER` when authenticating to the SMTP server. If either of these settings is empty, Django won't attempt authentication.

See also `EMAIL_HOST_USER`.

EMAIL_HOST_USER

Default: `' '` (empty string)

This is the username to use for the SMTP server defined in `EMAIL_HOST`. If it's empty, Django won't attempt authentication. See also `EMAIL_HOST_PASSWORD`.

EMAIL_PORT

Default: 25

This is the port to use for the SMTP server defined in `EMAIL_HOST`.

EMAIL_SUBJECT_PREFIX

Default: `'[Django] '`

This is the subject-line prefix for e-mail messages sent with `django.core.mail.mail_admins` or `django.core.mail.mail_managers`. You'll probably want to include a trailing space.

FIXTURE_DIRS

Default: () (empty tuple)

This is a list of locations of the fixture data files, in search order. Note that these paths should use Unix-style forward slashes, even on Windows. It is used by Django's testing framework, which is covered online at `http://docs.djangoproject.com/en/dev/topics/testing/`.

IGNORABLE_404_ENDS

Default: (`'mail.pl'`, `'mailform.pl'`, `'mail.cgi'`, `'mailform.cgi'`, `'favicon.ico'`, `'.php'`)

This is a tuple of strings that specify beginnings of URLs that should be ignored by the 404 e-mailer. (See Chapter 12 for more on the 404 e-mailer.)

No errors will be sent for URLs that end with strings from this sequence.

See also `IGNORABLE_404_STARTS` and `SEND_BROKEN_LINK_EMAILS`.

IGNORABLE_404_STARTS

Default: ('/cgi-bin/', '/_vti_bin', '/_vti_inf')

This is just like IGNORABLE_404_ENDS except it applies to the end of URLs.
See also SEND_BROKEN_LINK_EMAILS and IGNORABLE_404_ENDS.

INSTALLED_APPS

Default: () (empty tuple)

A tuple of strings designating all applications that are enabled in this Django installation. Each string should be a full Python path to a Python package that contains a Django application. See Chapter 5 for more about applications.

LANGUAGE_CODE

Default: 'en-us'

This is a string representing the language code for this installation. This should be in standard language format—for example, US English is "en-us". See Chapter 19.

LANGUAGES

Default: A tuple of all available languages. This list is continually growing and any copy included here would inevitably become rapidly out of date. You can see the current list of translated languages by looking in django/conf/global_settings.py.

The list is a tuple of two-tuples in the format (*language code, language name*)—for example, ('ja', 'Japanese'). This specifies which languages are available for language selection. See Chapter 19 for more on language selection.

Generally, the default value should suffice. Only set this setting if you want to restrict language selection to a subset of the Django-provided languages.

If you define a custom LANGUAGES setting, it's OK to mark the languages as translation strings, but you should *never* import django.utils.translation from within your settings file, because that module itself depends on the settings, and that would cause a circular import.

The solution is to use a "dummy" gettext() function. Here's a sample settings file:

```
gettext = lambda s: s

LANGUAGES = (
    ('de', gettext('German')),
    ('en', gettext('English')),
)
```

With this arrangement, make-messages.py will still find and mark these strings for translation, but the translation won't happen at runtime—so you'll have to remember to wrap the languages in the *real* gettext() in any code that uses LANGUAGES at runtime.

MANAGERS

Default: () (empty tuple)

This tuple is in the same format as ADMINS; it specifies who should get broken-link notifications when SEND_BROKEN_LINK_EMAILS=True.

MEDIA_ROOT

Default: ' ' (empty string)

This is an absolute path to the directory that holds media for this installation (e.g., "/home/media/media.lawrence.com/"). See also MEDIA_URL.

MEDIA_URL

Default: ' ' (empty string)

This URL handles the media served from MEDIA_ROOT (e.g., "http://media.lawrence.com"). Note that this should have a trailing slash if it has a path component:

- *Correct:* "http://www.example.com/static/"

- *Incorrect:* "http://www.example.com/static"

See Chapter 12 for more on deployment and serving media.

MIDDLEWARE_CLASSES

Default:

```
("django.contrib.sessions.middleware.SessionMiddleware",
 "django.contrib.auth.middleware.AuthenticationMiddleware",
 "django.middleware.common.CommonMiddleware",
 "django.middleware.doc.XViewMiddleware")
```

This is a tuple of middleware classes to use. See Chapter 17.

MONTH_DAY_FORMAT

Default: 'F j'

This is the default formatting to use for date fields on Django admin change-list pages—and, possibly, by other parts of the system—in cases when only the month and day are displayed. It accepts the same format as the now tag (see Appendix E, Table E-2).

For example, when a Django admin change-list page is being filtered by a date, the header for a given day displays the day and month. Different locales have different formats. For example, US English would have "January 1," whereas Spanish might have "1 enero."

See also DATE_FORMAT, DATETIME_FORMAT, TIME_FORMAT, and YEAR_MONTH_FORMAT.

PREPEND_WWW

Default: False

This setting indicates whether to prepend the "www." subdomain to URLs that don't have it. This is used only if CommonMiddleware is installed (see Chapter 17). See also APPEND_SLASH.

ROOT_URLCONF

Default: Not defined

This is a string representing the full Python import path to your root URLconf (e.g., "mydjangoapps.urls"). See Chapter 3.

SECRET_KEY

Default: Generated automatically when you start a project

This is a secret key for this particular Django installation. It is used to provide a seed in secret-key hashing algorithms. Set this to a random string—the longer, the better. django-admin.py startproject creates one automatically, and most of the time you won't need to change it.

SEND_BROKEN_LINK_EMAILS

Default: False

This setting indicates whether to send an e-mail to the MANAGERS each time somebody visits a Django-powered page that is 404'ed with a nonempty referer (i.e., a broken link). This is used only if CommonMiddleware is installed (see Chapter 17). See also IGNORABLE_404_STARTS and IGNORABLE_404_ENDS.

SERIALIZATION_MODULES

Default: Not defined

Serialization is a feature still under heavy development. Refer to the online documentation at http://docs.djangoproject.com/en/dev/topics/serialization/ for more information.

SERVER_EMAIL

Default: 'root@localhost'

This is the e-mail address that error messages come from, such as those sent to ADMINS and MANAGERS.

SESSION_COOKIE_AGE

Default: 1209600 (two weeks, in seconds)

This is the age of session cookies, in seconds. See Chapter 14.

SESSION_COOKIE_DOMAIN

Default: None

This is the domain to use for session cookies. Set this to a string such as ".lawrence.com" for cross-domain cookies, or use None for a standard domain cookie. See Chapter 14.

SESSION_COOKIE_NAME

Default: 'sessionid'

This is the name of the cookie to use for sessions; it can be whatever you want. See Chapter 14.

SESSION_COOKIE_SECURE

Default: False

This setting indicates whether to use a secure cookie for the session cookie. If this is set to True, the cookie will be marked as "secure," which means browsers may ensure that the cookie is sent only under an HTTPS connection. See Chapter 14.

SESSION_EXPIRE_AT_BROWSER_CLOSE

Default: False

This setting indicates whether to expire the session when the user closes his browser. See Chapter 14.

SESSION_SAVE_EVERY_REQUEST

Default: False

This setting indicates whether to save the session data on every request. See Chapter 14.

SITE_ID

Default: Not defined

This is the ID, as an integer, of the current site in the django_site database table. It is used so that application data can hook into specific site(s) and a single database can manage content for multiple sites. See Chapter 16.

TEMPLATE_CONTEXT_PROCESSORS

Default:

```
("django.core.context_processors.auth",
"django.core.context_processors.debug",
"django.core.context_processors.i18n",
"django.core.context_processors.media")
```

This is a tuple of callables that are used to populate the context in RequestContext. These callables take a request object as their argument and return a dictionary of items to be merged into the context. See Chapter 9.

TEMPLATE_DEBUG

Default: False

This Boolean turns template debug mode on and off. If it is True, the fancy error page will display a detailed report for any TemplateSyntaxError. This report contains the relevant snippet of the template, with the appropriate line highlighted.

Note that Django displays fancy error pages only if DEBUG is True, so you'll want to set that to take advantage of this setting.

See also DEBUG.

TEMPLATE_DIRS

Default: () (empty tuple)

This is a list of locations of the template source files, in search order. Note that these paths should use Unix-style forward slashes, even on Windows. See Chapters 4 and 9.

TEMPLATE_LOADERS

Default: ('django.template.loaders.filesystem.load_template_source', 'django.template. loaders.app_directories.load_template_source')

This is a tuple of callables (as strings) that know how to import templates from various sources. See Chapter 9.

TEMPLATE_STRING_IF_INVALID

Default: '' (Empty string)

This is output, as a string, that the template system should use for invalid (e.g., misspelled) variables. See Chapter 9.

TEST_DATABASE_NAME

Default: None

This is the name of database to use when running the test suite. If a value of None is specified, the test database will use the name 'test_' + settings.DATABASE_NAME. See the documentation for Django's testing framework, which is covered online at http://docs. djangoproject.com/en/dev/topics/testing/.

TEST_RUNNER

Default: 'django.test.simple.run_tests'

This is the name of the method to use for starting the test suite. It is used by Django's testing framework, which is covered online at http://docs.djangoproject.com/en/dev/topics/ testing/.

TIME_FORMAT

Default: 'P' (e.g., 4 p.m.)

This is the default formatting to use for time fields on Django admin change-list pages—and, possibly, by other parts of the system. It accepts the same format as the now tag (see Appendix E, Table E-2).

See also DATE_FORMAT, DATETIME_FORMAT, TIME_FORMAT, YEAR_MONTH_FORMAT, and MONTH_DAY_FORMAT.

TIME_ZONE

Default: 'America/Chicago'

This is a string representing the time zone for this installation. One relatively complete list of time-zone strings can be found at http://www.postgresql.org/docs/8.1/static/datetime-keywords.html#DATETIME-TIMEZONE-SET-TABLE.

This is the time zone to which Django will convert all dates/times—not necessarily the time zone of the server. For example, one server may serve multiple Django-powered sites, each with a separate time-zone setting.

Normally, Django sets the os.environ['TZ'] variable to the time zone you specify in the TIME_ZONE setting. Thus, all your views and models will automatically operate in the correct time zone. However, if you're using the manually configured settings (described earlier in the section "Using Settings Without Setting DJANGO_SETTINGS_MODULE"), Django will *not* touch the TZ environment variable, and it will be up to you to ensure your processes are running in the correct environment.

■**Note** Django cannot reliably use alternate time zones in a Windows environment. If you're running Django on Windows, this variable must be set to match the system time zone.

URL_VALIDATOR_USER_AGENT

Default: Django/<version> (http://www.djangoproject.com/)

This is the string to use as the User-Agent header when checking to see if URLs exist (see the verify_exists option on URLField; refer to Appendix A).

USE_ETAGS

Default: False

This Boolean specifies whether to output the ETag header. It saves bandwidth but slows down performance. This is used only if CommonMiddleware is installed (see Chapter 17).

USE_I18N

Default: True

This Boolean specifies whether Django's internationalization system (see Chapter 19) should be enabled. It provides an easy way to turn off internationalization for performance. If this is set to False, Django will make some optimizations so as not to load the internationalization machinery.

YEAR_MONTH_FORMAT

Default: 'F Y'

This is the default formatting to use for date fields on Django admin change-list pages— and, possibly, by other parts of the system—in cases when only the year and month are displayed. It accepts the same format as the now tag (see Appendix E).

For example, when a Django admin change-list page is being filtered by a date drill-down, the header for a given month displays the month and the year. Different locales have different formats. For example, US English would use "January 2006," whereas another locale might use "2006/January."

See also DATE_FORMAT, DATETIME_FORMAT, TIME_FORMAT, and MONTH_DAY_FORMAT.

■ ■ ■

Built-in Template Tags and Filters

Chapter 4 lists a number of the most useful built-in template tags and filters. However, Django ships with many more built-in tags and filters. This appendix covers them.

Built-in Tag Reference

autoescape

Controls the current autoescaping behavior. This tag takes either on or off as an argument, which determines whether autoescaping is in effect inside the block.

When autoescaping is in effect, all variable content has HTML escaping applied to it before placing the result into the output (but after any filters have been applied). This is equivalent to manually applying the escape filter to each variable.

The only exceptions are variables that are already marked as "safe" from escaping, either by the code that populated the variable or because it has had the safe or escape filters applied.

block

Defines a block that can be overridden by child templates. See Chapter 4 for more information on template inheritance.

comment

Ignores everything between {% comment %} and {% endcomment %}.

cycle

Cycles among the given strings or variables each time this tag is encountered.

Within a loop, cycles among the given strings each time through the loop:

```
{% for o in some_list %}
    <tr class="{% cycle 'row1' 'row2' %}">
        ...
    </tr>
{% endfor %}
```

You can use variables, too. For example, if you have two template variables, rowvalue1 and rowvalue2, you can cycle between their values like this:

```
{% for o in some_list %}
    <tr class="{% cycle rowvalue1 rowvalue2 %}">
        ...
    </tr>
{% endfor %}
```

Yes, you can mix variables and strings:

```
{% for o in some_list %}
    <tr class="{% cycle 'row1' rowvalue2 'row3' %}">
        ...
    </tr>
{% endfor %}
```

In some cases, you might want to refer to the next value of a cycle from outside of a loop. To do this, just give the {% cycle %} tag a name, using as like this:

```
{% cycle 'row1' 'row2' as rowcolors %}
```

From then on, you can insert the current value of the cycle wherever you'd like in your template:

```
<tr class="{% cycle rowcolors %}">...</tr>
<tr class="{% cycle rowcolors %}">...</tr>
```

You can use any number of values in a {% cycle %} tag, separated by spaces. Values enclosed in single quotes (') or double quotes (") are treated as string literals, whereas values without quotes are treated as template variables.

For backward-compatibility, the {% cycle %} tag supports the much inferior old syntax from previous Django versions. You shouldn't use this in any new projects, but for the sake of the people who are still using it, here's what it looks like:

```
{% cycle row1,row2,row3 %}
```

In this syntax, each value gets interpreted as a literal string, and there's no way to specify variable values. Or literal commas. Or spaces. Did we mention you shouldn't use this syntax in any new projects?

debug

Outputs a whole load of debugging information, including the current context and imported modules.

extends

Signals that this template extends a parent template.

This tag can be used in two ways:

- `{% extends "base.html" %}` (with quotes) uses the literal value `"base.html"` as the name of the parent template to extend.

- `{% extends variable %}` uses the value of `variable`. If the variable evaluates to a string, Django will use that string as the name of the parent template. If the variable evaluates to a `Template` object, Django will use that object as the parent template.

See Chapter 4 for more information on template inheritance.

filter

Filters the contents of the variable through variable filters.

Filters can also be piped through each other, and they can have arguments just as in variable syntax.

For example:

```
{% filter force_escape|lower %}
    This text will be HTML-escaped, and will appear in all lowercase.
{% endfilter %}
```

firstof

Outputs the first variable passed that is not `False`. Outputs nothing if all the passed variables are `False`.

For example:

```
{% firstof var1 var2 var3 %}
```

This is equivalent to the following:

```
{% if var1 %}
    {{ var1 }}
{% else %}{% if var2 %}
    {{ var2 }}
{% else %}{% if var3 %}
    {{ var3 }}
{% endif %}{% endif %}{% endif %}
```

You can also use a literal string as a fallback value in case all passed variables are `False`:

```
{% firstof var1 var2 var3 "fallback value" %}
```

for

Loops over each item in an array. For example, to display a list of athletes provided in athlete_list:

```
<ul>
{% for athlete in athlete_list %}
    <li>{{ athlete.name }}</li>
{% endfor %}
</ul>
```

You can loop over a list in reverse by using {% for obj in list reversed %}.

If you need to loop over a list of lists, you can unpack the values in each sublist into individual variables. For example, if your context contains a list of (x,y) coordinates called points, you could use the following to output the list of points:

```
{% for x, y in points %}
    There is a point at {{ x }},{{ y }}
{% endfor %}
```

This can also be useful if you need to access the items in a dictionary. For example, if your context contained a dictionary data, the following would display the keys and values of the dictionary:

```
{% for key, value in data.items %}
    {{ key }}: {{ value }}
{% endfor %}
```

The for loop sets a number of variables available within the loop (see Table E-1).

Table E-1. *Variables Available Inside {% for %} Loops*

Variable	Description
forloop.counter	The current iteration of the loop (1-indexed)
forloop.counter0	The current iteration of the loop (0-indexed)
forloop.revcounter	The number of iterations from the end of the loop (1-indexed)
forloop.revcounter0	The number of iterations from the end of the loop (0-indexed)
forloop.first	True if this is the first time through the loop
forloop.last	True if this is the last time through the loop
forloop.parentloop	For nested loops, this is the loop "above" the current one

The for tag can take an optional {% empty %} clause that will be displayed if the given array is empty or could not be found:

```
<ul>
{% for athlete in athlete_list %}
    <li>{{ athlete.name }}</li>
```

```
{% empty %}
    <li>Sorry, no athlete in this list!</li>
{% endfor %}
<ul>
```

The preceding is equivalent to but shorter, cleaner, and possibly faster than the following:

```
<ul>
  {% if athlete_list %}
    {% for athlete in athlete_list %}
      <li>{{ athlete.name }}</li>
    {% endfor %}
  {% else %}
    <li>Sorry, no athletes in this list.</li>
  {% endif %}
</ul>
```

if

The {% if %} tag evaluates a variable, and if that variable is true (i.e., exists, is not empty, and is not a false Boolean value), the contents of the block are output:

```
{% if athlete_list %}
    Number of athletes: {{ athlete_list|length }}
{% else %}
    No athletes.
{% endif %}
```

In the preceding code, if athlete_list is not empty, the number of athletes will be displayed by the {{ athlete_list|length }} variable.

As you can see, the if tag can take an optional {% else %} clause that will be displayed if the test fails.

if tags may use and, or, or not to test a number of variables or to negate a given variable:

```
{% if athlete_list and coach_list %}
    Both athletes and coaches are available.
{% endif %}

{% if not athlete_list %}
    There are no athletes.
{% endif %}

{% if athlete_list or coach_list %}
    There are some athletes or some coaches.
{% endif %}
```

```
{% if not athlete_list or coach_list %}
    There are no athletes or there are some coaches (OK, so
    writing English translations of boolean logic sounds
    stupid; it's not our fault).
{% endif %}
```

```
{% if athlete_list and not coach_list %}
    There are some athletes and absolutely no coaches.
{% endif %}
```

if tags don't allow and and or clauses within the same tag because the order of logic would be ambiguous. For example, this is invalid:

```
{% if athlete_list and coach_list or cheerleader_list %}
```

If you need to combine and and or to do advanced logic, just use nested if tags. For example:

```
{% if athlete_list %}
    {% if coach_list or cheerleader_list %}
        We have athletes, and either coaches or cheerleaders!
    {% endif %}
{% endif %}
```

Multiple uses of the same logical operator are fine, as long as you use the same operator. For example, this is valid:

```
{% if athlete_list or coach_list or parent_list or teacher_list %}
```

ifchanged

Checks to see whether a value has changed from the last iteration of a loop.

The ifchanged tag is used within a loop. It has two possible uses:

- Checks its own rendered contents against its previous state and only displays the content if it has changed. For example, this displays a list of days, only displaying the month if it changes:

  ```
  <h1>Archive for {{ year }}</h1>

  {% for date in days %}
      {% ifchanged %}<h3>{{ date|date:"F" }}</h3>{% endifchanged %}
      <a href="{{ date|date:"M/d"|lower }}/">{{ date|date:"j" }}</a>
  {% endfor %}
  ```

- If given a variable, check whether that variable has changed. For example, the following shows the date every time it changes, but only shows the hour if both the hour and the date have changed:

```
{% for date in days %}
    {% ifchanged date.date %} {{ date.date }} {% endifchanged %}
    {% ifchanged date.hour date.date %}
        {{ date.hour }}
    {% endifchanged %}
{% endfor %}
```

The ifchanged tag can also take an optional {% else %} clause that will be displayed if the value has not changed:

```
{% for match in matches %}
    <div style="background-color:
        {% ifchanged match.ballot_id %}
            {% cycle red,blue %}
        {% else %}
            grey
        {% endifchanged %}
    ">{{ match }}</div>
{% endfor %}
```

ifequal

Outputs the contents of the block if the two arguments equal each other.

For example:

```
{% ifequal user.id comment.user_id %}
    ...
{% endifequal %}
```

As in the {% if %} tag, an {% else %} clause is optional.

The arguments can be hard-coded strings, so the following is valid:

```
{% ifequal user.username "adrian" %}
    ...
{% endifequal %}
```

It is possible to compare an argument only to template variables or strings. You cannot check for equality with Python objects such as True or False. If you need to test whether something is true or false, use the if tag instead.

ifnotequal

Just like ifequal, except that it tests that the two arguments are not equal.

include

Loads a template and renders it with the current context. This is a way of "including" other templates within a template.

The template name can either be a variable or a hard-coded (quoted) string in either single or double quotes.

This example includes the contents of the template "foo/bar.html":

```
{% include "foo/bar.html" %}
```

This example includes the contents of the template whose name is contained in the variable template_name:

```
{% include template_name %}
```

An included template is rendered with the context of the template that includes it. This example produces the output "Hello, John":

- Context: variable person is set to "john".
- Template:

  ```
  {% include "name_snippet.html" %}
  ```

- The name_snippet.html template:

  ```
  Hello, {{ person }}
  ```

See also: {% ssi %}.

load

Loads a custom template tag set. See Chapter 9 for more information on custom template libraries.

now

Displays the date, formatted according to the given string.

Uses the same format as PHP's date() function (http://php.net/date) with some custom extensions.

Table E-2 shows the available format strings.

Table E-2. *Available Date Format Strings*

Format Character	Description	Example Output
a	'a.m.' or 'p.m.' (Note that this is slightly different from PHP's output because it includes periods to match Associated Press style.)	'a.m.'
A	'AM' or 'PM'.	'AM'
b	Month, textual, three letters, lowercase.	'jan'
B	Not implemented.	
d	Day of the month, two digits with leading zeros.	'01' to '31'
D	Day of the week, textual, three letters.	'Fri'
f	Time, in 12-hour hours and minutes, with minutes left off if they're zero. Proprietary extension.	'1', '1:30'
F	Month, textual, long.	'January'

Format Character	Description	Example Output
g	Hour, 12-hour format without leading zeros.	`'1'` to `'12'`
G	Hour, 24-hour format without leading zeros.	`'0'` to `'23'`
h	Hour, 12-hour format.	`'01'` to `'12'`
H	Hour, 24-hour format.	`'00'` to `'23'`
i	Minutes.	`'00'` to `'59'`
I	Not implemented.	
j	Day of the month without leading zeros.	`'1'` to `'31'`
l	Day of the week, textual, long.	`'Friday'`
L	Boolean for whether it's a leap year.	`True` or `False`
m	Month, two digits with leading zeros.	`'01'` to `'12'`
M	Month, textual, three letters.	`'Jan'`
n	Month without leading zeros.	`'1'` to `'12'`
N	Month abbreviation in Associated Press style. Proprietary extension.	`'Jan.'`, `'Feb.'`, `'March'`, `'May'`
O	Difference to Greenwich time in hours.	`'+0200'`
P	Time, in 12-hour hours and minutes, and 'a.m.'/'p.m.', with minutes left off if they're zero and the special-case strings `'midnight'` and `'noon'` if appropriate. Proprietary extension.	`'1 a.m.'`, `'1:30 p.m.'`, `'midnight'`, `'noon'`, `'12:30 p.m.'`
r	RFC 2822 formatted date.	`'Thu, 21 Dec 2000 16:01:07 +0200'`
s	Seconds, two digits with leading zeros.	`'00'` to `'59'`
S	English ordinal suffix for day of the month, two characters.	`'st'`, `'nd'`, `'rd'`, or `'th'`
t	Number of days in the given month.	28 to 31
T	Time zone of this machine.	`'EST'`, `'MDT'`
U	Not implemented.	
w	Day of the week, digits without leading zeros.	`'0'` (Sunday) to `'6'` (Saturday)
W	ISO-8601 week number of year, with weeks starting on Monday.	1, 53
y	Year, two digits.	`'99'`
Y	Year, four digits.	`'1999'`
z	Day of the year.	0 to 365
Z	Time zone offset in seconds. The offset for time zones west of UTC is always negative, and for those east of UTC is always positive.	-43200 to 43200

For example:

```
It is {% now "jS F Y H:i" %}
```

Note that you can backslash-escape a format string if you want to use the "raw" value. In this example, "f" is backslash-escaped because otherwise "f" is a format string that displays the time. The "o" doesn't need to be escaped, because it's not a format character:

```
It is the {% now "jS o\f F" %}
```

This would display as "It is the 4th of September."

regroup

Regroups a list of like objects by a common attribute.

This complex tag is best illustrated by use of an example: say that people is a list of people represented by dictionaries with first_name, last_name, and gender keys:

```
people = [
    {'first_name': 'George', 'last_name': 'Bush', 'gender': 'Male'},
    {'first_name': 'Bill', 'last_name': 'Clinton', 'gender': 'Male'},
    {'first_name': 'Margaret', 'last_name': 'Thatcher', 'gender': 'Female'},
    {'first_name': 'Condoleezza', 'last_name': 'Rice', 'gender': 'Female'},
    {'first_name': 'Pat', 'last_name': 'Smith', 'gender': 'Unknown'},
]
```

And you want to display a hierarchical list that is ordered by gender, like this:

- **Male:**
    - George Bush
    - Bill Clinton
- **Female:**
    - Margaret Thatcher
    - Condoleezza Rice
- **Unknown:**
    - Pat Smith

You can use the {% regroup %} tag to group the list of people by gender. The following snippet of template code would accomplish it:

```
{% regroup people by gender as gender_list %}

<ul>
{% for gender in gender_list %}
    <li>{{ gender.grouper }}
    <ul>
        {% for item in gender.list %}
        <li>{{ item.first_name }} {{ item.last_name }}</li>
        {% endfor %}
    </ul>
    </li>
{% endfor %}
</ul>
```

Let's walk through this example. {% regroup %} takes three arguments: the list you want to regroup, the attribute to group by, and the name of the resulting list. Here, we're regrouping the people list by the gender attribute and calling the result gender_list.

{% regroup %} produces a list (in this case, gender_list) of group objects. Each group object has two attributes:

- grouper: The item that was grouped by (e.g., the string "Male" or "Female")
- list: A list of all items in this group (e.g., a list of all people with gender='Male')

Note that {% regroup %} does not order its input! Our example relies on the fact that the people list was ordered by gender in the first place. If the people list did *not* order its members by gender, the regrouping would naively display more than one group for a single gender. For example, say the people list was set to this (note that the males are not grouped together):

```
people = [
    {'first_name': 'Bill', 'last_name': 'Clinton', 'gender': 'Male'},
    {'first_name': 'Pat', 'last_name': 'Smith', 'gender': 'Unknown'},
    {'first_name': 'Margaret', 'last_name': 'Thatcher', 'gender': 'Female'},
    {'first_name': 'George', 'last_name': 'Bush', 'gender': 'Male'},
    {'first_name': 'Condoleezza', 'last_name': 'Rice', 'gender': 'Female'},
]
```

With this input for people, the previous example {% regroup %} template code would result in the following output:

- **Male:**
  - Bill Clinton
- **Unknown:**
  - Pat Smith
- **Female:**
  - Margaret Thatcher
- **Male:**
  - George Bush
- **Female:**
  - Condoleezza Rice

The easiest solution to this gotcha is to make sure in your view code that the data is ordered according to how you want to display it.

Another solution is to sort the data in the template using the dictsort filter if your data is in a list of dictionaries:

```
{% regroup people|dictsort:"gender" by gender as gender_list %}
```

spaceless

Removes whitespace between HTML tags (this includes tab characters and newlines).

For example:

```
{% spaceless %}
    <p>
        <a href="foo/">Foo</a>
    </p>
{% endspaceless %}
```

This example would return this HTML:

```
<p><a href="foo/">Foo</a></p>
```

Only space between *tags* is removed; not space between tags and text. In this example, the space around Hello won't be stripped:

```
{% spaceless %}
    <strong>
        Hello
    </strong>
{% endspaceless %}
```

ssi

Outputs the contents of a given file into the page.

Like a simple include tag, {% ssi %} includes the contents of another file that must be specified using an absolute path in the current page:

```
{% ssi /home/html/ljworld.com/includes/right_generic.html %}
```

If the optional "parsed" parameter is given, the contents of the included file are evaluated as template code within the current context:

```
{% ssi /home/html/ljworld.com/includes/right_generic.html parsed %}
```

Note that if you use {% ssi %}, you'll need to define ALLOWED_INCLUDE_ROOTS in your Django settings as a security measure.

See also {% include %}.

templatetag

Outputs one of the syntax characters used to compose template tags.

Because the template system has no concept of "escaping," to display one of the bits used in template tags, you must use the {% templatetag %} tag.

See Table E-3 for the available arguments.

Table E-3. *Available Arguments for templatetag Filter*

Argument	Output
openblock	{%
closeblock	%}
openvariable	{{
closevariable	}}
openbrace	{
closebrace	}
opencomment	{#
closecomment	#}

url

Returns an absolute URL (i.e., a URL without the domain name) matching a given view function and optional parameters. This is a way to output links without violating the DRY principle by having to hard-code URLs in your templates:

```
{% url path.to.some_view arg1,arg2,name1=value1 %}
```

The first argument is a path to a view function in the format `package.package.module.function`. Additional arguments are optional and should be comma-separated values that will be used as positional and keyword arguments in the URL. All arguments required by the URLconf should be present.

For example, suppose that you have a view, `app_views.client`, whose URLconf takes a client ID (here, `client()` is a method inside the views file `app_views.py`). The URLconf line might look like this:

```
('^client/(\d+)/$', 'app_views.client')
```

If this app's URLconf is included into the project's URLconf under a path such as this:

```
('^clients/', include('project_name.app_name.urls'))
```

you can create a link to this view like this in a template:

```
{% url app_views.client client.id %}
```

The template tag will output the string `/clients/client/123/`.

widthratio

For creating bar charts and such, this tag calculates the ratio of a given value to a maximum value, and then applies that ratio to a constant.

For example:

```
<img src="bar.gif" height="10" width="{% widthratio this_value max_value 100 %}" />
```

If `this_value` is 175 and `max_value` is 200, the image in the preceding example will be 88 pixels wide (because 175 / 200 = .875, .875 * 100 = 87.5, which is rounded up to 88).

with

Caches a complex variable under a simpler name. This is useful when accessing an "expensive" method (e.g., one that hits the database multiple times).

For example:

```
{% with business.employees.count as total %}
    {{ total }} employee{{ total|pluralize }}
{% endwith %}
```

The populated variable (in the example above, total) is only available between the {% with %} and {% endwith %} tags.

Built-in Filter Reference

add

Adds the argument to the value.

For example:

```
{{ value|add:"2" }}
```

If value is 4, the output will be 6.

addslashes

Adds slashes before quotes. Useful for escaping strings in CSV, for example.

capfirst

Capitalizes the first character of the value.

center

Centers the value in a field of a given width.

cut

Removes all values of arg from the given string. For example:

```
{{ value|cut:" "}}
```

If value is "String with spaces", the output will be "Stringwithspaces".

date

Formats a date according to the given format (same as the {% now %} tag). For example:

```
{{ value|date:"D d M Y" }}
```

If value is a datetime object (e.g., the result of datetime.datetime.now()), the output will be the string 'Wed 09 Jan 2008'.

When used without a format string, as follows, the formatting string defined in the DATE_FORMAT setting will be used:

```
{{ value|date }}
```

default

If value evaluates to False, use given default. Otherwise, use the value.

For example:

```
{{ value|default:"nothing" }}
```

If value is "" (the empty string), the output will be nothing.

default_if_none

If (and only if) value is None, use the given default. Otherwise, use the value.

Note that if an empty string is given, the default value will *not* be used. Use the default filter if you want to fallback for empty strings.

For example:

```
{{ value|default_if_none:"nothing" }}
```

If value is None, the output will be the string "nothing".

dictsort

Takes a list of dictionaries and returns that list sorted by the key given in the argument.

For example:

```
{{ value|dictsort:"name" }}
```

If value is:

```
[
    {'name': 'zed', 'age': 19},
    {'name': 'amy', 'age': 22},
    {'name': 'joe', 'age': 31},
]
```

then the output would be:

```
[
    {'name': 'amy', 'age': 22},
    {'name': 'joe', 'age': 31},
    {'name': 'zed', 'age': 19},
]
```

dictsortreversed

Takes a list of dictionaries and returns that list sorted in reverse order by the key given in the argument. This works exactly the same as the previous filter, but the returned value will be in reverse order.

divisibleby

Returns True if the value is divisible by the argument.
   For example:

```
{{ value|divisibleby:"3" }}
```

   If value is 21, the output would be True.

escape

Escapes a string's HTML. Specifically, it makes these replacements:

- < is converted to <
- > is converted to >
- ' (single quote) is converted to '
- " (double quote) is converted to "
- & is converted to &

   The escaping is applied only when the string is output, so it does not matter where in a chained sequence of filters you put escape: it will always be applied as if it were the last filter. If you want escaping to be applied immediately, use the force_escape filter.
   Applying escape to a variable that would normally have autoescaping applied to the result will result in only one round of escaping being done. So it is safe to use this function even in autoescaping environments. If you want multiple escaping passes to be applied, use the force_escape filter.

escapejs

Escapes characters for use in JavaScript strings. This does *not* make the string safe for use in HTML, but does protect you from syntax errors when using templates to generate JavaScript/JSON.

filesizeformat

Formats the value like a 'human-readable' file size (i.e., '13 KB', '4.1 MB', '102 bytes', etc).
   For example:

```
{{ value|filesizeformat }}
```

   If value is 123456789, the output would be 117.7 MB.

first

Returns the first item in a list.

For example:

`{{ value|first }}`

If value is the list `['a', 'b', 'c']`, the output will be `'a'`.

fix_ampersands

Replaces ampersands with & entities.

For example:

`{{ value|fix_ampersands }}`

If value is Tom & Jerry, the output will be Tom & Jerry.

floatformat

When used without an argument, rounds a floating-point number to one decimal place (but only if there's a decimal part to be displayed). See Table E-4.

Table E-4. *Example Output of floatformat Tag*

Value	Template	Output
34.23234	`{{ value|floatformat }}`	34.2
34.00000	`{{ value|floatformat }}`	34
34.26000	`{{ value|floatformat }}`	34.3

If used with a numeric integer argument, floatformat rounds a number to that many decimal places. See Table E-5.

Table E-5. *More Example Output of floatformat Tag*

Value	Template	Output
34.23234	`{{ value|floatformat:3 }}`	34.232
34.00000	`{{ value|floatformat:3 }}`	34.000
34.26000	`{{ value|floatformat:3 }}`	34.260

If the argument passed to floatformat is negative, it will round a number to that many decimal places, but only if there's a decimal part to be displayed. See Table E-6.

Table E-6. *Even More Example Output of floatformat Tag*

Value	Template	Output
34.23234	{{ value|floatformat:"-3" }}	34.232
34.00000	{{ value|floatformat:"-3" }}	34
34.26000	{{ value|floatformat:"-3" }}	34.260

Using floatformat with no argument is equivalent to using floatformat with an argument of -1.

force_escape

Applies HTML escaping to a string (see the escape filter for details). This filter is applied *immediately* and returns a new escaped string. This is useful in the rare cases where you need multiple escaping or want to apply other filters to the escaped results. Normally, you want to use the escape filter.

get_digit

Given a whole number, returns the requested digit, where 1 is the rightmost digit, 2 is the second digit, and so on. Returns the original value for invalid input (if the input or argument is not an integer or if the argument is less than 1). Otherwise, output is always an integer.

For example:

```
{{ value|get_digit:"2" }}
```

If value is 123456789, the output will be 8.

iriencode

Converts an Internationalized Resource Identifier (IRI) to a string that is suitable for including in a URL. This is necessary if you're trying to use strings containing non-ASCII characters in a URL.

It's safe to use this filter on a string that has already gone through the urlencode filter.

join

Joins a list with a string such as Python's str.join(list).

For example:

```
{{ value|join:" // " }}
```

If value is the list ['a', 'b', 'c'], the output will be the string "a // b // c".

last

Returns the last item in a list.
>   For example:

`{{ value|last }}`

>   If value is the list `['a', 'b', 'c', 'd']`, the output will be the string "d".

length

Returns the length of the value (this works for both strings and lists).
>   For example:

`{{ value|length }}`

>   If value is `['a', 'b', 'c', 'd']`, the output will be 4.

length_is

Returns `True` if the value's length is the argument, or `False` otherwise.
>   For example:

`{{ value|length_is:"4" }}`

>   If value is `['a', 'b', 'c', 'd']`, the output will be `True`.

linebreaks

Replaces line breaks in plain text with appropriate HTML; a single newline becomes an HTML
line break (`<br />`) and a new line followed by a blank line becomes a paragraph break (`</p>`).
>   For example:

`{{ value|linebreaks }}`

>   If value is `Joel\nis a slug`, the output will be `<p>Joel<br />is a slug</p>`.

linebreaksbr

Converts all newlines in a piece of plain text to HTML line breaks (`<br />`).

linenumbers

Displays text with line numbers.

ljust

Left-aligns the value in a field of a given width.
>   **Argument:** field size

lower

Converts a string into all lowercase.
>   For example:

```
{{ value|lower }}
```

>   If value is Still MAD At Yoko, the output will be still mad at yoko.

make_list

Returns the value turned into a list. For an integer, it's a list of digits. For a string, it's a list of characters.
>   For example:

```
{{ value|make_list }}
```

>   If value is the string "Joel", the output would be the list [u'J', u'o', u'e', u'l']. If value is 123, the output will be the list [1, 2, 3].

phone2numeric

Converts a phone number (possibly containing letters) to its numerical equivalent. For example, '800-COLLECT' will be converted to '800-2655328'.
>   The input doesn't have to be a valid phone number. This will happily convert any string.

pluralize

Returns a plural suffix if the value is not 1. By default, this suffix is 's'.
>   For example:

```
You have {{ num_messages }} message{{ num_messages|pluralize }}.
```

>   For words that require a suffix other than 's', you can provide an alternate suffix as a parameter to the filter.
>   For example:

```
You have {{ num_walruses }} walrus{{ num_walrus|pluralize:"es" }}.
```

>   For words that don't pluralize by simple suffix, you can specify both a singular and plural suffix, separated by a comma.
>   For example:

```
You have {{ num_cherries }} cherr{{ num_cherries|pluralize:"y,ies" }}.
```

pprint

A wrapper around the Python standard library's pprint.pprint function for debugging, really.

random

Returns a random item from the given list.

For example:

```
{{ value|random }}
```

If value is the list `['a', 'b', 'c', 'd']`, the output could be `"b"`.

removetags

Removes a space-separated list of [X]HTML tags from the output.

For example:

```
{{ value|removetags:"b span"|safe }}
```

If value is `"<b>Joel</b> <button>is</button> a <span>slug</span>"` the output will be `"Joel <button>is</button> a slug"`.

rjust

Right-aligns the value in a field of a given width.

Argument: field size

safe

Marks a string as not requiring further HTML escaping prior to output. When autoescaping is off, this filter has no effect.

safeseq

Applies the safe filter to each element of a sequence. Useful in conjunction with other filters that operate on sequences, such as join. For example:

```
{{ some_list|safeseq|join:", " }}
```

You couldn't use the safe filter directly in this case because it would first convert the variable into a string instead of working with the individual elements of the sequence.

slice

Returns a slice of the list.

Uses the same syntax as Python's list slicing. See http://diveintopython.org/native_data_types/lists.html#odbchelper.list.slice for an introduction.

For example:

```
{{ some_list|slice:":2" }}
```

slugify

Converts to lowercase, removes nonword characters (only alphanumerics and underscores are kept), and converts spaces to hyphens. Also strips leading and trailing whitespace.

For example:

`{{ value|slugify }}`

If value is "`Joel is a slug`", the output will be "`joel-is-a-slug`".

stringformat

Formats the variable according to the argument, a string-formatting specifier. This specifier uses Python string-formatting syntax, with the exception that the leading % is dropped.

See `http://docs.python.org/library/stdtypes.html#string-formatting-operations` for documentation of Python string formatting.

For example:

`{{ value|stringformat:"s" }}`

If value is "`Joel is a slug`", the output will be "`Joel is a slug`".

striptags

Strips all [X]HTML tags.

For example:

`{{ value|striptags }}`

If value is "`<b>Joel</b> <button>is</button> a <span>slug</span>`", the output will be "`Joel is a slug`".

time

Formats a time according to the given format (same as the `now` tag). The `time` filter will accept parameters in the format string that relate to the time of day, not the date (for obvious reasons). If you need to format a date, use the `date` filter.

For example:

`{{ value|time:"H:i" }}`

If value is equivalent to `datetime.datetime.now()`, the output will be the string "`01:23`".

When used without a format string, the format string defined in the `TIME_FORMAT` setting will be used:

`{{ value|time }}`

timesince

Formats a date as the time since that date (e.g., "4 days, 6 hours").

Takes an optional argument that is a variable containing the date to use as the comparison point (without the argument, the comparison point is *now*). For example, if `blog_date` is a date instance representing midnight on 1 June 2006, and `comment_date` is a date instance for 08:00 on 1 June 2006, then `{{ blog_date|timesince:comment_date }}` would return "8 hours".

Comparing offset-naive and offset-aware datetimes will return an empty string.

Minutes is the smallest unit used, and `"0 minutes"` will be returned for any date that is in the future relative to the comparison point.

timeuntil

Similar to `timesince`, except that it measures the time from now until the given date or date-time. For example, if today is 1 June 2006, and `conference_date` is a date instance holding 29 June 2006, then `{{ conference_date|timeuntil }}` will return `"4 weeks"`.

Takes an optional argument that is a variable containing the date to use as the comparison point (instead of *now*). If `from_date` contains 22 June 2006, then `{{ conference_date|timeuntil:from_date }}` will return `"1 week"`.

Comparing offset-naive and offset-aware datetimes will return an empty string.

Minutes is the smallest unit used, and `"0 minutes"` will be returned for any date that is in the past relative to the comparison point.

title

Converts a string into titlecase.

truncatewords

Truncates a string after a certain number of words.

Argument: Number of words to truncate after.

For example:

```
{{ value|truncatewords:2 }}
```

If `value` is `"Joel is a slug"`, the output will be `"Joel is ..."`.

truncatewords_html

Similar to `truncatewords`, except that it is aware of HTML tags. Any tags that are opened in the string and not closed before the truncation point are closed immediately after the truncation.

This is less efficient than `truncatewords`, so should be used only when it is being passed HTML text.

unordered_list

Recursively takes a self-nested list and returns an HTML unordered list *without* opening and closing `<ul>` tags.

The list is assumed to be in the proper format. For example, if var contains `['States', ['Kansas', ['Lawrence', 'Topeka'], 'Illinois']]`, then `{{ var|unordered_list }}` would return the following:

```
<li>States
<ul>
        <li>Kansas
        <ul>
                <li>Lawrence</li>
                <li>Topeka</li>
        </ul>
        </li>
        <li>Illinois</li>
</ul>
</li>
```

upper

Converts a string into all uppercase.

For example:

```
{{ value|upper }}
```

If value is `"Joel is a slug"`, the output will be `"JOEL IS A SLUG"`.

urlencode

Escapes a value for use in a URL.

urlize

Converts URLs in plain text into clickable links.

Note that if `urlize` is applied to text that already contains HTML markup, things won't work as expected. Apply this filter only to *plain* text.

For example:

```
{{ value|urlize }}
```

If value is `"Check out www.djangoproject.com"`, the output will be `"Check out <a href="http://www.djangoproject.com">www.djangoproject.com</a>"`.

urlizetrunc

Converts URLs into clickable links, truncating URLs longer than the given character limit.

As with `urlize`, this filter should be applied only to *plain* text.

Argument: Length to truncate URLs to.

For example:

```
{{ value|urlizetrunc:15 }}
```

If value is "Check out www.djangoproject.com", the output would be 'Check out <a href="http://www.djangoproject.com">www.djangopr...</a>'.

wordcount

Returns the number of words.

wordwrap

Wraps words at a specified line length.

Argument: number of characters at which to wrap the text.

For example:

```
{{ value|wordwrap:5 }}
```

If value is Joel is a slug, the output would be the following:

```
Joel
is a
slug
```

yesno

Given a string mapping values for True, False, and (optionally) None returns one of those strings according to the value (see Table E-7).

Table E-7. *Examples of the yesno Filter*

Value	Argument	Output
True	"yeah,no,maybe"	yeah
False	"yeah,no,maybe"	no
None	"yeah,no,maybe"	maybe
None	"yeah,no"	"no" (converts None to False if no mapping for None is given)

■ ■ ■

The django-admin Utility

django-admin.py is Django's command-line utility for administrative tasks. This appendix explains its many powers.

Usually you'll access django-admin.py through a project's manage.py wrapper. manage.py is created automatically in each Django project and is a thin wrapper around django-admin.py. It takes care of two things for you before delegating to django-admin.py:

- It puts your project's package on sys.path.

- It sets the DJANGO_SETTINGS_MODULE environment variable so that it points to your project's settings.py file.

The django-admin.py script should be on your system path if you installed Django via its setup.py utility. If it's not on your path, you can find it in site-packages/django/bin within your Python installation. Consider symlinking it from some place on your path, such as /usr/local/bin.

Windows users, who do not have symlinking functionality available, can copy django-admin.py to a location on their existing path or edit the PATH settings (under Settings ➤ Control Panel ➤ System ➤ Advanced ➤ Environment) to point to its installed location.

Generally, when working on a single Django project it's easier to use manage.py. If you need to switch between multiple Django settings files, use django-admin.py with DJANGO_SETTINGS_MODULE or use the --settings command-line option.

The command-line examples throughout this appendix use django-admin.py to be consistent, but any example can use manage.py just as well.

Usage

Here's how to use django-admin.py:

```
django-admin.py <subcommand> [options]
manage.py <subcommand> [options]
```

subcommand should be one of the subcommands listed in the "Available Subcommands" section of this appendix. options, which is optional, should be zero or more of the options available for the given subcommand.

Getting Runtime Help

Run django-admin.py help to display a list of all available subcommands. Run django-admin.py help <subcommand> to display a description of the given subcommand and a list of its available options.

App Names

Many subcommands take a list of *app names*. An app name is the base name of the package containing your models. For example, if your INSTALLED_APPS contains the string 'mysite.blog', the app name is blog.

Determining the Version

Run django-admin.py --version to display the current Django version.
    Here are some examples of output:

```
1.1
1.0
0.96
0.97-pre-SVN-6069
```

Displaying Debug Output

Use --verbosity to specify the amount of notification and debug information that django-admin.py should print to the console.

Available Subcommands

cleanup

This can be run as a cron job, or directly to clean out old data from the database (only expired sessions currently).

compilemessages

The compilemessages subcommand compiles .po files created with makemessages to .mo files for use with the built-in gettext support. See Chapter 19.

--locale

Use the --locale or -l option to specify the locale to process. If this option is not provided, all locales are processed.

Here is a usage example:

```
django-admin.py compilemessages --locale=br_PT
```

createcachetable

This subcommand creates a cache table with a given name for use with the database-cache back-end. See Chapter 15.

Example usage:

```
django-admin.py createcachetable my_cache_table
```

createsuperuser

This creates a superuser account (a user who has all permissions). This is useful if you need to create an initial superuser account but did not do so during syncdb, or if you need to generate superuser accounts programmatically for your site(s).

When run interactively, this command will prompt for a password for the new superuser account. When run non-interactively, no password will be set, and the superuser account will not be able to log in until a password has been set for it manually.

The username and e-mail address for the new account can be supplied by using the --username and --email arguments on the command line. If either of these is not supplied, createsuperuser will prompt for it when running interactively.

This command is available only if Django's authentication system (django.contrib.auth) is in INSTALLED_APPS. See Chapter 14.

dbshell

dbshell runs the command-line client for the database engine specified in your DATABASE_ ENGINE setting, with the connection parameters specified in your DATABASE_USER, DATABASE_ PASSWORD, and other such settings:

- For PostgreSQL, this runs the psql command-line client.

- For MySQL, this runs the mysql command-line client.

- For SQLite, this runs the sqlite3 command-line client.

This command assumes the programs are on your PATH so that a simple call to the program name (psql, mysql, sqlite3) will find the program in the right place. There's no way to specify the location of the program manually.

diffsettings

Use this to display differences between the current settings file and Django's default settings. Settings that don't appear in the defaults are followed by "###". For example, the default settings don't define ROOT_URLCONF, so ROOT_URLCONF is followed by "###" in the output of diffsettings.

Note that Django's default settings live in django/conf/global_settings.py, in case you're ever curious to see the full list of defaults.

dumpdata

This outputs to standard output all data in the database associated with the named application(s). If no application name is provided, all installed applications will be dumped. The output of dumpdata can be used as input for loaddata.

Note that dumpdata uses the default manager on the model for selecting the records to dump. If you're using a custom manager as the default manager and it filters some of the available records, not all of the objects will be dumped.

Here is a usage example:

```
django-admin.py dumpdata books
```

Use the --exclude option to exclude a specific application from the applications whose contents are output. For example, to specifically exclude the *auth* application from the output, you would call:

```
django-admin.py dumpdata --exclude=auth
```

If you want to exclude multiple applications, use multiple --exclude directives:

```
django-admin.py dumpdata --exclude=auth --exclude=contenttypes
```

By default, dumpdata will format its output in JSON, but you can use the --format option to specify another format. Currently supported formats are listed in the Django documentation.

By default, dumpdata will output all data on a single line. This isn't easy for humans to read, so you can use the --indent option to pretty-print the output with a number of indentation spaces.

In addition to specifying application names, you can provide a list of individual models, in the form of appname.Model. If you specify a model name to dumpdata, the dumped output will be restricted to that model, rather than the entire application. You can also mix application names and model names.

flush

flush returns the database to the state it was in immediately after syncdb was executed. This means that all data will be removed from the database, any post-synchronization handlers will be re-executed, and the initial_data fixture will be reinstalled.

Use the --noinput option to suppress all user prompting, such as "Are you sure?" confirmation messages. This is useful if django-admin.py is being executed as an unattended, automated script.

inspectdb

This subcommand introspects the database tables in the database pointed to by the DATABASE_ NAME setting and outputs a Django model module (a models.py file) to standard output.

Use this if you have a legacy database with which you'd like to use Django. The script will inspect the database and create a model for each table within it.

As you might expect, the created models will have an attribute for every field in the table. Note that inspectdb has a few special cases in its field-name output:

- If inspectdb cannot map a column's type to a model field type, it'll use TextField and insert the Python comment 'This field type is a guess.' next to the field in the generated model.

- If the database column name is a Python reserved word (such as 'pass', 'class', or 'for'), inspectdb will append '_field' to the attribute name. For example, if a table has a column 'for', the generated model will have a field 'for_field', with the db_ column attribute set to 'for'. inspectdb will insert the Python comment 'Field renamed because it was a Python reserved word.' next to the field.

This feature is meant as a shortcut, not as definitive model generation. After you run it, you'll want to look over the generated models yourself to make customizations. In particular, you'll need to rearrange models' order so that models that refer to other models are ordered properly.

Primary keys are automatically introspected for PostgreSQL, MySQL, and SQLite, in which case Django puts in the primary_key=True where needed.

inspectdb works with PostgreSQL, MySQL, and SQLite. Foreign-key detection works only in PostgreSQL and with certain types of MySQL tables.

loaddata <fixture fixture ...>

This subcommand searches for and loads the contents of the named fixture into the database.

What's a Fixture?

A *fixture* is a collection of files that contain the serialized contents of the database. Each fixture has a unique name, and the files that compose the fixture can be distributed over multiple directories, in multiple applications.

Django will search in three locations for fixtures:

- In the fixtures directory of every installed application
- In any directory named in the FIXTURE_DIRS setting
- In the literal path named by the fixture

Django will load any and all fixtures it finds in these locations that match the provided fixture names.

If the named fixture has a file extension, only fixtures of that type will be loaded. For example:

```
django-admin.py loaddata mydata.json
```

would load only JSON fixtures called `mydata`. The fixture extension must correspond to the registered name of a serializer (e.g., `json` or `xml`). For more on serializers, see the Django docs.

If you omit the extensions, Django will search all available fixture types for a matching fixture. For example:

```
django-admin.py loaddata mydata
```

would look for any fixture of any fixture type called `mydata`. If a fixture directory contained `mydata.json`, that fixture would be loaded as a JSON fixture.

The fixtures that are named can include directory components. These directories will be included in the search path. For example:

```
django-admin.py loaddata foo/bar/mydata.json
```

would search `<appname>/fixtures/foo/bar/mydata.json` for each installed application, `<dirname>/foo/bar/mydata.json` for each directory in `FIXTURE_DIRS`, and the literal path `foo/bar/mydata.json`.

When fixture files are processed, the data is saved to the database as is. Model-defined `save` methods and `pre_save` signals are not called.

Note that the order in which fixture files are processed is undefined. However, all fixture data is installed as a single transaction, so data in one fixture can reference data in another fixture. If the database back-end supports row-level constraints, these constraints will be checked at the end of the transaction.

The `dumpdata` command can be used to generate input for `loaddata`.

Compressed Fixtures

Fixtures may be compressed in `zip`, `gz`, or `bz2` format. For example:

```
django-admin.py loaddata mydata.json
```

would look for any of `mydata.json`, `mydata.json.zip`, `mydata.json.gz`, or `mydata.json.bz2`. The first file contained within a ZIP-compressed archive is used.

Note that if two fixtures with the same name but different fixture types are discovered (for example, if `mydata.json` and `mydata.xml.gz` were found in the same fixture directory), fixture installation will be aborted, and any data installed in the call to `loaddata` will be removed from the database.

MYSQL AND FIXTURES

Unfortunately, MySQL isn't capable of completely supporting all the features of Django fixtures. If you use MyISAM tables, because MySQL doesn't support transactions or constraints, you won't get a rollback if multiple fixture files are found or if validation of fixture data fails.

If you use InnoDB tables, you won't be able to have any forward references in your data files—MySQL doesn't provide a mechanism to defer checking of row constraints until a transaction is committed.

makemessages

This runs over the entire source tree of the current directory and pulls out all strings marked for translation. It creates (or updates) a message file in the `conf/locale` (in the Django tree) or `locale` (for projects and applications) directory. After making changes to the messages files, you need to compile them with `compilemessages` for use with the built-in `gettext` support. See Chapter 19 for details.

--all

Use the `--all` or `-a` option to update the message files for all available languages.

Here's an example of its usage:

```
django-admin.py makemessages --all
```

--extension

Use the `--extension` or `-e` option to specify a list of file extensions to examine (default: ".html").

Here's a usage example:

```
django-admin.py makemessages --locale=de --extension xhtml
```

Separate multiple extensions with commas or use `-e` or `--extension` multiple times:

```
django-admin.py makemessages --locale=de --extension=html,txt --extension xml
```

--locale

Use the `--locale` or `-l` option to specify the locale to process.

Here's a usage example:

```
django-admin.py makemessages --locale=br_PT
```

--domain

Use the `--domain` or `-d` option to change the domain of the messages files. These are currently supported:

- `django` for all `*.py` and `*.html` files (default)
- `djangojs` for `*.js` files

reset <appname appname ...>

This subcommand executes the equivalent of `sqlreset` for the given app name(s).

--noinput

Use the `--noinput` option to suppress all user prompting, such as "Are you sure?" confirmation messages. This is useful if `django-admin.py` is being executed as an unattended, automated script.

runfcgi [options]

This starts a set of FastCGI processes suitable for use with any Web server that supports the FastCGI protocol. See Chapter 12 for details. Requires the Python FastCGI module from flup: `http://trac.saddi.com/flup`.

runserver

This starts a lightweight development Web server on the local machine. By default, the server runs on port 8000 on the IP address 127.0.0.1. You can pass in an IP address and port number explicitly.

If you run this script as a user with normal privileges (recommended), you might not have access to start a port on a low port number. Low port numbers are reserved for the superuser (root).

Do not use this server in a production setting. It has not gone through security audits or performance tests. (And that's how it's gonna stay. We're in the business of making Web frameworks, not Web servers, so improving this server to be able to handle a production environment is outside the scope of Django.)

The development server automatically reloads Python code for each request, as needed. You don't need to restart the server for code changes to take effect.

When you start the server, and each time you change Python code while the server is running, the server will validate all of your installed models. (See the `validate` command later in this appendix.) If the validator finds errors, it will print them to standard output, but it won't stop the server.

You can run as many servers as you want, as long as they're on separate ports. Just execute `django-admin.py` `runserver` more than once.

Note that the default IP address, 127.0.0.1, is not accessible from other machines on your network. To make your development server viewable to other machines on the network, use its own IP address (e.g., 192.168.2.1) or 0.0.0.0 (which you can use if you don't know what your IP address is on the network).

Use the `--adminmedia` option to tell Django where to find the various CSS and JavaScript files for the Django admin interface. Normally, the development server serves these files out of the Django source tree magically, but you'd want to use this if you made any changes to those files for your own site.

Here's an example of usage:

```
django-admin.py runserver --adminmedia=/tmp/new-admin-style/
```

Use the `--noreload` option to disable the use of the auto-reloader. This means any Python code changes you make while the server is running will *not* take effect if the particular Python modules have already been loaded into memory.

Here's an example:

```
django-admin.py runserver --noreload
```

Examples of Using Different Ports and Addresses

Port 8000 on IP address 127.0.0.1:

```
django-admin.py runserver
```

Port 8000 on IP address 1.2.3.4:

```
django-admin.py runserver 1.2.3.4:8000
```

Port 7000 on IP address 127.0.0.1:

```
django-admin.py runserver 7000
```

Port 7000 on IP address 1.2.3.4:

```
django-admin.py runserver 1.2.3.4:7000
```

Serving Static Files with the Development Server

By default, the development server doesn't serve any static files for your site (such as CSS files, images, things under MEDIA_URL, and so forth).

shell

shell starts the Python interactive interpreter.

Django will use IPython (http://ipython.scipy.org/), if it's installed. If you have IPython installed and want to force use of the "plain" Python interpreter, use the --plain option, like so:

```
django-admin.py shell --plain
```

sql <appname appname ...>

This prints the CREATE TABLE SQL statements for the given app name(s).

sqlall <appname appname ...>

This prints the CREATE TABLE and initial-data SQL statements for the given app name(s).

Refer to the description of sqlcustom for an explanation of how to specify initial data.

sqlclear <appname appname ...>

This prints the DROP TABLE SQL statements for the given app name(s).

sqlcustom <appname appname ...>

This prints the custom SQL statements for the given app name(s). For each model in each specified app, this command looks for the file `<appname>/sql/<modelname>.sql`, where `<appname>` is the given app name and `<modelname>` is the model's name in lowercase. For example, if you have an app news that includes a `Story` model, `sqlcustom` will attempt to read a file `news/sql/story.sql` and append it to the output of this command.

Each of the SQL files, if given, is expected to contain valid SQL. The SQL files are piped directly into the database after all of the models' table-creation statements have been executed. Use this SQL hook to make any table modifications or insert any SQL functions into the database.

Note that the order in which the SQL files are processed is undefined.

sqlflush

This prints the SQL statements that would be executed for the `flush` command.

sqlindexes <appname appname ...>

This subcommand prints the `CREATE INDEX` SQL statements for the given app name(s).

sqlreset <appname appname ...>

This prints the `DROP TABLE` SQL then the `CREATE TABLE` SQL for the given app name(s).

sqlsequencereset <appname appname ...>

This prints the SQL statements for resetting sequences for the given app name(s).

startapp <appname>

`startapp <appname>` creates a Django app directory structure for the given app name in the current directory.

startproject <projectname>

This creates a Django project directory structure for the given project name in the current directory. This command is disabled when the `--settings` option to `django-admin.py` is used, or when the environment variable `DJANGO_SETTINGS_MODULE` has been set. To re-enable it in these situations, either omit the `--settings` option or unset `DJANGO_SETTINGS_MODULE`.

syncdb

`syncdb` creates the database tables for all apps in `INSTALLED_APPS` whose tables have not already been created. Use this command when you've added new applications to your project and want to install them in the database. This includes any apps shipped with Django that might be in `INSTALLED_APPS` by default. When you start a new project, run this command to install the default apps.

SYNCDB WILL NOT ALTER EXISTING TABLES

syncdb will only create tables for models that have not yet been installed. It will *never* issue ALTER TABLE statements to match changes made to a model class after installation. Changes to model classes and database schemas often involve some form of ambiguity and, in those cases, Django would have to guess at the correct changes to make. There is a risk that critical data would be lost in the process.

If you have made changes to a model and wish to alter the database tables to match, use the sql command to display the new SQL structure and compare that to your existing table schema to work out the changes.

If you're installing the django.contrib.auth application, syncdb will give you the option of creating a superuser immediately.

syncdb will also search for and install any fixture named initial_data with an appropriate extension (e.g., json or xml). See the section on loaddata in the official Django documentation for details on the specification of fixture data files.

--noinput

Use the --noinput option to suppress all user prompting, such as "Are you sure?" confirmation messages. This is useful if django-admin.py is being executed as an unattended, automated script.

test

This subcommand runs tests for all installed models. See the Django documentation for more on testing.

--noinput

Use the --noinput option to suppress all user prompting, such as "Are you sure?" confirmation messages. This is useful if django-admin.py is being executed as an unattended, automated script.

testserver <fixture fixture ...>

This runs a Django development server (as in runserver) using data from the given fixture(s). For more information, see the Django documentation.

validate

This validates all installed models (according to the INSTALLED_APPS setting) and prints validation errors to standard output.

Default Options

Although some subcommands may allow their own custom options, every subcommand allows for the following options.

--pythonpath

This adds the given filesystem path to the Python import search path. If this isn't provided, django-admin.py will use the PYTHONPATH environment variable.

Here is a usage example:

```
django-admin.py syncdb --pythonpath='/home/djangoprojects/myproject'
```

Note that this option is unnecessary in manage.py, which takes care of setting the Python path for you.

--settings

This explicitly specifies the settings module to use. The settings module should be in Python package syntax, for example mysite.settings. If this isn't provided, django-admin.py will use the DJANGO_SETTINGS_MODULE environment variable.

Here is a usage example:

```
django-admin.py syncdb --settings=mysite.settings
```

Note that this option is unnecessary in manage.py, which uses settings.py from the current project by default.

--traceback

By default, django-admin.py will show a simple error message whenever an error occurs. If you specify --traceback, django-admin.py will output a full stack trace whenever an exception is raised.

Here is a usage example:

```
django-admin.py syncdb --traceback
```

--verbosity

Use --verbosity to specify the amount of notification and debug information that django-admin.py should print to the console.

- 0 means no output.
- 1 means normal output (default).
- 2 means verbose output.

Here is a usage example:

```
django-admin.py syncdb --verbosity 2
```

Extra Niceties

Syntax Coloring

The `django-admin.py` / `manage.py` commands that print SQL to standard output will use pretty color-coded output if your terminal supports ANSI colors. It won't use the color codes if you're piping the command's output to another program.

Bash Completion

If you use the Bash shell, consider installing the Django bash completion script, which lives in `extras/django_bash_completion` in the Django distribution. It enables tab completion of `django-admin.py` and `manage.py` commands, so you can, for instance

- Type `django-admin.py`
- Press the Tab key to see all available options
- Type `sql`, then press the Tab key to see all available options whose names start with `sql`

■ ■ ■

Request and Response Objects

Django uses request and response objects to pass state through the system. When a page is requested, Django creates an HttpRequest object that contains metadata about the request. Then Django loads the appropriate view, passing the HttpRequest as the first argument to the view function. Each view is responsible for returning an HttpResponse object.

We've used these objects often throughout the book; this appendix explains the complete APIs for HttpRequest and HttpResponse objects.

HttpRequest

HttpRequest represents a single HTTP request from some user-agent. Much of the important information about the request is available as attributes on the HttpRequest instance (see Table G-1). All attributes except session should be considered read-only.

Table G-1. *Attributes of HttpRequest Objects*

Attribute	Description
path	A string representing the full path to the requested page, not including the domain—for example, "/music/bands/the_beatles/".

method	A string representing the HTTP method used in the request. This is guaranteed to be uppercase. For example:
	
	`if request.method == 'GET':`
	`    do_something()`
	`elif request.method == 'POST':`
	`    do_something_else()`

encoding	A string representing the current encoding used to decode form submission data (or None, which means the DEFAULT_CHARSET setting is used). You can write to this attribute to change the encoding used when accessing the form data. Any subsequent attribute accesses (such as reading from GET or POST) will use the new encoding value. Useful if you know the form data is not in the DEFAULT_CHARSET encoding.

Continued

Table G-1. *Continued*

Attribute	Description
GET	A dictionary-like object containing all given HTTP GET parameters. See the "QueryDict Objects" section later in this appendix.
POST	A dictionary-like object containing all given HTTP POST parameters. See the "QueryDict Objects" section later in this appendix. It's possible that a request can come in via POST with an empty POST dictionary— if, say, a form is requested via the POST HTTP method but does not include form data. Therefore, you shouldn't use if request.POST to check for use of the POST method; instead, use if request.method == "POST" (see the method entry in this table). Note: POST does not include file-upload information. See FILES.
REQUEST	For convenience, a dictionary-like object that searches POST first, and then GET. Inspired by PHP's $_REQUEST. For example, if GET = {"name": "john"} and POST = {"age": '34'}, REQUEST["name"] would be "john", and REQUEST["age"] would be "34". It's strongly suggested that you use GET and POST instead of REQUEST, because the former are more explicit.
COOKIES	A standard Python dictionary containing all cookies. Keys and values are strings. See Chapter 14 for more on using cookies.
FILES	A dictionary-like object that maps file names to UploadedFile objects. See the Django documentation for more.
META	A standard Python dictionary containing all available HTTP headers. Available headers depend on the client and server, but here are some examples: • CONTENT_LENGTH • CONTENT_TYPE • QUERY_STRING: The raw unparsed query string • REMOTE_ADDR: The IP address of the client • REMOTE_HOST: The hostname of the client • SERVER_NAME: The hostname of the server • SERVER_PORT: The port of the server Any HTTP headers are available in META as keys prefixed with HTTP_, converted to uppercase, and substituting underscores for hyphens. For example: • HTTP_ACCEPT_ENCODING • HTTP_ACCEPT_LANGUAGE • HTTP_HOST: The HTTP Host header sent by the client • HTTP_REFERER: The referring page, if any • HTTP_USER_AGENT: The client's user-agent string • HTTP_X_BENDER: The value of the X-Bender header, if set

Attribute	Description
user	A `django.contrib.auth.models.User` object representing the currently logged-in user. If the user isn't currently logged in, `user` will be set to an instance of `django.contrib.auth.models.AnonymousUser`. You can tell `user` and `AnonymousUser` apart with `is_authenticated()`, like so: ```python\nif request.user.is_authenticated():\n # Do something for logged-in users.\nelse:\n # Do something for anonymous users.\n``` `user` is available only if your Django installation has `AuthenticationMiddleware` activated. For the complete details of authentication and users, see Chapter 14.
session	A readable and writable dictionary-like object that represents the current session. This is available only if your Django installation has session support activated. See Chapter 14.
raw_post_data	The raw `HTTP POST` data. This is useful for advanced processing.

Request objects also have a few useful methods, as shown in Table G-2.

Table G-2. *HttpRequest Methods*

Method	Description
__getitem__(key)	Returns the `GET`/`POST` value for the given key, checking `POST` first, and then `GET`. Raises `KeyError` if the key doesn't exist. This lets you use dictionary-accessing syntax on an `HttpRequest` instance. For example, `request["foo"]` is the same as checking `request.POST["foo"]` and then `request.GET["foo"]`.
has_key()	Returns `True` or `False`, designating whether `request.GET` or `request.POST` has the given key.
get_host()	Returns the originating host of the request using information from the `HTTP_X_FORWARDED_HOST` and `HTTP_HOST` headers (in that order). If they don't provide a value, the method uses a combination of `SERVER_NAME` and `SERVER_PORT`.
get_full_path()	Returns the path, plus an appended query string, if applicable. For example, `"/music/bands/the_beatles/?print=true"`.
is_secure()	Returns `True` if the request is secure; that is, if it was made with HTTPS.

QueryDict Objects

In an `HttpRequest` object, the `GET` and `POST` attributes are instances of `django.http.QueryDict`. `QueryDict` is a dictionary-like class customized to deal with multiple values for the same key. This is necessary because some HTML form elements, notably `<select multiple="multiple">`, pass multiple values for the same key.

QueryDict instances are immutable, unless you create a copy() of them. That means you can't change attributes of request.POST and request.GET directly.

QueryDict implements all standard dictionary methods because it's a subclass of dictionary. Exceptions are outlined in Table G-3.

Table G-3. *How QueryDicts Differ from Standard Dictionaries*

Method	Differences from Standard dict Implementation
__getitem__	Works just like a dictionary. However, if the key has more than one value, __getitem__() returns the last value.
__setitem__	Sets the given key to [value] (a Python list whose single element is value). Note that this, as other dictionary functions that have side effects, can be called only on a mutable QueryDict (one that was created via copy()).
get()	If the key has more than one value, get() returns the last value just like __getitem__.

update()	Takes either a QueryDict or standard dictionary. Unlike the standard dictionary's update method, this method appends to the current dictionary items rather than replacing them:
	
	``python
	>>> q = QueryDict('a=1')
	>>> q = q.copy() # to make it mutable
	>>> q.update({'a': '2'})
	>>> q.getlist('a')
	['1', '2']
	>>> q['a'] # returns the last
	['2']
	``

items()	Just like the standard dictionary items() method, except this uses the same last-value logic as __getitem()__:
	
	``python
	>>> q = QueryDict('a=1&a=2&a=3')
	>>> q.items()
	[('a', '3')]
	``

values()	Just like the standard dictionary values() method, except this uses the same last-value logic as __getitem()__.

In addition, QueryDict has the methods shown in Table G-4.

Table G-4. *Extra (Nondictionary) QueryDict Methods*

Method	Description
copy()	Returns a copy of the object, using copy.deepcopy() from the Python standard library. The copy will be mutable—that is, you can change its values.
getlist(key)	Returns the data with the requested key, as a Python list. Returns an empty list if the key doesn't exist. It's guaranteed to return a list of some sort.
setlist(key, list_)	Sets the given key to list_ (unlike __setitem__()).
appendlist(key, item)	Appends an item to the internal list associated with key.

Method	Description
setlistdefault(key, a)	Just like setdefault, except it takes a list of values instead of a single value.

lists()	Like items(), except it includes all values, as a list, for each member of the dictionary. For example:
	
	>>> q = QueryDict('a=1&a=2&a=3')
	>>> q.lists()
	[('a', ['1', '2', '3'])]

urlencode()	Returns a string of the data in query-string format (e.g., "a=2&b=3&b=5").

A Complete Example

For example, given this HTML form

```
<form action="/foo/bar/" method="post">
<input type="text" name="your_name" />
<select multiple="multiple" name="bands">
    <option value="beatles">The Beatles</option>
    <option value="who">The Who</option>
    <option value="zombies">The Zombies</option>
</select>
<input type="submit" />
</form>
```

if the user enters "John Smith" in the your_name field and selects both The Beatles and The Zombies in the multiple-select box, here's what Django's request object would have:

```
>>> request.GET
{}
>>> request.POST
{'your_name': ['John Smith'], 'bands': ['beatles', 'zombies']}
>>> request.POST['your_name']
'John Smith'
>>> request.POST['bands']
'zombies'
>>> request.POST.getlist('bands')
['beatles', 'zombies']
>>> request.POST.get('your_name', 'Adrian')
'John Smith'
>>> request.POST.get('nonexistent_field', 'Nowhere Man')
'Nowhere Man'
```

Note The GET, POST, COOKIES, FILES, META, REQUEST, raw_post_data, and user attributes are all lazily loaded. That means Django doesn't spend resources calculating the values of those attributes until your code requests them.

HttpResponse

In contrast to HttpRequest objects, which are created automatically by Django, HttpResponse objects are your responsibility. Each view you write is responsible for instantiating, populating, and returning an HttpResponse.

The HttpResponse class lives at django.http.HttpResponse.

Construction HttpResponses

Typically, you'll construct an HttpResponse to pass the contents of the page, as a string, to the HttpResponse constructor:

```
>>> response = HttpResponse("Here's the text of the Web page.")
>>> response = HttpResponse("Text only, please.", mimetype="text/plain")
```

But if you want to add content incrementally, you can use response as a filelike object:

```
>>> response = HttpResponse()
>>> response.write("<p>Here's the text of the Web page.</p>")
>>> response.write("<p>Here's another paragraph.</p>")
```

You can pass HttpResponse an iterator rather than passing it hard-coded strings. If you use this technique, follow these guidelines:

- The iterator should return strings.

- If an HttpResponse has been initialized with an iterator as its content, you can't use the HttpResponse instance as a filelike object. Doing so will raise Exception.

Finally, note that HttpResponse implements a write() method, which makes it suitable for use anywhere that Python expects a filelike object. See Chapter 8 for some examples of using this technique.

Setting Headers

You can add and delete headers using dictionary syntax:

```
>>> response = HttpResponse()
>>> response['X-DJANGO'] = "It's the best."
>>> del response['X-PHP']
>>> response['X-DJANGO']
"It's the best."
```

You can also use has_header(header) to check for the existence of a header.

Avoid setting Cookie headers by hand; instead, see Chapter 14 for instructions on how cookies work in Django.

HttpResponse Subclasses

Django includes a number of HttpResponse subclasses that handle different types of HTTP responses (see Table G-5). Like HttpResponse, these subclasses live in django.http.

Table G-5. *HttpResponse Subclasses*

Class	Description
HttpResponseRedirect	The constructor takes a single argument: the path to redirect to. This can be a fully qualified URL (e.g., 'http://search. yahoo.com/') or an absolute URL with no domain (e.g., '/search/'). Note that this returns an HTTP status code 302.
HttpResponsePermanentRedirect	Like HttpResponseRedirect, but it returns a permanent redirect (HTTP status code 301) instead of a "found" redirect (status code 302).
HttpResponseNotModified	The constructor doesn't take any arguments. Use this to designate that a page hasn't been modified since the user's last request.
HttpResponseBadRequest	Acts just like HttpResponse but uses a 400 status code.
HttpResponseNotFound	Acts just like HttpResponse but uses a 404 status code.
HttpResponseForbidden	Acts just like HttpResponse but uses a 403 status code.
HttpResponseNotAllowed	Acts like HttpResponse but uses a 405 status code. It takes a single, required argument: a list of permitted methods (e.g., ['GET', 'POST']).
HttpResponseGone	Acts just like HttpResponse but uses a 410 status code.
HttpResponseServerError	Acts just like HttpResponse but uses a 500 status code.

You can, of course, define your own HttpResponse subclass to support different types of responses not supported out of the box.

Returning Errors

Returning HTTP error codes in Django is easy. We've already mentioned the HttpResponseNotFound, HttpResponseForbidden, HttpResponseServerError, and other subclasses. Just return an instance of one of those subclasses instead of a normal HttpResponse in order to signify an error, as in this example:

```
def my_view(request):
    # ...
    if foo:
        return HttpResponseNotFound('<h1>Page not found</h1>')
    else:
        return HttpResponse('<h1>Page was found</h1>')
```

Because a 404 error is by far the most common HTTP error, there's an easier way to handle it. When you return an error such as HttpResponseNotFound, you're responsible for defining the HTML of the resulting error page:

```
return HttpResponseNotFound('<h1>Page not found</h1>')
```

For convenience, and because it's a good idea to have a consistent 404 error page across your site, Django provides an Http404 exception. If you raise Http404 at any point in a view function, Django will catch it and return the standard error page for your application, along with an HTTP error code 404. Here's an example:

```
from django.http import Http404

def detail(request, poll_id):
    try:
        p = Poll.objects.get(pk=poll_id)
    except Poll.DoesNotExist:
        raise Http404
    return render_to_response('polls/detail.html', {'poll': p})
```

In order to use the Http404 exception to its fullest, you should create a template that is displayed when a 404 error is raised. This template should be called 404.html, and it should be located in the top level of your template tree.

Customizing the 404 (Not Found) View

When you raise an Http404 exception, Django loads a special view devoted to handling 404 errors. By default, it's the view django.views.defaults.page_not_found, which loads and renders the template 404.html.

This means you need to define a 404.html template in your root template directory. This template will be used for all 404 errors.

This page_not_found view should suffice for 99% of Web applications, but if you want to override the 404 view, you can specify handler404 in your URLconf, like so:

```
from django.conf.urls.defaults import *

urlpatterns = patterns('',
    ...
)

handler404 = 'mysite.views.my_custom_404_view'
```

Behind the scenes, Django determines the 404 view by looking for handler404. By default, URLconfs contain the following line:

```
from django.conf.urls.defaults import *
```

That takes care of setting handler404 in the current module. As you can see in django/conf/urls/defaults.py, handler404 is set to 'django.views.defaults.page_not_found' by default.

There are three things to note about 404 views:

- The 404 view is also called if Django doesn't find a match after checking every regular expression in the URLconf.

- If you don't define your own 404 view—and simply use the default, which is recommended—you still have one obligation: to create a 404.html template in the root of your template directory. The default 404 view will use that template for all 404 errors.

- If DEBUG is set to True (in your settings module), then your 404 view will never be used, and the traceback will be displayed instead.

Customizing the 500 (Server Error) View

Similarly, Django executes special-case behavior in the case of runtime errors in view code. If a view results in an exception, Django will, by default, call the view `django.views.defaults.server_error`, which loads and renders the template `500.html`. This means you need to define a `500.html` template in your root template directory. This template will be used for all server errors.

This `server_error` view should suffice for 99% of Web applications, but if you want to override the view, you can specify `handler500` in your URLconf, like so:

```
from django.conf.urls.defaults import *

urlpatterns = patterns('',
    ...
)

handler500 = 'mysite.views.my_custom_error_view'
```

Index

You Need the Companion eBook